THE EUROPEANISATION
OF CONFLICT RESOLUTION

Manchester University Press

GENERAL EDITORS: THOMAS CHRISTIANSEN AND EMIL KIRCHNER

The formation of Croatian national identity
ALEX J. BELLAMY
The European Union and the accommodation of Basque difference in Spain
ANGELA K. BOURNE
Theory and reform in the European Union, 2nd edition
DIMITRIS N. CHRYSSOCHOOU, MICHAEL J. TSINISIZELIS, STELIOS STAVRIDIS AND KOSTAS IFANTIS
From integration to integrity: administrative ethics and reform in the European Commission
MICHELLE CINI
The transatlantic divide
OSVALDO CROCI AND AMY VERDUN
Germany, pacifism and peace enforcement
ANJA DALGAARD-NIELSEN
The changing European Commission
DIONYSSIS DIMITRAKOPOULOS (ED.)
Supranational citizenship
LYNN DOBSON
Reshaping Economic and Monetary Union
SHAWN DONNELLY
The time of European governance
MAGNUS EKENGREN
Adapting to European integration? Kaliningrad, Russia and the European Union
STEFAN GÄNZLE, GUIDO MÜNTEL, EVGENY VINOKUROV (EDS)
An introduction to post-Communist Bulgaria
EMIL GIATZIDIS
Mothering the Union
ROBERTA GUERRINA
Non-state actors in international relations: the case of Germany
ANNE-MARIE LE GLOANNEC
Globalisation, integration and the future of European welfare states
THEODORA ISMENE-GIZELIS
European internal security: towards supranational governance in the area of freedom, security and justice
CHRISTIAN KAUNERT
Turkey: facing a new millennium
AMIKAM NACHMANI
Europolis: constitutional patriotism beyond the nation state
PATRIZIA NANZ
The changing faces of federalism
SERGIO ORTINO, MITJA ŽAGAR AND VOJTECH MASTNY (EDS)
The road to the European Union
Volume 1 The Czech and Slovak Republics JACQUES RUPNIK AND JAN ZIELONKA (EDS)
Volume 2 Estonia, Latvia and Lithuania VELLO PETTAI AND JAN ZIELONKA (EDS)
A political sociology of the European Union: reassessing constructivism
MICHEL MANGENOT AND JAY ROWELL (EDS)
Democratising capitalism? The political economy of post-Communist transformations in Romania, 1989–2001
LILIANA POP
Europe and civil society: movement coalitions and European governance
CARLO RUZZA
Constructing the path to eastern enlargement
ULRICH SEDELMEIER
Governing Europe's new neighbourhood: partners or periphery?
MICHAEL SMITH, KATJA WEBER, AND MICHAEL BAUN (EDS)
Two tiers or two speeds? The European security order and the enlargement of the European Union and NATO
JAMES SPERLING (ED.)
Recasting the European order
JAMES SPERLING AND EMIL KIRCHNER
Political symbolism and European integration
TOBIAS THEILER
Rethinking European Union foreign policy
BEN TONRA AND THOMAS CHRISTIANSEN (EDS)
The Europeanisation of the western Balkans: EU justice and home affairs in Croatia and Macedonia
FLORIAN TRAUNER
The European Union in the wake of Eastern enlargement
AMY VERDUN AND OSVALDO CROCI (EDS)
Democratic citizenship and the European Union
ALBERT WEALE
Inclusion, exclusion and the governance of European security
MARK WEBBER

Boyka Stefanova

THE EUROPEANISATION OF CONFLICT RESOLUTION

Regional integration and conflicts in Europe from the 1950s to the twenty-first century

MANCHESTER UNIVERSITY PRESS

Copyright © Boyka Stefanova 2011

The right of Boyka Stefanova to be identified as the author of this work has been asserted by her in accordance with the Copyright, Designs and Patents Act 1988.

Published by Manchester University Press
Altrincham Street, Manchester M1 7JA, UK
www.manchesteruniversitypress.co.uk

British Library Cataloguing-in-Publication Data is available

ISBN 978 1 5261 1703 8 *paperback*
ISBN 978 0 7190 8339 6 *hardback*

First published by Manchester University Press in hardback 2011

This edition first published 2017

The publisher has no responsibility for the persistence or accuracy of URLs for any external or third-party internet websites referred to in this book, and does not guarantee that any content on such websites is, or will remain, accurate or appropriate.

Printed by Lightning Source

To Marina

Contents

	List of figures and tables	*page* ix
	Preface	xi
	List of abbreviations	xiii
1	Introduction	1
2	The Europeanisation of conflict resolution: theory and framework	22
3	The early years: European integration as a system of conflict resolution in the Franco-German relationship (1950–63)	44
4	Northern Ireland: Europeanisation breakthrough	79
5	The case of Cyprus: unmet expectations	116
6	Kosovo: Europeanisation in the making	148
7	Conclusion	186
	Bibliography	203
	Index	227

Figures and Tables

Figures

3.1	Generational differences in attitudes towards issues of European integration: net support for integration in youth minus adult cohorts	68
3.2	The emergence of empathy between France and Germany, 1954–63	68
4.1	Line graph of voter turnout rates at European elections, NI compared to the UK average: net difference in voter turnout rates between Northern Ireland and the UK (NI minus UK) at elections for Members of the European Parliament and UK general elections, 1979–2009	109
4.2	Vote distribution in the elections for Members of the European Parliament in Northern Ireland, 1979–2009	110

Tables

3.1	The economic importance of the Ruhr: coal production by basins in the ECSC, 1952–58 (million tons)	56
3.2	Historical and comparative data on coal production in the Community, 1938–58 (million tons)	60
3.3	Steel production in the Community, 1938–58 (million tons)	60
4.1	EU regional policy instruments assisting conflict resolution in Northern Ireland	93
4.2	Northern Ireland's performance in comparison with the UK, Ireland, EU-27, and five similar EU regions	95
4.3	The European Union in Northern Ireland's political discourse: the Europeanisation of conflict resolution and the domestication of Europe	106
6.1	The European perspective and the Kosovo conflict in Serbia's political discourse	174
6.2	The European perspective in EU political discourse	178

Preface

This project draws on my standing interest in the political implications of European integration. It belongs to a research agenda that is both historically and analytically inspiring. While studying the influence of the European Union on the security dynamics in Europe through its self-styled mission of projecting security and stability across borders, I realised not only the enormous complexity of the process, but also its major challenges and opportunities. I found that the macro-process of order and security creation embodied in the European Union as a political actor, a civilian and a normative power, and a 'force for good', creates a type of ecological fallacy for the concrete settings of conflicts. While the systemic objectives of European integration remain uncompromised, it is also important to explain how this regional system functions to restore peace at the unit level, when the fundamental condition of equilibrium and political stability is broken in the real-life settings of irreconcilable claims over territory and belonging. The second realisation was that regardless of the ups and downs of institutional breakthroughs and unfulfilled promises oscillating between the EU's 'presence' and 'actorness' in international politics, the European construction has one standing meaning which links the macro-system to the group by offering the unique European experience, that of reconciliation. The ability to draw on the politics of the post-Second World War reconciliation between France and Germany through European integration is a standing resource for scholars and practitioners in the field.

This book developed by bringing together the challenge of explaining how peace is restored and the opportunity of recreating the founding politics of reconciliation through European integration. I am thankful for the ideas and support of colleagues and professionals, and for their involvement in the project. I feel greatly enriched by their vast expertise and touched by their willingness to share insight and provide valuable comments on issues and earlier drafts. I am indebted to Mark Miller for the inspiration to study European integration as a peace project and to Robert Denemark for helping me shape the concepts and approach which transformed this research into a book.

I would like to thank Series Editors Thomas Christiansen and Emil Kirchner for their support for the ideas developed in this book and the entire team at Manchester University Press, and especially Tony Mason for his active cooperation throughout the process. My special thanks go to the staff at the Central Library of the European Commission in Brussels for their help and advice. I am grateful to the Department of Political Science and Geography at the University of Texas at San Antonio for research support for the completion of the project. I thank Sean Anderson for assisting with the editing process. Finally, I would like to thank my family for their patience and unfailing support throughout the years.

List of Abbreviations

AIA	Anglo-Irish Agreement
CAP	Common Agricultural Policy
CARDS	Community Assistance for Reconstruction, Development and Stabilisation
CDU	Christian Democratic Union
CFSP	Common Foreign and Security Policy
CoE	Council of Europe
CPS	Comprehensive Proposal for the Kosovo Status Settlement
CTP	Republican Turkish Party
DKBL	*Deutsche Kohlenbergbauleitung*
DKV	*Deutsche Kohlen-Verkaufsgesellschaft*
DS	Democratic Party
DSS	Democratic Party of Serbia
DUP	Democratic Unionist Party
EAGGF	European Agricultural Guidance and Guarantee Fund
ECJ	European Court of Justice
ECSC	European Coal and Steel Community
EDC	European Defence Community
EEC	European Economic Community
EESC	European Economic and Social Committee
EP	European Parliament; European Partnership
EPC	European Political Cooperation
ERDF	European Regional Development Fund
ERP KiM	Serbian Orthodox Church (Kosovo and Metohia)
ESDP	European Security and Defence Policy
EU	European Union
EULEX	EU rule of law mission
EUPT	European Union Planning Team
EUSR	European Union Special Representative Office
FJME	Fondation Jean Monnet pour l'Europe
FRY	Federal Republic of Yugoslavia
GAERC	General Affairs and External Relations Council
GDP	Gross Domestic Product
GFA	Good Friday Agreement
HA	High Authority (of the ECSC)
IAR	International Authority for the Ruhr

ICG	International Crisis Group
ICJ	International Court of Justice
ICO	International Civilian Office
ICR	International Civilian Representative
ICTY	International Crime Tribunal for the Former Yugoslavia
IFI	International Fund for Ireland
IFIs	International financial institutions
INTERREG	Interregional Cooperation Programme
IPA	Instrument for Pre-Accession
IRA	Irish Republican Army
KLA	Kosovo Liberation Army
KPC	Kosovo Protection Corps
MEP	Member of the European Parliament
MLA	Member of Legislative Assembly
NATO	North Atlantic Treaty Organisation
NI	Northern Ireland
NSMC	North–South Ministerial Council
OEEC	Organisation for Economic Cooperation in Europe
OFMDFM	Office of the First Minister and Deputy First Minister
OSCE	Organisation for Security and Co-operation in Europe
PEACE	Special Support Programme for Peace and Reconciliation
PISG	Provisional Institutions of Self-Government
RoC	Republic of Cyprus
SAA	Stabilisation and Association Agreement
SAP	Stabilisation and Association Process
SDLP	Social Democratic and Labour Party
SEA	Single European Act
SEUPB	Special European Union Programmes Body
SF	Sinn Féin
SFIO	Section Française de l'Internationale Ouvrière
SFRY	Socialist Federal Republic of Yugoslavia
SG	Secretary General
SG/HR	Secretary-General/High Representative for CFSP
SNS	Serbian Progressive Party
SPD	Social Democratic Party of Germany
SPS	Socialist Party of Serbia
SRS	Serbian Radical Party
SRSG	Special Representative of the UN Secretary General
STM	Standards Tracking Mechanism
TCC	Turkish Cypriot Community
TRNC	Turkish Republic of Northern Cyprus
UBP	National Unity Party, Turkey
UDI	Kosovo's unilateral declaration of independence
UNFICYP	United Nations Peacekeeping Mission in Cyprus

List of Abbreviations

UNMIK	United Nations Mission in Kosovo
UNSC	United Nations Security Council
UNSCR	United Nations Security Council Resolution
UNSG	United Nations Secretary-General
UNSRSG	Special Representative of the UNSG (Kosovo)
UUP	Ulster Unionist Party
WEU	Western European Union

1

Introduction

> I am now going to say something that will astonish you. The first step in the re-creation of the European family must be a partnership between France and Germany. In this way only can France recover the moral and cultural leadership of Europe. There can be no revival of Europe without a spiritually great France and a spiritually great Germany.
>
> Winston Churchill[1]

European integration as a peace project

The proposition that European integration may be historically relevant to conflict resolution is not new. Integration is inseparable from the intellectual traditions of European political thought in search of new forms of political organisation to secure Europe's peace. References to a European union as a peace project are present in the writings of Maximilian de Béthune, Duc de Sully, reflecting on the role of a regional union to avoid the catastrophes of war, Bernardin de Saint-Pierre, Gottfried-Wilhelm Leibnitz, and Jean-Jacques Rousseau on the project of perpetual peace in Europe, Novalis on Christian unity, Victor Hugo on the United States of Europe, and Friedrich Nietzsche on Europe's destiny. These references are also dominant in the intellectual currents of the early twentieth century represented by Georges Sorel, Paul Valéry, Heinrich and Thomas Mann, Edouard Herriot, Romain Roland, and Richard Coudenhove-Kalergi (Lefort 2001). All these perspectives share the proposition that integration would provide the economic foundations of the natural convergence of European societies into a regional federation, a United States of Europe.

Ever since it was implemented as a political project of the post-Second World War reality in Europe, the workings of European integration have been credited with performing conflict resolution functions. Early in its contemporary evolution, integration unfolded as a process of creating regional interdependencies by expanding across issue areas and increasing the number of participating countries. European integration allegedly transformed the long-standing adversarial relationship between France and Germany into a strategic partnership. Conflict in Western Europe became obsolete. The end of the Cold War further reinforced the role of integration as a regional peace project. Its institutional embodiment, the European Union (EU)[2] developed as a proxy to the historic reunification of the European continent by extending peace, reconciliation, and prosperity to Eastern Europe. As the EU evolved, it acquired a self-proclaimed vocation to serve peaceful development and formulated special policies to address such issues (Voorhoeve 2007: 163).

While these evolutionary dynamics are uncontested, they remain largely unexplained. The deeper meaning of the process, its transformative power, is still to be elucidated. How does European integration restore peace when its equilibrium is broken and conflict or the legacies of enmity persist? This book sets out to explore the peace and conflict-resolution role of European integration by testing its somewhat vague, albeit well-established, macro-political rationale of a peace project in the practical settings of conflicts. The question it asks is: how does European integration contribute to conflict resolution?

Explaining this historical puzzle may be disaggregated into several researchable questions: is there an inherent conflict resolution mechanism to European integration, a consistent model applicable across cases? If so, what is its *modus operandi*? What kind of conflict resolution effects are created through integration? Are they historically consistent? Do they depend on the status of conflict – interstate versus intercommunal – or on the presence of a negotiated settlement? What does the EU's influence on conflict resolution tell us about the time and the proximity factor in Europeanisation? Are conflicts located 'closer' to the EU more likely to be resolved as a result of its influences? Should one argue (should we accept) that European integration is in the process of subsuming conflict resolution in Europe, as the EU progressively consolidates its foreign policy domain and political relevance through enlargement? These questions have yet to receive a systematic treatment as the literature exploring the significance of European integration to conflict resolution in a variety of contexts has come to represent a high-growth area (Blockmans *et al.* 2010; Coppieters *et al.* 2004; Diez *et al.* 2006, 2008a; Diez and Tocci 2009; Kronenberger and Wouters 2005; Tocci 2004, 2007, among others).

A renewed focus on conflict resolution is highly relevant to Europe's regional dynamics. There is a widely recognised need for revitalisation of the classical model of international conflict resolution based on negotiation and third-party mediation. Efforts to date have focused on constitutional designs based on self-determination and the protection of minority rights in conflict. Post-conflict reconstruction strategies in the war-torn region of the Western Balkans and the Caucasus demonstrate that under conditions of sheer asymmetry in the ethnic composition of societies, constitutional arrangements are inadequate even in cases of significant power sharing and autonomy (du Toit 2003, Lijphart 2004; Roeder and Rothchild 2005). Partition or secession, although sustained by democratic theory, does not automatically result in reconciliation due to the lack of political culture reflecting the changed territorial realities (Franck 1992).

As a factor of conflict resolution, European integration itself is not immune from the conceptual and practical issues emerging on the path to securing the irreversibility of the process. Regardless of its universalist values of peace and reconciliation, integration is not the only or guaranteed strategy for resolving Europe's outstanding conflicts. Facts on the ground suggest that the workings of integration towards restoring peace are not theoretically necessary and empirically consistent. The EU was not an official party to the peace process in Northern Ireland. It gained visibility in the Cyprus conflict only at a later stage when its enlargement and membership criteria were transposed in the UN peace plans. The EU was not the principal initiator of settlement in the Kosovo conflict. As in Cyprus, it acquired a role through the UN negotiation process. In all contemporary conflicts examined in this study – Northern Ireland, Cyprus, and Kosovo/Serbia – national legacies and group identities have persisted. None of these conflicts has been fully resolved or ultimate intercommunal reconciliation accomplished. The historical precedent of the Franco-German reconciliation has yet to repeat itself. In the context of historical evidence that both validates and questions the peace rationale of European integration, the objective of this book is to revisit the puzzle of how integration may contribute to resolving conflicts. It does so in a study of critically important cases: the exemplary process of the Franco-German reconciliation during the 1950s, the EU's involvement in reconstructing peace in Northern Ireland, the conflict in Cyprus, and the efforts assisting Kosovo's independence.

The literature lacks a comprehensive study on the relationship between regional integration and conflict resolution, although earlier work points to the integrative functions of conflict (North *et al.* 1960), the relevance of integration as an alternative to the distributive effects of peace settlements (Mitchell 1991), and the capacity of international communication to redefine actors' preferences within a cooperative multilateral framework (Deutsch *et al.* 1957; Jandt 1973).

For most contemporary theories the conflict resolution effects of integration are unproblematic. The functionalist approach to international organisation explains the creation of agencies for the management of international issues, and by extension the resolution of conflicts, by the ability of international institutions to transcend sovereignty through function and attract loyalties. Functionalism is only broadly relevant to integration – inasmuch as it is concerned with transnational processes responding to objective needs. Its founder, David Mitrany, was himself against regional integration. 'The need to unite is not obvious,' he argued. Mitrany regarded international conflict as inevitable due to the anarchy of the nation-state system. The task of international organisation was to provide for the functional replacement of sovereignty and move international politics 'away from the system of enclosed armed units' towards a system of 'beneficial common action' (Mitrany 1975: 228). Mitrany's idea of voluntary issue-based international agencies sought to reconcile power asymmetries with the ultimate objective of preventing and resolving conflict.

By contrast, the federalist logic of peace is based on the proposition that only political unity based on a regional federal order is capable of removing conflict inherent to sovereignty and nationalism. All intellectual currents of the otherwise eclectic post-Second World War European Federalist Movement recognised that a treaty-based peace was inadequate to the political realities in Europe. The various branches of federalism differed with regard to the ways of achieving a European federation: directly, by creating larger units according to the principle of transferability and ceding of sovereignty, power sharing and division of power; or gradually, through the creation of institutions for managing individual sectors following a pluralistic societal model (Brugmans 1965; Forsyth 1967; Haas 1970).

The federalist project became unrealisable after the creation of the intergovernmental structures of the Council of Europe in 1949, yet functionalist approaches survived as alternatives for securing Europe's peace. Integration theory, in its classical neofunctionalist version, regards conflict resolution as an automatic by-product of the process of spillover across functional domains, leaving little space for political action designed at the regional level (Haas 1968). Still, neofunctionalism contributes to conflict resolution understood as a political process (negotiation) and a process of governance (management), the theoretically informed argument that European integration cannot be separated from domestic politics, that elites cannot isolate European issues (Pentland 1973: 247), and that the distribution of domestic preferences for integration is an indicator of the relevance of integration to domestic politics. More recent versions, such as institutionalist propositions of supranational governance (Sandholtz and Stone Sweet 1998), also suggest that conflict resolution should be inherent to the process. They posit the capacity of the supranational institutions of European integration to affect outcomes at the domestic level of politics. The alternative to neofunctionalism, intergovernmentalism, allows for conflict resolution outcomes, although it posits the instrumental influence of the institutions of European integration as nation-states remain the driving force of the process. In its realist and liberal versions, intergovernmentalism allows for conflict resolution outcomes in the process of interstate bargaining due to the inherent peace interest of the state (Hoffmann 1966) or the credibility of supranational institutions (Moravcsik 1998).

The prevalent approaches are drawn from international relations theory and examine the EU's conflict resolution capacity in terms of power (Barnett and Duval 2005), actorness (Ginsberg 1999), regional interdependence (Tavares 2004), security community building (Deutsch et al. 1957; Wæver 1998), reconciliation as a result of a common European identity (Parsons 2004), or desecuritisation (Diez et al. 2008a). The actor–process dichotomy in international relations understandably conceptualises European integration as a phenomenon of a dual nature. Most studies present the EU as an international institutional actor and integration as a process of regionalism. Actor-centred approaches regard the EU as a civilian or a normative power (Diez and Pace 2007; Duchêne 1972; Harpaz 2007; Manners 2002, 2008; Sjursen 2006). They examine its effectiveness in resolving conflicts as an external benevolent third-party mediator, a factor of conflict prevention and management, or a source of economic assistance in reconstruction and reconciliation (Ginsberg 2001; Hill 1996). Regionalism explains peace and conflict resolution in terms of security externalities which help to mitigate ethnic, nationalist, or communal conflict (Hurrell and Fawcett 1995: 313, Tavares 2004).[3] Through the lens of regionalism, European integration represents an incentive structure for the reformulation of contested interstate incompatibilities into benefits derived from interdependence and cooperation.

This book aspires to go beyond the simple coming to terms with the duality of integration and explain how the EU is causally important to conflict resolution by using analytical tools specific to integration studies, drawing upon theories and frameworks explaining the *modus operandi* of European integration. The task meets a number of challenges. The European experience with conflict resolution illustrates the difficulty of untangling the effects of integration from other influences. The formative stages of regional integration in Europe were embedded in a network of multilateral agreements securing the peace between France and Germany: great power politics, alliances, and influential actors. The choice of integration as a conflict resolution strategy was neither evident, nor self-explanatory. Similar limitations have remained valid in more recent cases of conflict in Europe. Outside the provisions of the Common Foreign and Security Policy (CFSP) formulated in terms of safeguarding common values, fundamental interests, preserving peace and strengthening security, there are no explicit treaty-based autonomous EU competences in the area of conflict resolution.[4]

The argument

Analytically, identifying the sources and causal significance of integration to conflict resolution relative to other factors is a task similar to that of assessing the power status and capabilities of the EU. However, this 'actorness' approach raises certain ontological and epistemological issues. European integration itself is a product of actors' preferences. The study of its outcomes belongs to the post-ontological stage of inquiry which transforms integration from 'effect' into 'cause' (Pierson 1993). A study of the conflict resolution effects of European integration suggests that it needs to be treated as an independent variable and therefore belongs to the post-ontological stage of inquiry, a type of influence more complex than the 'second image reversed' path of outcome creation (Gourevitch 1978) or the basic institutionalist premise that 'institutions matter' (Hasenclever *et al.* 2008: 2).

From an epistemological point of view, the link between European integration and conflict resolution transcends the agency-structure dichotomy without prioritising either of these categories. Integration is both an actor-centred process and a source of institutional influence. At the same time, despite a high level of institutionalisation, the EU is not a typical institution. It combines a variety of institutional settings and behavioural logics into 'a complex ecology' (Olsen 2007: 45). Since its formative stage, it has been intended to have political consequences and logically has developed in a political direction (Forsyth 1967; Scheingold 1970), although domestic mobilisation around it remains low (Parsons 2007). Its principal embodiment, the European Union, has emerged as an international actor with evolving competences, capabilities, and influence in world politics (Ginsberg 2001; Hill 1993; Smith 2004).[5] Actorness, however, does not grant a systemic quality to European integration. Its coherence as an entity and as a locus of power, consequential for other actors and processes, remains problematic. The EU is not a coherent polity (Caporaso and Stone Sweet 2001: 228; Risse-Kappen 1996). It lacks the authority structures of a state and is at best a would-be polity (Lindberg and Scheingold 1970), a multiperspectival polity (Ruggie 1993), a cosmopolitan polity (Eriksen 2006), or a non-unitary polity (Weiler 1991).

Yet another problem occurs due to the fact that although European integration originated as a peace project, it is by nature an economic and transactions-based process. The political effects of integration are not theoretically necessary or obvious, also because its institutional embodiment, the EU, is more readily associated with structural qualities than politicisation. The question with regard to conflict resolution is whether such effects are intrinsic to the integration process or are the product of purposive political action.

In order to respond to the limitations imposed by the ontological status of integration, the book advances a dual historical and analytical argument. It argues that European integration as a peace project cannot be explained by macro-level theories as they tend to prioritise individual aspects of the phenomenon – the underlying structural process or the institutional form of the EU – leaving aside the potential interaction effects of these attributes. The consequential nature of integration is explained more accurately by middle-range theorising based on the interaction between actors and structures, identities and opportunity structures, inherent to the way European integration creates outcomes. By definition, this interactive process is governance: a process of building political capacity to address policy challenges; a process of steering, of setting common goals, incentives, and constraints; and a network-type of resource exchange and output creation (Cole 2004: 354–5).

The governance perspective reverses prior analyses which posit proximity, top-down pressures, and actor-based strategies as the explanatory variables of the EU's impact on conflict resolution. From this perspective, conflict resolution represents an outcome (and variation of outcomes) created through interactions between the domestic and the EU level. Depending on the mode of outcome creation, the EU's inputs into conflict resolution may be policy-, polity-, or politics-related.

The central argument of the book is that the evolution of the dynamic mix of policy tools, resources, framing influences and political opportunities through which European integration affects conflicts and processes of conflict resolution (on the example of the Franco-German relationship, Northern Ireland, Cyprus, and Kosovo/Serbia) demonstrates a historical trend. It proceeds from the pooling together of policy-making at the European level for the management of particular sectors (early integration in the European Coal and Steel Community and the EEC customs union) through the functioning of core EU sectoral and horizontal policies (Northern Ireland) to the conditionality and incentive instruments of enlargement (Cyprus) to the externalisation of governance under the EU's integration strategy for the Western Balkans (Kosovo). The book argues that, in contrast to the interdependence literature, this historical pattern is political in nature. It is sustained by the presence of a European space (with a varying degree of salience across cases) which requires compliance, and provides reference, guidance, incentives, resources, and opportunities for political actors to pursue interest maximisation, modify cost–benefit calculations, mobilise political action, and accommodate value and identity change. The governance perspective posits such institutional and behavioural change at the domestic level as 'Europeanisation'. By extension, the EU's influences on interstate or intercommunal conflicts implemented through the tools and resources of European governance may be studied as a potential process of Europeanisation which alters actors' interests, values, and needs and is conducive to conflict resolution and reconciliation.

In this sense, EU governance has a paradigmatic effect. It is the creation of the political sphere of European integration, institutionalised and embodied in the EU, which is conducive to change in conflict dynamics and actors' behaviour and has the potential to induce the transformation of conflict into a peaceful relationship. This regional domain was originally conceptualised by Jean Monnet as 'new politics'. It has evolved historically through the discourse and norm of reconciliation, the institutionalisation of interdependencies, and the pluralisation of public space enabling domestic political actors to advance new interests and create new relationships.

The historical hypothesis holds that the conflict resolution effects of European integration are inseparable from the EU's evolution as a form of new politics. Its impacts may not directly and immediately translate into conflict resolution outcomes, but they shape the context of interstate and intercommunal relations, build a connection between economics and politics, create opportunities for critical junctures in the path-dependent processes of protracted conflicts, and provide political actors with resources to initiate positive dynamics. Binding together the historical and the analytical dimension of the argument, the working hypothesis is that European integration is historically necessary for conflict resolution and reconciliation in Europe through the systemic nature of its governance. Conflicts that occur in proximity to the EU are increasingly subsumed under an EU-generated dynamic. European integration alters the logic of conflict resolution and actors' behaviour in it. This is the broadest level of Europeanisation which Ginsberg (1999: 444) understands as moving closer to EU norms, policies, and habits.

Why would the parties to a conflict respond to EU influences in the direction of conflict resolution? Answering this question requires a definition of the possible domain of application of EU governance tools, pressures, and discourses in conflict situations in the objective of their resolution. Analysis needs to establish the root causes of conflicts, the type of relationships and issues that characterise them, the sources of conflict transformation into a peaceful relationship, and the interface between such processes and European integration.

The domain of application: conflict resolution in theory

Conflicts are multi-layer and multi-factor phenomena (Whittaker 1999: 107). Conflicts are due to incompatible interests, values, or needs and unfold as contested incompatibilities concerning territory, government, and belonging (Wallensteen and Axell 1994: 333). Whittaker (1999) posits conflicts as dynamic configurations. Conflicts evolve as a result of external influences. Third-party involvement may alter the pattern of communication between the parties, their cost–benefit calculations, values, and identities, ultimately leading to a compromise or a new bargain. Even frozen conflicts in which such sources of change are absent, are susceptible to evolution.

International conflict resolution represents a political process of removing the tensions between the parties due to previous mutually incompatible claims. It includes the act of settlement and sustaining elements to make it irreversible. Conflict resolution occurs as a result of preference or value change or a change in conflict dynamics (Wallensteen 2002). In order to be resolved, conflict should be replaced by other preferences, values, or needs. The process is one of transformation of a prior conflictual relationship into a different strategic game. It is comprised of political, social, and institutional aspects including competition, integration, or cooperation (Udalov 1991). As the dependent variable in political inquiry, conflict resolution may be measured beyond the binary outcomes of success and failure as a continuum of values representing stages of reduction of conflict intensity or positive change in conflict dynamic, secession of violence, and/or sustained management by peaceful means. Conventional conflict resolution takes place through negotiation, third-party mediation, and (authorised) intervention (Whittaker 1999: 4). The external sources of conflict resolution are coercion, creation of supranational authority, or socialisation. Such strategies are applied through different tools: indirect, such as facilitating bilateral negotiations; nonbinding third-party settlement, such as good offices, inquiry, conciliation, or mediation; and binding, including adjudication and arbitration (Mitchell 2002: 750). As a result of restructuring of the contested incompatibility, conflict ends by several possible outcomes: a free-will agreement or withdrawal from contestation, domination or conquest by one of the parties, compromise, a deceptive agreement, or integration on the basis of equality. All of these outcomes are achieved either by the parties themselves, or via third-party involvement.

Regional integration is associated with alternative methods of conflict resolution, beyond a fixed and final settlement, in which the conflict parties may develop mutual interests without removing their grievances. It is rather associated with the reconceptualisation of parties' preferences and the reformulation of their interests through tangible benefits. Integration may serve also as a sustaining mechanism for settlements which necessarily represent a distributive outcome. It permits the creation of new interests and offers a macro-political solution in which problem-solving and compromise may be embedded.

A separate dimension of conflict resolution, less discussed in the international relations literature, is based on the relationship between the status of the conflict and the domestic politics of the parties involved. Conflict resolution is inseparable from the domestic conditions, political regime, elite-mass relationships, and potential for political change in communities that are parties to a conflict. The external transactions of the state, including conflicts, have differential impact upon domestic groups. In pluralistic societies these consequences are contested or negotiated (North *et al.* 1960: 364). Processes of domestic contestation, changes in the power position of political groups, and interest reformulation during conflict help the parties to revise the status quo in the direction of peace (North *et al.* 1960: 356). It is logical to expect that conflict is easier to resolve when the parties are pluralistic societies.

Reconciliation is the final stage of conflict resolution. It represents the long-term societal process of addressing conflictual and fractured relationships, a sum of the humanising relations among adversary elites, the creation of a domestic environment conducive to peace, and the development of cooperation linkages (Montville 1990: 535). In substance, reconciliation represents the creation of an integrated community whereby conflict is replaced by tolerance and civilised behaviour (Hamber and Kelly 2004; Whittaker 1999: 7, 114). Reconciliation includes political arrangements and psychological processes. From a policy perspective, reconciliation is a process of establishing structures and procedures for durable peace at the post-settlement phase (Ackerman 1994). The relative salience of interests versus morality determines two varieties of reconciliation processes: rapprochement and forgiveness (Feldman 1999a). Whittaker (1999: 91–2) has argued that the methods of reconciliation, whether political, policy, or psychological, may be applied through legislative, corporate, or grassroots channels.

Regional integration is viewed as an international factor facilitating reconciliation. It acts either as a form of institutional influence generating actors' compliance with the rules and norms of peaceful coexistence (Pevehouse and Russett 2006), or as a process of interdependence conducive to reconciliation through strategic calculus: an estimate that the costs of war are prohibitively high relative to the benefits of economic cooperation (Feldman 1999b). By positing European integration as a pluralist process, we would expect that it would contribute to change in loyalties, legitimation discourses, and creation of new interests. Basic issues, such as improvement in needs, public amenities, public order, reconstituting governance, betterment, reconstruction, and shared values are all components of reconciliation. Reconciliation is different from a hurting stalemate in which both sides are 'reconciled' to 'futility and finality' (Whittaker 1999: 8). It depends on the possibility of developing a shared vision of an interdependent and fair society, acknowledging and dealing with the past, building positive relationships, and creating cultural, attitudinal, social, economic, and political change (Hamber and Kelly 2005b: 28).

The presence of protracted conflicts in Europe and the variation in the type of EU impact and outcomes suggests that such influences are not automatic. Existing theories explain certain aspects of the process, leaving out unexplained variation or providing conflicting predictions by either separating conflict resolution from the process or suggesting that the outcome is deterministic, or dichotomous. Such premises do not permit the evaluation of variation in a systematic way. The role of European integration as an agent of change is often underestimated due to the fact that its contributions historically have been long term, affecting root causes, grievances, and needs. They are less obvious when tracking short-term change in conflict dynamics. Due to the analytical distinctions between actors and processes, agents and structures, the literature has yet to establish a connection between the classical case of the Franco-German relationship of the 1950s and the contemporary dynamics of conflict resolution through integration in Europe. It is necessary to contextualise conflict resolution beyond the dichotomous measures of success and failure to include an assessment of critical junctures and intermediate outcomes. These include reduction in conflict intensity, interruption of violence, change in the domestic political opportunity structures, emergence of new actors, ideas, and demands, and indicators of societal reintegration. These outcomes have a distinct governance, institutional, discursive, and political content.

The new approach: Europeanisation through governance

As a purposive process based on political action, European integration is designed to create authority structures and competences for problem-solving–that is, to function as a system of governance (Harmsen and Wilson 2000). At first glance, European governance is at odds with the conceptualisation of integration as an institutional entity, an international actor, or an agent of change. The problem is that of granting the qualities of an actor, typically affecting outcomes through individual actions, to a process variable. The governance perspective, however, does just that. It recasts European integration from an instance of transnationalism into a source of impact without reducing it to an actor or a process. The systemic quality of European integration in a governance perspective is that of a non-hierarchical web of overlapping networks of public and private, national and supranational agents, i.e. 'deliberative and apolitical governance' (Hix 1998: 54).

The consequential nature of European governance
Although the integration literature conventionally associates EU governance with the workings of multi-level networks and is less concerned with the consequences of decision-making (Pollack 2005; Wiener and Diez 2004), the analytical potential of the governance perspective is significant. Governance is based on shared values, norms, and a culture of reciprocity (Rhodes 2003: 65–6). The emphasis is less on its non-hierarchical nature than on its objectives and the substantive qualities of resource exchange. Viewed through a governance lens, the EU's policy process emerges as a factor in domestic politics reflecting the foundational premise that 'policies create a new politics' (Schattschneider 1935: 288). The governance perspective reorients the classical research agenda of EU studies from the puzzle of why regional integration emerged as a preferred state strategy to explaining how it affects the domestic level of politics (Rittberger 2001). Besides an emphasis on networks, governance is amenable to study the transformative power of European integration (Checkel 2005; Weiler 1991), its politicising effects (Christiansen 1997; Daviter 2007), and impact on the structures of domestic political opportunities (Laffan 2006). The general hypothesis is that the rule-making activities of the EU create adaptational pressures at the domestic level (Knill and Lehmkuhl 1999). Its principal value added is the opportunity to open the black box of European integration as a political process of competition, resource distribution, and allocation of values conducive to the differential empowerment of actors (Mair 2004). Governance captures well the EU's extension into the wider Europe as a process of policy-making in the context of interdependence with the external system (Lavenex 2004: 685). Consequently, the independent effects of European integration may be kept substantively and analytically separate from exogenous international factors (Matlary 1997).

By focusing on the interaction between domestic politics and EU-level policies, governance is amenable to a new type of theorising, which transcends the international relations/comparative politics dichotomy in European Union studies (Hix 1998; Jupille *et al.* 2003; March and Olsen 1984). Its implications for research design are significant. Governance permits moving beyond competitive testing of rival explanations to examine the additive effects of strategic action and ideational factors. It reconciles the logic of consequentialism with that of appropriateness and contributes to the ontology of mutual constitution. Governance adopts the premise of commensurability between rational choice and constructivist theorising, reflected in the turn towards a new institutionalism in European integration theory (Aspinwall and Schneider 2001; Jupille *et al.* 2003; Zürn and Checkel 2005) and the institutionalist claim of the transformative effects of the EU institutions (Kohler-Koch and Eising 1999; Sandholtz 1993; Sbragia 2000; Stone Sweet *et al.* 2001).[6]

Governance has developed its own research agenda for the study of domestic change induced by integration. Organised around the proposition that 'Europe matters', Europeanisation constitutes a branch of the governance literature which examines the creation of rules and structures at the EU level and their consequences for the domestic political systems.[7] While theories of integration, preference formation, and even governance *per se* seek to explain why states integrate and how outcomes are created, Europeanisation transforms the dependent variable in such causal relationships into an independent variable. It advances integration research to the post-ontological stage of examining the outcomes of the process rather than its determinants (Graziano and Vink 2007). Europeanisation studies the impact of integration on the domestic political systems. In other words, if we are trying to determine whether European integration has influenced certain aspects of the domestic systems – policies, institutions, actors, and politics – we need to determine whether a process of Europeanisation is in place and provide an assessment of the extent to which the object of inquiry is Europeanised (Buller 2006). Europeanisation captures well the essence of the European Union. While there is no single locus of authority, the EU exists as a system of governance. It therefore derives its power, authority, and legitimacy through a governance process, rather than actorness.

By transforming integration from an outcome into an explanatory variable, Europeanisation offers important conceptual and analytical advantages. It shows that the influences of integration are multidirectional and unfold according to multiple logics. Most importantly, in contrast to institutionalist theorising, it demonstrates that European integration is not only a system of rule-making but also a resource and an opportunity for domestic actors to make reference to Europe and solve problems even in the absence of direct EU-level pressures. Europeanisation advances the new institutionalism in integration studies by adding a political perspective. It looks beyond institutional outcomes, conventionally defined as compliance and identity change, and focuses on political processes of choice, implementation, and empowerment (Olsen 2007). In short, Europeanisation contributes to uncovering the sources, causal paths, and influences of integration as a political, rather than as an economic or an institutional process.

This analysis presents conflict resolution as an area susceptible to Europeanisation effects. Applied as an organising framework for the study of the conflict resolution effects of European integration, Europeanisation permits one to address the subject-matter from the point of view of 'what the EU does', in contrast to conventional approaches which explain its political influence by 'what it is', an international actor and a process of regionalism (Hettne and Söderbaum 2005; Manners 2002). It is applicable to conflict resolution because it permits the linking of changes in conflict dynamics to domestic politics and the analysis of how domestic change reduces conflict intensity even if it does not affect settlement. Conflicts are Europeanised when the institutional processes that guide their resolution are reframed, reoriented, and reshaped to reflect the primacy of EU norms and governance processes, and when influential actors adopt the modalities of European integration to resolve conflicts relative to other inputs.

The analytical capacity of Europeanisation permits the untangling, to the extent possible, of the EU's sources of impact from those of other regional institutions, influential players, or universal processes. Besides an evaluation of impact, it also permits the examination of the possible homogenisation of political systems as a result of their interaction with EU governance (Page 2003: 167) and thus address the big question about the influence of European integration on conflict resolution: is there an EU-specific model of conflict resolution and is the EU itself a model regional system of conflict resolution?

The novelty of research

Recasting the study of the conflict resolution effects of European integration through the analytical lens of Europeanisation does not constitute *per se* novelty in the field. Both the Europeanisation agenda and the EU's role in conflict resolution have asserted themselves as important research areas in the EU literature. A number of publications, among them Coppieters *et al.* (2004), Tocci (2004), Axt *et al.* (2006a, 2006b), Papadimitriou *et al.* (2007), and Zaborowski (2004) have applied the concept of linking conflict resolution to the prospects of some form of integrative association between the EU and conflict parties. These works tend to adopt specific substantive definitions that treat conflict resolution as a precondition to EU membership and thus posit Europeanisation as identical to membership conditionality. Where this book would claim novelty is the application of Europeanisation to model-building and the argument that the EU's impacts on conflict resolution take place through the interconnected arenas of policy, politics, and polity interactions, as opposed to the prevalent treatment of Europeanisation as a strategy for resolving conflicts through the conditionality of EU membership.

Europeanisation has made significant advances as a research agenda which now permits engagement in thematic analyses. A number of publications and, in particular, works evoking the bottom-up and other complex trajectories of Europeanisation (Börzel and Risse 2007; Graziano and Vink 2007; Quaglia and Radaelli 2007) have focused on methodological issues in Europeanisation research. While Europeanisation has established itself into a mainstream agenda in EU studies, empirical research integrating its policy, politics, and polity dimensions is still in its infancy. By adopting an approach examining the cross-cutting influences of European integration, this book presents a novel treatment of Europeanisation with regard to conflict resolution. It contends that the influences of European integration are not limited to conditionality and norm adoption, as prior studies suggest. If applied systematically, the definition of Europeanisation permits the examination of the entire range of potential integration influences on conflict resolution beyond membership conditionality. This book problematises claims in the literature that conditionality can serve as a common instrument of conflict resolution and that the EU has failed in its conflict resolution efforts due to the lack of consistency in the application of its conditionality and incentive structures.

There is therefore a need to revisit the application of Europeanisation as an analytical framework for the study of the EU's role in conflict resolution. This first-generation, or 'classical' Europeanisation, predominantly applied with regard to the secessionist conflicts in Southeastern Europe, is linked to the incentives and conditionality structure of enlargement and institutional rapprochement to the EU. Since the completion of the Eastern European enlargement cycle (1997–2007), the prospect of membership in exchange for compliance with the EU's preference for resolving outstanding conflicts has lost its credibility. In a major decision to support Kosovo's declaration of independence through a rule of law mission launched in 2008, the EU reversed its prevalent preference to discourage secession (as was the case in Bosnia-Herzegovina, Serbia/Montenegro, and Cyprus).

What is the continued relevance of the EU to conflict resolution? If the argument that due to its inconsistent application and low credibility, membership conditionality is of limited utility to induce positive change in the dynamics of conflict resolution, does that mean that the EU's impact is declining, in the absence of an alternative strategy? Europeanisation can no longer remain conceptually and empirically linked to the incentive structure of the EU's enlargement policy and membership conditionality. The disconnect between the definitional qualities of Europeanisation and its application in the literature on conflict resolution limits the opportunities to examine the EU's influence on conflicts as a substantive area of European governance in which the EU institutional actors interact to formulate policy tools, discourses, and political action and apply them in their interaction with conflict parties. A broadly based definition of Europeanisation beyond membership conditionality improves the analytical utility of the concept and connects the study of conflict resolution to processes of preference formation, policy formulation, and implementation testing for variation and consistency across time. The process is one of linking the system of governance to the contested incompatibilities of conflict through agenda-setting, institutional processes, and material, cognitive, and ideational resources.

Beyond this analytical dimension, the broader objective is to conceptualise Europeanisation as a paradigm of peace: a matrix of principles, norms, and political processes beyond interdependence which transform a conflictual relationship (France–Germany), sustain settlement (Northern Ireland, potentially Cyprus) or make it redundant (Kosovo). The Europeanisation of conflicts does not suggest that all conflicts in Europe are resolved by European integration only. The argument is that there is a trend of subsuming conflicts into the dynamics of regional integration even outside processes of EU accession or association.

Method and case selection

This research presents an alternative to the 'variable-oriented' approach (Ragin 1987). It traces and compares how European integration, as an independent variable conceptualised as EU governance, performs across cases. The research design is not explicitly one of hypothesis testing because European integration is not a fully autonomous process or a single factor at work to allow operationalisation as a single independent variable. Methodologically, analysis relies on process tracing, an approach alternative to causation, which examines the sequence of events to establish links between plausible causes and the values of the dependent variable (George and Bennett 2005: 6). Also applicable to the study is the method of qualified historical analogy and comparison. By evoking the classical case of conflict resolution and reconciliation between France and Germany, the discussion of subsequent cases is amenable to across-case comparisons.

Consistency in the implementation of the research design is maintained through data collection based on triangulation. Evidence in all case studies is derived from a combination of primary, secondary, and media sources. Primary sources include official documents, such as communications among the European institutions, official reports of the UN Secretary-General and the Security Council, written comments, testimony, press releases, and statements by influential political actors in international conflict resolution involved in the decision-making process, as well as personal interviews conducted by the author during the periods March–June 2008 and June–August 2010 with representatives of the EU institutions, member states, and societal actors. Special emphasis is placed on primary sources pertaining to the EU institutions, including audit reports, Council Conclusions, communications of the European Commission to the Council and the European Parliament, press releases, documents of the European Economic and Social Committee (EESC), the Bulletin of the EU, European Parliament resolutions, debates, and interviews with Members of the Parliament, the European Commission, and members of working groups in the Council and the EESC, as well as everyday communication among the institutions: parliamentary questions and answers, joint sessions of the EP and the Commission, and joint reporting as evidence of institutional exchange and decision-making.

By applying the analytical framework of Europeanisation, the book relies on evidence located both at the EU and at the domestic/individual level of analysis which accounts for an interactive research design and fits well with the methodological principle of data source triangulation. Triangulation improves the external validity of the analysis by using multiple sources and interpretation of data. It produces a complex picture of the social phenomena under examination and contributes to the reliability of the conclusions we draw (Mathison 1988). This approach to treating the evidence complements the methodological pluralism characteristic of the field, as research tends to privilege either actor-centred perspectives by relying primarily on interview data, or comprehensive policy analyses of the EU conflict resolution domain which examine evidence located at the EU level.

With the objective of representativeness and consistency, the book applies a multiple case study design based on intentional case selection. Although the number of cases is limited and the Europeanisation thesis itself is confined to the membership and association mechanism of European integration, they comply with the criteria for multiple case study designs and permit the examination of a variety of integration influences. The resulting selection is a set of case studies independent of one another: France/Germany, Northern Ireland, Cyprus, and Kosovo/Serbia. Bias can be avoided by including cases representative of all historical periods of the European construction and the corresponding mechanisms of EU governance: the early years of integration reflected in the Europeanisation of policy-making and the evolution of the EU's regional, enlargement, and foreign policies. From a conflict resolution perspective, the cases comprise a variety of conflict situations: interstate conflict, intercommunal conflict, self-determination, and secession, representative of incompatible claims to territory, identity, and governance.

Regardless of the level of analysis, all conflicts have a broader regional relevance and involve international mediation as a method of conflict resolution. Furthermore, they all involve EU participation beyond conventional peacemaking and negotiation. All conflicts permit the application of a dynamic perspective by tracing their various stages: grievances, initial stages and escalation, management, settlement, resolution, and reconciliation. Last but not least, they share a status of proximity to the EU, although differentiated as membership, accession, privileged association, or a European perspective broadly defined. Proximity is a necessary condition for applying the Euroepanisation matrix. Europeanisation presupposes some form of integrative relationship between the EU and the parties to a conflict: membership, association, or partnership. If integrative links are lacking, the influence of regional integration would be similar to that of other international actors and should be treated as a case of international socialisation, interdependence, and mediation (Diez et al. 2006).

The case studies refer to a large variety of choices and outcomes of European integration at key stages of its functioning as a system of regional governance. Its early history represents a process of transformation of the historical enmity between France and Germany by binding together their war industries into a multilateral economic and political framework. In this version of 'old' Europeanisation (Diez 2000) actors Europeanise policy-making with a view to establishing an irreversible relationship based on multilateral bargaining and open-ended compromise. Cyprus and Northern Ireland represent two cases of protracted intercommunal conflict. The conflict in Northern Ireland gradually emerged from an internal member state issue into a matter of intercommunal negotiation embedded in a European context and amenable to the instruments of EU policy-making. Cyprus experienced a transition from a matter of foreign policy to a case of externalisation of governance under the EU enlargement policy and, ultimately, EU membership. The Kosovo/Serbia conflict, since its beginnings labelled a European problem, is representative of the externalisation of EU governance and its international crisis management capabilities, the development of a regional approach to the Western Balkans, and the limitations of conventional integration mechanisms.

Although the Franco-German case represents the 'archetypal' case of conflict resolution in Europe, it cannot be applied as a standard of evaluation in subsequent cases. The book builds an alternative comparative approach by focusing on the sources of variation historically and across cases. Case selection is designed to provide a detailed examination of individual integration mechanisms as they become, or fail to become, applicable to conflict resolution.

Structure of the book

The book proceeds with a theoretical chapter, titled 'The Europeanisation of conflict resolution: theory and framework', which discusses Europeanisation as a construct of middle-range theorising. The chapter examines the scope, causal processes, and outcomes of Europeanisation with a particular emphasis on their implications for model-building. A separate section discusses the Europeanisation of conflict resolution as a non-traditional area of Europeanisation related to the capacity of EU policies and discourses to alter or subsume the organisational logic of the process and induce behavioural change on behalf of the conflict parties. Following the conceptualisation of Europeanisation as a matrix of top-down, bottom-up, and discursive influences, the chapter outlines the necessary stages of the Europeanisation of conflict resolution, applied as an analytical framework to the case studies in subsequent chapters.

Chapter 3 examines the formative stage of European integration as a system of conflict resolution. This is the classical case of the design of regional integration as a peace process. Europeanisation takes place as the pooling together of policy-making in individual areas. The timeframe of the chapter is set with the beginnings of integration as a strategy of Franco-German reconciliation from the late 1940s and the 1950s to the signing of the 1963 bilateral Treaty for Cooperation, the Elysée Treaty. The introductory section traces early attempts to break the cycle of punitive peace between France and Germany. It then reflects on the meaning of Europeanisation during the 1950s as a strategy of peace-building accomplished through joint policy-making in the European Coal and Steel Community and the irreversible institutionalisation of a customs union through the European Economic Community. Europeanisation is traced through the problem-solving capacity of integration with regard to the Ruhr and the Saar issue and the signing of the Elysée Treaty. The concluding section reflects on the significance of Europeanisation for domestic political pluralism and for the politicisation of economic interdependence.

Chapter 4 discusses the EU's role in the conflict in Northern Ireland as a case of Europeanisation breakthrough: the gradual expansion of the tasks and competences of European integration affecting the institutional logic of the Northern Ireland peace process. The chapter begins with a historical overview of the European dimension of the conflict: nation-building in the European state system, nationalism, and the post-Second World War evolution of the welfare state. It then outlines the EU's involvement following the 1973 accession of the UK and Ireland through the gradual application of the instruments of the EU structural policies. The focus of the chapter is the incremental nature of establishing a role for European integration in the conflict resolution process through policy tools, resources, and political opportunities. Analysis examines the roles of the EU institutions, especially the debates and resolutions of the European Parliament and the programming initiatives of the European Commission, for inducing change in the domestic political opportunity structure conducive to intercommunal reconciliation. The chapter finds that relative to other actors involved in the conflict, the importance of European integration has grown and concludes that it has produced significant long-term transformative effects by enhancing communication, societal interaction, and interest disaggregation.

Chapter 5 is devoted to the study of the EU's influence on the intercommunal conflict in Cyprus. The introductory section provides an overview of the conflict and maps out integration strategies implemented over the course of the EU–Cyprus relationship. A process-tracing approach is followed in order to establish the growing centrality of a European space with regard to the conflict. Analysis identifies changes in the institutional logic of the UN-sponsored process towards negotiated settlement as a result of the evolution of the the EU–Cyprus relationship by tracing the early stages of the Association Agreement (1973), application for EU membership (1990), prospect and instruments of the EU enlargement policy (1995), decoupling of conditionality and membership incentives (1999–2002), EU accession (2004), Turkey's accession negotiations (2005), and resumption of intercommunal talks (2008). This case addresses specifically the issue of conditionality and the limitations of its application.

Chapter 6 discusses Europeanisation effects in the context of a failed, or non-negotiated, settlement in the case of the Kosovo/Serbia conflict as an instance of Europeanisation in the making. The chapter outlines the long-term perspective of the EU's involvement in the conflict since 1990. Analysis examines the precursors of Europeanisation through political and diplomatic instruments, international negotiation and mediation within the Contact Group on Kosovo, and UN-based initiatives, as well as EU integration mechanisms, such as the Regional approach (1997), Stability Pact for Southeast Europe (1999), Stabilisation and Association Process (2000), the instruments of the EU integration strategy for the Western Balkans (2003), and the European civilian rule of law mission EULEX. The chapter finds weak direct effects but a strong positive association between the EU influences and the institutional dynamic of the conflict resolution process, measured as political change and reform in Serbia and progress in state-building in Kosovo. It argues that despite significant limitations, the EU has become an indispensable agent of conflict resolution in Kosovo.

The concluding chapter reviews the empirical findings and discusses their implications for the theoretical debates in EU studies and international conflict resolution. It presents an argument about the potential of the concept of Europeanisation and the governance perspective in EU studies to explain the effects of European integration on conflicts. The chapter comments on the limitations of the top-down adaptational pressures and functional expediencies of integration to induce domestic change, if removed from processes of political resources and opportunities, and ideological legitimation.

By tracing the evolution of the dynamic mix of policy tools, resources, framing influences, and political opportunities which European integration creates in the diverse settings of conflict resolution, the book is able to demonstrate a historical trend. It proceeds from the creation of instruments of joint policy-making for the management of particular sectors (early integration in the European Coal and Steel Community and the EEC) through the functioning of the EU regional policy (Northern Ireland) to the inconclusive application of the conditionality and incentive instruments of the EU eastern enlargement (Cyprus) to the externalisation of EU governance under the European perspective of the Western Balkans (Kosovo). In contrast to the interdependence literature, the book argues that this historical pattern is political in nature. It is sustained by the presence of a European space relevant to conflict resolution (with varying degrees of salience across cases), which requires compliance and provides incentives, resources, opportunities, and legitimation for political actors to pursue interest maximisation, alters their preferences and lowers the domestic costs of acceptance of EU-sponsored proposals for conflict resolution, mobilises political action, and accommodates value change conducive to a positive evolution in conflict dynamics.

Notes

1 Winston Churchill, speech delivered at the University of Zurich, 19 September 1946. Strasbourg: Council of Europe. Available at: www.coe.int/T/E/Com /About_Coe/DiscoursChurchill.asp,http://www.ena.lu?lang=2&doc=22347.
2 The designation 'European Union' was introduced in the Maastricht Treaty (1992) to replace the term 'European Economic Community' (EEC), the international organisation created under the Treaty of Rome (1957). As a result of the Merger Treaty (1967), the European Economic Community, together with the European Coal and Steel Community (ECSC), and Euratom emerged as the European Communities (EC). The Maastricht Treaty subsumed the EC as the first pillar of the European Union (EU) and developed also a foreign policy domain, the Common Foreign and Security Policy (CFSP), and an internal security dimension, the Justice and Home Affairs (JHA) domain. For the sake of consistency and historical continuity, 'European Union' will be used as an umbrella term throughout, as appropriate. Individual chapters apply the terms 'European Economic Community' and 'European Communities' (EC) with reference to the historical period 1957–1965 and 1965–1992, respectively.
3 The terms 'regionalisation', 'regionalism', and 'integration' are analytically distinct. Regionalisation is an objective trend of enhanced interdependence in areas of geographical proximity with an emphasis on micro- or market processes, while regionalism and integration imply a political process. Regionalism is an 'an ideology about how the world should be organised to follow an example of pioneering region-alising regions and adapt to "a slicing up" of interdependence' (Hettne 1991: 282). Regional integration is a consciously guided process reflecting a regionalist approach insofar as it creates viable regions. Integration as an outcome is 'the voluntary creation of larger political units involving the self-conscious eschewal of force in relations between participating institutions' (Rosamond 2000: 12).
4 Provisions on the CFSP in the Treaty on European Union, Art. 21–22 (European Union 2008a: 28–30). See also Part Five 'External Action by the Union', Treaty on the functioning of the European Union (European Union 2008b).
5 For a summary and principal contributions to the actorness perspective in EU studies, see Ginsberg (1999), Hill (1996), Hill and Wallace (1996), Kirchner (2006), Kirchner

and Sperling (2007), Sjøstedt (1977), Wæver (1998), and Zielonka (1998, 2007), among others. For a contrasting view, arguing that the EU lacks the autonomy of an actor, see Bull (1982).
6   On the governance perspective, see also Bulmer (1983), Eberlein and Kerwer (2002, 2004), Kohler-Koch (1996, 2003), March and Olsen (1995), Marks *et al.* (1996), Pierre and Peters (2000), Pollack (2005), and Wallace *et al.* (2005), among others.
7   The early literature examining the domestic influences of European integration proceeds from the premises of supranationalism and institutionalism. See Bulmer (1983, 1985), Sandholtz (1996), Sandholtz and Stone Sweet (1998), Stone Sweet *et al.* (2001), and Usher (1985).

2

The Europeanisation of conflict resolution: theory and framework

Introduction

The purpose of this chapter is to develop an analytical framework for the study of the ways in which European integration affects conflict resolution processes. If integration is causally significant to resolving conflicts, then it must possess certain attributes and mechanisms of action which would distinguish it from other actors and processes, such as influential third powers, international organisations, structural interdependence, and liberal internationalism. The objective is to identify the elements and causal paths of integration with a capacity to resolve conflict and to contribute new insights into the intriguing relationship between European integration and peace. Building upon the proposition about the transformative nature of European governance and the relationship between the EU and the domestic level of politics, this analysis applies Europeanisation as an analytical framework for examining the impacts of European integration on conflict resolution. To the extent that EU governance, understood as a process of institution- and capacity building, provision of policy tools, and legitimation of collective understandings of peaceful coexistence affects the dynamics of the conflict resolution process inducing positive change in the preference and behaviour of conflict parties, such effects may be examined as a thematic area of Europeanisation.

Recasting the conflict resolution and reconciliation effects of integration as a process of Europeanisation is a challenging task. As an institutional embodiment of integration, the EU lacks explicit competences for dealing with conflicts although it possesses certain policy, normative, and cognitive resources, especially in the area of conflict prevention (European Commission 2001). At the same time, the EU has acquired a growing stake in the political stability and economic prosperity of Europe maintained through its external, enlargement, and neighborhood policies, and through a network of institutionalised relations with the majority of European states. Such relations, including their policy, political and conflict-related aspects are subsumed under the Europeanisation framework. Europeanisation fills the gap between settlement and resolution in conflict resolution analysis, as well as between constitutional and political approaches to resolving conflicts, by shedding more light on actors' responsiveness to international conflict resolution strategies.

The argument of the chapter is that by introducing governance initiatives relevant to conflict resolution, which engage the parties to a conflict in institutional processes and provide them with policy tools and resources, European integration is conducive to opening up the single-issue context of conflicts. The core proposition is that Europeanisation is associated with increasing domestic pluralism, as the network-type, multi-actor EU governance process tends to disaggregate domestic interests. If such processes of pluralisation take place in the process of conflict resolution as a result of the EU's involvement, and if the principal contested incompatibility of the conflict may be disaggregated into individual high-salience issues, such as economic development, nondiscrimination, social disparities, and minority/majority rights represented by diverse societal interests, the chances for conflict resolution increase. This analysis posits that conflict resolution is 'Europeanised' when a European 'space' of policy-making and political interaction emerges and gains centrality relative to other agents of conflict resolution, and when EU conditionality and compliance mechanisms, norms, and discourses prescribe the appropriate standard of behaviour, offer the preferred form of resources, and are recognised by the conflict parties as a legitimate and desirable source of political action.

How can this argument be linked to the existing literature on Europeanisation? In order to do this, the chapter proceeds as follows. It begins with an examination of the definitional attributes of Europeanisation, its principal domains of application, sources of influence, causal mechanism, and possible outcomes. It then adapts the framework to the thematic study of conflict resolution, situating it within prior research examining the conflict resolution effects of European integration. Based on the conceptualisation of Europeanisation as a matrix of top-down, bottom-up, and discursive influences which potentially affect the institutional process of conflict resolution and actors' behaviour, the chapter outlines the elements of the Europeanisation matrix of conflict resolution: European space of resources and interaction, a causal mechanism, and the conversion of Europeanisation outcomes into policy, political, or institutional sources of conflict resolution.

Why Europeanisation? Defining the term

Europeanisation is not a grand theory. It is a construct of middle-range theorising and a heuristic device (Mair 2004). According to Caporaso (2007: 33), Europeanisation is a component of integration theory together with classical integration and theories of the EU as polity. Europeanisation and integration theory share several common assumptions: that the development of European integration is voluntary and purposeful, and that integration fulfils functional expediencies (Olsen 2007; Schmitter 1996). Political pluralism constitutes another shared premise (Aspinwall and Schneider 2001; Haas 2001). The EU represents an arena of policy-making and open-ended compromise where actors compete based on the domestic distribution of political and economic power (Olsen 2002: 930). Although domestic pluralism and democratic government are foundational principles of European integration (Hoffmann 1966), the latter in turn reinforces the pluralist nature of domestic politics and the openness of political space by adding a transnational dimension (Della Porta and Caiani 2006).

Europeanisation has 'many faces' (Olsen 2002). It consists of two-directional processes of institutionalisation of European norms and governance structures (European integration *per se*) and the penetration of EU-level rules and principles of governance in the domestic political systems. Europeanisation spans across several layers of politics: expansion of the territorial boundaries of European integration, creation of governance institutions, national adaptation and rule-following, export of political organisation outside the territorial boundaries of the European Union, and political unification (Olsen 2002).

The concise definition of Europeanisation is that of a process term implying the reorientation of domestic politics in the context of regional integration so that the EU's political and economic dynamics 'become part of the organisational logic of national politics and policy-making' (Ladrech 1994: 69). Historically this definition has evolved. Diez (2001: 7) posits a distinction between 'old' and 'new' Europeanisation. Old Europeanisation is a synonym for the transfer of competences in select policy areas to the supranational level (Forsyth 1981; Geiger 2000; Milward 1992). New Europeanisation examines the influence of EU governance on the domestic political systems. The governance perspective grants Europeanisation an expanded analytical ability to address questions of interaction, feedback effects, and variation in domestic outcomes (Kohler-Koch and Eising 1999; Marks *et al.* 1996; Radaelli and Francino 2004; Scharpf 2001).

Spanning across the old/new typology, Risse *et al.* (2001: 3) define Europeanisation as 'the emergence and development at the European level of distinct structures of governance, that is, of political, legal, and social institutions associated with political problem-solving that formalize interactions among actors, and of policy networks specializing in the creation of authoritative European rules'. This definition combines the process of communitarisation of select policies and practices at the EU level (Prange 2003) and their subsequent effects (Schmidt 2002). A similar two-directional definition posits Europeanisation as the transfer of institutional arrangements, norms, and beliefs from the European to the domestic level and the process of building a European capacity to act (Bulmer 2007: 47).

Radaelli (2003: 30) formally distinguishes between the two directions of the process by defining Europeanisation as 'processes of (a) construction, (b) diffusion, and (c) institutionalization of formal and informal rules, procedures, policy paradigms, styles, "ways of doing things", and shared beliefs and norms which are first defined and consolidated in the making of EU public policy and politics and then incorporated in the logic of domestic discourse, identities, political structures, and public policies'. Other definitions prioritise a domain of application approach. From the perspective of polity-building, Schmidt (2004) conceptualises Europeanisation as a process of transcendence of state boundaries and the historical convergence of the European nation-states towards a higher-order configuration. Paraskevopoulos (2001) describes it as the opening up of the nation-state to formal and informal rules originating at the supranational level and as a challenge to its territorial order related to devolution, restructuring, and expansion of institutional capacity at the local level of politics. Following institutionalist premises, Olsen defines it as 'change in the core domestic institutions of governance as a consequence of the development of European-level institutions, identities, and policies' (Olsen 2007: 227). Graziano and Vink (2007: 7) understand Europeanisation as 'the domestic adaptation to European regional integration'.

The most important attribute of Europeanisation is its interactive nature: first, because member states both shape EU policies and adapt to them (Börzel 2002a: 194) and second, because the influences of integration are contingent upon social, political, and economic processes at the domestic level. The interaction between the domestic and the EU level represents a process of policy 'uploading', whereby states transfer their policy preferences and styles to the EU level, 'downloading', as they adapt to or internalise EU governance rules and norms, and 'cross-loading', as they interact in the process (Howell 2004). State behaviour affects the patterns and scope of Europeanisation. High-regulation countries seek to upload their governance model ('pace-setting'); low-regulation states seek to contain the EU's top-down pressures ('foot-dragging'); others prefer ambivalent positions which tend to produce flexible coalitions ('fence-sitting') (Börzel 2002b).

All of these perspectives are relevant to the thematic study of EU influences on conflict resolution as the EU has no single blueprint, predefined competences, or an established *modus operandi* in that area. According to the general Europeanisation hypothesis, if there is an identifiable EU source and mechanism of action which produces conflict resolution effects, then changes in the institutional process of conflict resolution and actor behaviour in conflict can be defined as Europeanisation.

Who is Europeanised and by whom: by European integration or by the EU?

There is a consensus in the literature that Europeanisation is not limited to the EU member states but is a valid framework for the study of the EU's influence on candidate countries and other actors bound to the EU by some form of association (Grabbe 2001, 2006; Lippert *et al.* 2001; Magen 2006; Schimmelfennig 2007; Schimmelfennig and Sedelmeier 2005; Sciarini *et al.* 2004). The extended territorial relevance of Europeanisation is a product of the externalisation of the system of EU governance whereby third countries adopt EU-designed policy instruments, styles, and paradigms, as well as norms and principles of political behaviour in the expectation of getting closer to Europe (Farrell 2005; Treib 2008).

Because it refers to interaction and sources of influence both at the regional and the domestic level, Europeanisation risks conceptual stretching (Radaelli 2000b). It has evolved into a synonym for the democratising influences of the Western institutions. Europeanisation in this sense is no longer bound by the EU proximity criterion. The process is broader and less coherent than Europeanisation in the context of EU integration. The causal path approximates that of international socialisation (Schimmelfennig *et al.* 2006). Problematic analytical overlap exists between European integration as a process of creation of EU-level structures of governance and Europeanisation. Cowles *et al.* (2001) consider the creation of EU institutional rules a component of Europeanisation while Schmidt (2002) places an ontological distinction between the two. European integration is regarded as a process of rule-making and Europeanisation as the influence of EU-level rules on the domestic systems.

Defining the independent variable: the EU, European integration, or EU governance?

Which are the sources of Europeanisation: macro-political processes of territorial restructuring, interdependence, or simply the EU? The theoretical literature explains the confounding uses of the terms 'European integration' and 'European Union' by the multidimensional nature of integration reflected in the dependent variable problem in integration theory and the level of analysis issue in European studies. Rosamond (2000: 13) posits integration as a dual concept, a process and an outcome, and points to the differences between the structural dimensions of integration as a process of economic interdependence and 'formal', or 'legal', integration as the construction of institutions for cooperation which the EU represents. Integration is also an arena of policy-making dynamics. The policy system of the EU is defined by the interactions of actors and processes of agenda-setting, policy formulation, legislative activities, interest mediation, and policy implementation (Rosamond 2000: 15). This system represents European governance, which takes place through policy networks and institutional roles in overlapping national and supranational political arenas.

According to Rosamond, the appropriate term depends on 'where we locate our analysis', that is, on how we answer Rosenau's famous question: 'Of what is this an instance?' (Rosamond 2000: 14). The ordering of integration as an instance of regionalism, international organisation, or governance reflects the level-of-analysis issue in integration studies (Rosamond 2000: 112). Rosamond suggests that the appropriate term for the macro-process at the super-systemic level is European integration. At the system level, the unit of analysis is European Union as an institution and a political entity. EU governance is located at the meso-level as a meeting place of demand and supply of roles, decision-making, and resource allocation. Although it has systemic features, governance moves away from the macro-aspect of integration. It represents the level of analysis closest to the creation of outcomes and is therefore anchored in the EU-specific theoretical literature. By contrast, an examination of integration as a super-systemic process is amenable to broader theories of international relations. The level-of-analysis issue demonstrates why, as a concept of EU governance, Europeanisation may be better positioned to explain the relevance of European integration to conflict resolution than international relations theory approaches based on power, interdependence, or contractual relations. Systemic theories explain state preferences for integration but are less amenable to examining the workings of integration as rule creation and adaptation at the unit level. Due to across-level interaction, it is often difficult to separate Europeanisation effects from broader influences, such as globalisation, comparative advantage, interdependence, and national preferences (Bulmer 2007). The outcomes of Europeanisation are 'subtle, indirect, incremental, and difficult to measure and assess' (Olsen 2007: 242–3). As a result, the influences of European integration often are subsumed under the insights of organisation theory (Olsen 2002), sociology (Grote and Lang 2003; Schimmelfennig *et al.* 2006), social constructivism (Checkel 2001), and regionalism (Hettne and Söderbaum 2000; Tavares 2004).

The object of Europeanisation: what is being Europeanised?
The literature distinguishes between three domains of EU-level impacts on the domestic systems: policies, politics, and polity (Featherstone and Radaelli 2003). The Europeanisation of public policies constitutes the most widely researched domain. The sources of Europeanisation influences are multiple and differ according to the policy sector and type of EU governance: whether they are hierarchical, consensual, or deliberative (Bulmer and Radaelli 2005). The proposition that the different modes of governance determine differences in the autonomy, cohesiveness, and centrality of EU actions, is integral to the study of the conflict resolution effects of European integration. The community method and regulatory governance are associated with the prescriptive rules of the system of EU law in the economic and political domain and result in policy transfer (Radaelli 2000a, 2003). The open method of coordination provides diverse horizontal rules and norms which affect the domestic systems by altering the ways in which resources are mobilised and deployed (De Bièvre and Neuhold 2007). There is therefore no single model

of outcome creation through integration. We would expect that the more consensus-based the respective EU mode of governance is, the more actor-based the model of outcome-creation would be. The mode-of-governance proposition explains why top-down Europeanisation models are more readily applicable towards non-members. The closer actors are drawn to the EU, the more likely it is that the model of outcome creation would be actor-based.

The polity effects of Europeanisation are measured in terms of change at the level of domestic institutions, inter-governmental relations, and legal systems, as well as the cognitive structures of the state, such as traditions, norms, values, and identities (Anderson 2002; Auel and Benz 2005; Cole and Drake 2000; Kassim 2003, 2005). Europeanisation influences the domain of politics along two dimensions: the structure of societal cleavages and public discourse (Schmidt 2004). It expands the opportunity for the transnationalisation of collective action in a European public space and acts as a source of supranational impact on the openness of the domestic realm (Della Porta and Caiani 2006; Imig and Tarrow 2000). By altering the structure of domestic political opportunities, the regional dimension of political space reshapes the equilibrium among elites and their capacity and chances for success in political mobilisation (Goldsmith 2003; Vassallo 2003).

As a discursive practice, Europeanisation is inseparable from the significance of European integration as a historical process. According to Diez (1999: 610), institutions cannot be isolated from the discourses they are embedded in. The role of discourse is to frame policy development, advance agendas, and grant legitimacy to the adoption of European rules and norms (Wincott 2004). Policy and politics is thus a part of discourse, not only a consequence of framing influences (Diez 2001: 6–7). According to Schmidt (1997), political discourse produces a coherent vision of integration capable of convincing the public that change is necessary. Its normative significance is informed by the logic of appropriateness. Its cognitive content is related to the relevance of ideas as policy solutions, or the logic of necessity (Schmidt 2005: 7). The role of discourse is not automatic. Its capacity to affect actor behaviour and identities depends on the extent to which it resonates with public norms (Radaelli and Schmidt 2004).

Although analytically appropriate, treating the politics, policy, polity, and framing effects of Europeanisation as separate and independently created limits the opportunity to apply the concept in a dynamic perspective. Prior findings suggest that Europeanisation affects simultaneously all domains of social interaction because policies, politics, and polity constitute interconnected arenas (Bulmer and Radaelli 2005; Bursens 2007: 125). The policy effects of European integration have nontrivial polity-building and political relevance with a capacity to alter inter-institutional relations and the relative positioning of political actors (Knill 2001). Rules inducing similarity in policy styles and paradigms of development affect the authority structures of the state (Massey 2004: 26). By inducing change in the domestic functional cleavages and access to political participation the European level affects the settings of domestic political interaction. According to Daviter (2007), the principal outcome of the Europeanisation of the politics of contention is increasing pluralism, as the less rigidly organised EU governance process disaggregates domestic interests, rather than confront them directly. The analytical advantage of Europeanisation is the opportunity to look for interactions across its policy, polity, and political impacts. Similarly, Ladrech's (1994) definition evokes measures of Europeanisation pertaining to the organisational logic of politics and policy-making. EU-derived policy instruments may alter the constellation of domestic political actors as they empower pacifist and reform-oriented elites, provide them with new discourses, and change their strategic calculations even without clear prospects for EU membership and immediate benefits. Such reordering of preferences, objectives, and relationships at the domestic level is conducive to altering polity traditions, as well as perceptions of belonging, identity, and needs. The proposition of across-domain interactions is thus relevant to the argument that Europeanisation is an appropriate framework for examining the conflict resolution effects of European integration.

Establishing causality

Causality is central to the study of Europeanisation in a variety of aspects. The claim that European integration affects the domestic level of politics needs to be theoretically justified (Bulmer 2007: 47). The alternative view is that, as an actor-centred phenomenon, integration has a limited or no capacity to affect the domestic systems (Goetz 2000). Because of the actor-centred nature of European integration, we need to demonstrate that at least one variable in the model of outcome creation is exogenous. Furthermore, integration is not isolated from broader influences. As an embedded process, it may act either as an independent or an intervening variable. Establishing its net effect is not a straightforward task also due to the need to control for competing explanations (Goetz 2000: 19; Haverland 2005).

In order to establish the theoretical necessity of causation, the core of the Europeanisation research agenda consists of identifying the sources of integration influences while taking into account that integration is not a single-stream event. Next, such influences need to be causally linked to domestic change. Due to the presence of mediating factors and reciprocal pressures emanating from domestic politics, it is necessary to identify possible interaction effects. Last but not least, the research task is to explain (variation in) Europeanisation outcomes. Often an account of direct causation is replaced by an account of the logic of EU action.

How do we evaluate the potentially causal links between the EU's input and domestic change? Moravcsik (1994) has argued that international institutions reallocate political resources by changing the informational, ideological, and institutional context within which policy decisions are made at the domestic level. Initiatives which establish control over the agenda and the institutional procedure for deliberation, informational asymmetries, and ideological and cognitive resources providing legitimacy for a European agenda serve as causal links which translate EU pressures into domestic adaptation in line with EU-level initiatives. According to Moravcsik (1994: 9), the EU's influence over domestic decision-making tends to limit the opportunities for societal actors to introduce alternative procedures, practically imposing a procedure of 'closed rule' in the decision-making process. Control over the agenda increases the credibility of EU initiatives by creating opportunities for linkages and side payments. Such situations tend to expand the win-set of domestic actors in international negotiation and increase the chances of adoption of EU-inspired policy initiatives (Moravcsik 1994: 9). The discursive and ideological influences of the EU take place by reallocating ideational and cognitive resources in the direction of providing legitimation for a given policy outcome. Through its historical discourses and value system, the EU introduces broader philosophical, political, and economic considerations which change actors' preferences (Moravcsik 1994: 13). Such outcomes are possible due to declining costs for acceptance of change and, conversely, increasing the costs of non-adoption of EU-based initiatives. Moravcsik (1994: 13) has argued that domestic perceptions of European integration and the EU's emergence as a high-salience issue in domestic politics lowers the costs for public acceptance of the outcomes of international negotiation.

Because European integration is a process of institutionalisation of interdependencies, Europeanisation lends itself to institutionalist theorising (Knill 2001). Rational choice and sociological institutionalism make different claims with regard to its causal paths. Both logics are actor-centred. Rationalist accounts posit the causal logic of consequentialism, according to which European incentives and constraints trigger adaptational pressures at the domestic level. The top-down path of impact induces actor responses of rule compliance, inertia, resistance, or accommodation. Domestic institutional setups are key intervening variables acting as veto points or mediating factors (Tsebelis and Yataganas 2000). A widely shared claim of the top-down model is that a policy, institutional, or cognitive misfit between the EU and the domestic level constitutes a necessary condition for Europeanisation to take place (Cowles *et al.* 2001; Kohler-Koch 2002). Top-down pressures and the resulting domestic adaptation increase proportionally to the degree of misfit (Börzel and Risse 2003: 61). The misfit proposition has come to represent the most problematic element of the top-down model. Empirical research concludes that it is reductionist and constitutes neither a necessary, nor a sufficient condition for Europeanisation (Héritier and Knill 2001; Sturm and Dieringer 2005: 284). Research findings also suggest that European integration may not directly require adaptation but that it may still induce change (Héritier and Knill 2001; Jacquot and Woll 2003; Kohler-Koch 1999; Schimmelfennig and Sedelmeier 2005). It may affect non-members, for whom misfit does not apply, inducing change even under conditions of low institutional capacity or crisis (Sciarini *et al.* 2004). According to Mastenbroek and Kaeding (2006), Europeanisation is an entirely actor-centred process. Regardless of the presence of misfit, its influences depend on actors' responses alone. The importance of the actor-centered hypothesis is that it exogenises Europeanisation (Quaglia and Radaelli 2007: 926). The unit of analysis is actors, their preferences and interests, norms and values, and behavioural dynamics.

The sociological institutionalist model explains Europeanisation through the logic of appropriateness. Social change involves thick forms of learning and socialisation whereby actors' interests are reconceptualised in the process of norm internalisation and identity transformation (Checkel 2001; Risse *et al.* 2001). Here the misfit hypothesis does not operate in the same direction as in the rationalist model. If the resonance between norm structures at the European and domestic level is low, local political institutions will resist change and the Europeanisation effect will be minimal. Domestic change is more profound under conditions of high resonance between the domestic and European level and where top-down pressures are moderate (Börzel 2002a; Börzel and Risse 2003).

The two logics of Europeanisation are not mutually exclusive (March and Olsen 1998). They function as a combination of rationalist, normative, and framing influences. Multiple veto points at the domestic level restrict the opportunity for European integration to induce domestic change under both types of causal logic. On the contrary, a pluralist domestic framework with dispersed preferences and/or no high-intensity preference actors in key mediating positions facilitate the mobilisation of coalitions favouring change (Börzel and Risse 2000). Socialisation and learning mechanisms are more likely when actors are uncertain about their preferences but are clear about their identities. A rationalist path of outcome creation is more likely under conditions of well-defined domestic preferences, aggregated interests, and the presence of veto points (Börzel and Risse 2000: 13).

In an examination of Europeanisation in the policy domain, Knill and Lehmkuhl (1999, 2002) have argued that its causal path depends on the nature of integration. Positive integration creates direct adaptational pressures. It leaves little discretion to domestic political actors in selecting a course of action. Europeanisation takes place as a top-down process based on conditionality and prescriptive rules.[1] Organisational and behavioural change takes place as a result of coercion, rewards and incentives, and socialisation processes (Schimmelfennig *et al.* 2006). Negative integration consists of liberalisation and harmonisation directives without direct EU-level legislation and induces a bottom-up process of adaptation. It alters the domestic political opportunity structure and differentially empowers political actors for mobilisation and change. The causal logic is that of resource exchange or coalition-building, whereby domestic actors do not simply comply with EU rules but respond by mimetic adaptation, professionalisation, and policy commitments (Massey 2004: 25).

The causal chain of Europeanisation in the compliance model begins with the EU level and ends with domestic adaptation (exogenous model). By contrast, the coalition-building model begins and ends with domestic actors. Here integration does not directly induce adaptational change. It affects the distribution of resources, institutional capacity, and actors' perceptions. The sufficient condition for Europeanisation to take place is the ability of domestic actors to avail themselves of the opportunities presented by European integration resulting in the creation of new equilibrium patterns (endogenous model) (Grote and Lang 2003: 226; Risse *et al.* 2001: 9–10).[2]

Outcomes and variation
The outcomes of Europeanisation are measured in terms of institutional change whereby the 'organisational logic' of domestic politics becomes subsumed under a European process, and behavioural change, measured as actors' adaptation to Europe (Ladrech 1994: 69). These outcomes are not deterministic. Although the process of rule-making at the EU level is conventionally associated with convergence and harmonisation pressures, Europeanisation implies neither an uninterrupted transfer of decision-making competences towards the EU institutions, nor an automatic adoption of rules at the unit level. Empirical studies concur that the outcomes are mixed and that the system of EU governance has a differential impact on the components of the domestic political systems – constitutional orders, distribution of resources, modes and outcomes of policy-making – although some cross-national convergence cannot be excluded (Börzel and Risse 2003; Bulmer and Lequesne 2005; Haverland 2005). Outcomes vary between inertia or the lack of change, absorption and accommodation measuring the degree of adaptational change, transformation or paradigmatic change, and retrenchment as a direct opposition to change (Radaelli 2003). Variation in outcomes does not permit the establishment of a trend, as a result of which Europeanisation is associated more often with clustered effects (Goetz 2006), segmented outcomes (Sifft *et al.* 2007), increased interdependence, and the emergence of winners and losers (Radaelli and Pasquier 2007).

A broadened Europeanisation agenda: the Europeanisation of conflict resolution

Theories of conflict resolution explain such outcomes as a result of change in conflict dynamics, actors' strategic calculus, needs, or identities (Schellenberg

1996; Wallensteen 2002). Europeanisation may be causally important to all these components. Even if conflict resolution is not an explicit EU competence, the effects of governance, measured as policy tools, resources, and influential discourse, may affect actors' interests, perceptions, and behaviour in conflict. EU-induced change may occur by changing certain dimensions of the conflict, the preferences of the parties, and the situation itself. The Europeanisation of conflicts may occur also in the absence of direct EU pressures, incentives, or resources, as the power of attraction or framing causes actors to change their perceptions without coercion or formal mediation (Töller 2004: 7).

The Europeanisation agenda has established itself as an important dimension in the literature examining the relevance of European integration to peace and reconciliation in Europe. These analyses inform two principal areas of research exploring, respectively, the systemic nature of the process and its mechanism. The former represents the peace rationale of European integration associated with processes of geopolitical consolidation, learning, and socialisation as a historical process. The latter examines its problem-solving capacity determined by power capabilities, decision-making competences, and interactions.

Regional integration and conflict resolution in empirical analysis

The systemic dimension examines the historical link between European integration and conflict resolution. Olsen's so-called 'reconciliation' hypothesis posits that European states have chosen integration because, through past experience with conflict and violence, they have learned that institutionalised cooperation is preferable to war (Olsen 2007). Conflict resolution has established itself as a source of legitimacy for European integration (Banchoff and Smith 1999; Feldman 1999b). This legacy has had a formative influence in extending European integration to Eastern Europe after the end of the Cold War, making the Europeanisation of conflict resolution a pan-regional process (Feldman 1999a and b; Ginsberg 1999, 2001).[3] In parallel with the legitimising force of peace and reconciliation, the impact of European integration on conflict has become inseparable from the institutional and political dynamics of the EU. The EU's evolution towards explicit competences and involvement in conflict resolution is an outgrowth of member state cooperation. This process is conventionally regarded as Europeanisation of their foreign policies (Koenig-Archibugi 2004; Ruggie 1993; Tonra 1997, 2001) reflected in the development of the EU's Common Foreign and Security Policy (CFSP) (Charillon 2005; Jørgensen 1997; Rieker 2006; Stetter 2004). The increasing centrality of European integration in regional geopolitics, the EU's Eastern European enlargement, and its involvement in ethnopolitical conflicts in the wider Europe has established integration as a gravitational model for the democratisation of Eastern Europe (Ágh 1999; Emerson and Noutcheva 2004; Glenn 2004; Kelstrup 1990; Schimmelfennig and Sedelmeier 2005; Schimmelfennig and Wagner 2004a; Vachudova 2005).

The second dimension of the relationship between European integration and conflict resolution examines the problem-solving capacity of the EU. The large number of publications attests to the significance of the topic, the research interest it generates, and its relevance to the study of European Union politics (Axt *et al.* 2006a; Coppieters *et al.* 2004; Diez *et al.* 2008a; Tocci 2007, among others). These works emphasise either the process or actorness qualities of European integration with regard to conflict resolution (Tocci 2004, 2005). In contrast to systemic account on the role of European integration in conflict resolution and peace in Europe, these works examine variation in the EU's effectiveness to act as an agent of conflict transformation. Diez *et al.* (2008a), Bourne (2004), Coppieters *et al.* (2004), and Schimmelfennig *et al.* (2006) have argued that the relationship between integration and peace is not necessarily a positive one and that European integration creates unintended consequences.

Research focused on variation and modelling posits different sources of the conflict resolution capacity of European integration through the concept of power: structural power (Galtung 1973), ability to generate learning and reconciliation discourses (Feldman 1999b), institutional power derived from the coherence of the EU decision-making process, normative power (Manners 2002, 2008), or perturbator to conflicts (Diez *et al.* 2008a). Other perspectives link the EU's role in conflict resolution to identity change in conflict (Bourne 2003b: 531) or regard it as a type of compulsory impact (Laffan and Payne 2003).

Tocci (2007) adopts a different angle of an actor-based model. The argument is that the effectiveness of the EU's involvement in conflict resolution is determined by the nature and quality of its contractual relations with the parties in conflict. This analysis finds that despite its potential to contribute to conflict resolution, the EU's performance has been disappointing (Tocci 2007: 173) and sets out to examine the determinants of the gap between objectives and effective performance. The study finds that underperformance is due to the specific manner in which the EU conducts its contractual relations with the parties in conflict. Intervening variables, such as actors' calculations of the value of the benefits, costs of compliance, timeframe of benefits offered, credibility of EU conditionality, the clarity of conditions, and the political management of the EU's contractual relations, emerge as the valid determinants of the effectiveness of the EU's impact on conflict resolution.

Process-centred research posits integration as a framework of interdependence (Eilstrup-Sangiovanni and Verdier 2005) and a post-national order (Diez 2002a; Laffan 1996, 1997). According to this view, European integration transforms the meaning of sovereignty through the pooling of resources and interests and thus removes the basic tenet of competition among groups in identity and secessionist conflicts (Coppieters *et al.* 2004; Tocci 2004).

Diez *et al.* (2006, 2008a) reconcile the actor/process dichotomy by adapting the concept of transformative power from international relations theory, a fundamentally actor-centred construct, to the examination of the impacts of integration as a process of interactions. This research proceeds from an understanding that as a single stream of influence actorness does not fully explain the causal relevance of European integration and that 'a mix of pathways is the most effective way for significant EU impact' (Stetter *et al.* 2008: 225). Féron and Lisaniler (2009: 198) similarly posit a multidimensional impact: the transformative power of Europeanisation on identities, the effects of EU policies, especially the CFSP, and more subtle roles for the EU institutions and norms on conflict management.

While these works are important, they tend to recast European integration into a structure, process, actor, value system, or path dependency. They rely on a single logic of impact and underestimate the possibility for interaction effects. By contrast, Europeanisation possesses the analytical tools to measure interactive and integrative effects. Applied as a framework for the study of conflict resolution outcomes, Europeanisation permits the examination of more complex trajectories of impact while taking into account intervening variables and facilitating factors.

Coppieters *et al.* (2003) test the hypothesis that Europeanisation can contribute to conflict resolution by triggering critical political, security, economic and societal developments in a manner that can transform the interests of the conflict parties (Coppieters *et al.* 2003: 1). This analysis examines the development of institutional frameworks, such as multi-tier federal models and division of sovereignty. Coppieters *et al.* (2004) define Europeanisation of conflicts as 'a process which is activated and encouraged by the European institutions, primarily the European Union, by linking the final outcome of the conflict to a certain degree of integration of the parties involved in it into European structures' (Noutcheva *et al.* 2004: 7). Conflict resolution is explained as the product of EU conditionality and socialisation mechanisms. The emphasis on compliance and incentives regards Europeanisation as a linkage between the requirement to resolve conflicts and the benefits of a privileged relationship with the EU.

More broadly, the Europeanisation of conflicts is understood as a process of adaptation to the explicit and implicit EU norm system (Axt *et al.* 2006a). The effects of Europeanisation are measured as rule adoption, cultural adaptation, and lesson drawing, whereby actors reconcile interest calculation with norm legitimacy. This study argues that the likelihood of conflict resolution increases as Europeanisation transcends the formal institutions of the state to affect civil society and state–society relations. This argument is important as it suggests that European integration is not an automatic process or agent of conflict resolution and that there is variation in its effectiveness.

The definitional qualities of Europeanisation permit the examination of the effects of European integration beyond conditionality or norm legitimacy by including multiple sources of influence. Furthermore, Europeanisation permits a focus on interactions, rather than capabilities, without prioritising either actors or processes. The research design is necessarily intensive, tracing top-down EU pressures and bottom-up sequences in actors' behaviour (Haverland 2005, 2007). By adapting Ladrech's (1994) definition to the thematic area of conflict resolution, the Europeanisation of conflict resolution may be conceptualised as an incremental process in which the political and economic dynamics of European governance become part of the 'logic' of the conflict resolution process.

Hypothesising the Europeanisation of conflicts
The null hypothesis associates potential EU-level influences on conflict resolution with random or no effects. Any positive change in conflict dynamic is induced by other actors and sources of impact. The alternative hypothesis posits the systematic effects of European integration measured as improved communication between the conflict parties, reduction in conflict intensity, settlement and/or settlement sustaining dynamics, compromise in exchange for the benefits of a privileged relationship with the EU, and reconciliation.

The categories of the independent variable, EU-level resources of conflict resolution, are policy prescriptions, norms, resources, or EU-related reconciliation discourse. These categories are measured according to their clarity and prescriptive guidance (Checkel 2001: 183), the extent to which they subsume the conflict dynamics under an EU perspective, and make it clear and possible for actors to develop preferences for conflict resolution and reconciliation.

From the perspective of European integration, all conflicts represent an institutional and behavioural misfit between actors' preferences and EU-level norms of rule of law, democracy, human rights, and protection of minorities, as well as the peace and reconciliation rationale of European integration. According to the general Europeanisation hypothesis, we should expect EU-level pressures, actor-centred domestic processes, strategic and cognitive paths of outcome creation, nontrivial incidence of intervening variables, and differential outcomes. To the extent that the EU develops a design for conflict resolution or deploys political action, an incentive and constraints structure, or a discourse legitimising a particular solution, the causal path of integration influences will be top-down, a function of conditionality and direct pressures. The causal path is one of actors' internalisation of EU influences on conflict dynamics generating interest change, adjustment, absorption, or resistance.

Although the misfit proposition implies a domain-of-application approach, the Europeanisation of conflicts is not a type of policy, politics, or a polity influence. Interaction effects between these domains are possible and desirable suggesting that EU influences may act synergistically (Emerson and Noutcheva 2004: 4). The Europeanisation of conflict resolution pertains to the domain of policies to the extent that it involves issue-specific EU policy instruments, styles, constraints, and discourses; to the domain of politics through its impact on societal cleavages, interest formulation, mobilisation, and coalition-building; and to the polity domain to the extent that it affects national and subnational institutions, legacies, identities, and intergovernmental and state–society relations.

The top-down model takes into account that European integration may not act as a single independent variable, and may not produce clear-cut effects but rather chains of events, mutual influence, triggering mechanisms, and reiterated games (Natali 2004: 1079–80). Integration may enter into a causal process at some point, as it does in all ongoing conflict resolution processes discussed in the case studies, as a conditioning variable providing impetus, challenges, and political change causally related to the original stimulus (Natali 2004: 1080).

If the EU's input into conflict resolution is that of a solution, such as a resource or opportunity for learning and political action on behalf of the conflict parties, Europeanisation will take place as a bottom-up resource-based process. Actors internalise EU policy concepts as a resource, not a constraint or a threat (Radaelli and Franchino 2004: 944). The outcomes are new strategies, political change, and actor empowerment. We would expect the influences of European integration to alter domestic political space in the direction of increased openness. If the EU endows more resources and legitimising discourse to actors favouring settlement and reconciliation, the likelihood of conflict resolution would increase. The model of Europeanisation as a solution starts at the level of interactions in the context of conflicts and traces their institutional logic: actors' perceptions of problems, references they make to European integration, and EU-based problem-solving tools they adopt to advance conflict resolution. European variables become integrated into the domestic level of interactions (Radaelli and Franchino 2004: 948). The success of conflict resolution will be affected by mediating factors, such as opportunity structures, type and aggregation of domestic interests, and issue context. In contrast to the compliance hypothesis, these factors do not have the status of intervening variables, as the sources of Europeanisation influences in this model are indirect. Restricted political space and the presence of dominant players, social norms and adversarial identities, well aggregated domestic interests, and tight circles of elites interested in preserving the status quo approximate the role of veto points. By contrast, the presence of cross-cutting demands facilitates the empowerment of actors with a European agenda, as well as public responsiveness to Europeanisation influences. Such conditions contribute to political mobilisation and coalition-building around new ideas and norms and are conducive to positive change in conflict dynamics.

Because of variation in proximity, mode of governance considerations, and the status of European integration as a conditioning variable, we would expect that the framework of Europeanisation of conflict resolution would be primarily resource- rather than compliance-based, and that the top-down and bottom-up paths of outcome creation would converge towards resources and coalition-building.

Besides the status of the independent variable, the framework needs to specify and accommodate specific issues related to the dependent variable, conflict resolution outcome. The latter is affected by the context and status of the conflict. The issue context constitutes a component of political space which affects actor-centred processes of change. Conflict is likely to be conceptualised as a single-issue politics. The status quo is maintained by legacies, discourses, and social norms favouring intolerance and exclusivity, especially ideologies of nationalism. In such cases bottom-up mobilisation for change is less likely to occur. By contrast, if the conflict issue can be disaggregated into individual high-salience issues, such as economic development, social disparities, and minority/majority rights represented by diverse societal interests and with a varying degree of intensity for elites and publics, the chances for conflict resolution would increase.

Conflict status also affects the capacity of European integration to alter its dynamics. In conflicts at a pre-settlement stage with a high degree of interest aggregation and the presence of dominant players, the opportunities for change are low. Top-down pressures and conditionality are likely to be more effective in inducing strategic adaptation but less likely to lead to conflict transformation. If the preferred form of influence is a compliance strategy, bottom-up processes of change would be slow and difficult to generate. According to the sociological hypothesis, we would expect resistance to top-down pressures. Conversely, if the instruments and discourses of integration create conditions for political mobilisation by enhancing dialogue, power sharing, and participation in common projects, the chances for long-term change in conflict dynamics would increase. This type of Europeanisation influence is compatible with the 'peace through interdependence' thesis in international relations theory (Boulding 1972; Frost 1991). However, in contrast to interdependence, which assumes actors' strategic unitary calculation of the benefits of trade versus the costs of war, the underlying causal process of Europeanisation is that of political disaggregation and pluralism. Economic interdependence, communication, and participation in EU projects opens up a European dimension of domestic political space. A broadened arena of domestic contestation and mobilisation facilitates the emergence of new political actors and agendas within a European perspective, which increases the likelihood of conflict transformation (Jeong 2005).

Political openness and interest disaggregation are integral to the politics of conflict resolution. If conflict is by definition a function of incompatible interests, values, or needs, then settlement tends to represent a suboptimal outcome for all parties. Its principles and conditions are not always willingly accepted. A re-ranking of individual preferences is necessary in the process. Following North *et al.* (1960), we expect that conflicts would be easier to resolve when the parties are pluralistic societies. Empirical studies of Europeanisation in the policy domain have found that the configuration of domestic interests is a key determinant of the scope and direction of change. As Héritier and Knill (2001) suggest, strong integrated local leadership may ignore EU inputs or may initiate change without direct EU support. Even informal pressure groups may make change improbable (Radaelli 2003: 47). Discursive influences are inseparable from this path of Europeanisation. Euro-discourse may act as an agent of change triggering coalition-building even in the absence of resource reallocation, side payments, and other specific instruments.

The Europeanisation framework of conflict resolution

The hypothesised path of conflict resolution through integration permits the construction of a matrix of the Europeanisation of conflicts comprised of the necessary elements for a causal process linking the sources of integration influences to conflict resolution outcomes (Bulmer and Radaelli 2005). According to the premises of Europeanisation, the framework applies to cases characterised by the presence of some form of an integrative relationship between the EU and countries or communities in conflict. It demonstrates how links occur between European integration and conflict resolution dynamics by connecting sources (European space), processes (links) and outcomes (effects). The framework rests on two assumptions. First, the presence of stimuli or a triggering mechanism, such as the misfit proposition as a necessary condition for EU action; second, the transposition of the outcomes of Europeanisation as actions transcending the incompatibility of the conflict, such as creation of new interests, compromise, acceptance of each other's existence, and secession of violent action against each other (Wallensteen 2002: 8).[4]

The Europeanisation framework consists of three elements necessary for outcome-creation: European space of policy actions, resources, or discourse; a social process of application of EU resources, and development of institutional instruments, such as monitoring, European partnerships, institutional bodies, principles of additionality and conditionality, or devolution; and outcomes of adaptation, politicisation, absorption, or transformation which potentially change the institutional dynamics or actors' behaviour in processes of conflict resolution.

The first element of the framework is the presence of a 'European space' of policy, polity, and political influences on conflict dynamics potentially conducive to conflict resolution. When applied to case study evidence, this element requires one to determine whether a European dimension of conflict resolution is present and to order the categories of integration as the independent variable. The European space is comprised of potential sources of

Europeanisation: EU rules, norms, crisis management capabilities, learning opportunities, and resources. The sources differ according to the type of influence they generate: top-down pressures and incentives for compliance or bottom-up sources of mobilisation, learning, and political opportunities. The next task is to establish the degree of their autonomy versus other instruments of conflict resolution. As Quaglia and Radaelli (2007: 925) have argued, we need to demonstrate that there is 'something sufficiently distinct and coherent up there in Brussels to require adoption' – a structure or process of governance, norm, discourse, or resource – that is recognised and accepted by other actors (Sifft *et al.* 2007). The salience of the distinctive EU-level system of interaction is a necessary condition for Europeanisation to occur (Radaelli and Pasquier 2007: 41). Centrality involves dual measures. At the EU level, its attributes are intensity, autonomy, coherence, and robustness over time. At the domestic level, centrality is measured relative to other influences in terms of dominance, credibility, recognition, and legitimacy (Caporaso and Wittenbrinck 2006). We can expect a higher likelihood of outcome creation if there is a historically robust, coherent, automatic, and resource-rich policy process, widely recognised as the preferred conflict resolution strategy; if the EU institutions are accepted as a legitimate source of influence; if there is a dominant European discourse, and if social norms resonate with European ones.

Measuring the scope of integration influences as top-down impact approximates conventional estimates of the conflict-related capacity of the EU, for example in the actorness perspective (Ginsberg 1999). The bottom-up dimension, which provides an estimate of 'what actors make of it', is less straightforward. The guiding principle is determining the scope of actors' encounters with Europe (Quaglia and Radaelli 2007: 928). The latter is measured by examining whether political actors are willing to exploit EU resources and whether they adapt to European rules or initiate change conducive to the transformation of the incompatibility of the conflict.

The second element determines whether a social mechanism is in place to link the European arena to the local context (Checkel 2005). In order to establish causality, the evidence needs to connect the influences of integration to the object of Europeanisation: conflict dynamics, actors' preferences, identities, and needs (Quaglia and Radaelli 2007: 926). If the sources of integration influences are robust, autonomous, and enjoy recognition, do they trigger change in the domestic political structure, actors' preferences and values, and learning opportunities? The appropriate method is that of process tracing and establishing the congruence between EU-level inputs and domestic change while controlling for rival explanations (Haverland 2007). According to the causal paths of Europeanisation, we can expect the process to take place either as an EU policy design for conflict resolution requiring some form of rule compliance or as a resource of coalition-building conducive to political mobilisation, actor empowerment, and learning with the potential to change the configuration of factors sustaining the conflict.

Based on Moravcsik's (1994) typology of causal mechanisms, such as agenda-setting, institutional procedure of decision-making, and ideational/informational context, we may unpack the two principal dimensions of Europeanisation – institutional logic and actor behaviour – into a series of causal links which translate EU pressures and resources into change in the status of conflict through control and initiative in agenda-setting, institutional procedure, and informational and ideational context.

By affecting the agenda, procedure, and ideational context, the EU in practice 'Europeanises' the conflict resolution process. The agenda determines the strategy of conflict resolution: a peace process, negotiated settlement, federalised solution, integration, or a new bargain. Control over the institutional procedure of conflict resolution implies setting the rules for acceptance of a proposed solution and discussing alternative proposals. Does the EU's involvement in conflict resolution provide the conflict parties with alternatives for discussing other proposals and include other actors: bilateral negotiations, UN intervention, a regional format, etc.? Or, on the contrary, does it limit the options actors have to delay and dilute the conflict resolution agenda? The second causal mechanism of affecting the institutional logic of conflict resolution is influence over the institutional procedure: the method of reaching agreement – through debate, amendment, or in a 'take it or leave it' fashion. Because in its enlargement policy the EU relies on conditionality, the procedure of linking the resolution of outstanding conflicts to receiving the benefits of a privileged relationship has emerged as an exemplar of the EU impact on international conflict resolution (Coppieters *et al.* 2004).

The third element of the framework transposes the effects of Europeanisation into sources of conflict resolution. The principled effects of Europeanisation, such as adaptation, transformation, politicisation, and retrenchment closely overlap with the main sources of conflict resolution: communication, strategic calculus, and needs. The reconceptualisation of the outcomes of Europeanisation as change in the dynamics of conflict resolution constitutes the ultimate measure of change in the dependent variable: conflict status. If integration produces inertia or retrenchment, then we cannot expect a corresponding Europeanisation of conflict resolution. These outcomes correspond to the lack of domestic responsiveness to integration influences resulting in preservation of the status quo or outright resistance potentially leading to re-escalation of the conflict. The logical conclusion in this case is that integration induces only random effects. European rules and discourses contrast with actors' priorities and the latter resist change despite exposure to EU governance or, in the case of positive change, the sources of conflict resolution do not pertain to the integration process; for example, conflict resolution is the result of third party involvement or actors' preferences alone. Interest change is likely to result in change in conflict intensity, negotiation, or settlement, but not conflict transformation, societal reintegration, or long-term reconciliation. By contrast, preference and value change have a transformative influence on conflict by changing actors' identities or needs. In this case, change affects the structural aspects of conflict, such as root causes, grievances, and values.

The Europeanisation framework permits determination of the scope and effectiveness of the EU's involvement in a variety of contexts by establishing a referent for evaluation of the source of influence, direction of a potentially causal link, and resulting institutional or behavioural change in conflict. The chapters that follow apply the Europeanisation framework in an examination of prominent cases of conflict resolution in Europe: the Franco-German relationship of the 1950s, Northern Ireland, Cyprus, and Kosovo. These cases discuss a variety of integration influences.

Conclusion: why Europeanisation?

The principal objective of this chapter has been to outline the analytical qualities of Europeanisation as a device for organising empirical analysis and modelling conflict resolution effects. Although there is some scepticism about the analytical capacity of Europeanisation, described as 'fashionable' and 'contested' (Olsen 2007: 68), its definitional attributes and mechanism of action examined here demonstrate that the concept can be used in a variety of ways to examine the empirical complexity of change in Europe (Goetz 2000). Thematic studies offer a significant update to the domain-of-application approach to Europeanisation across its policy, political, and polity dimensions. The issue area of conflict resolution offers an opportunity to unpack Europeanisation as a process of creation of EU-level rules and structures of governance relevant to conflicts and as a stream of pressures and opportunities conducive to change in conflict dynamics. As is the case in other areas of inquiry in Europeanisation research, the question is to determine whether integration influences on conflict are present and whether they are causally significant to change at the unit level; in the case of conflicts, to change in the institutional process of conflict resolution and actors' behaviour in it.

Europeanisation traces the causal links between scope conditions, policy designs, norms, and practices and potential change in conflict dynamics. Its analytical contribution to the study of conflicts is the ability to examine the politics of the process. The model permits a move beyond static analyses of the influence of European integration on conflict following an actor- or a process-centred approach. Such approaches build on the already established contribution of Europeanisation to the normalisation of research on European integration (Radaelli 2000a). It permits the refocusing of theory-building from metatheoretical issues toward a problem-driven inquiry which seeks to uncover causal links between actions and outcomes and evaluates their intensity. Europeanisation thus advances the governance perspective in European studies from 'thick description' to hypothesis testing and causal relationships (Pollack 2005: 380).

Notes

1 Conditionality is defined as material incentives to bring about change in the behaviour of a target actor (Checkel 2005: 809).
2 According to Knill and Lehmkuhl (2002), the framing influences of European integration constitute a third causal path of outcome creation. Its underlying logic is neither purely consequentialist, nor that of appropriateness. Framing has enabling, legitimising, and mediating qualities. The effects of framing are nonhierarchical and take place as a cognitive input into domestic opportunity structures to produce a governance effect (Knill and Lehmkuhl 2002: 262; Radaelli 2003: 44).
3 For the opposite view, see Obradovich (1996).
4 These actions constitute the definition of conflict resolution in Wallenstein (2002).

3

The early years: European integration as a system of conflict resolution in the Franco-German relationship (1950–63)

> The coal-steel settlement is like a spherical wooden puzzle held together by interlocked parts. When taken apart and laid out piece by piece on a table, reassembly seems impossible; yet after patient, frustrating, mostly blind manipulation the thing will eventually, unexpectedly, and inexplicably snap into place, forming a tight round object almost as hard to pull asunder as it once had been to put together [...] The precise way in which the various pieces fit into one another, however, and the interconnections that give the puzzle inner strength can only be visualized. The solution will always remain partly a mystery.
>
> John Gillingham (1991: 364)

> The predatory behavior of the past is finished. This is a Germany of the Bundesrepublik; the country has been 'Europeanized.'
>
> Markovitz and Reich (1997: XI)

Introduction

This case study examines the original application of regional integration as a system of conflict resolution in the example of the Franco-German relationship of the 1950s. The process of Franco-German reconciliation is critically important for ordering the history of European integration. It offers important insights into the formative stages of the European construction and its importance relative to other designs of international organisation. It also informs much of the contemporary understandings of the political relevance of integration to European politics and societies.

A specific feature of the Franco-German relationship is the historical continuity of enmity and war. Rivalry dates back to the division of Charlemagne's Carolingian Empire in the early ninth century and the creation of the contested middle realm of Lorraine. Later the Treaty of Westphalia gave France limited control over Alsace and Lorraine which determined a long-term pattern of contestation over these territories. French occupation in 1680, the War of the Palatinian Succession, and the Napoleonic Wars marked further stages of rivalry and conflict throughout the nineteenth century. The pattern of revanchism became particularly pronounced after the Franco-Prussian War of 1870–71 in which France lost Alsace and a quarter of Lorraine and had to pay an indemnity of 5 billion francs to the German Empire. During the 70-year period after that France and Germany fought against each other in the two world wars. At the end of the First World War the Versailles Treaty imposed reparations and territorial annexation on Germany, inducing a new cycle of nationalism and enmity which led to Hitler's occupation of one-third of French territory during the Second World War.

The Second World War ended without an immediate settlement but established a process leading to the conclusion of a Franco-German peace treaty in 1955. The initial stage was one of building security and preventive measures through four-power occupation, division, and administrative control over Germany's war industries. By 1949, the Franco-German relationship had evolved into an element of superpower politics and containment, placing new demands on the process of reconciliation between the former adversaries. European integration entered the Franco-German relationship in 1950. As this chapter will argue, it became indispensable to all stages of conflict resolution, the final settlement, and reconciliation between France and Germany reflected in the conclusion of the bilateral peace treaty in 1955 and the Franco-German (Elysée) Treaty on Friendship (22 January 1963).

The main argument of this chapter is that European integration had a transformative influence on post-Second World War Franco-German relations. It subsumed the institutional logic of conflict resolution and actors' preferences in the process replacing alternative strategies. Integration affected the key outstanding issues of the conflict: territorial claims, annexation, and external control. It first created a sectoral arrangement binding the French and German war industries into the European Coal and Steel Community (1951). The European Economic Community (1957) ensured the continued expansion of integration into a systemic open-ended process of building common institutions and policies. As a result of incremental institutional growth, the desirability of European integration in maintaining the Franco-German peace emerged as a shared preference. The Franco-German relationship became Europeanised.

The Franco-German case may be considered as a classical example of the Europeanisation of conflicts in Europe. Europeanisation occurred through the development of a European realm of interactions in the area of conflict resolution and reconciliation, its recognition on behalf of political actors, and growing centrality relative to other approaches to securing the Franco-German peace. Examined through the lens of Europeanisation, the impacts of integration represent a two-track process of construction of European-level institutions, policies, and political discourses of peace and reconciliation, and the use of integration resources by political actors to induce change in conflict dynamics through integration, rather than other frameworks.

In order to disentangle the role of integration from that of other factors, the chapter is organised as follows. The section that follows traces the history of attempts to break the cycle of punitive peace in the long-term conflictual relationship between France and Germany. Analysis then examines the institutions and governance process of European integration as strategies of conflict resolution. Key elements of the process are the pooling together of select policies under a common authority in the European Coal and Steel Community (ECSC), and the irreversible institutionalisation of a customs union through the European Economic Community (EEC), as well as the problem-solving capacity of European integration in the resolution of the key Ruhr and Saar issues and in the signing of the Elysée Treaty of Franco-German friendship and cooperation. The objective is to demonstrate that although a variety of designs for peace and reconciliation were tested within the same historical context, they remained secondary to European integration as a tool of conflict resolution.

The purpose of this analysis is neither to reconstruct the negotiating process leading to the creation of the European Communities, nor their institutional development or the details of the treaties. These processes are discussed in the literature on the formative period of European integration (Bitsch 1995, 2004; Forsyth 1967; Gerbet 2004; Haas 1968; Lindberg and Scheingold 1970; Lipgens and Loth 1988; Parsons 2004; Wilkens 2004, among others). The objective is rather to explain how the process of European construction affected actor preferences to end the historical enmity and laid down the structural components of Franco-German reconciliation. The chapter re-examines the historical evidence of the 1950s through the lens of the European construction and outlines the link between the advancement of the integration project and conflict resolution and reconciliation in the Franco-German relationship. Although it is generally accepted that the European context facilitated the bilateral process of negotiating the Saar settlement and the multilateral resolution of the Ruhr issue through the ECSC, the literature provides little analysis as to how exactly the design and process of European integration contributed to this outcome.

Political approaches toward securing the post-Second World War peace

The repeated cycles of war between France and Germany had catalytic effects on the search for change in their conflictual relationship during the twentieth century. The implementation of the post-First World War settlement reflects significant efforts to break the cycle of punitive peace institutionalised through the Versailles Treaty (Frevert 2005). One of the architects of post-

Second World War Franco-German peace, Konrad Adenauer, had argued, in the wake of the First World War, that the relationship between France and Germany was a pillar to European unity. In a speech to the National Assembly on 1 February 1919 and later at the University of Cologne (12 June 1919), Adenauer discussed the reconciliation issue as a method of preventing war from repeating itself (Adenauer 1965: 254–6).

Governments, industry, and intellectual circles advanced a number of initiatives, including some through international institutions and especially the League of Nations. The Locarno peace (1925), designed to correct the deficiencies of the distributive settlement of the Versailles Treaty, established equal security guarantees for France and Germany. Germany's admission to the League of Nations validated the principle of collective security in Franco-German relations. French evacuation of the Rhineland as a result of a series of diplomatic manoeuvres, including the Dawes and Young Plans, alleviated German reparations. The bilateral initiatives of Gustav Stresemann and Aristide Briand advanced political and moral arguments. The idealist approach of the French government's Memorandum for a European Union (1928) and the Kellogg-Briand Pact (1928) marked significant steps in the internationalisation of the process. These initiatives were effective public opinion events and depended more on the personal charisma of their architects, Stresemann and Briand, than on institutional mechanisms. By 1931, Hitler's electoral success and the project for a customs union between Germany and Austria affected negatively the Franco-German relationship. Although the pacifist spirit of the initiatives remained active for some time, the evasive reaction of the European states to the French memorandum on Europe demonstrated that they were weakening as a result of Briand's and Stresemann's withdrawal from politics (and Briand's death in 1932) (Muir 1966: 27). The Franco-German relationship did not transcend the cycle of concessions and personal compromises, although it received high publicity in the context of general pacifist predispositions. The creation of a web of private sector and economic initiatives, often considered as a forerunner to the process of economic integration of the post-Second World War period (Gillingham 1991), also failed to produce transformative effects.

The end of Second World War marked a renewed interest in institutional, political, and intellectual approaches to securing Europe's peace. It was obvious that negotiation and justice were not sufficient to address the root causes of conflicts. Since its beginnings, the post-Second World War conflict resolution process was based on the understanding that in order to secure peace, it was necessary to simultaneously place a limit on Germany's capacity to start a war and grant it a place in Europe.

The pursuit of peace by resolving the question of German power invited a variety of strategies. At one level, it was a question of political organisation and the locus of state authority. In his 1946 Speech at the University of Zurich, Churchill placed Franco-German reconciliation at the centre of

Europe's revival. The approach was to build peace on federalist principles, through the creation of a United States of Europe. As a parallel strategy, peace was sought by means of multilateralisation of control over Germany's war capabilities through joint supervision over its resources, deindustrialisation and demilitarisation, territorial dismemberment and occupation, and incremental advances towards a peace treaty. At the level of domestic politics, the Franco-German peace was the object of political debate in France and Germany and emerged as the core of their respective European policies.

French views were guided by *Realpolitik* arguments aimed at achieving a sincere and practical agreement (Loth 1988a). Although these initiatives reflected also humanistic considerations, they did not transcend the distributive-punitive approach to peace. France's main concerns were security, territorial control, and administration of Germany. The original French approach to reconciliation was at odds with the American concept of a western bloc against the Soviet Union with Germany as a core asset. General de Gaulle supported a rapid solution to the Ruhr and the Saar issues and the dismantling of German industry. De Gaulle pointed to the need for equilibrium between France and Germany as a condition for peace and proposed a bilateral agreement – economic initially, followed by a cultural agreement: 'The foundation of [...] Europe must be a direct agreement, without intermediaries, between the French and German peoples' (Bromberger and Bromberger 1969: 78).[1]

Konrad Adenauer also preferred a direct approach to settlement and reconciliation with France. As early as 1946, with reference to the party platform of the Christian Democratic Union (CDU) and before Churchill's Zurich speech, Adenauer developed his post-First World War ideas of a United States of Europe. Adenauer supported the concept of a European federation based on economic integration (Lipgens and Loth 1988: 445). His idea about Franco-German reconciliation rested on a combination of approaches to building trust, bilateral political, economic, and cultural relations, addressing France's security concerns, and creating a political community. Although such an approach reveals the multidimensional aspect of reconciliation, the link between the uniting of Europe and Franco-German reconciliation at this stage remained underdeveloped. Such ideas lacked strategy and political weight to become influential. Germany was an occupied state and Adenauer was not an elected chancellor at that time. More importantly, these ideas had no practical meaning as to how to build the Franco-German pillar of Europe's unity.

Political actors in France understood both the need for German equality to prevent revanchism and the desirability of some form of governing powers above the nation-state as envisaged by federalist designs. The Socialists, Christian Democrats, and Liberals supported the federalist idea. Socialist (SFIO) leader André Philip[2] proposed a common market and was the first to argue in favour of a coal and steel authority as a durable solution to the

German problem.³ The French Consultative Assembly (1946) and later the National Assembly debated the institutions of a federal Europe. On 11 April 1946 the Consultative Assembly adopted a constitutional provision stating that France agreed to the limitation of sovereignty necessary for the 'organisation and defence of peace'.⁴

In Germany itself, political debate on the German problem was cast along federal lines (Gruner 2007). The key issue was whether European unification should precede German unification. The German parties differed in their preferences for the political organisation of Europe (Marcussen *et al.* 1999). Karl (Carlo) Schmidt, prominent member of the Social Democratic Party (SPD), supported the thesis that German and European federalism were related.⁵

Wide societal interests supported the idea of a federalist solution to the German problem in France and Germany. People-to-people initiatives were on the rise after the Second World War, including psychological approaches to reconciliation, encounters, and the creation of parapublic organisations as a method of granting a European meaning to collective memories (Ackermann 1994; Feldman 1999a; Krotz 2007). State policies, however, continued to reflect the principles of distributive settlement. Political outcomes were shaped by diplomatic means.

A number of intergovernmental organisations were created in the 1945–49 period on a functional consultative basis. The Organisation for Economic Cooperation in Europe (OEEC) was founded on 16 April 1948 as the institution responsible for administering the Marshall Plan. It operated according to multilateralist principles but had no powers of joint decision-making, programming, or market integration. NATO was founded on 4 April 1949 as a collective defence alliance. On 22 April 1949, together with the Benelux countries, the Western occupying powers created the International Authority for the Ruhr (IAR) which guaranteed equal access to the coal and steel of the Ruhr to countries cooperating for the common economic interest. The creation of the Ruhr Authority, as well as the merging of the French zone into the Anglo-American bizone before that, prepared the foundations for the creation of the Federal Republic of Germany on 23 May 1949.

The Council of Europe (CoE) was created on 5 May 1949 as a compromise between federalists and intergovernmentalists. Its Consultative Assembly was a parliamentary platform for dialogue and its executive organ, the Council of Ministers, was sidelined from defence, economic, and political matters. The establishment of the CoE as an intergovernmental consultative organisation, instead of a federalist arrangement, together with the alliance structure of NATO, seriously undermined the federalist movement by preserving the nation-state as the principal unit in the organisation of relations in Europe.

Although they did not go far towards creating a conceptually new political order, the intergovernmental institutions of the early post-Second

World War period were important precursors to European integration. They prepared the end of the occupation status of Germany and maintained the responsibility of the great powers over Germany. However, these organisations were not sufficient to secure the irreversibility of peace in Western Europe (Robertson 1973: 17). The principles of federalism and economic integration, although frequently proclaimed, remained unapplied. In 1949 Franco-German relations were bad, the federalist movement had suffered a decisive blow, and the materialisation of the Soviet threat during the Berlin blockade (1948–49) demonstrated that war in Europe was still not unthinkable.

The link between European integration and Franco-German reconciliation

The proposal by French Foreign Minister Robert Schuman for sectoral integration, announced in the Paris Declaration of 9 May 1950, was a surprise for political circles in France and Germany. Prior to that, regional integration had not been considered as an independent project and remained subsumed under federalist thinking. Although nominally designed to create a common economic space, the location of such processes outside the nation-state and the objective of building peace and reconciliation recast regional integration into a political project. According to Walter Hallstein:

> We are not in business to promote tariff preferences, to establish a discriminatory club, to form a larger market to make us richer, or a trading bloc to further our commercial interests. We are not in business at all: we are in politics. Our aim is to help ourselves, and so help others: to rid Europe of the crippling anomalies of the past, and enable her to pull her full weight in building tomorrow's world. (Hallstein 1961: 6–7)

The concept of European economic integration transpired from a reflection note Jean Monnet wrote as a member of the French Committee of National Liberation on 5 August 1943 in Algiers.[6] Monnet proposed the reconstitution of Europe by pooling together key industrial sectors relevant to national defence by creating a new authority. While Monnet followed a federalist model, he proposed a different political form for its implementation: by linking together economics and politics, rather than separating them, as federalism and earlier projects to secure the post-First World War peace had done.[7] The concept of shared sovereignty emerged as a new political principle of the organisation of interstate relations which transcended the division between former adversaries through a joint commitment to common projects.

Monnet shared the view that Germany's growth and the domination of its industry were a danger for Europe. As French needs for economic modernisation required an increase in German production in the coal and steel sectors, France's industry had to be protected from outside competition, in turn inducing a decline in trade liberalisation. Such trends would restore the cartels of the interwar period and potentially orient Germany's trade relations to the east. Only the pooling of production could create opportunities for both countries. For Monnet, the answer was to build a community. The core rationale of the integration of production was to lock France and Germany into an irreversible process.

The creation and workings of the European Coal and Steel Community (ECSC) during the 1950s thus emerged as a process of Europeanisation of Franco-German reconciliation. It was accomplished through the reorientation of their bilateral relationship toward the logic of integration as a type of new politics: of shared competences and decision-making so that a return to conflict and war would be unthinkable.

The institutionalisation of integration as a reconciliation strategy

The idea of integration provided European political elites with a capacity to act. It united plans for a direct union between France and Germany, impossible to accomplish along federalist lines, with conceptual approaches to the 'Europeanisation' of the key problem regions of Western Europe: Ruhr, the Saar, and the Rhineland. After the First World War Adenauer had proposed a merger of French and German coal mines and steel industries. In the wake of the 1948 London conference, Adenauer expanded this idea into an economic Franco-German union based on the merger of their entire coal and steel production. Monnet initially contemplated Franco-German reconciliation through an approximate economic reconstitution of the old Lotharingia. The idea was to link the territories of the former Lotharingia into a single complex with the extended Rhineland (Loriaux 2008) within a network of regional relationships, rather than a binary Franco-German frontier. The conceptual mapping of the European Coal and Steel Community passed first through the idea of creating an *economic* Lotharingia through the Ruhr–Saar–Lorraine complex. As it was impossible to isolate it from the broader geopolitics of the region without replicating the historical Franco-German rivalry, it was deemed necessary to place it within a market open to all interested countries.

The realisation that the Ruhr–Saar–Lorraine complex could not be isolated from France and Belgium, that a common market could not be limited to certain regions and that supranational control could not be based entirely on economic planning, led to the design of an open market and the competitive allocation of production. Its practical implementation was a community which bound together economics and politics. Such a design achieved simultaneously all objectives. It responded to the federalist idea of a union between France and Germany for the purpose of peace, created a common market of resources, and ensured the consolidation of Western Europe through unification.

The Dutch, the Belgians, the Rhinelanders, the people of the Saar, and the

Lorrainers all have a common origin; they share the same mine basin. Could they be made into a single state? [...] The Saar, the Ruhr – they are German. You can't tear them away from Germany. Lotharingia would not be a separation but a regrouping of Germans, Frenchmen, Belgians, and Dutch! (Jean Monnet in Bromberger and Bromberger 1969: 96–7)

Diez et al. (2008b: 4) similarly refer to the significance of European integration for resolving the Franco-German conflict conceptualised through the problematic 'border region of Alsace'. According to Diez et al. (2008b: 5), European integration was conducive to social interaction across the border, crucial for reconciliation. The border lost significance as contacts increased, and identities were restructured and no longer expressed in antagonistic terms. However, the rationale for an ECSC was not simply to dismantle the Franco-German border in Alsace. There was a need for an 'extended' Franco-German construct of conflict resolution. The Schuman Declaration of 9 May 1950 which launched the idea for the creation of the community was neither an act of settlement nor a crossborder arrangement. It was an open-ended multilateral process of economic projects and political solidarity accomplished through the fusion of markets and regulation:

> Considering that world peace can be safeguarded only by creative efforts commensurate to the dangers that threaten it [France and Germany] resolved to substitute for age-old rivalries the merging of their essential interests; to create, by establishing an economic community, the basis for a broader and deeper community among peoples long divided by bloody conflicts.[8]

The timing of the Schuman Declaration and of the creation of the ECSC was at odds with the historical context of Western European security a year after the creation of NATO and the pursuit of Germany's demilitarisation. For this reason, a number of historians have explained it as a pursuit of national economic interests, prioritising the need for German coal of the French post-war recovery programme, and the necessity to extend the welfare state to critically important industrial sectors (Gillingham 1991; Milward 1992).

The novelty of integration was its method of joint policy-making delivered through institutional means. The European institutions ensured the irreversibility and robustness of the process. Integration no longer reflected individual state interests but a framework of mutual adjustment. Diverse interests of producers, consumers, business organisations, and labour unions competed and were reconciled within the common projects managed through the common market of coal and steel (Haas 1968). The contribution of European integration was that of pluralisation of domestic politics in the member states in the process of Europeanisation of policy-making within the ECSC. At the macro-political level integration reflected a common preference: durable European peace through Franco-German reconciliation. At a later stage, the impact of integration was that of continued institutional initiatives to sustain the irreversibility of the process as a guarantee for peace in Europe.

Europeanisation as resources and opportunities for problem-solving: liquidating the International Authority for the Ruhr, Europeanising the Saar

The second dimension of Europeanisation is comprised of influences on the institutional process of constructing the Franco-German peace (the organisational logic argument in Ladrech 1994) and their explicit or implicit effects on actors' behaviour through constraints and opportunities, resources, and discourse. While the main rationale of creating a system of joint decision-making in the ECSC was to replace the long-standing Franco-German enmity with a cooperative relationship, the institutional process of the ECSC was crucial to the resolution of key issues on their bilateral agenda. The literature tends to privilege the proposition about the broad historical relevance of integration to the German problem to the detriment of the problem-solving argument. In reality, solutions to important issues accomplished through traditional diplomatic means were the result primarily of the opportunities and resources of European integration. Two major cases, the Ruhr problem and the Saar issue, point to the classical relevance of integration to problem solving in Franco-German relations. The Ruhr, the Saar, and the deconcentration of German industry as an instrument of demilitarisation were all part of the ECSC institutional process.

The Ruhr

The Ruhr occupied a central place in the search for a solution to the German question through demilitarisation and deindustrialisation. There were different ideas for resolving the dual issue of including Germany in the European order and suppressing its industrial-military potential. American proposals ranged from Morgenthau's plan for complete deindustrialisation to the Dulles proposal for the Europeanisation of the Ruhr through a federal solution.

The position of France diverged from that of its allies, the UK and the US. France was not interested in a complete destruction of Germany's industrial base (Gillingham 1991: 151). Monnet's Reconstruction and Modernisation Plan was based on access to German coal and steel with an objective of reaching 150 per cent of pre-war industrial production (Bossuat 2001: 124). In its 1945 and 1946 memoranda to the Council of Foreign Ministers of the Western powers, France stated its security concerns with regard to the three regions: the Ruhr, the Rhineland, and the Saar. The memoranda maintained that the mere internationalisation of the mines could not guarantee control of the war industries without a customs barrier and the determination of ownership in the coal and steel sectors.

The Marshall Plan (1947) changed the context of France's Ruhr policy (Defrance 2004: 127). In February 1947 France proposed an international authority for the Ruhr. In November 1947, Britain and the US established the *Deutsche Kohlenbergbauleitung* (DKBL) to manage the Ruhr mines. France protested against the return of management functions to German control (Gillingham 1991: 151). Expropriation of mines took place in parallel with customs control established between the Ruhr and German territory. The London Agreements of 3 June 1948 determined that the Ruhr would be part of Germany. The American delegation accepted the creation of an international authority to manage the coal and steel production of the Ruhr, provided that it would be responsible for the implementation of the Marshall Plan.

The Ruhr Statute was signed on 28 December 1948 as a multilateral agreement with the participation of the US, the UK, France and the Benelux countries. The International Authority for the Ruhr (IAR) was created as a transitional mechanism (together with the Office of Military Security). It was integrated into the Ruhr Statute on 28 April 1949. Germany became a member and acquired voting rights as a result of the Petersberg agreement (22 November 1949). The Agreement removed certain conditions on dismantlement of industrial capacity but preserved the cap on steel production, set at 11 million tons (Schwabe 2004: 90).

France's agreement to the IAR marked the first change in French foreign policy. France gave up the separation of its occupying zone and claims to the Ruhr as the core of French security interests. By agreeing, France relied on the transitional nature of the arrangement. The Ruhr issue remained unresolved.

The IAR was about multilateral access to the Ruhr but not about its place in Europe. France wanted to respond to German concerns as an element of normalisation of the Franco-German relationship. The Ruhr Statute and the IAR were regarded as a step towards providing Germany with some degree of economic sovereignty, but also towards international control over industrial areas in Europe and a mechanism of cooperation indispensable for a future United States of Europe. However, the Authority was to deal with products and exports, not the organisation of production. The German coal and steel industry was dominated by the *Konzerns* which accounted for more than 90 per cent of the steel and 60 per cent of the coal production of Germany.[9] Germany also maintained its pre-war system of double pricing which stimulated domestic consumption and was detrimental to the French industry (Gerbet 2004: 20).

The Ruhr Statute did not make provisions with regard to ownership assuming that all control, regardless of the nature of ownership, would fall under its jurisdiction. Property Law 75 of 10 November 1948 determined a new structure for the coal and steel of the Ruhr (Gillingham 1991: 225) which France protested. The law liquidated the *Konzerns* and passed the management of the mines to German control. Property issues were delegated to a future democratically elected German government. Because the question of property was not decided at the time, the cartelisation issue was not removed. Due to the basic corporatist mechanism of the German economy, especially strong in the coal and steel sectors, it could be expected that the coordinated management of prices and market share would continue.

Law 27 (16 May 1950), which replaced Law 75, provided the immediate context to the Schuman Declaration. It remained valid during the process of negotiation of the ECSC Treaty. The Law established the decentralisation of Germany in order to eliminate excessive industry concentration and prevent the development of its war potential. The Law extended the works of the Steel Trustee Association and planned for the reorganisation of assets and the creation of unit companies breaking down the DKBL which had managed the Ruhr mines and the *Deutsche Kohlen-Verkaufsgesellschaft* (DKV) which operated in sales. The Law also limited the extent to which German steel companies could have holdings in related industries and especially own coal mines.

Law 27 transferred assets in the steel industry to 29 newly created independent companies. The break-up of vertical integration was critically important to France, highly dependent on German coke. Germany's participation in the ECSC was contingent upon the provisions of the Law in the area of concentration and vertical integration in the steel industry. The future of the DVK was a critical issue due to its monopoly on the sales of Ruhr coal. As the reforms in the coal and steel sector reflected the mutually exclusive interests of France and Germany, treaty negotiations under the ECSC emerged as a focal point for the resolution of all outstanding issues. The Schuman Declaration and the negotiations of the ECSC Working Document initially did not envisage changes in its functioning.

The logic of a common market for coal and steel shifted the core of Franco-German industrial trade from balancing coal production between the Saar Ruhr to developing an open-ended relationship based on the complementarity of coal and steel production in Ruhr and Lorraine.[10] French and German industrial interests were better served under a common market which stimulated efficiency and competition and ensured the equality of the participating parties. The process of negotiating the ECSC Treaty revealed that the IAR was unsustainable as an institutional mechanism. There were important conceptual differences which ultimately brought about its elimination.[11] French policy-makers understood that there could be no continuity between the Ruhr Statute and the ECSC. It was an intermediate arrangement which could not resolve the German question either for France or for Germany. Germany insisted on the dismantling of the IAR where it felt discriminated against as the distribution of production in the Ruhr was dominated by external powers (primarily Britain and the US). The legal position of Germany under the IAR and the ECSC was different. The ECSC was a contractual arrangement in which Germany participated as an equal partner.

Although Franco-German trade relations conducted under the IAR and the tariff agreement of 11 February 1950 were returning to normal, they were not unproblematic. By 1950, Germany produced more steel than France (excluding the Saar). German coal exports were also on the increase with the Ruhr replacing the US as a principal supplier.[12] Regardless of the contribution of Saar coal to French industrial needs, by 1951 annual imports had grown to 15 million tons coal of which 3 to 4 tons were coke.[13] Supplies of coal from the Ruhr increased in 1950 from 388,000 tons per month on average in 1948 (versus 437,000 tons in 1938) to 656,000 tons per month in 1949 and 586,000 tons in 1950.

Such a complete reversal of the source base was accompanied by problems in the management of Franco-German coal and steel trade. German sales were under a DKV monopoly. The cartelisation of the German coal industry and vertical integration between steel *Konzerns* and coal mines were exposed to potential price discrimination and a possibility for the German *Konzerns* to determine the growth of the French steel industry. The development of the coal and steel industries of Lorraine under the ECSC as a counterbalance to the Ruhr was a condition for the acceptance of the Schuman Plan in France.[14] However, on the eve of launching the ECSC market, the competitiveness of the French coal and steel industry (including the Saar) was lagging behind the Ruhr. French coal production had increased from 47.2 million tons in 1947 to 57.5 million tons in 1952. Productivity increased by 40 per cent to 1,400 kg per worker per shift. In the Ruhr, labour productivity was 2,000 kg per shift, with a possibility of increasing to 2,500 kg by 1961.[15] Although productivity in the coal sector of Lorraine was close to that of the Ruhr, the quality of Lorraine coal was inferior to that of the Ruhr. The French National Assembly included the condition of the channelisation of the Moselle in the ratification of the ECSC Treaty as a way to ensure that deliveries of coal and coke from the Ruhr would be efficient and that Lorraine would have access to the cheap transportation routes.

Politically, there was significant German opposition to the rules of deconcentration of the German coal and steel industry under the Ruhr Statute which transferred to the negotiation of the ECSC Treaty. On two occasions Adenauer spoke of the danger of failure to conclude the agreement.

Table 3.1 The economic importance of the Ruhr: coal production by basins in the ECSC, 1952–58 (million tons)

Basin	1952	1956	1957	1958
Ruhr	114.4	124.6	123.2	122.3
Saar	16.1	17.0	16.3	16.3
Lorraine	12.2	13.3	14.3	15.0
Community	237.9	248.5	247.2	245.8

Source: *Mémento de statistiques*: Office statistique des Communautés européennes, 1959. ENA archive, p. 3. www.ena.lu/production_coal_steel_europe_1936_1958-2-36669.

Domestic opposition, notably on behalf of the SPD, led to a crisis in Adenauer's support for the Treaty. US and UK support for German rearmament led Adenauer to believe that German political and security needs in 1950 would be better served through an agreement on Western European defence rather than the ECSC Treaty (Schwabe 2004: 101). In contrast, France developed a linkage between the ECSC and Germany's participation in a Western European defence. It was in this context that the Pleven Plan for a European Defence Community (EDC) was formulated. Germany accepted the ECSC plan mainly due to US support for decartelisation (Schwabe 2004: 102). The opportunity to create new interests increased the win-set of the agreement both in France and in Germany despite sectoral opposition. The core issue of the Franco-German relationship in its economic, political, and institutional dimensions, decartelisation of Germany's coal and steel industry, was resolved through the ECSC. It is important to note that the US supported its policies. In the context of US approval, the ECSC demonstrated that the origins of Franco-German reconciliation were European in nature. As the ECSC resolved issues beyond economic growth, it also demonstrated that they were political and not economic.

The main accomplishment of the ECSC was that it provided a new institutional process for reconciliation on the basis of equality and the opportunity to develop new common interests. It removed the powers of external actors. On 18 October 1951 the governments, signatories of the Ruhr Statute, initialled a Protocol to liquidate the IAR by the time the ECSC became operational. The Ruhr Statute was terminated on 21 December 1951. Adenauer underlined that France and Germany were equal partners under the ECSC Treaty. This meant that Germany's status as an occupied country, the idea of a European union, and the opportunity to resolve the Saar issue was improving (Schwabe 2004: 97). The DKV also ceased to exist in 1953 and was replaced with smaller independent companies.

The ECSC acted as a successful institutional solution to the core of the German problem in Europe because it effectively, implicitly and through process, resolved the question about the normal functioning of the German economy represented by the Ruhr. The Ruhr was not only critical to the historical rounds of attempted settlement between France and Germany but also to welfare and prosperity in Europe (Gillingham 1991: 369). While the Schuman Declaration was being contemplated, the security situation changed with the outbreak of the Korean War. German rearmament had to be dealt with in a separate format which led to plans for an EDC. The relationship between Germany's economic power, its political weight, and war potential would have re-emerged with more intensity without the ECSC with negative effects on French support for reconciliation with Germany.

The Saar

While the Ruhr's importance to Franco-German reconciliation is determined by the structural aspect of the German question in Europe – the problem of peace as a result of Germany's economic power – the Saar issue reflects historical continuities of the Franco-German bilateral relationship shaped by conflict, revenge, irredentism, and *Realpolitik*. The ESCS's relevance to the issue is not obvious. The bilateral negotiations on the Saar, coterminous with the ECSC treaty negotiations, initially produced an impasse. The resolution of the Saar issue through its return to Germany was the result of a referendum organised by the Western European Union (WEU) according to a Europeanisation process designed by the Council of Europe. French acquiescence of the outcome did not make an explicit reference to European integration. However, the ECSC's role can be derived from the broader historical context of the process. The workings of the ECSC and the idea of economic integration made the concerns and challenges associated with the Saar redundant. The resolution of the Saar issue was intimately linked to the negotiations for the ECSC and ultimately resolved through its functioning. The ECSC's relevance to the Saar settlement represents an instance of its actual Europeanisation, although nominally the plan to 'Europeanise' the issue by embedding it in a European context belongs to institutional actors outside European integration.

During the nineteenth century the Saar emerged as a typical border region between France and Germany, a meeting-place of their conflicting territorial and economic claims. The two world wars of the twentieth century placed economic interests at the centre of the Franco-German relationship. According to the Versailles Treaty, France acquired rights to exploit the Saar coal mines. While Germany formally retained sovereignty, the territory was placed under a League of Nations Governing Commission including French, German, and Saar members. It was determined that a referendum, to be conducted in 1935, would decide which country the Saar would belong to. The Saar territory was used as a tool to breed nationalism and resentment against the French, accompanied by politically motivated workers' strikes (1923), expulsions, and an atmosphere of unrest which led to the 1935 plebiscite.[16] Even after the Saar was returned to Germany as a result of the victory of the pro-German group, trade with France continued.

The problem was that although politically and culturally it was part of Germany, the Saar's economy was connected to France.[17] Saar coal production in 1936 amounted to seven per cent of Germany's coal output and 25 per cent of France's. In combination with Lorraine iron ore, it produced 14 per cent of German cast iron and steel output and 35 per cent of that of France. After the Second World War, the status of the Saar was similar to that of the post-First World War settlement. France declined territorial annexation. It recognised the German ethnic nature of the Saar but wanted the Ruhr and the Saar to be separate from Germany by the establishment of a special regime. The Saar's permanent definition was to be determined by a peace treaty.[18]

The mines of the Saar passed under French administration in January 1946. A customs barrier with Germany followed in December. The Saar territory was included in a French customs union. A French-sponsored Constitution was adopted on 15 December 1947 giving France the responsibility for defence of the territory, foreign policy, and economic management. From January 1948 it was no longer considered an occupied zone.

There was no major opposition to French rights in the province, as they contributed to its economic reconstruction. Dismantling of industry did not take place, the Saar was removed from the French occupation zone as part of the economic and monetary union with France, and benefited from high levels of employment. The Franco-Saar economic union rested on the natural complementarity between the Saar, a producer of coal and steel and consumer of agricultural products, and Lorraine, a source of iron ore and farming. France absorbed all of the Saar's coal production (it was 50 per cent under the Versailles Treaty). Because of the economic and monetary union, France did not use foreign exchange to pay for imports from the Saar. A memorandum prepared for the French Foreign Ministry in 1952 estimated that the Saar supplied to France 75 billion francs' worth of commodities, namely coal and steel (Wilkens *et al.* 1997: 231–40). The savings from foreign exchange purchases, including the possibility for France to import coke from the Ruhr in the amount of around 10 billion francs, brought the overall Saar contribution to the French economy to 100 billion francs (300 million dollars).[19]

Despite such positive developments, the unsettled status of the Saar was at the origin of persisting problems. Because there was no territorial annexation, the Saar mines remained the property of the German state although they were operated by France. That prevented workers from participation in the management of the mines and led to protests by the trade unions. Such arrangements applied also with regard to the Warndt coal mine which possessed the richest resource. Without the Warndt mine, the price of Lorraine coke would increase significantly (by 500 francs per ton). The financial needs of the coke-burning industry were covered by French investment and the French financial sector was interested in securing its positions.

Despite its foundations in mutual complementarity, the Franco-Saar economic union displayed significant structural weaknesses. The Saar did not possess a competitive advantage relative to Germany. Ruhr coal and steel were cheaper that the Saar's. Its location relative to furnaces was not as convenient as the Ruhr's. That was the core of the French argument for a continued union between France and the Saar. With low production levels in the Ruhr as a result of demilitarisation and deindustrialisation policies, the Saar ensured French industrial needs under the Modernisation Plan and French parity with Germany in coal and steel production. Under the ECSC, France and the Saar accounted for 34 per cent of the coal and steel production of the Community; Germany for 35 per cent.

Table 3.2 Historical and comparative data on coal production in the Community 1938–58 (million tons)

Year	1938	1951	1952	1956	1957	1958
Germany	137.0	118.9	123.3	134.4	133.2	132.6
Saar	14.4	16.3	16.2	17.1	16.5	16.4
Belgium	29.6	29.7	30.4	29.6	29.1	27.1
France	46.5	53.0	55.4	55.1	56.8	57.7
Italy	0.6	1.2	1.1	1.1	1.0	0.7
Netherlands	13.5	12.4	12.5	11.8	11.4	11.9
Community	209.4	231.4	238.9	249.1	247.9	209.4

Source: Mémento de statistiques: Office statistique des Communautés européennes, 1959. ENA archive, p. 2. www.ena.lu/production_coal_steel_europe_1936_1958-2-36669.

Table 3.3 Steel production in the Community, 1938–58 (million tons)

Country	1938	1951	1952	1956	1957	1958
Germany	17.902	13.506	15.806	23.189	24.507	22.785
Saar	2.557	2.603	2.823	3.374	3.466	3.485
Belgium	2.296	5.070	5.170	6.376	6.267	6.007
France	6.221	9.835	10.867	13.441	14.100	14.633
Italy	2.323	3.063	3.535	5.911	6.787	6.271
Netherlands	0.052	0.553	0.693	1.051	1.185	1.437
Community	32.788	37.707	41.896	56.798	59.805	57.997

Source: Mémento de statistiques: Office statistique des Communautés européennes, 1959. ENA archive, p. 4, www.ena.lu/production_coal_steel_europe_1936_1958-2-36669.

The Franco-Saar economic and monetary union posed questions of autonomy, recognition, and representation in international and Community institutions. The Saar's presence in international organisations together or in parallel with France and Germany was a contested issue which adversely affected Franco-German cooperation.

On 3 March 1950, the Saar and France signed the Franco-Saar conventions which provoked negative reactions in Germany as they represented a *de facto* recognition of the treaty-signing powers of the Saar. The conventions brought the Saar issue to the centre of international deliberations. The German government produced a White Paper recommending the establishment of an international authority similar to the IAR, an Allied Control Council, and a special customs agreement with regard to the Saar. Germany was firmly against the Saar's autonomy which the conventions made obvious. The diplomatic argument was that recognising the political separation of German territory in the west would mean that Germany acquiesced in the annexation of territory by Poland and Russia in the east. After the dismantlement of the IAR in the process of establishment of the ECSC, Germany recommended the Europeanisation of the Saar through the CoE and proposed the expansion of a European territory to include several cantons of Lorraine. The proposal was unacceptable to France. It was in this context that bilateral Franco-German negotiations on the Saar started on 8 February 1950.

France preferred to downplay the Saar issue during the ECSC negotiations. A common market of coal and steel ensuring unproblematic French access to the Saar's resources (a French priority) overrode the constitutional and territorial status of the Saar (a German priority). Germany sought to obtain membership in the ECSC while avoiding recognition of the separate status of the Saar. Outside status recognition, however, the economic foundations of French preferences to maintain a special relationship with the Saar were changing. The rationale of the Franco-Saar economic union was weakened due to the fact that Germany was a more competitive supplier for the French market than the Saar. The French position was that the ECSC and a resolution of the Saar were separate issues and the advantages of the Franco-Saar economic union were not comparable to the common market. According to the 1952 memorandum, 'only the complete economic integration of Europe and a unification of currencies, or at least convertibility between them, would destroy the case for the Franco-Saar economic union'.[20]

Institutional reasons also determined the need for the continuation of the economic union. The ECSC Treaty partly reflected the relative market strengths of the member states. It provided members with representation on the Assembly based on market share. The Treaty referred to the European customs territories of the High Contracting Parties which included the Saar as a French customs territory. The combined contribution of the Saar and France was equal to the position of Germany. The Saar had representatives in the ECSC institutions, except for the intergovernmental Council of Ministers. In order to address German concerns, the Treaty recognised that the Saar's status would not be linked to its 50-year validity and that the Saar would be committed to it not independently but by virtue of its economic union with France.[21] In line with American preferences, Jean Monnet sought to preserve the solution of the Saar outside the ECSC, through a future Franco-German peace treaty.

Despite a political understanding that the ECSC and the Saar were separate issues, European integration had major implications for actors' interests in the process that led to the resolution of the Saar's status. In March 1952, France and Germany undertook a new process to reach a settlement in the context of the EDC negotiations and agreed that the Europeanisation of the Saar was the best option. Germany first proposed Europeanisation in return for a French promise to begin a debate on the EDC in the French National Assembly. For its part, France also used the Saar issue as a condition in the EDC negotiations under the so-called the *'préalable sarrois'*. France sought to obtain Germany's agreement that it would not seek control over the Saar in exchange for opening a parliamentary debate on the EDC treaty.

The ECSC could sustain the Saar autonomy as both France and Germany belonged to it. However, France was concerned about German rearmament due to the nationalist reactions in Germany which its economic union with the Saar provoked. Fears of a possible German claim on the Saar and a potential expansion of its war industries had a negative effect on the prospect for French approval of German participation in a European army under the EDC. The initial Europeanisation of the Saar thus emerged as a dual linkage to the conflicting French and German national interests in the negotiations of the EDC Treaty. However, Europeanisation was unsustainable for both parties. Germany regarded it as a way for France to attempt economic hegemony through the Saar. For France, Europeanisation was a tool ensuring Germany's economic penetration into the Saar. Bilateral negotiations stalled due to such contradictory perceptions.

In the impasse, Dutch delegate to the CoE Marinus van der Goes van Naters was entrusted with the task of developing a proposal for the Europeanisation of the Saar. The second Europeanisation attempt was multilateral in nature, embedded in the WEU and the CoE. Originally, the Saar was to become a European territory separate from Germany and its European status would be negotiated under the authority of a European political community. As no such institution existed at the time, the proposal created a temporary arrangement, the Saar Statute.[22] Under the Paris Agreements of 23 October 1953, France and Germany agreed to this method of 'Europeanisation' of the Saar until a peace treaty was signed.

A key amendment to the original van Naters proposal of 26 August 1953 addressed the economics of the relationship between France, the Saar, and Germany. The proposal rejected the historical practice of a simple reattachment of the Saar to either France or Germany and underlined the uncontested value of the ECSC as a point of departure. It was based on reciprocal compromise and the equality and interests of all parties: the Saar residents, France, Germany, and Europe. The van Naters Plan relied on a referendum. Its outcome would not change the economic union between France and the Saar. Only a peace treaty could do that. This version of the Europeanisation argument therefore could not function as a definitive political arrangement. Although initially Europeanisation referred to the territorial and constitutional approaches to resolving the Saar issue, ultimately it was economics that made the revised CoE proposal acceptable to the parties and the resolution of the issue sustainable.

The van Naters Plan recognised the economic nature of the Saar issue: the 'permanent disequilibrium' between its production and consumption patterns (Conseil de l'Europe 1953, Article 608). The Saar needed to be part of a larger market, concluded the proposal. Furthermore, as the experience of the Saar's return to Germany in 1935 had indicated, the Saar economy could not be reintegrated into Germany without its links to Lorraine (Article 611). The European solution was thus fundamentally about the economic embeddedness of the Saar territory in a market which included both France and Germany, regardless of its territorial and constitutional belonging. The proposal concluded that the Saar economy might benefit more that other regions from the ECSC due to the opportunity to establish broader links while remaining connected to both the German and the French market. Article 627 presented the Saar issue from a French perspective as one contingent upon the workings of the ECSC. If the ECSC was to perform its functions successfully, French economic benefits from the union with the Saar would be guaranteed. In the event of an ECSC failure, France had to consider the functioning of its steel industry in relationship to Germany. As the ECSC made obvious the limitations of the Saar's competitiveness relative to the German market and especially the Ruhr, the economic benefits for France within the ECSC would outweigh the disadvantages of a possible outcome of the Saar referendum in favour of Germany. The only limitation was the duration of the ECSC, originally signed for 50 years, which open-ended integration in the European Economic Community (EEC) would later make unproblematic.

The emphasis of the ECSC in the van Naters proposal underlined its own principal weakness in the economic domain. The Europeanisation plan did not satisfy French preferences for a permanent economic union and a permanent status for the Saar. The economic provisions of Europeanisation ensured the viability of a common market between Germany and the Saar. The Statute thus did not resolve the dilemma of the Franco-German relationship which the Saar temporarily helped mitigate. If economic cooperation between the Saar and Germany did develop (as the Statute encouraged), then the balance within the Franco-Saar economic union, as well as between France and Germany, would disappear. If the status quo of the economic union was to be preserved, then it would be impossible to implement the provisions of the Saar Statute for developing Saar–German economic relations similar to those existing between the Saar and France, the French economy being less competitive than Germany's at the time. Any triangular relationship including the Saar would fail to improve the situation. It would create political issues for Germany with regard to the Saar's autonomy and economic problems for France because of the competitiveness disadvantage. Only a common market between the three could correct this imbalance. The ECSC did just that. It substituted the economic costs incurred by the Saar with political gains of being reintegrated with Germany and provided institutional remedies to Franco-German imbalances by maintaining the parity between the two in the ECSC. The European option would not have removed the issue because it did not build a connection between political representation and economic integration. The actual Europeanisation of the Saar occurred through the maintenance of parity between French and German voting rights in the ECSC.

The Franco-German agreement of 23 October 1954 endorsed the option of a referendum on the Saar Statute. The referendum, held on 1 October

1955, produced 96.72 per cent voter turnout with 67.71 per cent of the vote against a European statute for the Saar and 32.29 per cent support for the proposal.[23] After the referendum, the key question was to restore a peaceful relationship between the Saar and France although the rejection of the Statute did not nullify the economic union. French economic interests in the Saar were to be protected by a broader political arrangement with Germany. The Luxembourg Treaty of 27 October 1956 linked the Saar issue to the channelisation of the Moselle and the management of the upper flow of the Rhine, both of which were economic, not territorial, issues. The Saar was reunified with Germany on 1 January 1957. Economic reunification took place on 1 January 1959.

Why did France agree with the CoE proposal although it did not secure French interests in the Saar? French political actors understood the differences between the politico-economic and the territorial-constitutional aspects of the Saar and Ruhr which determined the French and German preferences, respectively. The ECSC, which linked the regrouping in the core of Lotharingia to the rest of France, Germany, Belgium, and beyond had resolved the geopolitical and economic aspects of the Saar's belonging even before the modalities of its territorial status were determined. The intensity of French preferences for a permanent economic union with the Saar were changing as a result of economic integration in the ECSC. The latter made the Saar economic agreements stable by granting France access to the Ruhr which made it possible to diversify markets.

The ESCS institutions did not intervene in the status determination process (Haas 1968: 470). The narrow economic reference to the functioning of the coal and steel market in the bilateral Luxembourg Treaty (1955) was the Warndt mine, the system of trade, and the settlement in the area of inland waterway and rail transport. Under the treaty, Germany agreed to finance partly the construction of the Moselle canal which provided access for Lorraine's heavy industry to the sea under conditions similar to those enjoyed by the Ruhr. It also gave France preferential access to the Saar's Warndt mine deposits for a period stipulated in the Franco-Saar agreements. The resolution of the Saar issue by assuring Lorraine's access to the Warndt coal on a preferential basis was in conflict with ECSC rules. It was made possible by the agreement of the High Authority (HA) to supervise the process and support an amicable settlement (Haas 1968: 471). The ECSC also resolved significant institutional and political issues in Franco-German relations. There was a need for rearrangement of the voting rights in the ECSC Council of Ministers as a result of the Saar agreements. France was to lose voting rights, as without the Saar its market share was no longer at par with Germany. Changes in the ECSC institutional arrangements maintained the equilibrium between them by reducing the threshold for voting rights privileges. Article 28 was modified, replacing the prior one-fifth of votes necessary to obtain privileged status with one-sixth. Article 21, concerning votes on the Assembly, was amended as well.[24] Germany absorbed the three parliamentary representatives of the Saar in its delegation to the Common Assembly without a corresponding increase in its quota. The HA did not exercise supranational authority to induce a solution. It generated positive political effects by moderating outside political pressures and by offering institutional resources towards a consensus and continuity objective.

Having made arrangements with regard to the Warndt mine, the ECSC framework was sufficient to cover France's needs. It was through the ECSC that parity, a core premise of the Franco-German peace, was laid down. It was to be sustained at a number of occasions through the distribution of voting rights in the EEC and the EU.

Similarly to maintaining controls over Germany, the CoE plan for the Europeanisation of the Saar was incompatible with the efficiency and distributional functions of regional integration. The outcome of the Saar issue demonstrated that exclusive arrangements based on political separation – a practice typical of the history of territorial settlements between France and Germany – had become an obsolete policy. Outside voting rights, the logic of the common market was against strict balancing and matching of industrial production. The ECSC effectively re-established parity between France and Germany despite differences in size and economic potential. It sustained the principles of participation, equality, and joint decision-making crucial to Franco-German reconciliation. By the time the Saar issue was resolved, the economic relevance of the ECSC was uncertain. The importance of coal was on the decline due to the rising importance of oil and the prospects for nuclear energy. European integration, however, experienced sustained growth.

The EEC as continued Europeanisation: design and discourse
Despite the inconclusive economic results of the ECSC and the failure to expand sectoral integration by creating a defence community, political action for continued integration persisted. The election of pro-European politicians domestically and the creation of a transnational elite consensus on the desirability of integration contributed toward the sustained Europeanisation of the Franco-German reconciliation agenda.

The political and economic context of the mid-1950s did not make integration an inevitable or necessary peace strategy. The main issues of the Franco-German relationship were resolved through a peace treaty in 1955. Trade and industrial patterns in Western Europe were covered by the existing economic arrangements. In the steel trade, commercial flows reoriented from Lorraine and the Saar towards Germany. Despite trends of normalisation, it was at this moment that actors' choices turned toward European integration once again. Belgian Foreign Minister Spaak proposed a sustaining context to ensure reconciliation (Spaak 1969: 396). As Spaak explained: 'If our continent delays too long in uniting, if our old hostilities and our border quarrels get the upper hand [...] we shall go spiraling into an irremediable decline.'[25] Adenauer supported the idea: 'Undoubtedly, all risk of war is now excluded between European nations, but more needs to be done,' he stated.[26]

In order to prevent a trend towards national entrenchment and fragmentation of regional relations, Spaak initiated a transnational network including Adenauer, French Foreign Minister Pinay, Italian Foreign Minister Gaetano Martino, and the Benelux countries (Spaak 1969: 61–5). The process of continued integration rested on the same concepts of solidarity and unity which had defined sectoral integration. The Beyen Plan for a customs union served as a blueprint to the Benelux proposal for a relaunch of European integration. Beyen considered the fragmented nature of sectoral agreements as inadequate to the objectives of building solidarity and unity in Europe. The only way to accomplish these goals was Europeanisation of policy on a larger scale, through the creation of a customs union and a supranational authority. Germany made a 'conscious choice' to join the EEC project as a political commitment to a united Europe and abandoned the alternative idea of a free trade area (Gillingham 2006: 77). While the latter was a viable project due to its Atlanticist nature, the continental European elites chose a political organisation.

Paul-Henri Spaak chaired an intergovernmental conference in Messina (1–2 June 1955) which discussed plans for relaunching integration. The Messina Declaration emphasised the continuity in political choice defined as the prevention of war through welfare maximisation and the creation of common institutions. Despite the failure of the EDC, the integration project was relaunched on a comprehensive scale. 'It [was] hard to devise an alternative to the integration scenario ...', notes Gillingham (1991: 32). The Rome Treaty on the European Economic Community (EEC) stated the founding states' commitment 'to ensure the economic and social progress of their countries by action to eliminate the barriers which divide Europe' and the objective of 'pooling of resources to preserve and strengthen peace and liberty'.[27]

In contrast to the ECSC Treaty, signed initially for a period of 50 years, the Rome Treaty establishing the EEC was signed for an indefinite period of time. The Treaty accommodated the prospects for German reunification. It contained a Declaration on the applicability of its provisions for Berlin, although Germany had kept the unification issue outside the negotiations. The workings of the EEC had a cohesiveness effect (Hallstein 1961: 7). The Third General Report of the European Commission (1960) noted that the treaty-required proposals of the Commission were 'an autonomous political action by which the Commission [...] expresses what it considers to be the general interest of the Community' (European Commission 1960: 17).

The continued development of integration emerged as inseparable from a European discourse anchored in ideas of solidarity, peace, Franco-German reconciliation, and learning. Framing European integration as a peace project changed the way in which actors pursued their national interests. The Euro-discourse built new and affected existing attitudes both at the level of elites and the mass publics. European integration emerged as a constraint to nationalist attitudes, a symbolic reflection, and a way to mobilise support. It altered the way actors perceived integration. Puchala (1970) and Deutsch (1966) report elements of positive identification between the French and the German publics during the 1950s and 1960s reflected in the recognition that participation in the EEC was necessary. Puchala (1970: 198) notes sub-processes of community formation through measures of amity, the disappearance of barriers, economic transactions, and emergence of a 'we-feeling'. The presence of conflicting views on the robustness of the process and its desirability serve to demonstrate that European integration had become a dimension of national political space. Inglehart (1967b: 97–8) contends that the positive trends of trust between France and Germany and support for European integration were the result of a process of socialisation induced by the European movement, increased trade, and the European insti-tutions. On the contrary, Deutsch (1966: 355) has argued that integration stalled around 1958. Scheingold (1970) has noted that there was no evidence that French and German public opinion preferred a transfer of governance functions in critical areas to the EEC, rather than to a Western European government. According to Scheingold, such trends make it difficult to determine the role of European integration in bringing peace and prosperity to Europe and raise the empirical question of evaluating 'what difference it makes whether Europe integrates' (Scheingold 1970: 1002).

Despite the lack of consensus in the literature, a comparative examina-tion of the data suggests that public opinion in France and Germany during the 1950s and the 1960s experienced similar trends of rising approval for inte-gration. Generational differences in the two countries were converging. Deutsch (1966: 358) has found consistent convergence between French and German public opinion in terms of rate of approval of integration relative to Britain and Italy. French and German citizens were more likely to have similar perceptions and preferences for integration relative to citizens of the EEC member states. Figure 3.1. below shows that change in the aggregate 'index of European integration', comprised of measures of support for free trade, mobility, common foreign policy, and development assistance, is identical for France and Germany (+16%) and considerably higher than the value for the Netherlands (+5%).

In parallel with such similarities between France and Germany, Inglehart (1967b: 105) contends that a shared reorientation of public attention towards European integration was in place by 1962, that despite General de Gaulle's opposition to European integration, French elites shared a more favourable opinion, and that such measures reflected the role of integration in reshaping the political aspirations of major social groups. Deutsch (1966: 199) relates such measures of rapprochement between France and Germany to the

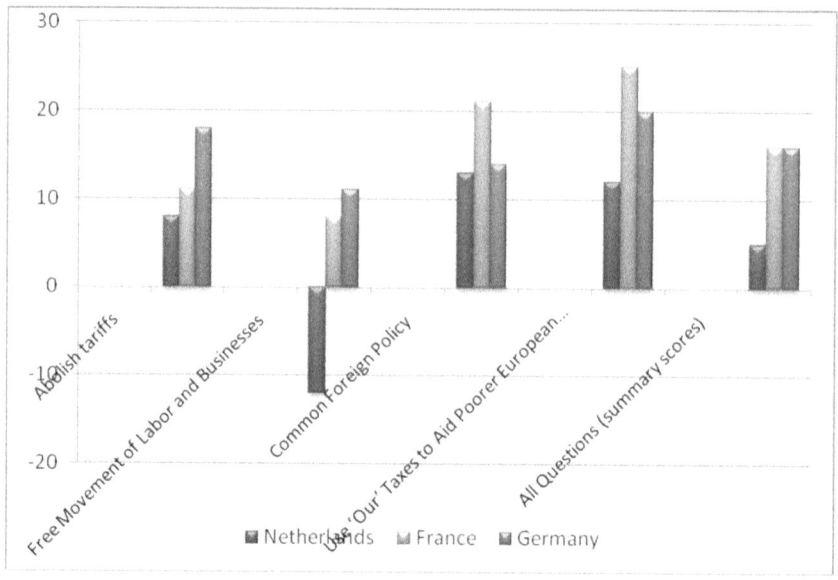

Figure 3.1 Generational differences in attitudes towards issues of European integration: net support for integration in youth minus adult cohorts

Source: Opinion polls: adults (1962–63); youth (1964–65). Derived from Inglehart (1967a: 49; 1967b: 92).

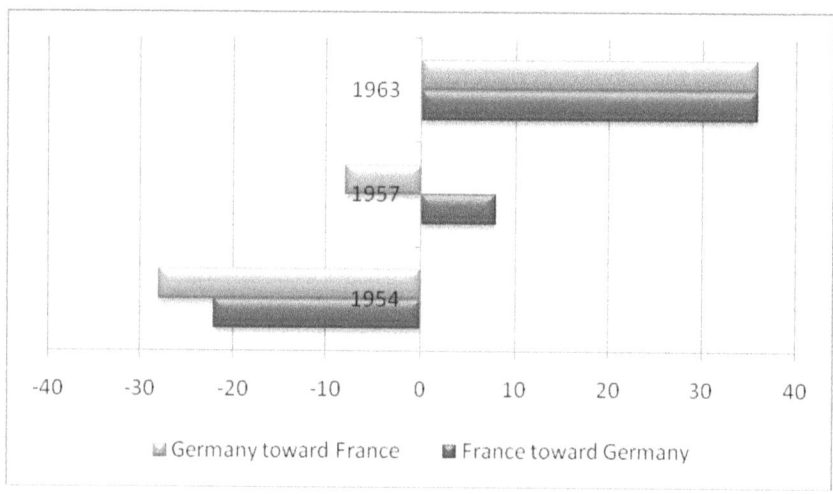

Figure 3.2 The emergence of empathy between France and Germany, 1954–63

Source: Based on data in Rabier (1965).

increased capacity for cooperative interaction as a result of integration. Building a capacity to act represents a measure of the Europeanisation of Franco-German reconciliation sustained by the institutions of European integration.

The Elysée Treaty of 22 January 1963: the 'crowning' of Franco-German reconciliation

The signing of the Elysée Treaty marked the final phase of the reconciliation process, allegedly making it irreversible.[28] The argument that European integration was a source of influence in this process is built on a paradox. The Franco-German treaty was not a part of European integration. On the contrary, its original design was the product of French reactions to the success of integration and the expanding competences of its institutions. While the long-term effects of the bilateral Franco-German Treaty of Cooperation and Friendship are inseparable from the institutional dynamics of European integration, the process leading to the conclusion of the Treaty is less discussed in connection with the EEC. The argument advanced here is that as an outcome of international negotiation, the Elysée Treaty was inseparable from the evolution of European integration, and namely, the discussion of political integration and the role of the Community institutions in it. The EEC had a tangible impact on its negotiation through design and political meaning. The signing of the treaty presents evidence of such Europeanising influences. There was a policy debate and a deliberate expression of political preferences by the EEC institutions in the objective of steering the political design of Western Europe. The conclusion of the Elysée Treaty in a limited bilateral form, reduced from a multilateral political arrangement designed to serve political cooperation, was a side effect of the established pattern of integration in the EEC.

After returning to power in 1958, President de Gaulle sought to create an institutional alternative to integration for a political union among the EEC member states. The global security situation at the time led him to believe that France had to build cooperation in Western Europe. According to de Gaulle, a political union among the Western European states would establish a pattern of intergovernmental cooperation and subsume economic integration achieved through the European Communities.

The project for a political community among the EEC member states which ultimately led to the Elysée Treaty was based on French foreign policy initiatives advanced around 1959. President de Gaulle first announced the plan for a political union in a televised speech on 5 May 1960.[29] Prior to that, a French government memorandum of 17 September 1958 elaborated on the idea of a political union as an intergovernmentalist replacement of the supranational designs for European integration. A Franco-Italian proposal of June

1959 envisaged regular consultations among the foreign ministers of the EEC member states in an intergovernmental framework. On 23 November 1959 in Strasbourg, the Foreign Ministers agreed to meet every three months to consult on foreign policy. Despite Belgian and Dutch reservations about the strictly continental-European format which excluded the UK and the US, the first meeting took place on January 1960 in Rome (Mayer 1996; Vanhoonacker 1989).

Outside broad considerations for an organised peace in Europe, de Gaulle's plan was anchored in the power configuration of the EEC. The objective was to create parallel intergovernmental structures diluting the power of the EEC institutions. But the failure of the project and the limited bilateral form which it took demonstrates that the institutions of European integration were already developing a life of their own. Political actors had different preferences with regard to the structures of political cooperation but they all – with the exception of the French leadership – sought to develop the political prospects of the EEC.

A series of government-related publications during the period 1960–61 were indicative of, or directly stated, de Gaulle's position that supranationalism no longer existed and 'could not work'. In a press conference on 5 September 1960 in Paris, de Gaulle denied the authority of the Community institutions. The idea of replacing the logic of European integration produced significant differences of opinion among the EEC members leading to various coalitions. The principal division occurred between France and Germany on the one hand, and the Benelux members and Italy on the other. President de Gaulle discussed the proposal during the Rambouillet meeting with Adenauer on 29 July 1960 and then relaunched the idea in an EEC format (Mayer 1996; Stelandre 1996).

The conference on the discussion of the joint Franco-German proposal for a political union was held during the Paris EEC Summit of 10–11 February 1961. The Paris Communiqué made explicit reference to the reconciliation objective of a political union:

> Amidst the crises and upheavals that beset the world, Western Europe, so recently ravaged by national rivalries and conflicts, is to become an area of understanding, liberty and progress. In this way, what Europe does will carry more weight in the world, which will be to the advantage of all countries and will, in particular, lead to closer cooperation with the United States. (European Parliament 1982: 106)

The Fouchet Committee was formed in the wake of the Paris Summit with a mandate to propose an institutional form for the political community. The Bonn Communiqué (18 July 1961) gave the Fouchet Committee a new mandate. It evoked the implicit political references in the Treaties establishing the European Communities and the resolution of the European Parliament (EP) of 28 June 1961 to that effect (European Parliament 1964: 9). The proposal for a political union among the EEC member states was formulated in the first Fouchet Plan (2 November 1961). The Plan was a revised version of the original French proposal of 19 October 1961. It envisaged the establishment of a Political Commission, a Council, consisting of the Heads of State or Foreign Ministers, a European Political Committee assisting the Council, and a Parliamentary Assembly, the same as that of the Community, entrusted with debating all questions concerning the Union and making recommendations to the Council.

Significant differences emerged on the role of the European Communities in the new institution. After the construction of the Berlin Wall (13 August 1961), Germany supported close political cooperation in Western Europe (Mayer 1996: 51). The Netherlands viewed the project as a form of Franco-German domination. Paul-Henri Spaak supported the agreement as it represented a movement towards political cooperation among the Western European countries and a way to keep Germany involved in it. At the same time, the EEC member states were aware that its intergovernmental basis diluted the principles of integration (Stelandre 1996: 31). The discussion of the Six on the modalities of political cooperation was therefore never completely separate from the workings of the Community institutions. The Paris and Bonn Conferences which negotiated the conditions for the political union were, respectively, the first and second summit sessions of the EEC member states. The European institutions were more than a point of deliberation. They were also a source of influence on the process. Even in a limited form, the proposal envisaged extending the work of the already existing EEC Parliamentary Assembly into the political domain. Its conditions were the object of deliberations in the European Parliament. The European institutions acted as a source of constraints on actor behaviour. The EEC member states sought to accommodate the French view in the spirit of solidarity but also sought to preserve the community method of integration. They declined to follow the logic of fragmentation of governance which had been overcome with the creation of the EEC.

The EP instructed its Political Committee to examine the Fouchet Plan. On 21 December 1961, based on a report by René Pleven, the EP adopted a recommendation on the draft Treaty in response to the Bonn Declaration. While stressing the importance of political cooperation in the area of foreign policy, defence, and the cultural field, the recommendation stated that the creation of new institutions was not to hinder the work of the already established European Communities:

> The Parliament wishes to avoid anything that might constitute or even merely appear to be a step back from the Treaties establishing the ECSC, EEC and Euratom. It recommends that no clause in the new Treaty should be capable of being interpreted as calling in question the subsequent existence, powers or impetus of the institutions of the European Communities. An explicit provision should be inserted in the new Treaty specifying that it does not modify the Treaties of Paris and Rome (I-3).
> [...]

The Parliament feels that the Union of the European peoples, as mentioned in the Bonn Declaration, should give effect to the desire for political union already implicit in the Treaties of Rome and Paris. For this reason, the Parliament is anxious to determine the relationships that should exist between the European Communities and the new organization. It is aware of the significance in this context of the extension of its own jurisdiction in new fields (II-7). (European Parliament 1982: 116–18)

The EP recommendation emerged as a basis for the five EEC members outside France to submit a counter-proposal to the Fouchet Plan, which reflected their disagreement with President de Gaulle's concept of a Europe of the nation-states. The proposal removed references to economics as an area of cooperation within the community and the future Political Commission, added a court of justice, opened a possibility for qualified majority voting in parallel with the unanimity rule, and embedded defence cooperation within the Atlantic Alliance (European Parliament 1982: 122). The proposal of the Five did not lead to the adoption of a final text. On 10 April 1962 the UK requested to be included in the negotiations. Belgium and the Netherlands blocked further negotiations until the UK joined the EEC. Negotiations on the Fouchet Plan were suspended on 17 April 1962 after a Belgian and a Dutch veto and international events pushed France to continue negotiations only with Germany (Vanhoonacker 1989).

The obvious failure of the effort to establish a political community among the EEC member states reflects the resilience of European integration. The discussion of a political union took place as the EEC had entered into a new stage of evolution. Although for different reasons, the member states chose not to dilute integration or to confine it to the economic domain. The five member states which rejected the plan did so because it failed to guarantee the continued development of integration and the competences of its institutions to act and provide governance.

The outcome demonstrated that European integration was not a power politics project, an alternative to the UK, the US, or NATO. Rather than seeking to create a 'third force' in Europe, the EEC adopted a strategy of strengthening its links with the Atlantic community which viewed European unification and the Atlantic Alliance as complementary processes (European Parliament 1964: 13–14). It similarly demonstrated that integration was not a federalist project, as the small states were not against unanimity in political matters (Stelandre 1996: 37–8).

The failure of the Fouchet Plan can be interpreted as a French reaction and retrenchment as a result of the emerging Europeanisation of the relations among the EEC member states. The political nature of the European Communities, despite their economic focus, was at odds with a conception of foreign policy based on the primacy of sovereignty which reduced integration to an intergovernmental trade negotiation process. President de Gaulle's initiatives represented an effort to stop the process of mutual adjustment, common decision-making, and institutionalisation by means of an alternative framework of intergovernmental cooperation.

Germany had supported France in the process. In a Declaration of 22 January 1963 France and Germany restated the historic role of reconciliation and put forward the new principle of consultation in bilateral cooperation (Gerbet *et al.* 1998: 141). The Franco-German (Elysée) Treaty was signed on 22 January 1963. It was perceived initially as a failure of the European concept of Franco-German reconciliation relative to bilateral negotiation:

> If what has been achieved today has failed to attract total support from all sides, this is because it sets us apart somewhat from our European partners and also from Great Britain and the United States. All the declarations and professions of faith in the world can do nothing to change that. Nothing much is left today of the European concept as it looked in the 1950s, of the community in which Schuman, De Gasperi, Monnet, Spaak and not least of all the Chancellor himself believed, a community founded on the notion of equal rights and equal obligations for all parties and embedded in the broader Atlantic community. (Blankenhorn 1980: 439)[30]

In reality, instead of neutralising the approach to embedding Franco-German reconciliation in a multilateral form through European integration, the Elysée Treaty itself adopted a European perspective. It was reoriented to serve as its guidance and reinforcement. The limitations of the Treaty from an intended political community into a bilateral treaty demonstrate that the communitarian perspective on Europe adopted through European integration acted as a constraint on actors' behaviour.

Germany accepted the plan that led to the signing of the Elysée Treaty not because it had a genuine interest in it but out of solidarity with France and in order to prevent her isolation. French retrenchment vis-à-vis the EEC is indicative of the fact that the workings of the European Communities, themselves a measure of the evolution of integration, were changing the nature of the foreign policies and decision-making of the member states. Although President de Gaulle tried to reform the method of cooperation within the EEC, he did not break with the Community. Actors' preferences for integration remained stable.

The Franco-German Treaty is the only durable consequence of the plans to create a political union among the EEC member states during the 1950s and the early 1960s. Its reconciliation spirit is reflected in the choice of a format to cooperate directly with Germany on a contractual basis, treating the latter as an equal partner. The Treaty was a strategy to adapt the pursuit of a French leadership to Germany's growing economic and political role in Europe. It was deeply embedded in European integration because the circumstances which led to it pertain to the integration process. The Preamble of the Treaty significantly modified the original draft as a result of the ratification by the German Bundestag on 16 May 1963. The final text restates close cooperation with the United States, common definition within NATO, and European unity through the EEC (Gerbet *et al.* 1998: 144).

The Elysée Treaty became stronger despite the limited scope of action as a result of European integration. It provided Franco-German political cooperation at all levels with a substantive foundation and a broad political purpose. The practice of bilateral political coordination, partnership, and rebalancing between France and Germany continued throughout the 1980s and emerged as a foundation of the EU's political domain from 1992. Perhaps the strongest argument that reconciliation between France and Germany was Europeanised is reflected in the fact that as an instrument of bilateral relations, the Elysée Treaty adopted the idea of a united Europe. It did not serve objectives of isolationism or domination. The long-term embeddedness of the treaty in European integration provided a sustaining mechanism for Franco-German reconciliation accomplished during the 1950s.

Conclusion

Conflict resolution became an explicit policy goal of the ECSC and was sustained through the EEC, not other actors (Wessels and Linsenmann 2002: 61). The EEC response to crises, such as the Elysée Treaty, and the emergence of the peace norm in European politics suggests that the European Communities developed into a peace structure (Galtung 1973: 57–8).

The evolution of the post-Second World War Franco-German relationship through European integration validates the Europeanisation thesis relative to alternative hypotheses, positing reconciliation as the product of influential actors, state interests, and domestic coalitions. Europeanisation does not measure impact by the extent to which the policies, procedures, and institutional consequences diverge from the actors' original intentions, as institutionalist analysis does, or whether institutions fulfil the purpose for which they are created (Cortell and Peterson 2001). It moves beyond the efficiency criteria of functionalism. Europeanisation captures the process of adaptation, learning, politicisation, and change in public perceptions (Olsen 2007). It fits well with the premises of domestic political pluralism. EEC governance structures and policies had tangible political relevance. They created pressures for reconsideration of interests, incentives for actors to pursue integration and constraints on actors to neutralise it – as President de Gaulle did – indirectly pointing to the transformative capacity of European integration.

What were the effects? The evidence suggests that the conflict resolution and reconciliation rationale of integration informed the choices of political actors. The purposeful application of European integration as a strategy of conflict resolution and reconciliation resulted first and foremost in institutional creation and growth. Integration was a process of construction of institutions for pooling interests, designing new projects, and creating and transferring rules. A European-level governance process created a sense of common purpose. The creation of the EEC demonstrates that the institutionalisation of integration acquired high salience in states' preferences even in the context of inconclusive substantive results. A second line of evidence reveals that European integration, either directly or indirectly, was a factor contributing to the resolution of the critical issues in the Franco-German relationship which multilateralism, consultation, external control, and alliance politics were unable to affect or transform. This mode of Europeanisation by design did not exert direct top-down influences. As Haas (1968: 471) has noted, the HA did not take a policy initiative even in cases within its competence. However, the institutional design of integration became the preferred arena for the resolution of outstanding issues by sustaining a common interest in integration, imposing constraints on actor behaviour, and creating opportunities to pursue conflict resolution objectives.

In addition to institutional processes of policy-making, European integration was a source of politicising effects. It emerged as a discourse in domestic politics which legitimised political action towards reconciliation. At a later stage, the impact of integration was that of a design, reflected in the initiatives of the EEC institutions to sustain the irreversibility of the process. Not only did integration under the EEC not retract, but it was expanded and made comprehensive through the customs union. Elite responsiveness to integration increased. Bargaining styles changed. The mobilisation of a transnational coalition to advance the European construction in the process of negotiation of the EEC Treaty and the Fouchet Plan demonstrated that political actors shared an understanding of the political necessity of the process.

The negotiation of the Plan shows that although the EEC member states were not prepared to adopt supranationalism, they similarly did not share a preference for intergovernmentalism (European Commission 2007c: 71). The ECSC had more concrete effects than conventional accounts suggest, if its outcomes are measured against goals, such as ending the occupation status of Germany, changing borders in Western Europe, or creating a new alliance. By binding together institutional logic and allowing for the adaptation of actors' interests within it, it produced a new method of structuring relations between France and Germany beyond the bilateral and multilateral agenda of negotiation and diplomacy, although it was achieved through diplomatic action. The new method of pooling together of resources opened up immediate political and problem-solving opportunities. As the case studies of the Ruhr, the Saar, and the Elysée Treaty indicate, European integration increased actors' capabilities to addresss pressing issues which conventional methods could not resolve. Direct problem-solving took place through Europeanisation of the Franco-German relationship within the ECSC's structures of decision-making and governance. The combination of political commitment and action, institutional creation, and policy-making within the ECSC and the EEC advanced the reconciliation agenda in key areas: the cartelisation of the German coal and steel industry, one of the sources of Germany's war mobilisation capabilities, the future of the Franco-Saar economic and monetary union vis-à-vis Germany's political and territorial claims to the region, and the choice to maintain integration as an overarching framework of interstate relations in Western Europe. The logic of integration Europeanised the Franco-German relationship through a governance process in the ECSC and later in the EEC, replacing prior frameworks based on settlement-style procedures, and the occupation rights of the allied powers, as well as alliances and intergovernmental organisations.

The Franco-German case established a tradition of applying the policy instruments of integration to create polity-related impacts in terms of legitimacy, state traditions, and identities. Although it was not a macro-constitutional process, European integration had major political effects measured primarily as an increased capacity to act. At this stage, the Europeanisation of conflict resolution took place through the deliberate design of policies that reconstituted interests, built new institutions, and changed public perceptions. France ultimately developed a policy towards Germany that was inseparable from European integration.

The Europeanisation of the Franco-German relationship of the post-Second World War period set a historical precedent for the relevance of European integration to conflict resolution. The justification of the process of European construction through the lens of peace, conflict resolution, and reconciliation created a positive momentum towards expanding the peace relevance of integration and established new foundations for the legitimacy of the process. The construction of meaning is reflected in the repeated reference to the past in all constitutive acts of European integration, pointing to the need to transcend past divisions, the logic of deepening integration in order to build peace, and the standing objective of creating an ever closer union among the peoples of Europe. As a result of the Franco-German constitutive relationship of the 1950s, the peace and reconciliation issue emerged as a fundamental norm of European construction and a legitimising discourse (Diez *et al.* 2008a; Ginsberg 2007, among others).

The case serves as an important referent to contemporary cases examined in the conflict resolution literature. Diez *et al.* (2008b: 4–5) evokes the Franco-German relationship as 'the one example of border conflict transformation that dominates the historical literature, but [...] also a common reference point in political speeches' and as a case that 'provides us with some initial clues about the relevance of European integration in the process of border conflict transformation'. The Franco-German case has featured prominently also in political statements relating the reconciliation process in Northern Ireland to the dynamics of Franco-German reconciliation in the context of European integration (Hume 1996; Salmon 2002). The peace and reconciliation discourse emerged as the core of an EU-level consensus on the Eastern European enlargement during the 1990s. The original integration design of pooling together policy-making in critical industrial sectors into the ECSC was replicated in the 2005 Treaty Establishing the Energy Community for Southeastern Europe.

Notes

1 See also public statements in de Gaulle (1970: 379–83).
2 French Section of the Workers' International (SFIO) representing the interests of Socialists.
3 André Philip, 'L'unification économique de l'Europe', *Cahiers du Monde Nouveau*, 5 (3) (March 1949): 32–8, in Loth (1988b: 88–90).
4 Article 46 of the Constitution, *Journal Officiel de la République Française*, Assemblé Consultative Provisoire, Débats 22 November 1946, p. 350, in Loth (1988b).
5 Carlo Schmidt, 'Europe: only possible as a federation' ('Europa – nur als Bund Möglich') in Lipgens and Loth (1988: 513–16).
6 Jean Monnet, 'Du cœur de la guerre', *Reflection Note*, 5 August 1943 (Algiers), in FJME (1985: 12–16).
7 The French Memorandum for the creation of a European union (1928) explicitly stated that politics had primacy over economics.
8 Preamble, *Treaty Instituting the European Coal and Steel Community* (18 April 1951) in European Union (2002).
9 Report by Albert Bureau on the demerging of the German steel industry (28 June 1951), translated by CVCE (ENA online archive: www.ena.lu (Ruhr)).
10 Albert Bureau, 'The Schuman Plan and the Lorraine', *Note*, 1 April 1951 (ENA online archive: www.ena.lu/note_albert_bureau_schuman_plan_lorraine_region_paris_april_1951-2–36384).
11 Anonymous French note on the coexistence of the IAR and the High Authority of the ECSC (7 November 1950), Archives Jean Monnet, FJME. Translated by CVCE (ENA online archive: www.ena.lu (Ruhr)).
12 'Initiative Française', *Le Monde*, 11 May 1950 (No. 1645), p. 3, translated by CVCE (ENA online archive: www.ena.lu (Ruhr)).
13 'General note on the ECSC' (29 August 1951), FJME (ENA online archive: www.ena.lu (Ruhr)).
14 Albert Bureau, note on the Schuman Plan and the Lorraine (2 April 1951), FJME (ENA online archive: www.ena.lu (Ruhr)).
15 'France's mining industry wants to beat the competition from the Ruhr', *Westdeutsche Allgemeine Zeitung* (10 February 1953), translated by CVCE (ENA online archive: www.ena.lu (Ruhr)).
16 M.M. 'The Status of the Saar', *Internationale Spectator* 19, 21 September 1949, pp. 4–8 (ENA online archive: www.ena.lu (Saar)).
17 Pierre Aycoberry, 'Le problème sarrois est-it résolu'?, *Cahiers des groupes Reconstruction* 15, December 1954, pp. 20–2.
18 France agreed to the provisions of the Potsdam accords on the decentralisation of the political structure of Germany. It sought to recreate and develop the regional entities as the basis for a future Germany but considered the conditions not right at the time.
19 Memorandum, p. 11 (Wilkens *et al*. 1997).
20 Memorandum, p. 3 (Wilkens *et al*. 1997).

21 There was a formal exchange of letters between France and Germany on the day of the signing of the ECSC Treaty, 18 April 1951, included as an annex. Luxembourg: Publishing Services of the European Community, complex pagination, pp. 1–4 (ENA online archive: www.ena.lu/mce.swf?doc=5129&lang=2).

22 See *Convention on relations between the Three Powers and the Federal Republic of Germany* as amended by Schedule I to the *Protocol on the Termination of the Occupation Regime in the Federal Republic of Germany*, signed at Paris on 23 October 1954, *Bundesgesetzblatt 1955 II*, 25.03.1955, No. 7, pp. 305–20. The system of the Bonn Agreements of 1952 regulated issues arising from the post-war occupation of Germany. The General Bonn Agreement was signed in anticipation of the EDC Treaty. As the latter failed to receive ratification in the French National Assembly and enter into force in 1954, the Bonn Agreement was replaced by the Paris Protocol of 23 October 1954.

23 As reported in 'Das Referendum in Saarland vom 23 Oktober 1955', *Saarländische Volkszeitung*, 24 October 1955, No. 247; 10 Jg, p. 1: www.ena.lu/results_referendum_saar_statute_23_october_1955-2-3072.

24 Note by Antoine Pinay, French Foreign Minister to German Foreign Minister von Brentano, during talks held on 12 December 1955. *Documents Diplomatiques Français*, Book II: 1955. Translated by CVCE (1988, ENA online archive: www.ena.lu (Saar)).

25 Quoted in Smets, P.-F. (1980), *La Pensée Européenne et Atlantique de Paul-Henri Spaak* (1942–1972). Volume 1. Brussels: Goemaere, pp. 427–31: www.ena.lu?lang=2&doc=12909.

26 Speech to the Grandes Conférences Catholiques, 26 September 1956, *Le Monde*, 3632 (27 September 1956), p. 5: www.ena.lu?lang=2&doc=942.

27 *Treaty Establishing the European Economic Community* (Preamble) (European Union 2002).

28 The reference to 'crowning' or conclusion of reconciliation was made by French Foreign Minister Maurice Couve de Murville, 'Partnerschaft statt Rivalität', *Europa-Archiv* (1983), 38 (4): 102, in Ackerman (1994: 250 n. 43).

29 The issue was discussed in a series of articles by Alain Peyrefitte in the series 'The Future of Europe', *Le Monde*, September 1960. See Mayer (1996: 44–5) and reflections of Herbert Blankenhorn (FJME 1985: 57–80).

30 Translated by CVCE (ENA online archive: www.ena.lu/herbert_blankenhorn_insights_understandings-2-13113).

4

Northern Ireland: Europeanisation breakthrough

> The basic architecture of the Good Friday Agreement was in evidence twenty-five years earlier at Sunningdale. Hence the main role of external players has been to act as honest brokers, or as facilitators of the peace process. They have accelerated change and influenced end-of-conflict negotiating positions [...] but they are not causal agents of the peace process.
>
> Murray and Tonge (2005: 265)

Introduction

The proposition that external actors facilitated but did not causally affect the peace process represents the null hypothesis on the EU's involvement in Northern Ireland. It posits that the sources of conflict resolution were endogenous only, with trivial or random external influence. From this standpoint, the task of examining the EU's role as a factor of peace and reconciliation in Northern Ireland is unproblematic. Most analyses agree that EU contributions have dwarfed the interventions of the UK and Ireland as principal stakeholders in the process and that in contrast to the United States, the EU has remained outside the negotiation of a political settlement. Although Hayward (2003, 2007) and Salmon (2002), among others, have found positive aspects in the EU's involvement through connective impact and institutional pressures, most of these works posit identity change as a critical factor for conflict transformation. Identities in Northern Ireland, however, have remained mostly fixed and a shared European identity has been slow to develop or is altogether lacking (Kennedy 1994: 187; McGarry 2006). Political mobilisation in Northern Ireland continues to be centred on the principal unionist–nationalist divide.

Identity change represents the most problematic aspect of the EU's influence on the conflict resolution process. The idea that, as a post-national political order (Kearney 1997), the EU may subsume the conflict issue by replacing conflicting notions of sovereignty and self-determination is not commonly shared. The EU has not induced significant enough change in sectarian identities to transcend the incompatibility of the conflict. Accordingly, the literature regards its relevance to conflict resolution as that of a 'material benefactor, not peacemaker' Hayward (2007: 685). Hayward and Wiener (2008: 56) conclude that 'the "reconstruction of identities" [...] is not occurring along the lines of what might be termed "Europeanisation".' European integration allegedly has failed to create a political space beyond the nation-state subsuming the conflicting national political projects (Bourne 2003b; Kennedy 2000; McGarry 2006).

This chapter argues that the EU's impact on conflict resolution in Northern Ireland should be examined through its role in sustaining the political settlement under the 1998 Good Friday (Belfast) Agreement (GFA) and the long-term process of intercommunal reconciliation in Northern Ireland. Based on the evolving politics of the peace process, in which European integration has gained political relevance and visibility, it finds that the generally assumed endogenous model of conflict resolution centred on internal dynamics alone is not fully recursive. The Northern Ireland peace process allows for the causal incidence of exogenous variables. European integration has emerged as the core external factor affecting the causal sequences of conflict resolution. The direction of change is that of increasing actor willingness to exploit the opportunities associated with European integration. By providing material, cognitive, and normative resources, the EU has created an indispensable 'unspoken' 'fourth strand'[1] of the political settlement. It sustains the underlying institutional process and binds together political actors and communal interaction.

While this analysis does not problematise the significance of domestic actors in generating conflict resolution outcomes, it argues that the EU is causally significant to conflict resolution and reconciliation in Northern Ireland. The institutional logic of the process has been increasingly subsumed under Europeanisation dynamics. The latter combine the EU's purposive political actions reflected in policy instruments, styles, and governance processes, and resources for domestic political actors to accomplish reconciliation objectives.

A Europeanisation perspective provides an alternative to both structural accounts of the EU's role in conflict resolution in Northern Ireland (Byrne 2001a: 10–11) and path-dependent processes (Ruane and Todd 2007). It permits the unpacking of conflict resolution along its principal dimensions, rather than relying on absolute measures of impact, such as identity change and success or failure. Indicators of repositioning of political actors, evidence of accommodation and adaptation to the evolving principles of EU governance, and changes in elite and public perceptions of the desired pattern of social interaction serve as more contextualised measures of the influences of European integration. Despite the fact that they reflect incremental change, such indicators permit one to determine that the European Union has emerged as an important actor in the peace process.

Analysis of the case proceeds from an interactive research design (Quaglia and Radaelli 2007: 926–7). Based on the Europeanisation matrix, it traces the evolution of the EU's reconciliation discourse and policy tools to address the conflict and looks for potential changes in the largely entrenched positions of political actors in the direction of tolerance and responsiveness to EU influences. The chapter finds that the EU's direct input and general facilitating impact on actor-centred strategies has fitted well with the complex dynamics of the Northern Ireland conflict. The latter has ceased to be a single-issue conflict of irreconcilable claims to sovereignty and self-determination. It has been deconstructed along the principal dimensions of governance and belonging to include diverse issues related to equality and nondiscrimination, political choice, and policy inclusiveness. Most importantly, the EU's influence has transcended the limitations imposed by the consociational nature of the settlement which achieved elite accommodation through power sharing but maintained separation at the communal level (Aughey 1990).

The chapter concludes that the Northern Ireland conflict has become Europeanised to the extent that there is both a trend of consistent opportunity and incentive creation at the EU level, as well as a corresponding process of shifting actors' attention toward Europe. Having reached settlement through classical instruments, such as external mediation and compromise, political actors agree that sustained EU assistance for the reconciliation process is needed, despite established networks of institutions and processes ensuring power sharing and local autonomy.[2] The understanding that their interests lie in Europe has triggered adaptation, learning, and orientation of strategies and behaviour toward compliance with and participation in the EU policy process. Against the background of the consistency and innovation in the EU's approach to conflict resolution and reconciliation, more traditional international roles in the Northern Ireland conflict, such as initiatives of third actors and institutional structures, tend to decline in importance as the peace process advances beyond the settlement stage.

The European dimension of the Northern Ireland conflict

The British–Irish quarrel, wrote John Hume, 'is European in its origins' (Hume 1996: 95). The conflict is a complex relationship with many strands: religion, national identity, and economic deprivation (Mitchell 1999: 12). According to Rose (1976), the interplay between religion, identities, and political loyalties position the Northern Ireland conflict within the dominant cases of war and conflict in Europe. From a European perspective, it represents a centre-periphery conflict of imperial dominance, secession, self-determination, and nation-building (Guelke 1988; Ruane and Todd 1996: 270). Its historical dimension can be traced to Henry VIII's decision to break with the Roman Catholic Church and establish the Church of Ireland in parallel with the Church of England. The religious schism produced irreconcilable cultural identities. The territorial dimension evolved as a result of competing Irish and British claims over Ireland dating back to William of Orange and his military victories on Irish soil in the seventeenth century. The simultaneous expansion of the Ulster plantations deepened the division between the settlers, loyal to the British Crown, and the Irish, who sought to regain independence.

The political struggle for Irish independence during the nineteenth century subsumed the cultural, colonial, and economic dimensions of the conflict. The struggle for independence culminated with the Government of Ireland Act of 1920 which granted independence to the 26 counties of Ireland to found the Free Irish State under the Anglo-Irish Treaty of 1921. The Act established a devolved administration in the six counties of Northern Ireland. Political life in the province was based on the divisions between Catholic/Protestant and Nationalist/Unionist identities.[3] The incompatible nature of identity-based political claims was reinforced by the particular constitutional position of Northern Ireland within the United Kingdom. The UK continued to exercise sovereignty with partially devolved governance functions to a local parliament and government. Northern Ireland emerged as a UK region with a distinct economic profile. The leading rationale of governance in Northern Ireland was to provide equal access of residents to services available to all British citizens. Since the beginning, such priorities led to the growing dependence of the province on the imperial subvention. Economic and political divergence between the North and the South of Ireland determined a historical pattern of uneven development (Goodman 2000).

The economic dimension of the conflict is embedded in the particular system of governance and sustained by its constitutional dimension. Rose (1971) has called the contested nature of governance in the province 'government without consensus'. Buckland (1979) contends that since the partition of Ireland in 1921, unionist monopoly over power created a system of unequal representation and inequality in economic opportunities, access to justice, and education. The governance perspective on the conflict explains the political economy of grievances by relating them to issues of representation and the policy-making process. It is broader than the political economy explanations which emphasise economic disparity and relative deprivation as a source of ethnic strife (Gurr 1968; Probert 1978). According to Rose (1976: 22), the problems with governance led to reinforcement of sectarian allegiances.

The post-Second World War intensification of the conflict reflected the long-term decline of the British Empire and the contradictory evolution of the European welfare state. The British economy was affected by the policy preferences of successive post-Second World War governments for wealth distribution, rather than wealth creation. As the welfare state and the public sector expanded, lower investment and growth rates and Britain's deteriorating external position increased the dependence of the Northern Ireland economy on the state subsidy. The discriminatory nature of its distribution and access to public services aggravated social conflict. Economic disparities led to a resurgence of nationalism among the Catholic minority. The historical continuity of domination, discrimination, and irreconcilable sovereignty claims in the Northern Ireland conflict accounted for high intensity perceptions of relative deprivation within the nationalist minority which culminated in the economic and political crisis of the late 1960s.

The Northern Ireland 'Troubles' commenced in 1969. The security situation deteriorated between 1969 and 1972 when the UK government assumed direct control over Northern Ireland. During the twenty-year period of political violence after 1969, the conflict resulted in 2,771 deaths, over 31,000 injuries, around 8,200 explosions, and 14,000 armed robberies (Arthur 1994: 404).

It was in the context of intensifying sectarian violence that the UK and Ireland became members of the European Communities (EC) on 1 January 1973. The fact that the crisis was a domestic issue, subject to the authority of a member state, precluded any political initiative on behalf of the EC institutions. The search for a political settlement, first reflected in the Sunningdale Agreement (1973), was marked by a closer cooperation between the UK and Irish governments resulting in the 1985 Anglo-Irish Agreement (AIA). The focus was on creating structures and mechanisms for negotiation and developing a consensus on the constitutional principles of settlement. In the Downing Street Declaration of 15 December 1993, the UK government agreed to the principle of consent in the exercise of the right to self-determination of the people of Northern Ireland. The main loyalist and nationalist paramilitary organisations declared a ceasefire in 1994. Multi-party talks, including the UK and Irish governments, began in 1996 on political and security issues. The comprehensive Good Friday (Belfast) Agreement (GFA) of 10 April 1998 restored devolved government to Northern Ireland.

The institutional arrangements under the GFA settlement allocated three strands of relationships. Northern Ireland's internal political organisation was established through the creation of a Northern Ireland Assembly proportional to party strength and an Executive based on power sharing (Strand 1). Arrangements between Northern Ireland and Ireland included a North–South Ministerial Council (NSMC) and North-South Implementation Bodies (Strand 2). East–West arrangements embedded Northern Ireland in an institutional structure comprised of the UK regions and Ireland in the British–Irish Council and, at the level of national governments, the British–Irish Intergovernmental Conference (Strand 3).

Elections to the Northern Ireland Assembly took place in June 1998. The Social Democratic and Labour Party (SDLP) and the Ulster Unionist Party (UUP) received the largest share of the vote. The devolved institutions were suspended in October 2002 due to mutual distrust and disagreement between the parties. Elections held in the interim period reflected significant shifts in voter support away from centrist parties. The Democratic Unionist Party (DUP) and Sinn Féin (SF) emerged as the largest parties in elections held in November 2003 and March 2007. Following the St Andrews Agreement on policing, criminal justice institutions, and power sharing, devolution was restored on 8 May 2007.

The impact of European integration: from transnationalism to peace dividend to Europeanisation

A variety of analytical perspectives have examined the EU's role in the Northern Ireland conflict. Historically, it has evolved from that of a benevolent external actor to a holistic process embedded in the economics and politics of integration (Arthur 1990; Hainsworth and Morrow 1993; O'Cleireacain 1983; Usher 1985). One approach posits the EU's role as a post-national, post-territorial order which reconciles incompatible claims to statehood and territory by rendering such political referents irrelevant (Diez *et al.* 2006; FitzGerald 1972; Hayward 2006). The Maastricht Treaty and the development of a political dimension in EU integration is seen as a tacit force which subordinates state preferences, erodes sectarian identities, and helps transform sectoral and class interests into regional ones. The EU's quasi-federal political system empowers regions to acquire more autonomy within a federated EU, leading to new political identities (McCall 1998) and the declining relevance of the border between Northern Ireland and Ireland (Byrne 2001b: 342; Delanty 1996; Stevenson 1998: 45).

From the perspective of the minority question in Europe, the EU contributes to conflict resolution by establishing a rights-based treatment of national minorities through autonomy, representation, and participation within existing nation-states, rather than irredentism, self-determination, and secession (Aughey 2005: 64; McGarry *et al.* 2006; McGarry and O'Leary 2004; Ruane and Todd 1996: 271). Laffan (1996) associates European integration with increased opportunities for accommodation of identities and emerging new dimensions in the national question through the reconfiguration of relationships between subnational units and the central government.

From an economic perspective, European integration generates conflict resolution effects in terms of positive externalities due to the shared vulnerabilities and opportunities created by its common policies for cross-border cooperation in an all-Ireland economy (Anderson and Goodman 1994a: 18), and the possibility for a political spillover (McSweeney 1996: 176).[4] The peace dividend literature evokes the EU economic incentives which create interdependencies and break up the cycle of violence due to the synergy between globalisation, peace, and economic growth (Ben-Porat 2005; Greer 2001; Irvin and Byrne 2004). In a related argument, Byrne (2001b) posits the EU's positive influence on civil society initiatives encouraging contact, reconciliation, and cross-border business cooperation. The opposite economic view holds that the uneven trends of transnationalism and a pan-European dimension of economic development in the EU have entered into conflict with the pattern of political conflict in Northern Ireland, creating tensions between the economic openness of integration and the territorial limits of nation-state sovereignty (Anderson and Goodman 1994b; Dixon 2000: 175; Goodman 2000).

Propositions that the tensions between the regional and national level of politics may be a source of conflict transformation are compatible with the Europeanisation thesis. They are based on the assumption that European integration is 'inconvenient' and at odds with established practices at the domestic level, and that it deepens domestic political divisions. Two conflicting conclusions follow from this observation: that due to entrenched divisions between unionists and nationalists, a permanent EU role in the internal governance of the region would be inappropriate (Teague 1996), and that domestic divisions may decrease as a result of the EU's involvement, becoming increasingly oriented towards the logic of integration (Kearney 1997).

The governance perspective adopts a different approach. It integrates economic and political influences to examine the EU's relevance to conflict resolution from the point of view of sources, policy-making processes, and mediating factors which explain how processes at the EU level may affect the domestic dynamics of the conflict. Governance recasts the EU's involvement in Northern Ireland from the primarily economic view which emphasises Northern Ireland's peripherality and economic issues to a peace-centred policy-making and political action designed to address conflict dynamics.

There was no single 'big bang' decision to establish a role for the EU in Northern Ireland but instead a process of debate, framing, initiative, and conceptual innovation. Northern Ireland introduced a new set of problems for the European Community which it had no direct competences to address: civil strife, disorder, terrorism, minority issues, and economic discrimination. At the early stages of the EC's institutional evolution as a common market, its relevance to the conflict resolution process was measured through the demand-side economic optimisation effects of integration, such as income transfer and redistribution. The EC regional policy acted as a distributional mechanism reducing the adverse effects of Northern Ireland's peripherality, improving economic structures, and removing barriers to cross-border cooperation with Ireland. European integration had no direct political influence.

The growing visibility of the EU structural policies was associated primarily with supply-side effects, such as added increased productive capacity and productivity rates (European Commission 2008a) and improvement of the quality of expenditure policies (Funck *et al.* 2003: 9). Through reform and policy innovation regional policy emerged as a source of influence on domestic structures and territorial politics, especially devolution. By empowering the subnational level, it assisted its participation in multi-level governance and regional networks. Such supply-side impacts provide a new set of resources and instruments for regional development and shape regional interactions by promoting networks, enhancing institutional capacity, and encouraging local initiatives (Eberlein and Kerwer 2004; Hooghe 1995; Paraskevopoulos and Leonardi 2004: 316). It reflects a shift towards the idea of collective goods (Wallace 2005: 84) away from the traditional focus on compensation for the impacts of integration on individual regions (Allen 2005: 214). The resulting domestic institutional and policy adaptation to EU policies is defined conventionally as a process of Europeanisation (Paraskevopoulos and Leonardi 2004: 315).

Northern Ireland was susceptible to the Europeanising influences of the EU regional policy. As this chapter will argue, such influences expanded the capacity for political action conducive to reconciliation both at the level of elites, by recreating a common interest in securing the benefits of European integration, and the public, by encouraging mobility, cross-border and intercommunal cooperation, and tolerance.

EU regional policy and the Europeanisation of conflict resolution dynamics in Northern Ireland

The EU's regional policy constitutes the first area of Europeanisation influences. It was at the origin of a European space of interaction and policy designs to address the Northern Ireland conflict. Regional policy combines the impact of positive integration generated by means of top-down influences in the area of Structural and Cohesion Funds with elements of negative integration pertaining to the liberalisation programme of the Single European Market and its implications for subnational mobilisation (Benz and Eberlein 1999; Hooghe 1995). The model of influence is that of policy transfer (Bache 2008). It takes place as norm diffusion of best practices, resources, and partnerships. Structurally, it represents an element of multi-level governance (Jeffery 2000: 20).

The regional and multi-level governance system of the EU emerged as a source of incentives and resources for the institutions of conflict resolution in Northern Ireland (Hayward 2003). Regionalism enhances cross-border cooperation, resulting in changes in opportunity structures for political action (Laffan and Payne 2003). This type of Europeanisation captures the transnational nature of integration in which the state loses exclusivity in regional transactions. Europeanisation unfolds in parallel with the evolution of territorial politics in Europe: intergovernmental, centre–periphery relations, and subnational-level processes, such as devolution, resolution of subnational issues through power sharing, subsidiarity, and regional autonomy. It occurs through enhanced transborder and transnational relations (Benz and Eberlein 1999: 333). Such processes may be linked to the governance agenda of the Northern Ireland conflict through their relevance to economic disparities, equal access, and societal reintegration.

Early references to conflict resolution in EC regional policy
The initiation of the policy measures to address socio-economic issues in Northern Ireland coincided with the 1973 accession of the UK and Ireland. Community involvement began at two levels: economic, by treating Northern Ireland as a region whose economic development lagged behind the EC average, and political, through the initiatives of the European Parliament (EP).

The cohesion policy was the main redistributive policy of the EC (Bache 2008: 39). Northern Ireland benefited from an Objective I status and was entitled to Structural Funds according to economic performance criteria and GDP per capita below 75 per cent of the EC average. This approach guaranteed that the EC would remain outside the constitutional issue of the conflict. The latter was the object of negotiations and settlement processes resulting in the Sunningdale Agreement (1973), the Constitutional Convention (1974) and the creation of the Northern Ireland Executive (1974). While the EC was not in a position to initiate free-standing policies for the political process of Northern Ireland, it provided resources and ideas which were later adopted by various stakeholders (Simpson 1984: 4). The measurable effects of the EC regional policy remained limited due to the approximate correspondence between Northern Ireland's attributed share in the UK contribution to the EC budget and its receipts under the European Regional Development Fund (ERDF), the European Social Fund, and the Common Agricultural Policy's (CAP) European Agricultural Guidance and Guarantee Fund (EAGGF). EC funding acted as a substitute resource, blurring the principle of additionality in ERDF funding (Bache 2008: 41). Similarly, Northern Ireland did not benefit from the British rebate, part of which it had earned through its own attributed contribution to the UK budget. Simpson (1984: 8) concludes that there was no major identifiable beneficial EC funding to Northern Ireland due to the distinctiveness of the redistributional policies of the UK government.

Politically, however, this stage established the normative and political foundations for the EU's subsequent policy involvement in the conflict resolution process. The rationale for an EC role was anchored in the reconciliation logic of integration in the historical Franco-German case and the Rome Treaty, which evoked peace and rapprochement among the peoples of Europe. A series of EP resolutions condemned political violence in Northern Ireland during the 1970s. The resolutions emerged as the first political instruments of the European institutions for addressing the conflict, despite the lack of direct EC competences.[5] The resolutions were at odds with the foundational premise that the domestic politics of the member states remained outside political discussion at the EC level. Such instruments had a limited impact as they failed to engage a process of political coordination reserved for the mechanism of European Political Cooperation at the time.[6]

The EP was at the origin of an EC policy process on the Northern Ireland conflict which exceeded conventional regional optimisation measures. Although the latter did not address the conflict directly, the distributional effects of the regional instruments were conducive to the emergence of a shared understanding about the need for targeted governance mechanisms. The latter gradually linked conventional policies to conflict resolution. The report of the EP Committee on Regional Policy and Regional Planning with rapporteur Ms Simone Martin (1979) was the first official statement on the relevance of the EEC regional policy to the Northern Ireland conflict beyond economic homogenisation considerations. The Martin Report referred to the obligations of the Community to assist the conflict resolution process recalling its historical tasks (European Parliament 1981).

In a resolution of 15 June 1981, the EP recognised that the EC had no competences to make proposals for constitutional change in Northern Ireland which the Council of Ministers confirmed. The European Commission had declared that it, too, had no role in the constitutional affairs in the province but was concerned with improving its economic and social conditions. Regardless of such formally restrictive statements, the pluralist nature of party politics within the EP was instrumental in developing debate and, subsequently, a policy process involving all EC institutions. A 1982 motion for a resolution tabled by Members of the European Parliament (MEPs) Lalor, Davern, Cronin, Junot, and Israel acknowledged the failure of the responsible authorities to restore peaceful conditions in Northern Ireland and called on the Council of Ministers to open discussions between the British and the Irish governments towards a plan for reconstruction.[7] In counter-motions for a resolution during the same period, independent MEPs Paisley and Taylor called for the EP to reaffirm that the EC had no competence to make proposals on the constitutional and political affairs of Northern Ireland.

Parliamentary politics connected the European institutions to the dynamics of the conflict. They pointed to the relative isolation of the EC from the domestic politics of the member states and its weakness to initiate independent action. Although the matter was formally outside the jurisdiction of the European Council, the debates in the EP and its communication with the Council made it possible to address issues concerning Northern Ireland in an inter-institutional framework. In the 1984 EP debate on the use of rubber bullets by the UK government, the then President of the European Council Irish Foreign Minister Martin, in mutually contradictory statements, first confirmed that the issue remained outside EC jurisdiction and then stated that such policies were unacceptable (European Parliament 1984b: 174–5).

The need to establish a link between the constitutional and policy aspects of the conflict was recognised in the Haagerup Report (European Parliament

1984a). The Report originated as a result of the political activities of the MEPs from Northern Ireland.[8] The Haagerup Report met with resistance among representatives of the two communities and the UK. It stated a need for cross-border cooperation at a time when regional policies were the prerogative of the member states. It also proposed that the EC assume greater responsibility for economic and social development in Northern Ireland and improve inter-governmental cooperation on security issues – areas which pertained to constitutional affairs and allegedly exceeded the EP's competences. The Report also endorsed a federal solution and common institutions, and called for a legitimate expression of the Irish dimension in the conflict even before the New Ireland Forum published its report on the need for joint authority over Northern Ireland in 1984.

As a result of the Haagerup Report the European Commission presented an assessment of the impact of community policies in Northern Ireland (European Commission 1984). The Assessment identified the province as a high-priority peripheral region, made reference to the difficult political situation, and established priorities for cross-border development. The EP found that cross-border links suffered from the uneven development between the North and the South and proposed to the Irish government devolution and regionalisation (European Parliament 1987: 7).

Outside political initiatives, acting upon its conventional economic assistance and peace dividend logic, the EC participated in the International Fund for Ireland (IFI) established following the Anglo-Irish Agreement (AIA) of 15 November 1985 for the purpose of encouraging contact and reconciliation between the two communities. The annual EC contribution amounted to 15 million ecus between 1989 and 1994, 17 million from 1995 to 1999, and 15 million euros from 2000 onwards (European Commission 2006: 2–3). By the end of 2006, EU support for the Fund represented 57 per cent of its total annual funding and 37 per cent of the cumulative contribution (European Commission 2006: 3).[9] While activities through the IFI addressed reconciliation through measurable interventions, the EU's participation shifted to a different model of conflict resolution. It developed specific programming and implementation instruments under the EU Structural Policy.

Europeanisation through policy instruments: formulation of the PEACE Programme

The reform of the EC regional policy following the Single European Act (SEA) (1986) provided Northern Ireland with new instruments of conflict resolution assistance. The concept of the regional policy of the 1970s was enriched by an emphasis on cohesion and new delivery instruments. The SEA granted competences for policy initiation to the European Commission, as well as the possibility to develop linkages between state aid policy and cohesion, and prioritised community projects towards fewer target groups and structurally underdeveloped regions (Wozniak Boyle 2006: 242–3). The process required devolution of competences towards the subnational level. The new approach established a link between the internal market programme and Community macro-policies.

The increasing independence of the Commission was derived partly from its capacity to enhance the participation of subnational actors to the detriment of national governments, strengthen the principle of additionality, and introduce new priorities (Rhodes 2003: 66). By reconfiguring territorial relationships, the reform of the regional policy had polity and political implications. European integration provided political actors with an opportunity to repackage polity ideas into policy positions and vice versa – EC-based policy tools assisted them to reconfigure polity traditions.

The structural objectives of removing economic disparities in the regions lagging behind, providing economic opportunities for industrial regions in decline, combating long-term unemployment, and promoting agricultural reform, fitted well with the EC outlook on the Northern Ireland conflict. According to Bache (2008: 152), the period 1989–97 marked a revival of the regional tier of governance. Partnership emerged as a delivery mechanism for EC funding and a new form of governance. Bache (2000, 2008) posits a direct link between the implementation of partnerships and Europeanisation understood as a process of change in the organisational logic of domestic politics by inducing behavioural adaptation to cross-national inputs (Bache 2000: 2).

Following the Joint Declaration of Peace (Downing Street Declaration) of the UK and Irish governments (1993), the Council of Foreign Ministers in Luxembourg (1993) appointed a Task Force to develop a distinctive programme for assisting the peace process. The EU institutional actors advanced policy innovation to develop a new understanding of the EU's role in conflict resolution in Northern Ireland beyond the peace dividend rationale of the IFI (Interview 1).[10] The new approach reflected the association between political violence and its origins in economic and social inequality (European Parliament 1990: 13). It also recognised that the Structural Funds could not attain the objectives of regional development independently of other policy tools and that the structural policies were amenable to an endogenous model of development and growth.

After the declaration of secession of violence by IRA and Loyalist paramilitary organisations in September 1994, acting upon a mandate from the Council, the European Commission created a Community Initiative (CI) as a Special Support Programme for Peace and Reconciliation (SSPPR), referred to as the PEACE Programme, with the objective of reinforcing peaceful relations and enhancing progress towards a stable society in Northern Ireland. European Commission President Jacques Delors personally took the initiative for an EU response to the peace opportunity. Although Delors had confirmed that the EU had no political role in Northern Ireland, he also referred to the future of Northern Ireland as a European matter.[11]

The innovative nature of the PEACE Programme reflects the policy initiative, autonomy, and cohesiveness of the EU governance process. It was based on the assumption that peace was more likely in an inclusive and open society, which determined the principle of consultation in securing social inclusion. The Programme was agreed between the Commission and the member states. It was embedded in the new rules and regulations on the criteria for the disbursement of funds under the reforms of the regional policies, the Delors I and Delors II Package.[12] PEACE applied the general principles of consultation and involvement of subnational actors significantly enriched by a direct conflict resolution component. It was 'a further gesture [...] to encourage the two communities to work together. After all, this was the intention of the founding fathers of the European Community [...] to make people work together in harmony, to understand each other and to make misunderstandings disappear.'[13] Funding under the PEACE Programme included conditions for developing horizontal relationships between local authorities and social partners.

Neither the idea of cross-border cooperation, nor the creation of partnerships, was new to governance in Northern Ireland. Cross-border cooperation was included in the 1920 Government of Ireland Act. It was discussed between the Prime Ministers of Northern Ireland and of Ireland, Terence O'Neill and Seán Lemass, in 1965 (Murray and Tonge 2005: 44). As a method of delivery of the PEACE Programme, however, partnership marked a conceptual innovation. It ensured that the EU would remain uninvolved in the political resolution, and therefore the constitutional issue of the Northern Ireland conflict, while building links among societal actors, including through North–South cooperation.

Decision-making under the PEACE Programme differed from the already established EU participation in the IFI. Its objectives moved beyond the task of bringing economic adjustment to disadvantaged areas. The Programme targeted urban and rural development and cross-border projects by focusing on areas and segments of the population most affected by the violence and suffering from acute deprivation (Court of Auditors 2000: 8; European Commission 1994). The balance of involvement of public and private actors shifted towards subnational actors and marginalised groups even though there was no clear mechanism for their identification. The consultation mechanism of the PEACE Programme differed from the open advertisement process of the IFI implemented through a secretariat and government agencies alone. From its inception, the Programme was designed as an outward-looking framework and justified as a source of experience in the fields of conflict resolution, respect for differences, and pluralism. From the point of view of regional policy, the PEACE Programme fitted well with the reform in EU regional policy to reflect objectives of cohesion which replace external models of growth with endogenous sources (Thielemann 2000: 4, n. 4).

After the GFA was signed in 1998, an extension to PEACE I was decided in 1999 as an Operational Programme within the Community Support Framework (CSF) for Northern Ireland and incorporated into the Structural Funds. It was extended at the request of the Irish and the UK government to match the duration of other programmes under the Structural Funds. In Regulation 1083/2006 of 11 July 2006[14] the Council of the EU determined that the PEACE Programme should be implemented as a cross-border programme to support the special effort of the peace process (SEUPB 2007: 6). PEACE II sought complementarity and synergies with the constitutional component of the GFA and devolution of powers to the Northern Ireland Assembly and Executive. The EU thus acquired substantive relevance to the constitutional provisions of the Northern Ireland settlement.

Measures of the growing centrality of EU-based conflict resolution activities can be derived from the core aspects of the functioning of PEACE II. The Programme included 'distinctiveness criteria' which underlined its uniqueness and specific focus on reconciliation (SEUPB 2007: 41). The European Commission applied a working definition of reconciliation (Hamber and Kelly 2004) in order to connect the conceptualisation of reconciliation to its practical implementation at the communal level through programming activities (Interview 2).[15] PEACE II acknowledged the long-term needs of funding (European Parliament 2005: 8) and was extended by two years in 2005 with an emphasis on economic growth and cross-community projects. The focus of the Programme continued to expand. PEACE II identified the opportunity to secure strategic linkages to other policy initiatives for Northern Ireland and the Border region, as well as to complement national policy development by the governments of Ireland and the UK: National Strategic Preference Framework in Northern Ireland and Ireland (on competitiveness and employment Structural Funds), INTERREG IV (territorial cooperation), IFI, Rural Development Programme, Taskforce on Active Citizenship (Ireland), The Irish National Development Plan (2007–13), National Anti-Poverty Strategy (Ireland), Neighbourhood Renewal Strategy (NI), European Fisheries Fund, National Spatial Strategy for Ireland (2002–20), A Shared Future and Equality Strategy (NI), and Investment Strategy for Northern Ireland, as well as policies for promoting equality in Northern Ireland and Ireland (SEUPB 2007: 85).

During that period, the EU became the most significant donor to the IFI. EU institutional actors, including the European Commission and the EP, established procedures for strengthening coordination with the Fund. After 2006, the IFI shifted its focus from economic-based to community-based, people-centred activities creating opportunities for closer coordination with EU programmes. In a parallel development, the European Commission acquired more visibility in IFI activities and pursued further alignment of PEACE with other Structural Funds programmes (Interview 3).[16] Networks at the local level were institutionalised by acquiring permanent secretariats as a result of EU-based rules for participation and funding (Laffan and Payne

Table 4.1 EU regional policy instruments assisting conflict resolution in Northern Ireland

Period	Reconciliation programme	Objective status	Structural Funds programmes	EU contribution million ecu/€	National contribution	Total programme	Total EU Structural Funds
1989–93	ERDF, ESF, EAGGF	Objective 1	CSF and 10 CIs	348			850
1994–99	PEACE I	Objective 1	Single Programming Document and 10 Is (including PEACE)	500	167	667	1917
2000–6	PEACE II	Objective 1 (transitional)	CSF and 4 Community Initiatives; PEACE II incorporated into CSF of both Northern Ireland and Ireland	609	386	995	1633
2007–13	PEACE III	Convergence, regional competitiveness and employment, European territorial cooperation	CSF through two Operational Programmes and 4 CIs	225	108	333	890

Source: European Parliament (1990: 12), SEUPB 2007: 11–12, European Commission, 'EU Funding Programmes 2007-2013', http://ec.europa.eu/unitedkingdom/about_us/office_in_northern_ireland/funding/eu_funding_programmes_2007-2013.pdf.

Notes: CSFs are Community Support Frameworks. CIs are Community Initiatives.

2003: 467). The need to comply with the requirement for inter-communal participation in cross-border programmes, control on funds, and movement to programming versus project-based activities (the mechanism predominant under IFI financing), developed into a system of 'financial carrots' in structuring EU funding (Laffan and Payne 2003: 466). The introduction of elements of compliance for EU and IFI funding monitored by the European Commission was designed to guarantee that EU programmes would not substitute public expenditure but would create additional impact. The EU also enhanced the conditional, compliance-based component by prioritising projects of cross-border and cross-community nature.

The third edition of the PEACE Programme was embedded in the 2007–13 framework of the EU Structural Funds. As Northern Ireland no longer qualified under the convergence objective of the Structural Policy, PEACE III was implemented as an operational programme under the Territorial Cooperation Objective (SEUPB 2007: 9).

The Europeanisation of reconciliation: embedding the PEACE Programme into regional objectives
The Europeanisation of conflict resolution assistance through PEACE III took place along two dimensions: strengthening of the core objective of the EU regional policy and increasing coherence of the EU institutional process relevant to conflict resolution in Northern Ireland (Interview 4).[17] The implementation of PEACE III provides evidence of the sustainability of the EU's involvement in Northern Ireland through mechanisms which have consolidated the PEACE programmes within the EU policy process. The weakness of PEACE I was that it fostered inter-communal activities on a project basis. It was not designed as a programme for building an economic model for Northern Ireland as the fundamental infrastructure of 'a real social economy' which would allow communities to develop a shared vision of an interdependent and fair society (Hamber and Kelly 2005b: 31; OFMDFM 2005). The new approach of the European institutions under PEACE III was to secure the adaptation of existing policies directly focused on the peace process towards future regional goals, such as competitiveness and economic growth. As of 2008, PEACE III was linked to programmes relevant to all member states, which supplement its conflict resolution specialisation with economic growth objectives under the Lisbon Agenda. Such an approach allows the Northern Ireland experience to be made relevant to other contexts and contributes to building an economic infrastructure embedded in the European economy (Interview 2).[18]

The embeddedness of PEACE III in the socio-economic objectives of national and European governance gradually moves from direct conflict resolution and reconciliation objectives towards anchoring the constitutional framework which it sustains into a working system of regional governance. The matching principle under PEACE III funding strengthened the require-

Table 4.2 Northern Ireland's performance in comparison with the UK, Ireland, EU-27, and five similar EU regions

Indicator	Unit	Year	EU27 ranking NUTS2	UK	Ireland	NI	Jihovychod (CZ)	Mittelfr anken (DE)	Poitou-Charentes (FR)	Sardegna (IT)	Vastsverige (SE)
GDP/head (PPS)	Index, EU27=100	2005	139	119.3	143.7	97.0	68.1	135.0	94.9	80.1	118.7
GDP growth	Average annual % change	1995–2004	91	2.9	7.6	3.0	1.9	2.3	0.5	1.3	3.1
Employment growth	Average annual % change	1995–2004	36	1.4	4.3	2.1	−0.4	0.5	1.3	1.4	0.9
GDP/person employed (euro)	Index, EU27=100	2004	103	123.0	159.4	115.4	32.7	121.7	117.8	100.1	124.2
Growth of GDP per person employed	Average annual % change	1995–2004	125	1.8	3.2	1.6	2.3	1.8	−0.6	−0.1	2.2
Population growth	Average annual % change	1995–2004	84	0.3	1.3	0.5	−0.2	0.3	0.5	−0.0	0.3
Population aged <15 yrs	% of total population	2004	8	18.2	20.9	21.6	15.3	15.3	16.8	13.4	18.1
Old age dependency rate	Population65+/population 15–64%	2005	49	23.7	16.3	20.0	20.6	28.1	26.9	24.5	25.3
Unemployment rate	% of active population	2006	223	5.3	4.4	4.4	7.1	7.8	7.8	10.8	6.8
Long-term unemployment	% of total number of unemployed	2006	177	22.4	32.3	33.9	52.0	49.7	42.9	52.5	14.3
Population aged 25–64 with low educational attainment	% of population aged 25–64	2005	119	14.8	35.4	25.7	9.6	19.4	35.2	58.9	17.7
R&D expenditure	% of GDP	2004	123	1.9	1.2	0.8	1.1	2.8	0.8	0.7	6.0
R&D expenditure in the business enterprise sector (BERD)	% of GDP	2004	98	1.2	0.8	0.5	0.6	2.3	0.5	0.1	5.3
R&D expenditure in the BERD, as % of GERD	% of total GERD	2004	88	66.8	64.6	56.6	55.8	80.4	56.0	7.9	87.3
Lisbon economic indicator	Relative to EU27 mean	2004–2005	NO	0.79	0.77	0.6	0.5	0.7	0.6	0.2	1.0

Source: Based on European Commission (2008: 6, 20)

ment for a direct focus on intercommunal reconciliation. As a result of devolution and in line with the neoliberal statist models maintained by the UK and Ireland, government-based initiatives to address the legacy of the conflict have been cast primarily under a 'peace dividend' discourse: the expectation that the cessation of violence would allow higher levels of investment fostering economic growth which Northern Ireland had lacked due to violence. Such strategies do not take into account the structural aspects of Northern Ireland's economic development and especially the inequalities existing on a sectarian basis and perpetuated by the nature of public spending (O'Hearn 2008: 102).

Institutional development under PEACE III constitutes the second aspect of the Europeanisation of conflict resolution through processes of regional governance. The activities of the EU institutions provide evidence of the growing centrality of a distinct EU space relevant to the Northern Ireland conflict. The policy initiatives of the European Commission, and the resolutions of the EP, as well as the European Economic and Social Committee (EESC) have been specifically designed to assist the reconciliation process (Interview 5).[19] At the early stages Northern Ireland was an object of the general interest of the European Communities in economic growth and social objectives; through analysis and debate the EU institutional actors framed the transition from EU assistance as non-interference in the political realities of the conflict to a decision to implement a peace dividend policy following the 1994 ceasefire to the PEACE Programme as an instrument enhancing Northern Ireland's competitive position. The latter stage of the process marked further conceptual transition: internally, by assisting the implementation of the constitutional provisions of settlement through the GFA and externally, by referring to the Northern Ireland experience as a best practice for other regions emerging from conflict. The EESC, which serves as a bridge between the EU institutions and civil society, presented an own-initiative opinion in 2008, recasting the EU's role in Northern Ireland as a model for implementation in other conflict situations (EESC 2008). Such developments represent the definitional attributes of Europeanisation as a method of exporting forms and principles of governance (Bulmer 2007: 47).

The policy and institutional aspects of the EU's involvement in sustaining the conflict resolution process provides evidence of the growing visibility of a European space emerging to address the needs of conflict resolution and reconciliation in Northern Ireland. The implementation of programmes through the policy tools of partnerships and an inter-communal component is more effective than instruments based on the peace dividend proposition because conflict resolution is more than economic opportunities and interdependence. It includes political, constitutional and structural issues. McCall and Williamson (2000) conclude that PEACE has been more successful in the delivery of a social partnership than a conventional cross-border programme, such as INTERREG.

The EU policy domain operates through direct policy tools and a resource-based model to reflect the particular mode of governance applicable to the case (Bulmer 2007: 56). As the EU policy mechanism with regard to conflict resolution in Northern Ireland is derived primarily from the structural policies, the latter determine both the mechanism of application and the social process through which outcomes are created. Policy-based Europeanisation takes place by providing resources and empowering local actors through devolution and partnerships. Its top-down pressures are limited and weak, as they are not designed to trigger adaptation but to address institutional and policy misfit through assistance. The EU model of conflict resolution influences is actor-centred, based on interaction, and endogenises change.

In line with the modalities of the EU regional policy, not only financial, but power, constitutional-legal, organisational, and political resources also are redistributed domestically (Bache 2008: 33). Resource dependence generates adaptational change but the causal process which links domestic adaptation to EU-based sources may not be direct or obvious due to the actor-centred mechanism of change. Instead of strategic adaptation, absorption or resistance, behavioural change takes place as a result of an enhanced capacity to act and local ownership. The policy relevance of European integration is not independent from processes of politicisation and institutional learning, both of which suggest interaction across the policy, polity, and political dimension of Europeanisation. An important political effect, inseparable from the implementation of EU policy instruments, is the opening of political opportunities for domestic actors to formulate their conflict resolution agenda and use EU resources to advance it and maintain constituency support.

Europeanisation as the creation of bottom-up opportunities: institutional logic and actor behaviour

The second dimension of the EU's impact on intercommunal reconciliation in Northern Ireland is comprised of the potential 'encounter' with Europe (Quaglia and Radaelli 2007: 926) of political actors relevant to conflict resolution. If analysis can demonstrate that the policy tools, resources, and the European 'way of doing things' (Quaglia and Radaelli 2007: 925) have a nontrivial impact on the institutional logic of the peace process and actors' strategies in it, then an argument can be made about the presence of Europeanisation influences.

This model of Europeanisation is entirely actor-centred. It traces actors' strategies in using the political opportunities, norms, or resources of European integration to steer the conflict resolution agenda either in the direction of advancing or resisting it. The hypothesised Europeanisation influences are measured through changes in the negotiation dynamics of the peace process, including references to the EU as a blueprint for structuring the peace, and by the ways in which political actors use EU-created opportunities to reconceptualise their interests in a European setting.

The institutional logic of conflict resolution: EU-related mechanisms in local, regional, and North–South relations

EC membership did not create immediate opportunities for local political actors to model the conflict resolution process according to European concepts and principles (Hainsworth 1981: 15). Initially, the UK did not use its 1981 EC Presidency to launch a conflict resolution initiative in an EU context, although there was an Irish proposal to that effect.

The EC was to emerge as an actor in the Northern Ireland conflict only gradually through its regional policy. The focus on economic governance became a resource for the conflict parties when new institutional forms of conflict resolution were tested. In 1976 Secretary of State for Northern Ireland Roy Mason reoriented the UK's policy to address the economic context of the conflict. In 1977 John Hume successfully persuaded US President Carter of the need for economic assistance to Northern Ireland. As Hume recollects, he himself suggested to Senator O'Neill that US assistance in the wake of the Anglo-Irish Agreement address the economic domain (Hume 1996: 159). Senator Mitchell's first mission as the Special Advisor of President Clinton to Northern Ireland focused on economic aid.

The regularisation of contacts between the UK and the Irish governments established the first political dimension of EC influences (Kennedy 1994: 177–8; Ruane and Todd 1996: 281) and of the resource model of Europeanisation. Intergovernmental cooperation began on the margins of the European Council. At the 1983 Council in Stuttgart, UK and Ireland government representatives discussed cross-border cooperation and security.

The EU economic homogenisation and redistribution policy tools acquired symbolic significance at the level of domestic political actors (Laffan and Payne 2003: 452). The operational concepts of the EU's political order offered a principled opportunity for transcending and unpacking the conflict issue without removing the underlying incompatibility of claims. Since 1994, the PEACE programmes offered a mechanism for correcting economic disparities and conflict legacies based on accommodation, local ownership, and joint projects. Such interactions do not automatically isolate and replace sectarian identities but enhance social interaction. In that sense, the expected impact may be contrary to the logic of consociationalism which emphasises elite accommodation but sustained communal division. Europeanisation has worked to facilitate that process at the top by providing elites with common references and at the communal level by addressing cross-cutting differences, such as economic inequality and social divisions.

Policy resources: actors accept EU policy preferences

The core concepts of European governance have been instrumental in strengthening devolution in UK territorial politics (Bache 2008: 103) by enabling direct expressions of the pursuit of actors' interests in Europe. Devolution raised important issues about Northern Ireland's dependence on the UK subsidy. According to O'Hearn (2008: 114), the implementation of devolution according to population-based principles has reversed the redistributional elements of UK public expenditure for Northern Ireland. Due to the neoliberal agenda of the devolved institutions centred on cutting costs, government spending has been insufficient to redress economic growth in Northern Ireland. The peace dividend is also insufficient to induce reconciliation as it is economic in nature with no social correctives (O'Hearn 2008: 115). In contrast to the project-based funding mechanism of the IFI and other economic initiatives, the EU's programmatic activities have brought a corrective mechanism to reconciliation and reconstruction in Northern Ireland by enhancing their social component, cross-border application, complementarity to national contributions, adherence to equality, and regional competitiveness.

The European Commission has acted as a policy entrepreneur shifting local policy agendas into a cross-border context. EU funding and policy styles have changed the existing three principal network players in the border region between Northern Ireland and Ireland and provided them with resources. Compliance-based access to funding has ensured that the cross-border networks transform themselves from an element of the local authority structure into civil society partnerships (Laffan and Payne 2003: 465). The creation of a Partnership Board and 26 District Partnerships under PEACE I brought together the partnership principle and cross-sectoral representation with the representative and participative democracy (European Commission 1998a: 18). Due to its bottom-up implementation, partnership no longer functions as a policy transfer but as a continuum of actions, including lobbying, advocacy, implementation, and service delivery (Laffan and Payne 2003: 460). The EU's policy preferences therefore induce general political effects with the long-term potential to sustain reconciliation.

Polity effects

Although the EU did not participate in the negotiations leading to the GFA, EU-based concepts of institution-building and policy designs were integral to the structure of the Northern Ireland settlement. As those resources were applied to its constitutional features and institutional setup, they had polity relevance. Such references were made at several levels: the spirit and design of the institutions, administrative structures, and the policy process (Murphy 2007).

The 1993 Joint Declaration on Peace of the Irish and UK governments endorsed a partnership between the UK and Ireland within the EU. The

Declaration marked an innovation in the conflict resolution process by referring to the context of EU membership as a norm and a constraint (Hume 1996: 168). 'The development of Europe will, of itself, require new approaches to serve interests common to both parts of the island of Ireland, and to Ireland and the United Kingdom as partners in the European Union' (Article 3). The Declaration acknowledged that the constitutional and political structures would 'include institutional recognition of the special links that exist between the peoples of Britain and Ireland as part of the totality of relationships, while taking account of newly forged links with the rest of Europe' (Article 9).[20]

As a consequence of the Maastricht Treaty, Ireland and the UK adopted the principle of subsidiarity, which fitted well with the devolution and cross-border initiatives of the 1990s. The EU's regional policies were conducive to a growing responsiveness to notions of deterritorialisation of politics. The partnership principle and idea for enhanced cross-border cooperation were embedded in the GFA. The PEACE programmes, INTERREG, and peripherality concepts reinforced the ideas of political actors for cross-border cooperation. Partnerships were not simply instrumental responses to the complexity of policy issues (Greer 2001: 14) but a policy paradigm of relationships and an extension to the fundamental concept of subsidiarity in EU governance. Partnership marks a transition from government to governance and facilitates coalition formation. It is a form of policy-induced pluralism. The principle of cross-border cooperation, integral to EU programming, underlies the functioning of the NSMC and is consistent with devolution and the confederal element of the GFA institutions (Interview 6).[21]

The institutional structure of the peace process represents another area of explicit and implicit reference to EU principles and designs. The Anglo-Irish Agreement of 1985 created an intergovernmental conference with a permanent secretariat which resembled a weak common executive similar to the Council of Ministers in the EC (Hume 1996: 118). The Anglo-Irish Secretariat at Maryfield was modelled on the European Commission. The constitutional provisions of the AIA lacked a sustaining policy process and were not amenable to the institutionalisation of a European dimension to the conflict. Although such North–South executive and consultative bodies followed the principles of institutional creation in the EC, they did not induce significant transnational dynamics (Ruane and Todd 1996: 281, n. 37).

The European perspective remained relevant to the conflict parties due to the understanding that the institutionalisation of cooperation through the agreement would replicate the post-sovereign politics of the EU model even without an explicit mention of its principles (Hainsworth and Morrow 1993: 141). The British–Irish Council under Strand 3 of the Agreement reflects EU principles of subsidiarity and post-nationalism. The North–South institutions under Strand 2 acquired direct functions in EU-related initiatives of cross-border cooperation. The North–South Implementation Bodies cover six areas of cooperation, institutionalised under provisions for dealing with EU matters, such as the Special EU Programmes Body (SEUPB). The latter became the managing authority for the PEACE III Programme and the Cross-Border Territorial Cooperation Programme (successor to INTERREG IIIa). The SEUPB is involved in the policy process in the area of agriculture, urban and rural development, cross-border cooperation, environment, the creation of linkages, and the domestication of Europe in domestic politics through cultural change and elite strategies.

The political effects of Europeanisation: political actors and agendas

The bottom-up model of Europeanisation is based on the proposition that EU resources and opportunities enhance actors' capacity to act and resolve problems. Evidence of such influences is derived from the political interaction between the EU institutions and political actors in Northern Ireland. It began with the allocation of three seats for Northern Ireland in the first elections for Members of the European Parliament (MEPs) in order to ensure representation of the nationalists, although the UK government had intended to grant it only one seat based on population criteria (Goodman 2000: 101).

The EU contributed to building a networking capacity among political actors with opposing views on the conflict issue by creating an additional dimension of domestic political space along the nationalist/unionist divide. It provided such actors with an opportunity to draw on the European experience, seek EU support, and upload their political agenda into the peace process with the potential to generate positive conflict dynamics. This path is one of recasting the Northern Ireland conflict as an element of the 'European power game' (Hume 1996: 137).

Actor-centred models point to two sources of EU influence of the conflict resolution process based on actors' references to the EU. Their dependence on the EU to formulate action and recognise its structural qualities represents one aspect of Europeanisation. Second is the political opportunity and resource model, whereby political actors draw on EU resources and apply active strategies to advance their interests. Such actor-centred processes result in linkages between European issues and the Northern Ireland political agenda (Hainsworth and Morrow 1993: 118). As a result, European norms become a resource for advocacy and coalition-building embedding reconciliation within European discourses.

There is no consensus in the literature on the extent to which political actors and agendas in Northern Ireland are Europeanised. Hainsworth and Morrow (1993: 137) posit a pragmatic approach to Europe. Murphy (2007) finds little evidence of Europeanisation outcomes in view of the resilience of political actors. Bew and Meehan (1994) posit the multi-level interaction between the EU and Northern Ireland as becoming intertwined with the conflict and thus attracting controversies.

The structure of the Northern Ireland party system follows the nationalist/unionist ideological divide but attitudes towards the EU do not coincide with the sectarian division. Most parties historically have been sceptical or openly oppose the political realities of European integration. The principal evidence of the EU's influence on the politics of conflict resolution in Northern Ireland therefore refers to changes in the political aspirations and strategies of domestic actors in principle hostile to the EU, that is, the majority of key civil society stakeholders in the reconciliation process (Interview 7).[22] These actors, the republican Sinn Féin (SF), as well as the unionist parties, the Democratic Unionist Party (DUP) and the Ulster Unionist Party (UUP) have been critical of European integration for diluting their national aspirations. The shift towards acceptance of the EU on behalf of such actors, as well as instrumental references to integration for the advancement of reconciliation, represent measures of the Europeanisation of the politics of conflict resolution in Northern Ireland. No other international input has received similar recognition.

Domestic political actors have become increasingly dependent on the EU for the formulation and accomplishment of their strategic goals, for maintaining a link with their constituencies, and for influencing the reconciliation dynamics. However, ideologically, there is a wide variation in the extent of misfit between the EU political project and the political agendas of individual parties. While the moderate nationalist Social Democratic and Labour Party (SDLP) has adopted an idea of reconciliation constitutionally and politically inspired by the EU model, the positions of other principal parties in the conflict have varied from resistance to instrumental use to ideological change in favour of the EU. Although traditionally, SF, the DUP, and the UUP have rejected integration, they have adjusted their attitude towards the EU based on perceptions of the opportunities it creates for their strategic goals.

The SDLP has maintained strong support for an EU-centred process of conflict resolution. Since its first publication on the issue, the 1972 programmatic document 'For a New Ireland' through the 1985 negotiations for the Anglo-Irish Agreement and the negotiations during the 1990s, the party showed little preference for an internal settlement. The SDLP sought to expand the EU's involvement in the constitutional framework and the process of power sharing by integrating the North–South dimension of conflict resolution with the European dimension (Ruane and Todd 1996: 136). The SDLP posited the EU institutions as a blueprint for a Northern Ireland government. The party's idea to follow the institutional model of the EEC was compatible with the creation of the Council of Ireland under the Sunningdale Agreement and the permanent Secretariat of the intergovernmental conference with functions in the area of consultation, harmonisation, and management.

Former SDLP leader John Hume built upon the parallel between Franco-German reconciliation of the 1950s and the situation in Northern Ireland. Hume's idea was that the EU would be an example and a path to follow, while understanding that an agreement between the parties would not bring conflict resolution by itself:

> I believe that we can follow the European example of evolution. How did [a united Europe] happen? It happened because the Europeans came to see that difference does not constitute a threat, that difference should in fact be respected, and that institutions should be built to work for our common interests ... I hope that we can achieve something similar in Ireland, that we can create a framework which respects our differences, but allows us to work together in our common interests. (Hume 1996: 118)

Hume's reference to the experience of European integration indicates that settlement alone (the 'instant package') is insufficient, if reconciliation is not institutionalised through participation in common trust-building projects. Hume elaborated on the importance of the European model of shared sovereignty to soften Sinn Féin's position on Britain's colonial presence in Northern Ireland (Hume 1996: 116). Such views contributed to the gradual adoption of European discourses in the peace process also in connection with ending Sinn Féin's electoral abstentionism.

In contrast to the SDLP, Sinn Féin's views on conflict resolution during the 1980s reflected a preference for democratic participation and consultation but did not evoke EU principles (Sinn Féin 1984: Art. 3.18). According to early SF views, European integration undermined the republican claim to self-determination. Later on, the position of Sinn Féin evolved. There is no early reference to European integration in party documents during the 1970s and the 1980s due to the policy of electoral abstentionism pursued until 1987. The perceived federalising influences of European integration were at odds with the traditional republican political and social philosophy of political representation of all Irishmen free from external interference. In parallel with the establishment of contacts between the SDLP and Sinn Féin, the latter's position towards the EU evolved.

Sinn Féin's positive approach to the EU emerged as primarily non-ideological. It has ranged from opposition to an acknowledgment that the EU is a structural factor for Irish unity to a strategy of cooperation with distrust, instrumental reference to European norms, and pursuit of political opportunities created by the EU. The signing of the Anglo-Irish Agreement,[23] the Single European Act, and EU membership, according to SF leader Gerry Adams, compromised Irish commitment to reunification. While the SDLP saw in the AIA a resemblance to the EC institutional model, Sinn Féin regarded the Agreement as a confirmation of Ireland's subservient nature. In 1992, while in growing isolation, Sinn Féin announced plans to seek help from the EC and the United Nations for the resolution of the conflict.[24] Subsequent references to the EU acknowledged that it created opportunities for Irish reunification: 'The political and economic transformation of Europe provides a golden opportunity for Ireland to finally resolve its British problem and embark on a process of economic and political reunification to the benefit of all its people' (Adams 1994: 179). In 2005, still facing isolation (prior to the IRA decommissioning process)[25] Sinn Féin leader Gerry Adams urged the EU to extend the PEACE Programme under the 2007–13 financial framework.[26] In 2006, Sinn Féin asked the EU to support tax breaks and exemptions from state aid rules following the example of Germany after the 1990 reunification, in order to promote an all-Ireland economy and political support for Irish reunification.[27]

SF's evolution from resistance to accommodation and proactive reference to the opportunities of European integration may be compared with the strategic behaviour of the unionist parties, the DUP and UUP. These parties have shared the position that European integration dilutes state sovereignty. For unionists, it interferes with UK sovereign rights, its territorial coherence, and claim on Northern Ireland. The DUP and UUP similarly regard the EU as a constraint for their policy choices (Bruce 2007: 47). Former DUP leader Ian Paisley was consistent in his opposition to Britain's EU membership, although he served as an elected MEP between 1979 and 2004.[28]

The unionist parties separate the economic from the political aspects of European integration. They are supportive of its economic benefits but reject the macro-process which undermines the relevance of the border. They also support selectively the institutional development which tends to concentrate governance competences at the regional level through devolution. For this reason, unionism has experienced relatively little change, showing ideological resistance but political pragmatism in its relationship with the EU institutions, especially as the unionist parties support devolved government in Northern Ireland.

The UUP shares an interest-based approach to using the funding opportunities of the EU's regional policies and to lobbying the EU institutions to 'get the best possible deal'.[29] It maintains a positive view of the constructive EU economic engagement, and especially the PEACE programmes. In his capacity as Northern Ireland's First Minister of the Northern Ireland Executive, UUP leader David Trimble appealed to the EU to maintain its support for Northern Ireland as a way to encourage the peace process.[30] The UUP is otherwise politically sceptical of the EU as it grants disproportionately high assistance to the nationalists. The UUP has moved to more traditional conservative positions and thus shares the typical Tory scepticism of the EU.

While the principled positions of the major parties, with the exception of the SDLP, have remained in opposition to European integration as a replacement of national sovereignty, they all increasingly refer to the EU to advance their respective political agendas, including that of conflict resolution. The following table presents a comparative summary of their views with regard to the desirability of an EU role in the reconciliation process, in shaping their policy positions, and cross-referencing between their domestic political agendas and European integration.

The preferences of political parties across the unionist/nationalist divide to use the material and cognitive resources of European integration, regardless of their ideological opposition to the EU, point to the presence of a resource model of Europeanisation. The unproblematic policy consensus on the EU's programmatic activities in Northern Ireland and on the latter's participation in EU governance demonstrates the growing relevance of European integration to enhancing actors' capacity for political action.

Parties across the nationalist/unionist divide participate in the Northern Ireland Executive. Assuming the position of the First Minister and Deputy First Minister of Northern Ireland, both the SDLP/UUP (1999–2002) and the DUP/SF (since 2007), respectively, have sought to adapt their positions to a common conception of a shared society as an attribute of reconciliation (Hamber and Kelly 2005a), which is not necessarily European in nature. Their common preferences as members of the Executive, however, have not translated into a consensus at the level of political parties.[31] The domestic political agenda of Northern Ireland's elites therefore remains contested. Against the background of such differences, the European agenda of the Northern Ireland Executive has emerged as unproblematic due to its governance nature. There is a shared non-ideological interest in the continued economic involvement of the EU in Northern Ireland combined with opposition to integration as a political order (UUP) and perceptions of the EU as a threat to national sovereignty (SF), the UK constitutional order and national democracy (DUP).

The dual perception of the EU as an economic benefactor and a political inconvenience is not entirely negative. It permits the contextualisation of elite opinions on the European Union and with it, to deconstruct the conflict issue along its economic, political, and ideological dimensions. Issues of economic opportunities, equality, human rights, and nondiscrimination are typical European issues. Agenda-setting in these horizontal EU policies ensures consistency of implementation. Due to the relevance of such issues to political conflict in Northern Ireland, the European agenda has been more prominent in electoral politics there compared to other UK regions. It is accordingly reflected in the policy positions of political parties. Political actors selectively adapt individual aspects of the EU agenda to their ideological preferences (Goodman 1998: 2–3). The evolving policy positions of SF, and to a lesser degree, the DUP, provide evidence that ideological change is possible. Unionists regard labour mobility (a principle of the European market) as conducive to reconciliation by undermining irredentist support from Ireland. Nationalists (since 1960) maintain that economic integration would facilitate union with Ireland. Elites in Northern Ireland approve the idea that the reconciliation process should play an active role in Europe by sharing experiences, and lessons learned, and based on its regional status (Interview 8).[32] In 2008, the EP adopted an own initiative report presented by Sinn Féin MEP Bairbre de Brún, emphasising local empowerment, an 'active citizenship'

Table 4.3 The European Union in Northern Ireland's political discourse: the Europeanisation of conflict resolution and the domestication of Europe

Indicator	SDLP	Sinn Féin	UUP	DUP
Perception of Europe	*A post-national order* The European Union commits all its members to an 'ever closer union' among the peoples of Europe. That includes an ever closer union between the people of Ireland, north and south, and between Ireland and Britain. Borders are gone all over Europe, including the Irish border. (Hume 1996: 68)	*Opposition and engagement with a dominant force* The European Union is a more dominant force than ever in the political, economic and social life of Ireland. (SF, Statement) ... to support or oppose the many and complex developments in the EU each on its own merits. (Statement)	*Pursuit of national interest* The serious point is, that in the EU [...] notwithstanding all the rhetoric about being 'good Europeans', other countries ruthlessly pursue their self-interest; and often at the expense of the United Kingdom.	*A threat: a sovereign super-state* ...a Europe of cooperating nations but not a Europe tied to the federalist approach of the Lisbon Treaty. (Dodds, Statement 16 Sept)
Attention to Europe: the EU on the political agenda	*High, standing* The Social Partnership Approach. Work to ensure that services currently dependent on EU funds, that reflect the priorities are in the future supported by new mainstream recurrent expenditure. (SDLP 2007: 11)	*Increasing* It is up to all of us to play our part in challenging the EU to become persuaders for Irish unity. (de Brún 2006)	*Increasing* ...There will be a Northern Ireland Executive Office in Brussels providing a direct voice in the European Union. (Trimble 2000)	*Increasing* This [EU] report clearly shows the way forward for Northern Ireland in Europe. The Taskforce has identified a number of areas in which it can assist us in making the most of the opportunities that Europe can offer. (Paisley, OFMDFM)
Interests lie in Key discourse	*EU membership as a benefit* There is no doubt that membership has been of major benefit to our region. (Hume 1996: 144)	*Critical but constructive engagement* Sinn Féin's approach to Europe is one of critical engagement. This entails interacting with the European Union at all levels to which we have access, in order to use our influence to ensure that our demands for national selfdetermination, democracy, and economic and social justice are addressed and advanced. (Sinn Féin 2003 entry 406)	*Pursuit of interests through mobilisation* It is vital that we build a pan-Union front, involving like minded parties who believe in the constitutional integrity of the United Kingdom. And it must spread to the European Parliament as well. (Empey)	*Interests of Unionism* [get] the best deal out of the EU. (Dodds, Launch). ...Keep unionism as the voice of Northern Ireland in Europe. (Robinson, Manifesto)

Resolving the conflict: source/factor	*Direct role for Europe* I believe that we can follow the European example of evolution. How did [a united Europe] happen? It happened because the Europeans came to see that difference does not constitute a threat, that difference should in fact be respected, and that institutions should be built to work for our common interests. (Hume 1996: 118)	*Reconciliation as a cross-border concept; learning from Europe* It should be remembered that the European project began following the mass destruction of two world wars. Its aim was to replace conflict with co-operation, peace and prosperity. We have much to learn from this approach and much to offer by way of our own experiences of reconstruction and conflict transformation. (McGuinness, OFMDFM Statement)	*Europe as context* … There were also some long-term factors at work. Attitudes in Western Europe to nationality have changed in the course of the last fifty years. The defeat of nazism, the reconstruction of West Germany within NATO as a modern liberal society, the greater ease and availability of travel both for business and leisure and the development of the European Community all produced a sense of integration and a more relaxed attitude to national differences. (Trimble 2001: 16–17)	*Reconciliation through representation* The concept of coordinated representation of Northern Ireland: 'the people of Northern Ireland have a strong and coordinated advocate at Brussels, Westminster and Stormont'. (Robinson, EP elections)
The domestication of Europe	*Embeddedness* The structures established by the Anglo-Irish Agreement reflected those of the European Union. (Hume 1996: 68–9)	*Resource* … We at this point have the opportunity to evaluate where we are now as a society, where we as a society want to be in 2013 and how PEACE III can help us bridge that gap. (SF 2006b on PEACE III)	*Challenge* What devolution has done – [it] has created the circumstances in which the Union could be damaged: damaged in the constituent parts by nationalist parties…; and damaged by the 'regionalism' strategy adopted by a European Union hierarchy which believes that it is easier to assimilate piece by piece rather than nation by nation.	*Constitutionalism, unionism* The European election is the only Province-wide poll and is regarded as a test of Northern Ireland's constitutional position. (Ibid)

approach, and the exchange of experience with other conflict regions based on the PEACE Programme.[33]

Public opinion
Besides elites, perceptions of European integration have undergone positive change also in public opinion. The background condition is that, similarly to other UK regions, Northern Ireland is characterised by a low level of knowledge and public interest in the EU. Measures of 'proximity' to Europe remain below the EU average. A 2003 study concluded that there was an 'alarming ignorance of the EU in Northern Ireland'.[34] However, since the 1980s, and especially since 1993, public opinion in Northern Ireland has become more receptive to European integration.[35] Eurobarometer data suggests that support for withdrawal from the EU in Northern Ireland has declined significantly since 1975. In the 1975 referendum on EC membership, 47.9 per cent of voters in Northern Ireland supported withdrawal versus 32.8 per cent in the UK. In 1991, 5.2 per cent of voters supported withdrawal from the EC in Northern Ireland versus 19.3 per cent in the UK. Goodman (1996: 87) concludes that Northern Ireland has established itself as the most Europhile region of the UK.

Opinion polls show that the residents of Northern Ireland show a higher level of awareness of developments at the EU level aimed at benefiting Europeans (European Commission 2007a: 64). A larger proportion than in the UK on average maintains a positive view on European integration. Similarly to the party elite, the public regards the EU as an asset in the national political agenda, rather than a factor directly contributing to conflict resolution. The Northern Ireland public historically has maintained higher voter turnout rates in European elections than UK voters (Figure 4.1). Public opinion data reinforce claims that the EU has become part of the political landscape in Northern Ireland (Bourne 2003b: 410).

The European elections have demonstrated significant repositioning among the Northern Ireland parties despite their relevance through the domestic, rather than a European agenda. It is significant that the elections for Members of the European Parliament have been treated as a referendum-style voting on the constitutional issue in Northern Ireland (Bruce 2007: 109).

The EU as a discourse: identity, post-national politics, and the legacy of reconciliation
The ideas and discourses of post-national politics in the EU have not acted as an independent source of influence on the Northern Ireland conflict. If the conflict is defined as an identity conflict (Albert *et al.* 2008: 18), then the logical conclusion would be that the EU has not been able to induce identity change. Political actors disagree on the need to replace the national project with a post-territorial and post-national one. Domestic actors rarely refer to the EU in their discourse to legitimise policies of conflict resolution (Stetter

Figure 4.1

Line graph of voter turnout rates at European elections, NI compared to the UK average: net difference in voter turnout rates between Northern Ireland and the UK (NI minus UK) at elections for Members of the European Parliament and UK general elections, 1979–2009.

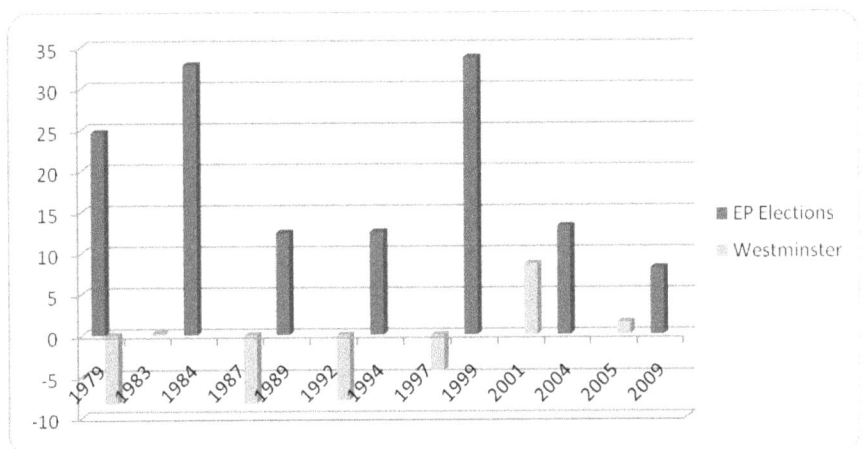

EP elections series: 1979, 1984, 1989, 1994, 1999, 2004, 2009.
Westminster elections series: 1979, 1983, 1987, 1992, 1997, 2001, 2005.

Source: Data from *Elections Northern Ireland:* www.ark.ac.uk/elections/fe09.htm, by year 1979–2009, European Parliament (European elections data), House of Commons, Research papers 01/54 and 05/33, UK Political Info: www.ukpolitical.info/Turnout45.htm (Westminster elections).

et al. 2008: 227). Neither the cooperative relationship between the UK and Ireland, nor the intercommunal institutions of power sharing possess mechanisms to overcome the salience of these divisions. However, EU discourse has been instrumental in fragmenting the conflict along multiple issue dimensions. Political actors have responded to such cognitive and normative references. While pursuing their individual interests, they have adopted EU discourses of peace, equality, participation in the EU institutions, and Northern Ireland's representation in the EU not because of an emerging common European identity or shared past experiences, but because of adherence to the non-exclusive conceptions of cooperation, political dialogue, and future interests.[36] As Harris (2003: 28) contends, European integration has altered the meaning of nationalism and national identities from concepts constructed around ethnicity to more inclusive, civic ones. Instead of belonging, common identification occurs with reference to EU policies, shared benefits of EU membership, compliance with its rules, and a political commitment to its institutions.

According to Harris (2003: 27–8), 'rivalry does not exclude future cooperation', social divisions 'can be overcome', and 'ethnic cleavages can result in "nested" nationalities'. Thus participation and cooperation constitute the foundations upon which identity-related differences can coexist without the need to disappear, as the identity change argument posits (McGarry 2006). Political elites have a strategic interest in participating in EU governance. European integration provides resources for political action: an opportunity to demonstrate leadership, mobilise constituencies to increase their vote share, and enhance the legitimacy of their ideological positions relative to their competitors while cooperating with them in the power-sharing institutions (Interview 9).[37]

Barry (2005: 202–3) contends that the EU provides a context within which traditional national identities can be expressed and rethought outside mutual exclusiveness and opposition. In this sense, Northern Ireland is not an exception to a broader trend of emerging middle-ground pluralism across the EU. While the EU does not command allegiances or induce identity change, it attracts a more positive general feeling as an institution even without a clearly defined European identity (Robyn 2005: 229). For this reason, measures of the vote distribution for opposing ideological blocs which demonstrate an increasing vote share for the hardliner parties (McGarry 2006) may be an inadequate measure of change in conflict dynamics. As the distribution of the vote in European elections in Northern Ireland demonstrates, electoral support for the parties has displayed variation in parallel with a changing party discourse on Europe.

Figure 4.2
Vote distribution in the elections for Members of the European Parliament in Northern Ireland, 1979–2009

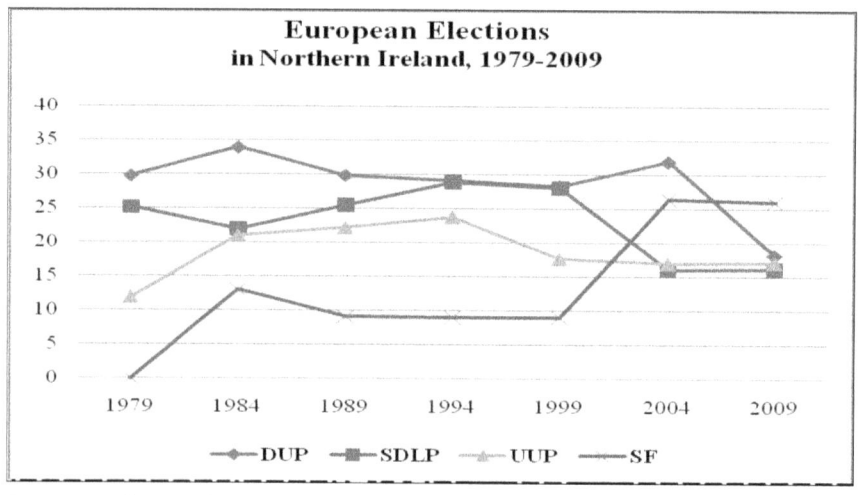

Source: Northern Ireland, Elections/European elections: www.ark.ac.uk/elections/gallsum.htm#top.

The persistence of opposing identities does not fully reflect the underlying shift towards domestic political pluralism. The broadened context of the reconciliation process is associated with actors' cost–benefit analysis, as well as learning to accommodate diversity and recognise the legitimacy of opposing claims (Hayward and Wiener 2008: 60). As a result, actors' perceptions about their own political priorities change. DUP leader Peter Robinson's statement in the 2009 European elections campaign demonstrates that interest change in the direction of party cooperation in the EU is possible and that political mobilisation may shift towards European issues:

> This election is also about Europe. While the DUP is opposed to European integration, we will still seek to use the EU in the interests of Northern Ireland. This is best achieved not by a lone maverick MEP but by an MEP who is working as part of a team represented at Westminster and along with the Northern Ireland Executive. Our capacity to influence decision-makers in Europe will be greatly enhanced by a joined-up approach in areas of common interest.[38]

The political application of Europe as a discourse helps to reinforce the inclusive nature of political actions but has not developed into an alternative to national/communal identities. According to Breakwell (2004), it remains an incomplete project. The lack of transformative impact on Northern Ireland's political elite illustrates its fundamental weakness. However, at the level of political constituencies, increasing public acceptance of the EU as an agent promoting reconciliation provides evidence of the Europeanising influences of the EU's policy contribution to conflict resolution. That this role is not transformative is to be expected, taking into account that the EU did not directly engage in the resolution of the security agenda of the peace process. The latter has persisted as its most problematic area, although the principles of organisation of police and internal security are based on European norms of equality, diversity, and nondiscrimination of employment. Such findings suggest that European integration contributes to the increase of the middle ground of pluralism with regard to integration: a sentiment of acceptance of the EU's involvement and its presence in European politics, while maintaining allegiances to the nation-state, the community, and ethno-cultural distinctiveness. Similar views place Northern Ireland in a comparative perspective, sharing trends valid for European public opinion (Robyn 2005: 13). The Northern Ireland case shows that elites are not necessarily more likely to be more pro-European or internationalist than mass public opinion.

Making sense of the evidence: Europeanisation through adaptation or political action?

The EU's involvement in the Northern Ireland conflict continues to evolve. It began with a declaration of the lack of competences to interfere in the political settlement and moved to support a peace dividend following 1985 AIA and the 1994 ceasefires. The PEACE programmes emerged as an instrument of governance correcting for the adverse socio-economic effects of the conflict and subsequently contributing towards Northern Ireland's competitive position as a European region. Finally, institutional actors reconceptualised the EU's experience in Northern Ireland into a best practice referent, a 'tool kit' for other regions emerging from conflict (EESC 2008). The emphasis on the process of developing tools for conflict resolution demonstrates that despite the lack of a formal role in the conflict, a European space emerged as a result of political discourse evoking the reconciliation rationale of European integration. EU institutional actors and member states developed a consensus which exceeded the economic foundations of the peace dividend and economic homogenisation policies to serve the political and social goals of reconciliation. The EU space acquired coherence, autonomy, and centrality relative to other international actors. Policy transfer emerged as the predominant mode of governance accomplished through partnerships and new policy ideas.

Although direct pressures have been low, this model of EU involvement produced adaptation in terms of institutional arrangements, governance methods (to maintain additionality), and actor behaviour. All political actors have adapted their political agendas to European integration, including those who traditionally downplay or resist the European idea in Northern Ireland politics. The EU concept and method of reconciliation through joint projects has been extended to other actors, demonstrated in the shift towards compatible objectives during the final stage of operation of the IFI. The policy and polity-relevant effects of European integration are measured through the increased salience of devolution which sustains the premises of the GFA political settlement, the cross-community method of programme implementation, and the cross-border concept.

The converging trajectories of the EU's policy, polity, and political effects point to the bigger question of whether Europeanisation has advanced conflict resolution and by how much. It may be argued that the EU's relevance to conflict resolution in Northern Ireland is determined by three main contributions: the acceptance of European integration as an element of domestic politics which sustains devolution and the institutions of power-sharing, programming activities that provide Northern Ireland with opportunities for increased competitiveness and economic growth without loss of resources due to sectarian divisions, and actors' perceptions that their interests lie in Europe.

The EU, although primarily referred to as a source of funding for reconciliation, is not only an economic project in Northern Ireland. It serves political interests. The evidence suggests that although the EU has been perceived as a threat (Hayward 2006: 680) actors seek engagement with it in order to advance their interests and in the process engage in cooperative behaviour. European integration has created opportunities for social partnerships. The EU programmes emerged as the only unifying projects when all others produced distributive effects reinforcing divisions (Pollak 1993: 207).

European integration has opened up a new dimension of political socialisation whereby elites and public opinion in Northern Ireland have developed a propensity to make cost–benefit calculations relative to their political prospects in the EU. The governance perspective has given more salience to these issues in the reconciliation process. Political actors increasingly emphasise the need for Northern Ireland – not as a part of the UK or a reunified Ireland – to be visible and represented in the EU. Although the EU's decision-making process and policy outcomes constitute an autonomous source of top-down influences, these sources have created only limited Europeanisation effects. Instead, while the policy-based incentives and pressures have not triggered adaptation, they have provided resources and opportunities for political action. Beyond altering the structure of incentives and funding eligibility requirements, European governance has served as an agent of domestic political change.

Notes

1 John Coakley argues that the British–Irish dimension, developed as Strand 3 of the Good Friday Agreement (GFA) had long become unproblematic and was thus less important to the settlement than the 'unspoken' 'fourth strand' of the European dimension, which had repositioned political relationships at lower levels. J. Coakley, 'Wise to put peacemaking at world's disposal', *The Irish Times*, 11 July 2007, p. 14.
2 Office of the First Minister and Deputy First Minister (OFMDFM), First Minister's Speech on the occasion of launching the PEACE III Programme, 29 October 2008: www.ofmdfmni.gov.uk/aqo_966–08.pdf.
3 The chapter will use the terms 'unionist' and 'nationalist' to identify the principal majority–minority division between Protestants and Catholics in Northern Ireland. While references to Catholic and Protestant identities are also all-inclusive and represent the theological base of the conflict (Ruane and Todd 1996: 23), the unionist/nationalist distinction is more readily applicable to the political dimension of inter-communal division, national identities, and allegiances. Further differentiation between loyalism and unionism, as well as between nationalism and republicanism, reflects conceptual and ideological differences. On the dimensions of difference, see Ruane and Todd (1996).
4 The concept of Ireland as an 'island economy' was advanced by Dr George Quigley, Chairman of the Ulster Bank and of the Northern Ireland Institute of Directors in 1992 in relation to the Single European Market programme, Speech to the Confederation of Irish industry, February 1992 (Anderson and Goodman 1994a: 17–18).
5 The EP denounced political violence in Northern Ireland in resolutions in 1975, 1979, and 1981. European Parliament, 'European Parliament Resolution on violence in Northern Ireland', 7 May 1981, *Official Journal* C 144, p. 90.
6 EP discussions on the Northern Ireland conflict sought to engage the mechanism of European Political Cooperation and the European Council on a regular basis. None

of these institutions provided input at the time due to the lack of jurisdiction over the issue. Examples include the use of plastic bullets in Northern Ireland, human rights, and treatment of prisoners. See Written question no. 1870/82 by Mr Mario Cana to the Council, *Official Journal* C 104, 18 April 1983, p. 0008, Question No. 90 by Mr Kappos (H-143/81) to the foreign ministers of the ten member states of the EC meeting in political cooperation, *Official Journal* C 172, 13 July 1981, p. 0064.
7 European Parliament, Document 1–752/82 (1982).
8 In 1978, the European Council voted to grant Northern Ireland three seats in the EP, which, under the principles of proportional representation, were to ensure the representation of the Catholic minority.
9 Community funding for the IFI was approved originally in 1989. The legal framework was established in 1994 through Council Regulation (EC) 2687/94 (Court of Auditors 2000: 3). The EU contributed 50 per cent of the funding, the US 47 per cent, and Australia 3 per cent. Northern Ireland received 75 per cent of the funding and Ireland 25 per cent.
10 Interview 1: MEP/ALDE, EP Committee on Regional Development (REGI), 21 May 2008, Brussels.
11 OFMDFM, First Minister's speech, 2008: www.ofmdfmni.gov.uk/eesc_-_fm_speech-3.pdf.
12 The PEACE Programme covers Northern Ireland and six border counties of Ireland: Donegal, Sligo, Leitrim, Cavan, Monaghan, and Louth.
13 Jacques Delors, quoted in George Brock and Nicholas Watt, 'Delors promises £240m EU peace bonus for Ulster', *The Irish Times*, 8 December 1994.
14 Following Regulation (EC) 1080/2006 on the ERDF, *OJ* L 210/1 (31 July 2006).
15 Interview 2: Member of the Commission Task Force on Northern Ireland, 18 June 2008, Brussels.
16 Interview 3: Expert 1, DG REGIO, 18 June 2008.
17 Interview 4: Expert 2, DG REGIO, 21 May 2008.
18 Interview 2: Member of the European Commission Northern Ireland Task Force, 18 June 2008, Brussels.
19 Interview 5: Member of the EESC, 24 June 2008, Brussels.
20 Joint Declaration on Peace (the Downing Street Declaration) of the governments of the UK and Ireland, 15 December 1993: www.dfa.ie/home/index.aspx?id=8734.
21 Interview 6: Member of the Commission of Territorial Cohesion, CoR/EPP, 30 June 2010, Brussels
22 Interview 7: Representative, NI community organisation, Brussels, 25 June 2008.
23 Adams (1994) refers to it as the Hillsborough Treaty.
24 See 'Sinn Féin makes peace bid to EC. Party leader says London and Dublin are stalemated', 23 February 1992, Associated Press.
25 See 'EU Chief, Deputy snub Adams' charm offensive', *Belfast News Letter* (Northern Ireland), 6 October 2005, p. 9.
26 Sinn Féin, 'Blair proposes 200 million PEACE III fund for 2007–2013', *Media Centre/News*, 7 December 2005: www.sfguengl.com/news/entry/73.
27 'EU conference discusses Irish unity', *Anphoblacht*, 19 October 2006: www.anphoblacht.com/news/detail/16383.
28 Paisley resigned his seat in the EP soon after the St Andrews Agreement (2007).
29 Jim Nicholson, 'Northern Ireland to lose out in EU enlargement', BBC News, 1 October 2003: http://news.bbc.co.uk/1/low/northern_ireland/3156992.stm.
30 '£940m EU package for NI', BBC News, 21 June 2000: http://news.bbc.co.uk/2/hi/uk_news/northern_ireland/800166.stm.
31 See publication of the Northern Ireland Office: www.asharedfutureni.gov.uk/2003_consultation_paper.pdf.

32 Peter Hain, MP, 'Peacemaking in Northern Ireland: A model for conflict resolution'?, *Lecture*, 12 June 2007, Northern Ireland Office (http://archive.nio.gov.uk), Mark Durkan, MLA, 'Northern Ireland must play an active role in Europe', *News Release*, Northern Ireland Executive, Department of Finance and Personnel, 9 May 2001: http://archive.nics.gov.uk/dfp/010509k-dfp.htm; Interview 8: Community worker, Brussels Economic Forum, 25 May 2010, Brussels.
33 'Learning the lessons of the PEACE Programme for Ireland', *Briefing page* (regional policy), 22 May 2008.
34 Press release, 'Alarming ignorance of EU issues in Northern Ireland – report says': http://news.ulster.ac.uk/releases/2003/946.html.
35 The period after 1992 marks a decline in public approval of the EU in the UK due to sovereignty concerns in the aftermath of the Maastricht Treaty.
36 On the distinction between shared identities and polity-based accommodation, past experiences, and future interests, see Harris (2003: 29).
37 Interview 9: MEP, Group of the Progressive Alliance of Socialists and Democrats (S&D), EP Committee on Regional Development (REGI), 15 June 2010, Brussels.
38 Peter Robinson, Manifesto launch speech, DUP, *European news*, 29 May 2009: www.dup.org.uk/default.htm.

5

The case of Cyprus: unmet expectations

Introduction

The Cyprus conflict[1] is another problematic case for Europeanisation. The evolution of the EU's involvement in its resolution is at odds with the historical reconciliation hypothesis on European integration. Against the evidence of Cyprus's EU accession in 2004 as a divided country and the lack of progress in conflict resolution at the post-accession stage, no immediate claim can be made with regard to the EU's positive role in it. The literature refers to the case as a failure of European integration to act as a credible incentive structure and induce conflict resolution in exchange for the benefits of EU membership (Tocci 2007). Such arguments posit membership conditionality as a tool for domestic adjustment to the rules and norms of European governance in candidate countries for EU membership (Schimmelfennig and Sedelmeier 2005). The Cyprus case, however, was not amenable to membership conditionality. The EU institutional actors explicitly removed conflict resolution as a condition for the Cyprus accession. Although the conflict did not reach a solution through conventional UN mediation, Cyprus became an EU member on 1 May 2004. The EU was not directly involved in the negotiations of a settlement during the post-accession stage. The 2009 Swedish Presidency acknowledged that the Union could not 'really play a role in the [...] negotiations'.[2]

The main argument of this chapter is that despite such developments, the null hypothesis on the EU's involvement in the Cyprus conflict, associating its impacts on conflict resolution with only marginal or random effects can be rejected. While no direct causal link exists between EU actions and advances in conflict resolution in Cyprus, historically and institutionally the process has been subsumed under the 'logic' of European integration. Conflict issues and actors' strategies have become inseparable from the modalities and discourses of EU membership pointing to the latter's Europeanisation.

As an interactive framework for examining the long-term evolution of conflict resolution, viewed as an institutional process and change in actor behaviour in the context of EU governance, Europeanisation is better positioned to explain the EU's role in Cyprus than single-variable accounts centred on membership conditionality or prior applications of the concept which prioritise actors' perceptions of the value of membership and direct EU effects on designing a settlement (Demetriou 2008; Tocci and Kovziridze 2004).

There is a need to re-examine the relevance of Europeanisation as an organising perspective for the study of potential EU impacts on conflict resolution in Cyprus. The Cyprus case presents a set of puzzles for the relationship between European integration and conflicts in Europe. The lack of Europeanising influences in the case is at odds with propositions about the socialisation of EU member states into a pattern of cooperative behaviour and a desire to compromise for unity. Synthetic analyses point to the Europeanisation of the EU political domain under the Common Foreign and Security Policy (CFSP), measured as a reflex of coordination, camaraderie, adherence to common values, and a preference for conflict prevention and resolution (Ginsberg 2007: 148–9). Such changes cannot be traced in the Cyprus case where individual interests and veto points have prevailed in decision-making at the EU level. Furthermore, as the protracted conflict in Cyprus represents a normative, policy, and institutional misfit with the EU's political order and governance system, in line with the Europeanisation thesis we should expect top-down pressures for conflict resolution prior to accession. In contrast to such expectations, the EU's policy preference has been to keep membership and conflict resolution separate. The lack of conditionality allowed for multiple linkages to develop, leading to suboptimal outcomes. The EU's failure to bring about the resolution of the Cyprus conflict thus was seen as a destabilising factor for security in the eastern Mediterranean (Oğuzlu 2002: 14). However, the persisting division of Cyprus did not produce negative geopolitical effects at the post-accession stage. A 'Euro-partition' of Cyprus did not materialise. Intercommunal talks resumed at the post-accession stage creating yet another puzzle in the process. The International Crisis Group (ICG) had noted that with the failure of the 2004 referendum on the UN-sponsored Annan Plan, all opportunities to maintain the process were exhausted, leaving unilateral action through confidence-building measures as the only possible option (ICG 2006: i). In reality, in the context of Cyprus's EU membership, the conflict resolution process experienced significant reconfiguration of actors and issues. Despite the missed opportunities to apply membership conditionality and the presence of veto powers blocking collective decisions towards conflict resolution, the EU remained the only external actor with a capacity to keep communication between the conflict parties open. The ICG later observed that the intercommunal negotiations which opened in 2008 were the 'best chance yet' to reach a political settlement (ICG 2008). Revisiting the conflict from the perspective of European integration is therefore warranted as it is apparent that the context of Cyprus's EU accession is associated with nontrivial change in the dynamics of the conflict.

Assessed relative to the accomplishment of objectives of conflict resolution, the EU's involvement was a policy failure. However, an examination of its relevance to the conflict within the logic of political action (Radaelli and Franchino 2004: 951) permits the development of a more contextualised assessment. Through its foreign and enlargement policies, as well as the underlying policy-making process, the EU has developed an autonomous arena of interaction with the conflict parties and the institutional process of conflict resolution. The Europeanisation model permits the identification of sources of EU influence as a combination of external stimuli, pressures, and resources with a capacity to alter the opportunities for political action related to the conflict. How such dynamics have translated or failed to translate into conflict resolution dynamics is an empirical question. The EU's involvement in the process was not based on an explicit competence or legislative decision. It was not inherent to the system of EU governance but developed through the politics and policies of integration in the process of Cyprus's EU accession.

The resolution of the Cyprus conflict is therefore closely related to issues pertaining to the attributes of European integration as a macro-political process, the autonomy and coherence of its policies, and the politics of EU membership. As in the case of Northern Ireland, the EU is regarded conventionally as a post-national order and framework for structuring regional interdependence (Diez 2002a; Tocci 2004). Such post-modern qualities are at odds with the incompatible claims to territory and self-determination of the two Cypriot communities anchored in modernity discourses. There is no theoretically necessary relationship between European integration and conflict resolution in Cyprus in the process of Cyprus's EU accession. At the systemic level, we may hypothesise that the EU would transform the conflict by recasting conflicting interests and identities into post-modern, post-territorial, and therefore non-conflictual categories (Diez 2002b: 7; Joseph 2006; Richmond 2002: 117; Tocci 2000: 46–7). Alternatively, we may also hypothesise that due to its post-national nature, in conflict with national claims anchored in modernity concepts of ethnopolitics and self-determination, the EU cannot induce meaningful change in the conflict (Diez 2002c; Richmond 2002: 134) but instead may reproduce 'conflictive identity patterns' (Stetter *et al.* 2008: 235). As the puzzles in the evolution of the conflict resolution process suggest, neither of the two paths of outcome creation has taken place.

At the meso-theoretical level, comprised of the system of policy inputs, decision-making, and outcomes of EU governance, the EU's relevance to the Cyprus conflict is more contextualised. The governance perspective permits an examination of the EU's role in conflict resolution through the two principal policy areas of enlargement and foreign policy. The domain of the Common Foreign and Security Policy (CFSP) formulates the EU's political interests in safeguarding democratic values, peaceful relations, and human rights (European Union 2008a). The Eastern European enlargement made it possible for this value system to be translated into the domestic politics of the applicant countries by means of rule adoption and adaptation (Nugent 1997a, 1997b). Grabbe (2006), Lippert *et al.* (2001), and Schimmelfennig and

Sedelmeier (2005), among others, posit domestic adaptation and political change in the applicant countries in the context of their EU accession as a process of Europeanisation. As enlargement is an example of hierarchical governance (Zielonka 2007: 195–6), it presupposes a top-down Europeanisation model. The latter is derived primarily from EU pressures, incentives and constraints, resource redistribution, public discourse, and identity change, without an opportunity for the candidate countries to upload their preferences onto the EU level and thus 'Europeanise' or upgrade their individual interests (Börzel and Risse 2007: 489). Because the direction of rule transfer proceeds from the EU to the domestic level, the Europeanisation of Eastern Europe is understood as a process of domestic adaptation as a result of the conditionality mechanism of the EU accession process (Grabbe 2003). In their classical study on conflict resolution in the wider Europe, Coppieters *et al.* (2004) define the Europeanisation of conflict resolution in terms of membership conditionality and institution-building in the context of the EU's eastward enlargement and neighbourhood policies.

The Cyprus conflict has emerged as a critical case of the Eastern European enlargement. EU membership conditionality represents the core of the European perspective on its resolution. Adaptation to the norms and modalities of European integration in exchange for the benefits of EU membership was expected to have a catalytic effect on the conflict (Güven-Lisaniler and Rodriguez 2002). As the EU separated the Cyprus accession from the conflict resolution process, the incentives and constraints impact of the EU enlargement policy did not perform in this case, explaining the lack of progress in the resolution of the conflict. The neglect of instruments linking conflict resolution to EU membership was a missed opportunity to advance the peace process (Tocci 2007: 28, 31). Verney (2009: 145) finds that membership conditionality and compliance with the accession criteria of the *acquis* have been insufficient as incentives for the parties to adhere to the EU's peace project. Bahcheli (2006) also emphasises the limits of the economic incentives to achieve settlement.

Beyond the failed conditionality of its enlargement policy, the positive, albeit insufficient, aspects of the EU's influence on the conflict are due to the multidimensional nature of European integration. Integration is comprised of perspectives coextensive with a variety of socio-economic, political, and institutional issues in the politics of intercommuninal relations, including citizenship, joint sovereignty, market liberalisation, and free movement of persons (Féron and Lisaniler 2009: 214). Christou (2006: 20) refers to the transformative effects of integration and the role of the EU governance system in the diffusion of core values. The literature concludes that the EU's influence along these dimensions has not been 'quite' a catalyst in the Cyprus case due to persistent nationalist policy outlooks within the Greek Cypriot and Turkish Cypriot elites and the use of the conflict for narrow political interests (Christou 2006: 25; Diez and Tocci 2009: 294). Diez (2002d) contends that the EU could induce a positive conflict dynamic only if it contributes to the desecuritisation of the relationship by mitigating the adversarial conceptualisation of identities in the process of its interaction with the conflict situation. Giegerich (2006: 279) concludes that the EU may support the conflict resolution process by improving the security of the communities and acquire more responsibility in other conflicts.

Such findings suggest that the EU's role in conflict resolution cannot be assumed, that enlargement has no 'magic touch' (Verney 2009: 145), and that it should be examined relative to specific policy instruments and political action. The Cyprus case is therefore amenable to a governance approach. Building upon the treatment of Europeanisation in prior research, this chapter examines the EU's involvement in the Cyprus conflict from a revised Europeanisation perspective (weak, failed, negative, or otherwise) based on the definitional qualities of the term across its policy, polity, and political dimensions.

Following the steps of the Europeanisation framework, the research task is to determine whether an autonomous, coherent, and visible European space has evolved with regard to the Cyprus conflict; how it has been defined – through policy instruments, political opportunities, or discourse; and which mechanisms, or logics of action, may have been relevant to the dynamics of the conflict. According to the misfit hypothesis, we would expect that the institutional, policy, and normative misfit of the conflict with the EU system of governance would trigger top-down pressures, incentives, specific policy tools, and policy blueprints. Based on the resource and coalition-building hypothesis, we would expect political actors to use EU resources and opportunities and adopt strategies with nontrivial effects on conflict resolution.

The evolution of the EU–Cyprus institutional relationship from association to membership also permits one to test the proximity thesis, prominent in the literature on Europeanisation, which posits a positive association between the EU's conflict resolution relevance and the proximity of the conflict parties to the EU as members or associated, acceding, or candidate countries (Diez *et al.* 2008b: 10; Noutcheva *et al.* 2004: 7; Schimmelfennig *et al.* 2006). The timeframe of this analysis is determined by the construction of the EU–Cyprus relationship proceeding from the conclusion of an Association Agreement (1972), membership application (1990), accession negotiations (1997–2002), accession (2002–4), and concluding with the resumption of intercommunal talks (2008–10).

Background for developing a European perspective on the Cyprus conflict

The Cyprus 'problem', 'conflict', or 'question' is a multidimensional phenomenon. It represents the irreconcilable claims of two ethnic communities (Bahcheli 2006) over territory and national independence, an instance of interethnic competition with international involvement (van Houten and Wolff 2008), and a conflict reflecting the complex relationship between ethnic identities and territory (Féron and Lisaniler 2009: 208). Tocci (2000) posits its dual nature as a delicate balance of elite interests and an underlying intercommunal dispute, both of which were reinforced by historical division and disparities.

The ethnopolitical nature of the Cyprus conflict cannot be separated from its statist and international perspectives. The conflict emerged as a case of incomplete, or imposed, state creation which permits its recasting as a conflict of national independence and self-determination sustained by the legacies of the Ottoman Empire. Its international dimension reflects issues of invasion, occupation, and territory (Constaninous and Papadakis 2002: 84). The complexity of the case is partly due to its relationship to other outstanding controversies in the European regional system, such as historical enmity in Greco-Turkish relations. Since the 1960s, the diverging paths of the European integration of the two countries altered the balance between them with major implications for the evolution of the conflict. Both Turkey and Greece established relations of association with the EEC in 1963. When Greece became a EC member in 1980, the asymmetry of the conflict increased, allowing for multiple linkages between economic, intercommunal, and European issues. The Greek and Greek Cypriot preference was for more European involvement in conflict resolution, as the Greek Cypriot side emphasised the international dimension of the conflict comprised of issues of sovereignty, territorial integrity, and occupation. Closer to the Turkish Cypriot side were issues of self-determination and communal perspectives positing the equality and separateness of two communities, nations, and states.

Cyprus's incomplete sovereignty was established in 1960, as the United Kingdom withdrew colonial control over the island (except for the two base areas of Akrotiri and Dhekelia). The Cyprus Constitution determined a consociational order between the Greek and Turkish Cypriot communities, comprising respectively 82 and 18 per cent of the Cypriot population. The UK, Greece, and Turkey acquired Guarantor status. Elite accommodation, initially achieved through the 1960 constitutional settlement, failed to resolve irreconcilable claims to territory and self-determination. The conflict began in 1963 with actions by the Greek Cypriot majority to move away from the principles of power sharing towards majority–minority relations. Such actions *de facto* suspended Cyprus's constitutional order based on a Turkish Cypriot veto power. In 1964, the UN deployed a peacekeeping force, the United Nations Peacekeeping Mission in Cyprus (UNFICYP), along the dividing UN buffer zone, the 'Green Line' between the north and the south of the island. The Green Line gradually consolidated distinct concentrations of Greek Cypriot (south) and Turkish Cypriot (north) communities.

The UN became involved in the conflict resolution process as a result of a set of proposals and the good offices of the special envoy of the Secretary-General who recommended direct negotiations through UN mediation. Talks on a political settlement began in 1968 in Beirut with no direct outcome (Hakki 2007: 651, n. 4). In 1974, the Greek junta organised a coup against Greek Cypriot President Makarios with the objective of *enosis*, a union with Greece. The coup was followed by a Turkish invasion justified according to the constitutive Treaty of Guarantee to protect the Turkish Cypriots. The coup and the invasion that followed resulted in a mass refugee wave and established areas of Greek Cypriot and Turkish Cypriot control leading to a partition of territory. This outcome was reinforced through the creation of a quasi-independent Turkish Federated State after the 1974 Turkish invasion. The Turkish Republic of Northern Cyprus (TRNC) was declared in 1983 but did not receive international recognition, except from Turkey. Successive UN Security Council (UNSC) resolutions established the legal-normative international framework for conflict resolution with an emphasis on issues of sovereignty, territorial integrity, and occupation.[3]

Although the two parties agreed on the federal, bicommunal and bizonal nature of the Cyprus state under the High-level Agreements of 1977 and 1979, such agreements at the level of elites did not produce a permanent settlement. In 1989, proposals on the three freedoms (of settlement, property, and movement) and communal security concerns were introduced, shaping a broadened agenda of political settlement (European Commission 1998b: 12). Despite its secondary role as an observer, facilitator, and agent of humanitarian assistance, the EU gradually acquired a unique role in the process. In 1990, the Republic of Cyprus, represented by the Greek Cypriot government, applied for EC membership.

The 1991–92 UN Secretary-General (UNSG) Boutros-Ghali's Set of Ideas on a framework agreement placed an emphasis on security-building measures and the political equality of the two communities. Intermittent communication and negotiations continued. The conflict entered the EU policy agenda with an increasing salience after 1993, when the European Commission issued an opinion that Cyprus was eligible to become a candidate for EU membership. The enmeshing of UN initiatives and EU-based discussions of the conflict issue intensified following the 1997 decision of the Luxembourg European Council which determined that Cyprus could begin accession negotiations. The 1999 Helsinki European Council de-linked the conflict resolution process from the prospects of Cyprus's EU membership. The Council determined that Cyprus would be eligible to become an EU member regardless of the status of the political settlement. Repetitive cycles of proximity talks and bilateral negotiations during the period 1999–2002 led to a proposal by UNSG Kofi Annan for a comprehensive settlement. The First Annan Plan was presented to Cyprus President Cleridis and Turkish Cypriot President Denktash on 11 November 2002. This plan established a confederal

(Swiss) model of a bizonal bicommunal arrangement. The Plan was inadequate to the needs of Cyprus's representation in the EU institutions due to the lack of provisions on the participation of the governments of the component states in policy-making at the EU level (Mallinson 2005: 165; Tocci and Kovziridze 2004). The parties failed to reach an agreement, although for reasons outside the EU agenda. Five cumulative versions of the Annan Plan were discussed during 2002–4. The Plans resolved the constitutional issue by establishing a bizonal bicommunal federation (Belgian model). They also resolved issues of governance, such as movement of persons, acquisition and adjustment of property, trade, economic conditions, compensation, and refugees. The constitutional and governance aspects of the Annan Plan became increasingly intertwined with the conditions for EU membership. EU-based rules on mobility and nondiscrimination, openness and investment were introduced as a part of the settlement agenda (Varnava and Faustmann 2009).

The successive versions of the Annan Plan demonstrated certain asymmetry between the obligations of the Greek and Turkish Cypriot communities. Ultimately, they left a mismatch between short-term gains which favoured the Turkish Cypriot community and long-term opportunities likely to accrue for the Greek Cypriot community. The Fifth Annan Plan for a 'Comprehensive Settlement of the Cyprus Problem'[4] was submitted to the two sides for approval at separate simultaneous referenda prior to the EU accession. The referenda produced conflicting results. A clear majority of Turkish Cypriots (64.9 per cent) approved the Plan. A similarly clear majority of Greek Cypriots (75.8 per cent) rejected it.[5] As the conflict issue was not part of the Cyprus EU accession, the Republic of Cyprus (RoC) became an EU member on 1 May 2004. The EU accommodated the lack of settlement by a provision in the Act of Adaptation to the Cyprus Accession Treaty. EU law (the community *acquis*) was suspended in northern Cyprus as the Cyprus government had no control over the northern part of the territory. In December 2004 the EU decided to open accession negotiations with Turkey. The conditions of membership, namely recognition of all EU member states, including Cyprus, on behalf of Turkey as an acceding country, extension of the EC–Turkey customs union to the new member states, and a requirement for Turkey's progress in resolving regional issues with regard to Cyprus entered into its accession negotiations. The scope of coverage and the number of actors relevant to the European perspective of the conflict increased.

Greek and Turkish Cypriot elites resumed talks in September 2008. Confidence-building measures and working groups and technical committees advanced a renewed negotiation agenda including power sharing, access to and acquisition of property, economic matters, security, and territory. The conflict resolution process entered into a new stage of bilateral, UN-assisted negotiations.

Evolution of a European space (1974–97): advancing Cyprus's candidacy for EU membership

The European Community (EC) signed an Association Agreement with Cyprus in 1972 with the objective of establishing a customs union. The EC viewed the Agreement through the prism of its Mediterranean policy and Cyprus's geopolitical importance. The developments in the conflict during the early 1970s, culminating with the 1974 coup and Turkish invasion, emerged as the first test for the mechanism of European Political Cooperation (EPC). Partition had no legal impact on the entry into force of the EC–Cyprus Association Agreement but delayed its implementation. The EPC had no mechanism of action outside coordination and dialogue. The EC had no specific competences except for political adherence to UN Security Council resolutions on the issue. The initial response to the 1974 crisis was to discuss humanitarian aid under the EC–Cyprus Association Agreement. The European Commission obtained a mandate for negotiations on the second phase of the Agreement in 1982. The scope of trade concessions was limited, demonstrating that the EC 'was not consistent with its political resolve' to respond to the geopolitical realities in the Eastern Mediterranean which had determined the conclusion of the Agreement in the first place (European Parliament 1983: 7). Similarly to the Northern Ireland conflict, the EU had no active position on the conflict at the time, although for different reasons. While both conflicts fell outside the competences of the EC institutions, the conflict in Northern Ireland was a conflict on the territory of a member state, by definition excluded from deliberation at the EC level. The Cyprus conflict was a political issue outside the scope of the Association Agreement. With its entry into force in 1973, the Agreement created the first precedent in the EU–Cyprus relationship whereby a suspended constitutional arrangement and domestic political stalemate was not taken into consideration when institutionalising a long-term association relationship.

The lack of consideration of Cyprus's constitutional and political issues during the 1970s created opportunities for a variety of linkages in the EC/EU's relations with the principal stakeholders in the Cyprus conflict. In 1986 Greece stated that it would not sign the fourth financial protocol between the EC and Turkey, a key component of the EC Mediterranean policy, unless Turkey withdrew its forces from northern Cyprus. The conditionality issue re-emerged in 1987, when Turkey submitted a membership application. While explicit linkages were absent at the time (Tocci 2004: 63, 115), political actors in the EC, initially member states, understood well the European context of the issue and Turkey's relevance to the Cyprus conflict as a Guarantor state. Outside deliberations in the EC, the British House of Commons Foreign Affairs Committee recommended freezing the application until a solution to the Cyprus problem was found. At the time, Turkey was not prepared to pay a political price on Cyprus, which it considered a matter of national interest, in order to advance its relationship with the EC.

The process of addressing Turkey's first EC membership application enhanced the role of Greece as an influential actor in the EC decision-making process with regard to Cyprus. In its dual capacity of a Guarantor state and an EC member state, Greece assumed centrality by establishing the linkage between Cyprus's EC membership and the modalities of conflict resolution. In 1989, Turkey's membership application was rejected without reference to the Cyprus conflict, citing lack of preparedness to adopt the Single Market programme and domestic reforms. A more active discussion of the Cyprus conflict under the EC agenda began in 1990, when the Republic of Cyprus submitted a membership application on behalf of the entire country, based on the international recognition of the Greek Cypriot government. The EC had no direct interest in becoming involved in the conflict resolution process as the prevalent view was that only a united Cyprus could become an EC member. The initial linkages were broad, actor-based, and had high potential to affect the outcomes of EC decision-making. There was no consensus on the treatment of the case in the intergovernmental institutions, the European Council and the Council of Ministers. A European space for addressing the issues was slow to develop as a common EC perspective on the conflict was lacking. The Cyprus membership application introduced a pattern of asymmetric treatment of the conflict parties: directly, as the EC application was submitted on behalf of the entire country while its power-sharing institutions were suspended and the preferences of two communities were not treated equally; and indirectly, through the EU's asymmetrical relationship with Greece and Turkey as Guarantor states and key stakeholders in the conflict. The Joint EC–Cyprus Parliamentary Committee, established in 1992, was the first institutional actor to adopt a recommendation that the resolution of the Cyprus conflict should not be linked to the accession process but should be pursued as an independent process.

The 1991–92 UN-based Set of Ideas on Cyprus introduced a communal aspect to the conflict resolution process by treating the authorities in northern Cyprus as a component of a two-zone federation and emphasising confidence-building measures. The prior one-dimensional conceptualisation of the Cyprus conflict as a problem of occupation and violation of territorial integrity, reflected in Resolutions 541/83 and 550/84, shifted to issues of intercommunal relations, recognition of the two communities, and governance, including economic opportunities, openness, human rights, freedom of movement, and access to public goods.[6]

Changes in the focus of the UN-mediated negotiations were instrumental to the emergence of a European arena for addressing the problem. The European Commission was influenced by the set of ideas when in 1993 it delivered a positive opinion on the eligibility of Cyprus to become an EC member. The Commission focused on Cyprus's capacity to adopt the *acquis* and the common policies under the Maastricht Treaty (European

Commission 1993: 4, Art. 9). It recognised that EU membership would help to reduce the gap in the economic development of the two parts of Cyprus. The intercommunal nature of the conflict became intertwined with the objectives of Cyprus's European integration.

The Commission opinion viewed the separation between the two communities as a violation of the sovereignty of Cyprus forced by the presence of Turkish troops. Institutional issues, such as the federal form of government and intercommunal relations, were not relevant to the community *acquis* at the time. The main preoccupation was the ability of Cyprus to assume responsibilities under the EU treaties, its membership in the non-aligned movement, and capacity to affect the relationship between the EU and Turkey (European Commission 1993: 12, Art. 22). Although such issues were secondary to the seemingly technical nature of the application review, they reflected the political nature of the opinion. The European Commission recommended negotiations with the objective of 'sending a positive signal' by endorsing Cyprus's European vocation (European Commission 1993: 23). It also recognised that a political settlement was necessary (Art. 24). The Opinion had a formative impact on the development of a European dimension to the Cyprus issue which was later to dominate UN proposals for a settlement through the Annan Plans. Despite references to Turkey and the Turkish Cypriot community in relationship to Cyprus's candidacy, the EU did not initiate a symmetrical institutional process vis-à-vis Turkey. The Opinion thus opened an opportunity for linkage politics rather than an autonomous policy process to address the conflict.

The first such linkage emerged at the Corfu European Council (1994) when Greece threatened to stop the eastward enlargement and the customs union with Turkey, unless Cyprus was included in the first wave of candidates. In 1994 the European Court of Justice (ECJ) imposed an embargo on northern Cyprus prohibiting direct flights and export of Turkish Cypriot goods to the EU (Anastasiou case). The Court ruled that only the customs authorities in Greek Cyprus were authorised to issue relevant documentation on the origin and phytosanitary certification of goods imported into the EU from the territory of Cyprus, thereby eliminating the possibility of authorities already in place in northern Cyprus issuing customs documentation (Hakki 2007: 533).

Similarly to the 1993 Commission opinion and the determinations of the European Council in 1994, the ECJ decision was political. It was a choice to recast trade issues as issues of recognition of Cyprus's territorial integrity represented by the Greek Cypriot government (Talmon 2001: 735). The ECJ decision introduced the Cyprus issue into the governance of the internal market. It deepened the asymmetry in the EU's relationship with the two communities which would require corrective measures later on.

During the General Affairs and External Relations Council (GAERC) (6 March 1995), France brokered an agreement whereby Greece lifted its veto on the customs union with Turkey. The Council concluded that Cyprus could engage in membership negotiations scheduled to begin six months after the 1996 Inter-governmental Conference. In a parallel development, the Council approved the customs union with Turkey. The Cyprus case was incorporated into the policy process of the EU eastward enlargement. The resolution of the customs union with Turkey together with Cyprus's advancement towards accession established an important precedent for the subsequent consideration of conditionality as a tool of conflict resolution.

The literature conventionally identifies a later decision, the conclusions of the 1999 Helsinki European Council, as critical for removing the requirement for conflict resolution from Cyprus's (or Turkey's) EU candidacy. However, the precedent of the 1995 General Affairs Council prior to that had introduced similar dynamics. The decisions of the Council significantly limited the opportunities to apply conditionality during the accession negotiations after 1997. Individual member states (UK, France, and Germany) and the European Parliament (EP) had posited a linkage between the customs union with Turkey and human rights but the issue was downplayed by the Commission and the Council in 1995. The EU institutions did not take into account Turkey's military presence in Cyprus, the Kurdish issue, or Islamic fundamentalism initially brought up in the deliberations. By contrast, they used the same argument of engaging Turkey in a European perspective as the 1993 Commission opinion has done with respect to Cyprus (Council of the European Union 1995).

The conflict parties also preferred to keep EU membership separate from the conflict issue. The Turkish Cypriot position, maintained until 2002, was that accession should not take place prior to conflict resolution. Although the Cyprus application for EU membership may be explained by a shared Greek and Greek Cypriot strategy to 'Europeanise' the conflict, in reality the Greek Cypriot elite did not have a specific preference to engage the EU institutional actors as a stakeholder in the conflict. There was a tacit consensus about keeping the conflict within a European context because the latter exemplified its international dimension, a long-established Greek approach to the issue.[7] The government of Greek Cyprus preferred the engagement of the UN as the guiding institution, in view of existing Security Council resolutions urging UN members not to recognise the Turkish Federated State (SC Resolution 367/75) and later the Turkish Republic of Northern Cyprus (Resolution 541/83). The Greek Cypriot government sought 'EU support and assistance' to that effect.[8] Greece used the Cyprus candidacy to gain leverage vis-à-vis Turkey and the Turkish Cypriots in the UN-based negotiations. Even following the Greco-Turkish rapprochement in 1999, Greece regarded the Cyprus issue as 'the "decisive element" that would either create good neighbourly relations or divide the two countries'.[9] The Greek Cypriot idea was to use the EU enlargement as a catalytic effect on the conflict. The literature views the 'catalytic-effect' strategy as an EU failure due to the fact that it created one-sided pressures on the Turkish Cypriot community and Turkey and failed to engage Greek Cypriots (Diez 2006: 222; Tocci 2004). The Greek government applied a consistent linkage strategy until 2004, by demanding a timetable of Cyprus accession, limiting subsidies to Turkey, and compensating Greek industry for losses related to the customs union.[10] According to Tocci (2004: 126), by introducing such broader linkages Greece emerged as the principal obstacle to direct settlement at the time.

The main outcome of the pre-accession stage was the institutionalisation of an EU policy process which included the resolution of the Cyprus conflict by default. The EU institutional actors had no established preference as to whether conflict resolution was a necessary condition for developing closer relations with the EU individually for Cyprus and Turkey, although both cases represented a misfit with the EU's normative context. There was no triggering mechanism for EU pressures which predetermined only a contingent, actor-centred model. The 1995 compromise created institutional prerequisites for introducing the EU integration agenda into the UN-sponsored negotiations. The most significant outcome at this stage was the emergence of a policy discourse pertaining to the EU–Cyprus and EU–Turkey relationship outside the constitutional dimension of the Cyprus conflict.

Europeanising conflict resolution through Cyprus's EU accession: institutional actors and policy tools in the EU enlargement (1997–2004)

The Eastern European enlargement introduced a separate dimension to the Cyprus conflict but it was not in the direction of conditionality and direct involvement as the hierarchical nature of this policy would suggest. In the course of the Cyprus accession negotiations, the number of stakeholders increased. Actors' positions evolved depending on the status of their relationship with the EU. The context of a future EU membership including the Turkish Cypriot community was at the origin of political change in northern Cyprus. The fact that Turkey acquired EU candidate status in 1999 induced a positive dynamic in the conflict resolution process. Greece remained a source of a coordinated policy with Cyprus directed towards keeping the EU accession separate from the conflict (Coufoudakis 2006: 61). At the same time, the EU institutional framework of the European Council, Council Presidency, and the General Affairs Council (GAERC) prevented Greece from the consistent application of its policy of leverage vis-à-vis Turkey.

The EU's eastward enlargement policy entered into a second stage in July 1997 when the European Commission recommended accession negotiations for six countries, including Cyprus.[11] Agenda 2000 (15 July 1997) marked the first instance at which the EU announced that conflict resolution would not constitute a condition for Cypriot membership and confirmed accession negotiations with the Republic of Cyprus as the recognised authority. It stated that the Union was determined to 'play a positive role in bringing about a just and lasting settlement in accordance with the relevant United Nations Resolutions' (European Commission 1998b: 4). The EU–Cyprus Joint Parliamentary Committee of 9 October 1997 supported accession without the conditionality of conflict resolution. GAERC and European Council deliberations influenced Greece to drop its veto on the implementation of the customs union with Turkey (European Council 1997). At the Luxembourg General Affairs Council (25–26 October 1997), the EU foreign ministers expressed a preference for the involvement of Turkish Cypriot representatives in the accession talks which Greece initially refused. The Luxembourg European Council (12–13 December 1997) noted in its conclusions:

> The accession of Cyprus should benefit all communities and help to bring about civil peace and reconciliation. The accession negotiations will contribute positively to the search for a political solution to the Cyprus problem through the talks under the aegis of the United Nations which must continue with a view to creating a bi-communal, bi-zonal federation. (European Council 1997)

In 1998, at the Edinburgh European Council, Greece threatened to block the Eastern European enlargement as France had insisted on a separate consideration of the Cyprus case, contingent upon progress in the involvement of the Turkish Cypriot community (TCC). Turkish Cypriot President Rauf Denktash refused to include representatives in the accession negotiations (when the Cypriot government followed up on the Council's request). Turkey did not positively address the issue because at the time, its aid package under the customs union was blocked by Greece. Most foreign ministers believed the prospect of a divided Cyprus joining the EU to be unrealistic. The modalities of conflict resolution thus remained isolated from the content of the accession agenda.

Despite the lack of consistent conditionality, the institutional process of the Eastern European enlargement offered an alternative route for the Europeanisation of the Cyprus conflict. The logic that as proximity to the EU increased, the incentives of membership and the attractiveness of European values would increase the likelihood of conflict resolution, did not materialise. Instead, Europeanisation occurred through the reframing of the constitutional issues of the conflict into a European perspective, expanded opportunities for political action within the TCC, a new Turkish discourse on the conflict, and accommodation of the institutional provisions of the UN settlement through the system of EU law and governance.

The introduction of European issues in the conflict resolution agenda was an element of the emerging European space as an autonomous source of influence on the conflict. As conditionality was not a valid policy tool in this case, top-down pressures and compliance requirements outside the community *acquis* were lacking. From a bottom-up perspective, however, the presence of a European dimension in the conflict resolution process created opportunities for political action and change in actors' preferences and strategies.

Cyprus's EU accession and the UN institutional process of conflict resolution: logic and issues

The first aspect of the Europeanisation of conflict resolution in Cyprus was reflected in the introduction of new issues on the UN-based negotiation agenda as a result of the EU accession negotiations. Direct trade, mobility, property acquisitions of foreigners, acknowledgement of the isolation of the TCC, and European elections entered the catalogue of topics discussed under the UN institutional process of conflict resolution. In its first progress report on the Cyprus accession, the European Commission noted the lack of conditions for the implementation of the community *acquis* in northern Cyprus due to adverse economic climate, declining demographic structure, and the status of economic and political rights (European Commission 1998b).

The work of the European Council continued to be determined by veto players. Not only Greece, but other member states also shaped the agenda and brokered decisions by uploading their preferences into EU decision-making. Greece was the major player supporting the separation between the Cyprus accession process and the resolution of the conflict. At the Helsinki European Council (1999), Greece agreed to a candidate status for Turkey only in exchange for removing the conditionality of conflict resolution from Cyprus's EU accession. The Helsinki Council granted Turkey candidate status and established the resolution of issues with Greece as a condition for the start of its accession negotiations (European Council 1999). The EP participated in the institutional process which developed the EU's position on Cyprus conflict by pursuing a consistent engagement with the issues pertaining to Cyprus's accession. On the one hand, the EP endorsed the policy initiatives of the Commission linking the elements of a future settlement to Cyprus's participation in the EU institutions and policy-making upon accession. On the other hand, Parliament communicated its own-initiative opinions and provided directions for the EU input into the conflict resolution process. The EP maintained that the Cypriot people had sovereign rights to resolve the conflict and recognised the EU's role as a catalyst, not a direct mediator. It also viewed political settlement as a compromise, rather than an ultimate resolution, therefore dependent on continued assistance. The EP's approval of the 1999 European Council decision was based on its preference to prevent Turkey from limiting Cyprus in the pursuit of EU membership. Parliament also understood that the lack of conditionality created a vicious circle in the distribution of pressures and incentives among the two communities (Interview 1).[12] It removed the pressures and incentives to cooperate towards settlement from the Greek Cypriots and placed them on the Turkish Cypriots while providing Greek Cyprus with veto power in the process.[13]

The preparation for accession negotiations with Turkey was instrumental in shifting attention towards Turkey as a critically important actor in the process. The conclusions of the Helsinki Council led to a series of principled decisions with regard to Turkey's status in the conflict. Council decisions included an obligation for Turkey to support the resolution of the Cyprus conflict. They moved the question about compliance into an EU context under the accession agenda. While formally Greece preserved its veto power, monitoring progress in Turkey's position was now subsumed under the EU policy process.

> Since the obligation to support a Cyprus solution was raised as part of the procedure for Turkey's alignment with Europe, it is not only a question of what Greece will say. The other European countries are also obliged to react and say to Turkey: Your accession course will not go ahead if you do not contribute to a Cyprus solution.[14]

Turkey's accession *acquis* included issues related to Cyprus in the area of the customs union and relations with neighbours (including member state recognition). Political discourse in the EU later downplayed these propositions, similarly to the question about the presence of Turkish troops in northern Cyprus. The accession negotiations with Turkey emerged as an important aspect of the Europeanisation of the Cyprus issue – if Europeanisation is understood as the application of EU-level governance tools or even the broader notion of 'bringing the issue closer' to EU norms, principles, and decision-making.

Turkey's Accession Partnership (December 2000) included a condition for Turkey to encourage the TCC to take a more conciliatory stance toward the Greek Cypriot community and be positive towards the UN mediation efforts. Such formulations were significantly affected by input from Greece but as Council decisions, they were part of the EU policy in the accession negotiations (Sepos 2008: 125). Greece argued that Turkey's candidacy implied adopting European standards, the *acquis* of the internal market, and standards of political behaviour. The issue was therefore also one of compliance with EU rules (with regard to the unresolved issue of Cyprus), rather than one susceptible to member state veto on the Council:

> I believe that Greece has every reason to raise the European aspect. There, Turkey will encounter an obligation to adopt European standards. These are not issues that Greece is going to raise to block Turkey's course. These are issues that Europe will raise, first, to establish a firm course for Turkey's route to Europe and, second, to secure regional stability ... [T]here are various stages, of a legal and political nature, concerning the relationship between Turkey and the EU. Within this framework there must be certainly issues that concern us, specific Greek sensitivities for example. These same issues are also of European interest. If Turkey had said 'I am not interested in Europe' possibly all these issues – the Cyprus issue ... International Court in the Hague, human rights, and so forth – would be different. When, however, Turkey says 'I want to join this family' this means that at the same time it states 'I am ready to face these issues.'[15]

The shift from a single-actor veto process to a multiple-point framework based on compliance with the accession *acquis* was a way to increase the salience of EU policy pressures, rather than political preferences. It took place as a process of uploading individual state preferences (in this case, Greece) to the EU level (Börzel 2002b), or bottom-up Europeanisation of critical elements of conflict resolution. It also reintroduced membership conditionality which linked Turkey's accession to the governance components of the Cyprus issues, such as internal market rules, openness, right to settlement, and regional stability.

Actor behaviour
The importance of European issues on the conflict resolution and actors' initial resistance to them, which was to change later on in conformity with the EU's preferences, also points to the Europeanisation of conflict resolution discourses and political action (Demetriou 2008: 76).

During that stage, Turkey continued to challenge the legality of the Cyprus accession. Turkey maintained that under the 1960 Constitution, Cyprus could not become a member of international organisations if both Guarantor states Greece and Turkey were not simultaneously members, nor enter into a political or economic union with other countries.[16] The Turkish position was that the EU accession constituted a *de facto* union with Greece and was unconstitutional. The government of northern Cyprus also criticised the decision of the Luxembourg European Council to open accession negotiations with Greek Cyprus. The EU accession negotiations were considered to be in contradiction with the negotiation framework under the 1992 UN Set of Ideas.[17]

The 1997 (Luxembourg) and 1999 (Helsinki) decisions of the European Council to approve the Cyprus accession without the conditionality of conflict resolution and to recognise Turkey as a candidate country, respectively, significantly altered the context of the conflict. As a reaction to the lack of advancement of its EU membership as a result of Agenda 2000 and the Luxembourg Council, Turkey initially announced a policy of partial integration with northern Cyprus and the creation of an Association Council. By contrast, the decisions of the Helsinki Council, which approved Turkey's candidacy status, created an improved climate positively affecting the position of the Turkish Cypriot elite in the negotiations.

As Turkey acquired an interest in its own accession, it was adjusting selectively to EU pressures about a constructive role in the Cyprus conflict. In November 2002, Turkish Prime Minster Erdogan acknowledged that the resolution of the Cyprus question would increase Turkey's chances for membership: 'No matter how much we say they're not related, solving the Cyprus issue will not just accelerate our EU process, it will also be a concrete and useful step to overcoming the problems between Greece and Turkey.'[18] The dual meaning of such statements is first that Turkey acknowledged the substantive link between its EU accession and the Cyprus conflict and, second, that it understood the accession negotiation not as rule adoption but as a process of mutual concessions, negotiations, and geopolitical considerations. Turkey had no motivation to end the conflict as its primary concern was the protection of the Turkish Cypriot community ensured through the presence of Turkish troops. For this reason, Turkey continued to oppose Cyprus's EU accession, as well as any connection between successful conflict resolution in Cyprus and the prospects of its own EU candidacy.[19]

The prospect of an imminent EU accession induced changes in the position of Turkish Cypriots. The Turkish Cypriot elite and President Denktash, in particular, initially insisted that EU membership was contrary to the spirit of the 1960 constitution. The 1997 Luxembourg Council decision worsened the relationship between the conflict parties and led to a hardening of the Turkish Cypriot position in the UN-based negotiations. The President of northern Cyprus Rauf Denktash called for a new approach to the negotiation process reflecting 'the realities pertaining to Cyprus, especially after the intervention of Greece and the EU, which had completely destroyed the political parity and symmetry needed for a solution of the conflict'.[20] The Turkish Cypriot position remained opposed to EU membership and considered the EU as a destructive influence, limiting the opportunities for a solution.[21] Turkish Cypriots feared the annexation of northern Cyprus under an EU framework through dominance and internal market rules on mobility and right to settlement. Such rules threatened the Turkish Cypriot identity of northern Cyprus and eroded the power-sharing principles of the federal arrangement (as Turkey was not an EU member).[22]

The first element of change in the position of elite retrenchment emerged in 1998. Turkish Cypriot negotiators proposed a confederal solution which included a separate bid for membership negotiations with the EU enabling northern Cyprus to attain the economic level of Greek Cyprus. According to the proposal, upon Cyprus's EU accession, Turkey would acquire rights in Cyprus similar to those of an EU member state. The fact that the Turkish Cypriot elite proposed an EU perspective for northern Cyprus independently of Turkey's membership prospects marked a reversal of prior policy positions of complete rejection of the Cyprus EU membership application. The Turkish Cypriot elite dropped their demands for recognition of a Turkish Cypriot state as a condition for negotiations in 2002.

The pre-accession period marked significant attitudinal changes also in public opinion (Tocci 2000: 12). The European context altered the domestic opportunity structure in northern Cyprus, reflected in growth in public approval for EU membership. Data reported in Polat (2002: 109) indicate that in 2000, when the EU context was still separate from the Annan Plans, 97 per cent of Turkish Cypriots supported EU membership in general, while 43 per cent opposed membership before settlement. There was no majority support for conflict resolution as a necessary condition for EU membership. Northern

Cyprus was hit by an economic crisis creating more demands for change. Popular sentiments associated demands for political change in northern Cyprus with the prospects for EU membership. By 2003, protests among the Turkish Cypriot community against the worsening economic situation, intransigence of the political elite, and frustration over the pariah state with over 100,000 settlers from mainland Turkey became frequent. Pro-European parties won the parliamentary elections in northern Cyprus in 2003.

Europeanisation effects on the institutional logic of conflict resolution: steering and accommodating the Annan Plan

The successive versions of the Annan Plan demonstrated the limitations of a negotiated settlement based on elite accommodation and mutual concessions. The EU accession emerged as a corrective in the process by adopting measures facilitating sustained communication between the conflict parties. In the absence of a new bargain, the asymmetry of the process led to its ultimate breakdown. The Annan Plans did not settle the constitutional issues despite a historical understanding between the Greek Cypriot and Turkish Cypriot elites. The more the revisions of the Plans accommodated the TCC in terms of reduced numbers of returns and postponement of troop withdrawal, the less the Greek Cypriots accepted the proposals. Among Greek Cypriots, the Annan Plan was perceived to give more power to the Turkish Cypriots (Ker-Lindsay 2007: 76).

Although the EU had no direct leverage over constitutional issues, it reshaped the settlement by ensuring that the Annan Plan allowed for the EU accession to take place. This process unfolded in two mutually exclusive frameworks. On the one hand, the EU made provisions to accommodate a possible Cyprus accession as a divided country in the event of a rejection of the Annan Plan. In 2003 it applied the 'symbolic' accession principle (Council of the European Union 2003), according to which Cyprus would join as one country with a partially suspended *acquis* on the territory of northern Cyprus in the case of a negative outcome of the negotiations on the Annan Plan. On the other hand, the ultimate version of the Plan accommodated the requirements for Cyprus's participation in the EU institutions and policy-making as a single actor and stipulated that the *acquis* would be enforced on its entire territory. The mutual adaptation and cross-referencing between UN and EU provisions effectively Europeanised the political settlement in line with European norms and guaranteed implementation through the EU governance process. The EU institutions regarded the issue of adapting the settlement to the values and norms of European integration as a question of their credibility (European Parliament 2004: point 13).

A significant compromise with the rules of the CFSP emerged as the EU accepted the provisions of the Annan Plan which postponed the withdrawal of Turkish troops. Even prior to that, in 2002, the Cyprus issue had created a problem in the development of the CFSP. It was only upon guarantees that

Cyprus would not participate in the EU Rapid Reaction Force that Turkey approved the use of NATO assets in EU peacekeeping operations.[23] The EU also made a commitment not to use force in conflicts between Greece and Turkey, including Cyprus and outstanding bilateral controversies.

The Cyprus EU Accession Treaty (2003) accommodated the settlement under the Annan Plan through special provisions for the TCC (Council of the European Union 2003). On the basis of Article 4 (Protocol 10) of the Act of Accession, the European Commission proposed an Act of Adaptation to the terms of accession of a reunified Cyprus. There was a link between the Foundation Document of the Comprehensive Settlement, the equal rights to settlement and ownership for Greek and Turkish nationals and the need to secure, through the EU mechanism of temporary derogations, the protection of national identities and economic opportunities for the Turkish Cypriots. Turkey and the TCC had demanded treaty-based guarantees to stand the challenges of the European Court of Justice in the area of freedom of settlement. The approach followed in the Cyprus Accession Treaty was to seek transitional periods through 'secondary legislation'. The Act of Adaptation reconciled the EU principles of mobility, right to settlement, non-discrimination, and political equality with the need to ensure the viability of the constituent states in Cyprus.[24] It agreed to restrictions on settlement and property acquisitions, and to safeguard measures to counteract adverse economic conditions.

The lack of EU pressure on the Greek Cypriot elite in the context of the 2004 referendum on the Annan Plan emerged as another area of compromise with EU policy objectives. After the failure of intercommunal talks on the first Annan Plan in 2003, the European Commission confirmed that Cyprus would become an EU member as represented by the Greek Cypriot government. The European Council maintained a strong preference for the EU accession of a united Cyprus and reiterated its readiness to accommodate the terms of the settlement (European Council 2004: 15). This highly asymmetrical situation shifted reward–punishment conditionality on the approval of the Annan Plan only to the TCC. The EU institutional actors otherwise did not take a political position in the campaign of the 2004 referenda, citing the need to secure the expression of democratic choice. The European Commission did state, however, that the settlement proposed by the Annan Plan was not 'this solution or another solution', but 'this solution or no solution at all for a very long time'.[25] There was evidence of manipulation of the vote in Greek Cyprus but EU statements from that period did not apply corrective pressure. The nationalist currents within the Greek Cypriot elite had a decisive input towards the outcome of the referendum relative to external influences (Ker-Lindsay 2007: 75).

The proximity hypothesis reversed: sustaining influence or decline in the EU's conflict resolution relevance at the post-accession stage?

Against the background of stalled conflict resolution, the Cyprus EU accession was as puzzling as was the actual EU membership of a divided country with foreign troops on its territory and areas with suspended application of the community *acquis*. There were several aspects to this outcome. It was not logical to expect that the failure of the referendum on the Annan Plan would permit a divided Cyprus to become an EU member, especially after the TCC approved the political settlement but was to remain excluded from the benefits of membership (ICG 2006: i). Conversely, it was logical to expect a crisis due to the failure to apply membership conditionality. The post-accession stage was at odds with the Europeanisation hypothesis. The presence of an unresolved conflict on the territory of an EU member state created a classical institutional and policy misfit with the system of EU governance. According to Europeanisation, we should expect membership to create adaptational pressures with the potential to resolve the conflict by exposing political actors to the influence of EU norms and principles. In reality, the likelihood of conflict resolution did not automatically increase as a result of Cyprus's EU membership.

Furthermore, the post-accession stage of the Cyprus conflict is contrary to the proximity thesis (Diez *et al.* 2006). As Cyprus became an EU member, Turkey commenced enlargement negotiations, and the EU made provisions for increased communication between the two Cypriot communities, all actors were drawn closer to the EU. How has this institutional and policy proximity affected conflict resolution? It may be expected that the closer to the EU the conflict parties are and the more significant the misfit with EU values and order, the stronger the EU pressures for resolving the conflict would be. The Cyprus case defies such expectations. While the policy process with regard to Turkey's accession became more coherently organised according to the requirements of the *acquis*, the credibility of the EU's commitment to Turkish membership declined. The lack of well-established institutional procedures allowed for alternative interests and proposals to gain salience which led to fragmentation and issue linkages. Low credibility has been cited as a key explanatory variable of the lack of conflict resolution in the process of Cyprus's EU accession (Stetter *et al.* 2008: 235; Tocci 2007).

Europeanisation offers an alternative explanation of this outcome. The post-accession stage of the Cyprus conflict provides evidence of the workings of a reversed model of Europeanisation: the use of conditionality by uploading member state preferences to the EU level, the pluralisation of actors as a result of the embeddedness of the conflict resolution process in an EU context, and a reconfigured mechanism of EU influence involving veto points and mediating factors.

Policy influences on the logic of conflict resolution

Upon rejection of the Annan Plan by the Greek Cypriots, the EU institutions responded by accommodating the lack of settlement with a special emphasis on measures with regard to the TCC (European Commission 2004c). The Council invited the Commission to develop proposals for improving the relationship between the two communities and promoting the economic integration of Cyprus. The set of proposals included the possibility for direct trade with northern Cyprus, aid regulation, and a special regime for trade across the Green Line.[26] On 4 May 2004 the Council of the EU adopted the Green Line Regulation establishing a regime under Article 2 of Protocol 10 of the Cyprus Act of Accession. The Regulation defined the terms under which EU law would apply to the line between the areas under the effective control of the government of the Republic of Cyprus and the areas outside its control (European Council 2004).

The Green Line Regulation and its subsequent amendments established a number of provisions facilitating the movement of goods and persons and trade in certain agricultural goods. As a result of the Green Line Regulation, Cyprus became the only EU member state with direct trade with northern Cyprus. Intra-island trade doubled in 2007 from 135 to 260 million euros (European Commission 2008b: 2). The most important quality of the Green Line regime was that of nondiscrimination, despite the presence of Turkish troops and limitations on the freedom of movement for Cypriots as EU citizens. Its nondiscriminatory nature was reflected also in the proposition that the Green Line did not constitute an external border of the EU. The EU removed the opportunity for the Cyprus government to adopt decisions contrary to the regime of openness (Preamble (10)).

The Green Line Regulation reinforced the policy relevance of the EU institutional actors to the creation of economic opportunities for the TCC. The regulation shifted control from the Greek Cypriot government towards EU-based policy implementation. The European Commission initiated a proposal for direct trade with northern Cyprus (European Commission 2004a). The Commission approximated the rules to other cases of member state regions outside the EU customs territory by proposing a regime under Article 133 of the Treaty establishing the European Community.[27] The proposal met with a Cyprus veto in the Council, thus preventing the EU from delivering on its promise to end the isolation of the TCC.

Acting upon the initiative of the European Commission to end the isolation of the Turkish Cypriot community, on 27 February 2006 the Council approved the Aid Regulation granting 259 million euros (effectively, 139 million) already earmarked in the event of settlement (European Council 2006a). A financial instrument was developed (European Commission: 2007b).[28] The Green Line Regulation and the Aid Regulation were directly implemented by the European Commission (not through member states). These regulations were approved despite Greek Cypriot demands for clarity on the parameters of application which established the possibility that the economic initiatives of the Commission would amount to an actual recognition of the sovereign status of northern Cyprus (Christou 2006: 27).

Major shifts occurred in the perceptions of the EP. Verney (2009: 144) contends that the EP emerged divided as a result of the 2004 failed settlement. However, conflicting ideological views did not prevent it from supporting Commission proposals and incentives for the TCC. The EP set up a High Level Contact Group for relations with the TCC. It was a source of political influence even though its policy relevance remained limited. The EP blamed the Greek Cypriot political elite for not endorsing the Annan Plan. Since 2004, the EP has consistently urged Turkey to engage positively in the resolution of the conflict (European Parliament 2006).

EU policy-making at the post-accession stage provides evidence of the limitations of the top-down pressures and incentives model to generate positive political effects. Although the EU-based measures to end TCC isolation were a necessary element of a visible and coherent EU space with regard to the Cyprus conflict, the case demonstrates the contradictory dynamics of Schattschneider's thesis that 'policy creates a new politics' (Schattschneider 1935). Structural policy measures, such as harmonisation, aid, and direct trade, are inseparable from territorial politics in Cyprus with the potential to develop into *de facto* recognition of northern Cyprus as an independent state. Accordingly, they have not been forcefully pursued in an EU policy format. On the other hand, the suspended *acquis* in northern Cyprus has limited the opportunities for the political representation of the TCC. As a result of the non-application of the *acquis*, elections for members of the European Parliament could not be held there in 2009. From an institutional point of view, the stalemate of the Direct Trade Regulation blocked by Cyprus demonstrates the limitations of EU institutional actors to transcend the veto status of the member states in the decision-making process (Hannay 2006: 99).

The lack of transition from the policy aspects to political change, as well as the impossibility for economic incentives to create interdependencies with the potential to transcend territorial ethno-national identities, represents a key indicator of the lagging Europeanisation of the Cyprus conflict.

Europeanisation of the institutional process of Turkey's enlargement

A separate dimension of EU impact on the conflict resolution process emerged in the course of Turkey's EU accession negotiations. The agenda-setting initiatives of the European Commission and institutional procedures in the Council effectively steered conflict resolution towards the politics of enlargement where the EU institutional actors had limited opportunities to advance alternative proposals through the accession *acquis*. The 1999 decisions of the Helsinki European Council had shifted the focus of EU pressures and incentives towards Turkey. The sources of the EU's willingness to address conflict resolution in Cyprus by engaging Turkey similarly shifted from Greek interests, dominant in the process of Cyprus's EU accession, towards a pluralist framework of diverse, often contradictory preferences of member states and EU institutional actors. The fragmentation of the conflict issue altered the core of the conflict from a focus on constitutional issues and a political settlement to issues of governance, such as mobility, economic opportunities, and isolation (Ker-Lindsay 2007: 73). From the perspective of conflict resolution, this new agenda could be expected to induce change in conflict dynamics. However, from a Europeanisation perspective, the lack of coherence diminished the authority of the EU's role in the process.

Even before the start of its accession negotiations, Turkey had rejected the link between conflict resolution in Cyprus and its EU membership:

> Cyprus is not a condition of the EU. The procedure, which has been implemented on every country that wanted to be a member of the EU, will also be implemented on Turkey... Cyprus is not determining our relations with the EU.[29]

The EU did not apply conditionality vis-à-vis Turkey consistently (Nugent 2006: 67). The 1999 recognition of Turkey's candidate status made no reference to its military presence in Cyprus or the need to recognise Cyprus. The EU institutional actors only subsequently introduced these issues due to their practical meaning for the *acquis*-related content of the negotiations. The first reference to the Cyprus conflict emerged in connection with the need to extend the EC–Turkey customs union, operational since 1995, to include the new member states of the Eastern European enlargement (the Ankara Protocol). The Commission's view was that the customs union was part of the accession framework and was therefore non-negotiable, while Turkey understood it as an element of reciprocity and mutual concessions in the negotiation process (Interview 3).[30]

Turkey refused to recognise Cyprus and extend the customs union by opening its air and sea ports to its vessels, as long as Cyprus blocked direct EU trade with northern Cyprus. It considered the EU's promise to end the isolation of the TCC as a necessary condition for its own compliance with the *acquis* on the customs union. The linkage between the two issues, which Turkey unilaterally introduced, shifted the focus from a direct EU responsibility to resolve the Cyprus conflict at the post-accession stage to an issue of membership conditionality towards Turkey. Against the background of the deliberate removal of conditionality during the Cyprus accession, such references to conditional application of measures with regard to Turkey were to remain without practical significance, undermining the EU's credibility in the process.

Turkey signed the Ankara Protocol extending the customs union to the ten new members adding a unilateral declaration of 29 July 2005 to the effect that its signature did not constitute a formal recognition of Cyprus.[31] As a result of Cypriot pressure, the EU issued a declaration restating the validity of

Turkey's obligations under the Additional Protocol. It maintained that recognition of all EU member states was a necessary component of the accession process (Council of the European Union 2005). Relations with Cyprus and input towards the resolution of the conflict emerged as a core regional issue when monitoring Turkey's progress under the Copenhagen political criteria (European Commission 2008c: 28). Due to a Cyprus veto on the proposed Direct Trade Regulation in the Council, the EU could not end the isolation of the TCC which the Council had promised prior to the 2004 referendum. Cyprus further blocked Turkey's accession negotiations by directly opposing discussions on eight policy areas related to the customs union. In 2006 Cyprus rejected Turkey's proposal whereby Cyprus was to open northern Cyprus air and sea ports to international trade in exchange for access for Cypriot ships to Turkish territory. The offer was interpreted as recognition of the independent status of northern Cyprus.

Cyprus was not the only country blocking the process in exchange for Turkish cooperation in the Cyprus issue. In December 2004, the EP did not support the position of the European Commission and the Council on the annual Progress Report on Turkey. The EP Foreign Affairs Committee criticised Turkey for the lack of progress on human rights and 'persistent shortcomings' with regard to Cyprus.[32] In 2005 the EP endorsed the beginning of membership negotiations with Turkey but stated that it would not ratify the EU–Turkey customs union because Cyprus was excluded access to Turkish ports.

More issue linkages emerged in the Council outside Cyprus where several member states (Austria, France, and Germany) saw an opportunity to link Turkey's intransigence on the Cyprus issue to their uncertainty about a fullyfledged EU membership for Turkey. In November 2006 the European Commission recommended suspending negotiations on chapters of the *acquis* related to the customs union (European Council 2006b).[33]

These measures failed to induce positive dynamics among the stakeholders in the Cyprus conflict. On the contrary, they resulted in Turkey's retrenchment demonstrating the limitations of top-down pressures to alter conflict dynamics even under conditions of high proximity to the EU.

'Negative' Europeanisation and the declining role of veto points
Cyprus has tried to 'project' its national priorities to the European level both historically and strategically (Sepos 2008: 124). EU membership created opportunities for Cyprus to upload its preferences with regard to Turkey's accession negotiations and the embargo on northern Cyprus (Ker-Lindsay 2007: 75). Greek Cypriot-based conditionality included demands for Turkey to adhere to a timeframe for fulfilling its obligations under the Ankara Protocol, such as recognise Cyprus, open its sea ports to Cypriot vessels, and abandon its policy of blocking Cypriot participation and cooperation with international organisations.

On the one hand, Cyprus's veto powers in the Council have permitted it to block EU institutional actors from advancing policy tools relevant to the conflict. On the other hand, the pluralist nature of EU governance has made it possible to propose measures transcending the veto points in the policy-making process. The Treaty on the functioning of the European Union (TfEU) (European Union 2008b) expanded the application of qualified majority voting in EU governance and the participation of the EP in legislating together with the Council, creating an opportunity for relaxing veto-based decision-making in the Council through the pluralisation of actors involved in the process (Interview 4).[34] The European Commission has maintained the application of corrective measures in the internal market to allow direct trade with northern Cyprus while ECJ decisions remain valid. Such developments are instrumental to the policy preferences of the EU institutional actors for ending the isolation of the TCC. Support for membership conditionality with regard to Turkey is also on the decline in the Council. The declining importance of veto points and conditionality marks a shift towards a more pluralist process and represents an element of the Europeanising influences of integration. Europeanisation has come to represent a process of change in the institutional dynamics of Turkey's accession. Support for Cyprus's policy preferences in the Council declined in parallel with a more constructive engagement with the TCC and qualified support for Turkey's European perspective. Change along all these dimensions points to a Europeanisation model based on resource allocation, pluralisation of resources, incentives, and opportunities for actor-centred strategies.

Due to the pluralist nature of EU governance Cyprus is limited in its capacity to upload its preferences and permanently block the decision-making process (Nugent 2006: 68). The European Commission did not withdraw the Direct Trade proposal, although the Council remained blocked from discussing it (Christou 2006: 28). While the Cyprus government had similarly threatened to block the Aid Regulation and demanded amendments, financial aid was released in line with the proposals of the European Commission. In 2005 the Commission proposed allowing export through the closed port of Famagusta as part of an effort to alleviate the isolation of northern Cyprus, which Cyprus later blocked in the Council. However, in 2008 Cyprus withdrew its appeal to the ECJ over eight tenders related to the Aid Regulation in order to facilitate the allocation of Community aid to areas in northern Cyprus. The Commission did not intervene when a direct ferry line opened between Famagusta and Latakia. Economides (2005: 487) contends that such developments of engaging in cooperative behaviour point to actor socialisation and adaptation.

There has been a trend of declining utility of the sustained application of veto power and the possibility for influential actors to determine EU decisions in the intergovernmental format of Council decision-making (Inteview 5).[35] In contrast to the high intensity of Greek Cypriot preferences to pressure Turkey in order to advance conflict resolution, the intensity of Greek pressures has declined. The Greek government did not oppose the Direct Trade Regulation. Such developments demonstrate that the politics of Greece and Cyprus diverged as Greece acquired a more positive perspective on Turkey's EU membership (Ker-Lindsay 2007: 76). EU member states have established contacts with the institutions of governance and the Turkish Cypriot elite despite the lack of international recognition of northern Cyprus (Interview 6).[36]

The broadened agenda combining actors and constitutional issues with governance demonstrates that from a European perspective the Cyprus conflict is not a matter of single-issue politics (Nugent 2006: 68). Collective policies and influential actors, including constructive ambivalence on behalf of Greece, have introduced a trend towards normalisation, denationalisation of the conflict issue, and acceptance of claims previously assumed as incompatible (Economides 2005: 484–5).

While EU membership was associated with actor empowerment in the case of Cyprus, it introduced contradictory dynamics in Turkish Cypriot politics. The realisation that their rights as EU citizens were incomplete provided Turkish Cypriots with opportunities and incentives for mobilisation to reverse their unfavourable treatment as Cypriot citizens. The dominant perception in northern Cyprus has been that the amount of financial aid is inadequate to its needs and that the lack of direct trade is limiting the economic opportunities. The core of political discourse emphasises the EU's failure to deliver on its pre-referendum promises to end the isolation of northern Cyprus (Christou 2006: 28).

In April 2005, despite disappointment over the 2004 outcomes, a pro-European and pro-settlement candidate, Mehmet Ali Talat, leader of the Republican Turkish Party (CTP) replaced Rauf Denktash to become Turkish Cypriot President. Turkish Cypriot leaders continued to challenge the legality of the Greek Cypriot government and the signing of the Accession Treaty (Coufoudakis 2006: 69). Trends of dissatisfaction with the ruling elite in northern Cyprus in 2002–3 and growing perceptions of the distinctiveness of the Turkish Cypriot community from Turkey which had shifted electoral support towards pro-European and pro-settlement parties (Lacher and Kaymak 2005: 159–60) were reversed in 2009–10. The failure to obtain the benefits of EU membership and continuing economic isolation led to the replacement of the pro-European Republican Turkish Party (CTP) with the pro-nationalist National Unity Party (UBP) as a governing party in the 2009 elections and of pro-European CTP leader Talat with nationalist UBP leader Derviş Eroğlu as President in 2010. Contrary to expectations, the shift in public and elite preferences towards ethnonationalist and uncompromising positions did not produce a reversal in Turkish Cypriot commitment to continued negotiations (Pope 2009: i). In the context of Turkey's EU accession negotiations, the theme of ending TCC isolation and pursuing bilateral talks on a settlement agenda have become inseparable in Turkish Cypriot political discourse, regardless of ideological views. While the limitations of the top-down model have prevented the EU from directly affecting the conflict resolution outcome, the resources and opportunities model of Europeanisation has performed well. It provides most of the problem-solving capabilities of the Greek Cypriot and Turkish Cypriot elite engaged in negotiations and contributes a capacity to act reflecting EU preferences, ultimately preventing political retrenchment.

Conclusion: analysing the evidence

From a conflict resolution and a Europeanisation perspective, respectively, the Cyprus case points to the validity of two opposite but not mutually exclusive conclusions. If conflict resolution is defined in terms of outcome creation, the lack of a definitive settlement demonstrates the limited effects of European integration despite the proximity of the conflict parties to the system of EU governance. The EU did not emerge as a critical actor in the process and did not impose a solution, as it had no direct competences in the area of conflict resolution. The Cyprus case demonstrates that European integration is not an automatic system of conflict resolution. It did not bring about settlement through Cyprus's EU membership. From a Europeanisation perspective this outcome points to a different conclusion. It reflects an actor-centred process of political change induced and sustained by European integration. Despite the EU's failure to establish a link between conflict resolution and the European integration of Cyprus, the conflict has become inseparable from the dynamics of integration through the EU's enlargement policy. Cyprus's candidacy for EU membership since 1990 has Europeanised the conflict resolution process. As a result of European integration, the only feasible options for settlement are those providing constitutional guarantees for Cyprus as a unified country and an EU member state.

Despite the lack of membership conditionality, the EU's influence is reflected in the increasing orientation of domestic politics towards Europe. The institutional logic of conflict resolution is determined by an EU agenda. As the negotiation process relapsed into a stalemate after the 2004 referendum, the EU emerged as the only actor with a capacity to introduce new dynamics and keep communication between the two communities open through issues of EU governance. This more flexible evolutionary framework may be contrasted with the prior diplomatic UN-sponsored process based on adversarial politics and compromise (Hadjipavlou-Trigeorgis and Trigeorgis 1993: 356). The lack of direct policy compliance and the failure to apply pressure through membership conditionality is due to the lack of coherence and autonomy of the European space with regard to the conflict.

The Cyprus case is at odds with the overall context of the Eastern

European enlargement, characterised by top-down pressures and incentives and little opportunity for political actors to upload their preferences (Grabbe 2006). If conflict resolution is regarded as an issue pertaining to the enlargement agenda, the lack of a coherent locus of authoritative decision-making in the EU points to the limitations of its enlargement policy to serve as a mechanism of conflict resolution. Instead, Europeanisation remains valid as a pluralist process of policy-making more likely to induce shifts in actors' preferences, neutralise veto points, and create opportunities for political mobilisation.

In parallel with a weak top-down dimension of Europeanisation, the context of Cyprus's EU accession provides evidence of its actor-centred nature. It is reflected in the capacity of member states to resist the policy initiatives of the EU institutional actors and 'upload' their own preferences in the formulation of EU policies (Börzel 2002b). From this perspective the Cyprus conflict represents a case of negative, or reverse, Europeanisation by means of which member states pursue national interests through a regional framework. Greece initially 'uploaded' its preferences for ensuring a Cyprus EU membership regardless of the resolution of the conflict by linking progress in the Eastern European enlargement to Cyprus's place in the accession process (Demetriou 2008; Tocci 2004, 2007). Already an EU member state, Cyprus used conditionality and the threat of a veto in the Council in order to induce change in Turkey's position on the conflict.

The Cyprus case reveals that even if Europeanisation influences are weak and veto points dominate, the pluralist nature of EU governance is likely to neutralise such limitations in the long term. The EU emerged as an indispensable actor. It induced change in the positions of the conflict parties in the existing stalemate which had been in place for 30 years before that. The application of a Greek Cypriot veto in the Council has reached its limits, as blocking Turkey's accession negotiations has decreased the value of EU membership.

Based on such considerations, an argument can be made about the indispensable nature of the EU's contribution to the Cyprus conflict despite the unfulfilled expectation of conflict resolution through EU membership. The evidence suggests that despite the lack of consistent application of conditionality, the modalities of European integration have altered the dynamics of conflict resolution and created a set of parallel processes which have altered the conventional model of conflict resolution based on proximity talks, unilateral confidence-building measures, and constitutional issues.

Notes

1. The literature defines the Cyprus case as a conflict, issue, or problem. This chapter will refer to it as a conflict based on the definitional qualities of the case as one of contested incompatibility over territory, identity, and governance. See also Diez (2002b: 4–5) and Joseph (2006), among others. The terms 'Republic of Cyprus' (RoC), 'Cyprus', and 'Greek Cyprus' will be used interchangeably with regard to the sovereign state in Cyprus created by the 1960 Constitution. References to the Turkish Cypriot community (TCC) and Turkish Cypriots are identical. Due to the lack of international recognition of the Turkish Republic of Northern Cyprus (TRNC) established in 1983, its political institutions (parliamentary assembly, government, and presidency) will be discussed with reference to 'northern Cyprus'.
2. Swedish Foreign Affairs Minister Carl Bildt presentation of Swedish Presidency's priorities to the EP Foreign Affairs Committee, 21 July 2009, European Parliament, *Press Release*, Document REF 2009072158591.
3. UNSCR 353 (20 July 1974), 367 (12 March 1975), and 541 (18 November 1983).
4. 'The Comprehensive Settlement of the Cyprus Problem', 31 March 2004: www.hri.org/docs/annan/Annan_Plan_April2004.pdf.
5. According to ICG (2006: 19), the Annan Plan was rejected by the Greek Cypriots due to the lack of definitive provisions with regard to the removal of Turkish troops, and an extension of citizenship for Turkish settlers, as well as the high economic costs of reunification.
6. UNSC Resolutions 716 (1991), 774, and 789 (1992). See Hakki (2007: 374–9).
7. 'Papandreou on *Financial Times* interview and Intercommunal talks', *BBC Summary of World Broadcasts*, 27 February 1982, ME/6965/C/1.
8. Statement by Cyprus Foreign Minister Alekos Mikhailidhis in response to Greek MEP Ioannis Karanidhiotis' offer to seek a solution to the conflict based on the joint action mechanism of the CFSP. CyBC Radio, 'Relations with EU: Parliamentarians oppose linking EU accession with Cyprus deadlock', *BBC Summary of World Broadcasts*, 14 April 1995, Cyprus EE/2278/B.
9. 'Cyprus solution is "decisive element" in relations with Turkey – foreign minister', *BBC Summary of World Broadcasts*, 8 March 2001, EE/D4092/B.
10. See Andrew Borowiec, 'Greece criticized for holding up EU pact with Turkey', *The Washington Times*, 16 February 1995, p. A17.
11. Those countries were: Cyprus, the Czech Republic, Estonia, Hungary, Poland, and Slovenia.
12. Interview 1: Former MEP, ALDE, Member of the EP Committee on Foreign Affairs, 12 June 2010, Brussels.
13. See summary of debate and motion for a resolution of the EP, 21 April 2004: www.eu-un.europa.eu/articles/fr/article_3421_fr.htm.
14. Greek Defence Minister Akis Tsokhatzopoulos (interview), 'Defence minister reaffirms joint defence doctrine with Cyprus', *BBC Summary of World Broadcasts*, 2 February 2000, EE/D3753/B.
15. Yeoryios Papandreou (interview), 'Minister says Greece could be Turkey's biggest ally in European integration', *BBC Summary of World Broadcasts*, 5 September 1999, EE/D3634/B.
16. See legal opinion of Professor M. H. Mendelson on the application of the RC to join the EU based on obligations pertaining to the Treaty of Guarantee (Hakki 2007: 571–88). For an opposing view emphasising the lack of conditions to approximate the EU as a state that would contradict the Cyprus Constitution and referring to *de facto*, rather than legal incompatibilities, see Mallinson (2005: 143) and opinion issued by

Professors Crawford/Pellet/Hafner with reference to estoppels (Hakki 2007: 588–604).
17 Government of northern Cyprus, statement, Ankara: Ministry of Foreign Affairs – Republic of Turkey, 14 December 1997: www.mfa.gov.tr/MFA/ForeignPolicy/MainIssues/Cyprus/Turkish++Republic+Of+Northern+Cyprus+Government+Statement.htm.
18 'Change of Turkish mood on Cyprus', *Irish Times*, 18 November 2002, p. 9.
19 'Turkish Premier: Cyprus issue, EU should not be linked', *Anatolia News Agency* (in Greek), 19 November 2003, *BBC Worldwide Monitoring* (English translation).
20 'Direct talks only way to settle Cyprus dispute, UN says', *Deutsche Presse-Agentur*, 21 May 1998.
21 Quoted in Declan Burke-Kennedy, 'An island still torn between conflicting outside forces', *The Irish Times*, 6 December 1999, p. 14.
22 Documents given by Mr Denktash to the UN Secretary-General, 28 March 1998 (Hakki 2007: 278–9).
23 Turkey demanded and received assurances that NATO assets would not be used by EU members states against its own interests.
24 Interview 2: Expert, DG Enlargement, 25 May 2008.
25 EU Enlargement Commissioner Günter Verheugen, Speech at the international Donors conference, 15 April 2004, SP04–232EN: www.eu-un.europa.eu/articles/fr/article_3394_fr.htm.
26 2576th Council meeting of the General Affairs, Luxembourg, 26 April 2004. Document PRES/04/115, p. 3.
27 The legal basis of Article 133 TEC in the proposal of the Commission (not accepted by the Council) referred to the discrepancy between the legal and policy determinations of territory. Cyprus became a member state in its full territory. However, the *acquis* was suspended in the areas not under effective control of the government of Cyprus according to Article 1(1) of Protocol 10 of the Act of Accession. The Community's customs code was not applicable in northern Cyprus. EU trade with these areas followed the rules applicable to third countries. This situation is not unique. It follows rules established for other territories of the EU which are not included in the EC customs territory, such as Ceuta, Melilla and Gibraltar, where special trade rules exist in parallel to Article 133 TEC (207 TfEU), and Büsingen, Campione d'Italia and Helgoland where third country rules apply generally.
28 The Instrument of Financial Support was established under European Council Regulation No 389/2006 (European Council 2006a). Due to a delay, 120 million could not be used.
29 Turkey's Foreign Minister and Deputy Prime Minister Abdullah Gul quoted by the *Anatolia News Agency* (in English), 30 September 2003 (in *BBC Worldwide Monitoring*, 30 September 2003).
30 Interview 3: DG External Relations, 29 June 2010, Brussels.
31 'Declaration by Turkey on Cyprus. Turkish Ministry of Foreign Affairs, Press Statement No. 123. Regarding the Additional Protocol to Extend the Ankara Agreement to All EU Members', 29 July 2005 (www.mfa.gov.tr/mfa). See Talmon (2006: 596–7).
32 European Parliament, *News Report*, 30 November 2004.
33 The eight chapters were: Free movement of goods, right of establishment and freedom to provide services, financial services, agriculture and rural development, fisheries, transport policy, customs union and external relations.
34 Interview 4: MEP, ALDE, Member of the EP Committee on Regional Development (REGI), 23 June 2010.
35 Interview 5: Member state representative, GAERC (General Affairs), Ad hoc Working

Party on the follow-up to the Council conclusions on Cyprus of 26 April 2004, 14 June 2010, Brussels.
36   Interview 5: MP, German Bundestag, SPD, 22 June 2010 (telephone interview).

6

Kosovo: Europeanisation in the making

> As history would have it, Kosovo won its independence from Serbia in the short window in which intractable ultranationalists in Belgrade drove the exasperated EU to approve Kosovar secession as the least worst solution in the Balkans and before an EU-friendly government in Belgrade would have voided EU support for independence. It now remains to be seen whether Kosovars and their European supervisors can build from scratch the kind of robust institutions and civil society in Kosovo that Serbia already enjoys and whether the Kosovars, like today's Serbs, can expel their own worst demons.
>
> Elizabeth Pond (2008: 110)

Introduction

In contrast to other conflicts in which its involvement has remained embedded in broader international influences, the EU's impact on the Kosovo/Serbia conflict is characterised by increasing autonomy and centrality. An EU role in Kosovo first emerged as a result of intergovernmental coordination and diplomacy, and evolved into a process of governance ultimately subsumed under the European perspective for the countries in the Western Balkans. The application of a variety of policy tools in this process, however, has not been unproblematic. There are two key aspects to the issue: how conceptually adequate to the needs of conflict resolution and how effective the EU's role in Kosovo has been.

Despite the long-term nature of the EU's involvement in conflict resolution in the Western Balkans, Kosovo represents a hard case for establishing the causal effects of integration. In the absence of a negotiated settlement, the positions of the conflict parties have remained mutually irreconcilable. The conflict issue, the status of Kosovo, has not been unequivocally resolved, despite an advisory opinion by the International Court of Justice (ICJ) which found that Kosovo's unilateral declaration of independence (UDI) of 17 February 2008 did not violate general international law as the latter does not prohibit processes of self-determination. The declaration of independence did not acquire the unanimous recognition of the EU member states. Cyprus, Greece, Romania, Slovakia, and Spain did not originally recognise the Republic of Kosovo due to considerations about legal inconsistency and assumptions that it would create a precedent for separatist regions. Despite the definitive outcome of secession and the benevolent ICJ opinion, Serbia continues to reject the outcome. The lack of internal EU consensus allegedly has limited the effectiveness, legitimacy, and normative justification of the EU's involvement in Kosovo (Noutcheva 2009).

Kosovo's status determination has remained unsettled. Although influential member states and the EU institutions have supported Kosovo's independence and declared its definitive nature, the act of independence denied Serbia territorial integrity, at odds with the principles of the UN system (van Meurs 2004: 72). Due to lack of uniform international recognition of Kosovo's independence, the case failed to emerge as a precedent for the doctrine of human rights and protection of minorities which had enabled Kosovo's separation from Serbia in the first place (Noutcheva 2009: 1073).

The politics of Kosovo's recognition point to the need to analyse the role of the EU on the evolution of the conflict in the context of the analytical challenges it poses. The case broadens our understandings of settlement and conflict resolution. Traditionally defined as incompatibility of claims over the status of the Kosovo province of former Yugoslavia, the conflict has shifted away from a negotiated settlement as a method of conflict resolution to securing internationally supervised independence, at odds with the concept of self-determination underlying a UDI. The Kosovo settlement was not a compromise between the two incompatible claims of the conflict parties. Conflict resolution was implicitly defined as a process of obtaining Serbia's acquiescence to the independence of Kosovo and implemented through international supervision. The case defies conventional models of conflict resolution based on negotiation, doctrines of humanitarian intervention, 'just secession' (Coppieters 2007), UN Security Council decision-making, and international arbitration, although all these options have been integral to its evolution.

The dynamics of the conflict point to the relevance of a political approach to settlement. There was strong international support for Kosovo's independence as a result of which the case appeared politically predetermined as the politics of conflict resolution preceded the legal determination.

> The question is whether or not there's going to be endless dialogue on a subject that we have made up our mind about. We believe Kosovo ought to be independent.[1]

> Kosovo will be independent one way or another.[2]

If we accept that according to the preferences of the international community the only possible conflict resolution outcome has been a definition of Kosovo's status in terms of independence – a *sui generis* case of the non-colonial application of the principle of self-determination – then the conflict resolution process should be understood as a process of assisting Kosovo's independence. The EU's role in that process should be evaluated relative to such objectives. In this case the dependent variable, conflict resolution, is not measured through the general categories or reduction in conflict intensity, change in the constellation of actors with positive impact on conflict dynamics, or decline in the salience and intensity of entrenched interests, but instead should adopt an operationalisation through the categories measuring success or failure in ensuring the sustainability of Kosovo's independence and Serbia's acquiescence to it.

The Kosovo case is also a test for the threshold of conflict transformation. According to Albert *et al.* (2008: 20), successful impact on conflict resolution is measured in terms of desecuritisation and regulation of the conflict issue through peaceful means. A similar view posits conflict resolution as a stage in which conflict may persist but is maintained through peaceful means within democratic debate and dialogue (Noutcheva *et al.* 2004: 10). While both Serbia and Kosovo have adopted democratic principles and renounced the use of violence as a method of achieving their goals in the conflict, can we make an argument that the Kosovo conflict has been resolved? When can we expect resolution to take place if Serbia has stated that it will never recognise Kosovo?[3] Independence in this case is not accurately defined, as Kosovo self-declared itself as a sovereign state, therefore independent from external interference, only to invite international presence and transform itself into a post-modern, voluntary US–EU protectorate.[4]

The theoretical literature does not offer sufficient criteria for evaluating the EU's role in the status determination process. The European perspective regards Kosovo as a European issue and a test for the EU's international credibility. Drawing upon analytical constructs in the field of international relations and conflict resolution, a number of studies have examined the Kosovo conflict as a case of self-determination, geopolitical interests, international socialisation, and problematic sovereignty. The regional approach posits the importance of the case for the stability of the Western Balkans and the EU's borders (ICG 2008; Pond 2006: 105). Smolnikov (2008) regards the EU as an agent of post-modernity and a state-creating entity empowering self-governing institutions and a market economy in Kosovo. Cortright (2007: 410) refers to the EU's efforts to induce harmony and prosperity among former rivals in line with its long-established strategy. Emerson (2002: 15) regards the conflict resolution properties of the EU multi-tier governance system as 'especially relevant for the secessionist conflicts of south-east Europe'. Avery and Balfour (2008: 14) argue that the EU possesses the tools to bring about the irreversible Europeanisation of South-East Europe. Similarly, the model of Europeanisation through Eurofederalism posits multi-level governance as a way to transform classical conceptions of sovereignty (Coppieters *et al.* 2004: 1). Coppieters *et al.* (2003: 16) regard the EU governance system as a facilitator in the search for constitutional solutions in secessionist conflicts by empowering subnational actors and developing cross-border cooperation. Emerson and Noutcheva (2004) evoke the benefits of the gravity model of institutional relationships between the EU and the countries in the Western Balkans. By contrast, Rupnik (2005) argues that the application of EU-related conceptions of order and governance to the resolution of conflicts in the region represents a process of 'Europeanisation of the protectorates'. Türkes and Gökgöz (2006) approximate the EU's role to a hegemonic project of extending neoliberal economy and democracy.

The presence of conflicting perspectives on the case illuminates the fundamental mismatch between the attributes of the conflict and the EU's role in its resolution based on conceptions of regionalism and political order. The Kosovo conflict is oriented towards a classical Westphalian notion of sovereignty. Due to the high value which both parties place on the sovereignty issue, traditional understandings of EU norms of pooled sovereignty or post-sovereign order are not applicable to the case. Neither party is prepared to reconcile to anything less than complete and exclusive sovereignty over the territory of Kosovo. Is the EU relevant under such conditions? The Kosovo case presents a challenge to Europeanisation as a framework of polity-related influences. How, if at all, does Europeanisation take place?

This chapter argues that conflict resolution in Kosovo represents a process of Europeanisation subsumed under the system of EU governance, understood as the EU's authority to make and implement rules in a specific domain (Smith 2004: 743). The governance perspective examines the EU's impact through the effectiveness of its external action, the relevance of the enlargement mechanism, and the institutional capabilities of EU decision-making to formulate and implement authoritative decisions.

EU foreign policy is a process of decision-making and allocation of values and resources with broad political, strategic, and moral aspects, and a mission that reflects the EU's political vocation to assist peacebuilding processes (Voorhoeve 2007: 161). The foreign policy domain posits a link between the system of EU rule-making and institutional processes with transformative effects on member states, non-members, and international organisations (Schimmelfennig and Wagner 2004b: 658). The EU's relationship with non-members is amenable to the Europeanising influences of the EU enlargement policy. As a component of EU foreign policy, enlargement is regarded as a process of bringing stability, peace, and security to the wider Europe. It is also the core mechanism of the Europeanisation of Eastern Europe through rule-making and rule transfer (Schimmelfennig and Sedelmeier 2005).

> Enlargement policy is one of the most powerful tools of the EU's foreign policy, [...] However, enlargement is not classical foreign policy in the strict sense of the word. It is essentially about preparation for EU accession and therefore, it has a strong link with internal policies of the EU.[5]

Enlargement and membership, however, are not an automatic method of conflict resolution. The Cyprus case demonstrates that the relationship between conditionality and conflict resolution is problematic (Avery and Balfour 2008:

38; Emerson 2008). Membership conditionality, a classical tool for achieving compliance and adaptation of the domestic political systems of the candidate countries and, by extension, conflict resolution in exchange for the prospect of EU membership, operates differently in the case of the Western Balkans. The EU's influence in the region departs from the strict conditionality of the enlargement model and is better understood as policy conditionality pertaining to the externalisation of governance (Buiter 2005; Epstein and Sedelmeier 2008). The framework of multidimensional EU influences ties together political conditions, economic adaptation, and community *acquis* into a policy-based monitoring mechanism ensuring long-term adaptation. Conditionality is explicitly removed from the conflict resolution process. Concrete policy transfer and rewards matter instead (Trauner 2009).

Examining the EU's relationship with the countries in the Western Balkans within the governance foundations of the EU's foreign and enlargement policy permits one to test for the presence of Europeanisation effects in the Kosovo conflict by tracing the link between the dynamics of conflict resolution and the European perspective of the conflict parties. Following Ladrech (1994), the Europeanisation of the Kosovo conflict may be understood as an incremental process in which the political and economic dynamics of European governance become part of the 'logic' of conflict resolution. Europeanisation effects are traced along three dimensions: domestic institutions, policies, and politics. These three dimensions of Europeanisation are mutually connected, as political change induced through the European perspective creates legitimacy for the acceptance of laws and policy change, and empowers reform-minded actors with interests in conflict resolution to implement policy change, further reinforcing European norms and principles of organisation of the polity.

In line with the Europeanisation thesis, we would expect the EU policy-making process to become part of the politics of conflict resolution in Kosovo (Ladrech 1994: 71). This hypothetical process of reorientation of conflict resolution within the logic of EU governance also means that key aspects of its political norms and principles, policy tools, paradigms, and discourses should be altering the dynamics of the conflict resolution process in its main components: actors' interests, values, and communication.

The chapter proceeds as follows. It examines the history of the EU's involvement in the Kosovo conflict as a component of the European perspective of the Western Balkans with a special focus on the post-2005 status determination process. The timeline of this analysis concludes with the 2009–10 period marked by the feasibility study of the European Commission on the prospects of the EU–Kosovo relationship at the post-independence stage and the ICJ advisory opinion on the case which established the international context of Kosovo's independence. The chapter finds that the conflict resolution process has become irrevocably bound within the EU system of governance.

The historical background of the European perspective on the Kosovo conflict

The Kosovo conflict is embedded in the geopolitical evolution of statehood in the Balkans as a history of sub-regional instability, incomplete nation-building, and dependence upon the stabilising patronage of external powers (Gallagher 2001; Krasner 1999; Larrabee 1977; Tziampiris 2000). Its contemporary stage is determined by the uneven federalism and divisive ethnic policies of communist rule in the former Socialist Federal Republic of Yugoslavia (SFRY). The two dimensions were entrenched in the contradictory nature of the 1974 Yugoslav Constitution. The latter distinguished between national communities defined through the concepts of the SFRY's nations (in the republics) and nationalities (in the autonomous provinces, such as Kosovo). Nations were granted the right to secede, nationalities not. The Constitution elevated the autonomous regions of Kosovo and Vojvodina to a federal status and provided them with rights equal to those of the republics. The surge of Serbian nationalist rhetoric in Kosovo during the 1980s led to a political process to limit Kosovo Albanian presence in decision-making. During the 1990s Kosovo experienced the oppressive policies of the socialist government of Slobodan Milosevic which established full control of the province, removing its autonomy.

Kosovo initiated a self-determination process after the end of the Cold War. Similarly to Slovenia, Croatia, and Bosnia-Herzegovina, a referendum on Kosovo's future led to a declaration of independence on 22 September 1991. The outcome was ignored by the international community due to the restrictive interpretation of the principle of self-determination in the Yugoslav Constitution (Weller 1999: 215). Sovereignty emerged as the core issue of the conflict due to incompatible claims by the Kosovo Albanian community and Serbia. The Kosovo Albanians framed it as independence and the creation of a Kosovo Albanian sovereign state. Serbia pursued it as Kosovo's preservation as an integral part of its territory. The search for a negotiated solution through elite accommodation internally was unsuccessful. The Kosovo Liberation Army (KLA) adopted an alternative strategy of armed resistance leading to increasing clashes with Serb forces after 1996. Serbia's policy of displacement and ethnic cleansing of the Kosovo Albanian population accelerated in 1998. The Rambouillet talks on Kosovo's autonomy within the Federal Republic of Yugoslavia (FRY)[6] sponsored by the Contact Group on Kosovo[7] in 1998–99, failed in March 1999 (Weller 1999). In the context of persistent ethnic cleansing on behalf of the Yugoslav army and paramilitary units, a NATO military campaign (26 March–11 June 1999) secured the withdrawal of the Serbian army from the province (Pond 2006).[8] The military intervention ended with UN Security Council (UNSC) Resolution 1244 separating the governance of Kosovo into a UN protectorate under the UN Mission in Kosovo (UNMIK).[9]

UNSC Resolution 1244 and UNMIK marked an important stage in the conflict resolution process but did not constitute a durable settlement. The conflict remained in its overt expression as both parties pursued strategies to induce change in their interest. In 2001, UNMIK created the Provisional Institutions of Self-Governance in Kosovo (PISG) but little actual improvement of governance took place. The inconclusive nature of the PISG led to a process of political mobilisation for independence. As the frustration of the Kosovo Albanians with the imposed system of governance grew, UNMIK opened an opportunity for a future status determination contingent upon implementation of standards of democratic governance under the 'Standards before Status' process in 2003 (United Nations 2005: 2–3). Ethnically motivated violence in 2004 accelerated the standards implementation and assessment procedure. The 2004 Report of Ambassador Kai Eide, Special Envoy of the UN Secretary-General (UNSG) to Kosovo, concluded that 'unfulfilled aspirations and ambitions cannot be handled by policies without a clear political perspective'.[10] The report recognised that the Standards before Status approach was untenable and had to be replaced with broader policy objectives. The report linked the future status process to European integration. It recommended a European perspective also for Serbia with a view of 'solving the problem in terms of European integration'.[11]

The UN proposed direct talks on status determination in 2005, although it acknowledged that 'there will not be any good moment for addressing Kosovo's future status. It will continue to be a highly sensitive political issue' (United Nations 2005: 4). Ambassador Eide's 2005 report outlined directions for the future 'Europeanisation' of conflict resolution in Kosovo:

> When status has been determined, the EU will be expected to take on a more prominent role. This relates to the police and justice, where a continued presence will be required, albeit smaller and more specialized; to monitoring and supporting the standards process, which will gradually be merged with established EU processes ... (United Nations 2005: 21)

In November 2005, UNSG Annan appointed Martti Ahtisaari as his Special Envoy in the future status process. The initial conditions for negotiations required that the future settlement would be acceptable to both parties and that deadlines would not be imposed (United Nations 2005). Direct talks between the parties started in February 2006 but failed to reach a solution.

In February 2007 UNSG Special Envoy Ahtisaari submitted a report and a plan for action. The Ahtisaari Plan under the title 'Comprehensive Proposal for the Kosovo Status Settlement' (CPS) did not explicitly mention either the term 'independence' for Kosovo or 'sovereignty' for Serbia. The Plan provided Kosovo with all attributes of a sovereign state, despite the element of international supervision. In a separate recommendation, Martti Ahtisaari proposed supervised independence as the only possible solution to Kosovo's status. The EU supported the plan.[12] In the absence of a consensus in the UN

Security Council, direct negotiations on the CPS began in August 2007 and concluded without an agreement by the end date of 10 December 2007.

Kosovo declared independence on 17 February 2008 upon consultation with the Western powers. A process of negotiated reconfiguring of UNMIK commenced, as it had no legal grounds to continue to function in the context of the unilaterally declared independence. The supervisory powers of the international community were to be vested in an International Civilian Representative (ICR), head of the International Civilian Office (ICO), replacing the international presence in Kosovo formerly ensured through UNMIK. The ICR was to serve simultaneously as the EU Special Representative in Kosovo (EUSR). The Kosovo Constitution entered into force on 15 June 2008. Both foundational documents, the Declaration of Independence and the Constitution, adopted the conditions of the CPS (which only the Kosovo Albanians had accepted during the negotiations on a settlement), including an invitation to the EU and NATO to assume monitoring missions during the initial stages of independence. The UNSC did not reach an agreement to recognise or endorse the outcome. UNSC Resolution 1244 remained formally valid. Due to Serbia's opposition to plans for replacing UNMIK with an EU civilian rule of law mission (EULEX), UNSG Ban Ki-moon proposed the Six-Point Plan for UNMIK's reconfiguration. The Plan adapted EULEX to UNSC Resultion 1244 by defining it as a status-neutral mission. On 8 October 2008, acting upon Serbia's request, the UN General Assembly endorsed a resolution requesting the advisory opinion of the International Court of Justice on the legality of the Kosovo secession. Despite continuing divergence of opinion among the permanent members of the UNSC, a resolution was passed in December 2008 to endorse UNMIK's transfer of functions to EULEX.

EULEX was deployed throughout Kosovo on 8 December 2008. It became fully operational on 6 April 2009. By May 2009, EULEX had reached 2,569 staff (1,651 international and 918 local staff).[13] All UNMIK residual powers were transferred to the European civilian mission. The ICR functions as the final authority in Kosovo. The creation of EULEX marked the culmination of the EU's involvement in the Kosovo conflict as a process of governance with significant policy and polity effects, at the same time ensuring the sustainability of the constitutional form of the conflict resolution outcome under the UDI. Arguably, by combining the latter's governance and constitutional aspects, EULEX has come to represent the core component of Europeanisation in the Kosovo/Serbia conflict. Its tasks in border management secure the regional dimension of Kosovo's independence in the wake on the ICJ opinion of 22 July 2010 which posited that the declaration of independence was not contrary to international law, as the latter does not contain provisions on self-determination.

Evolution of the conflict prior to the Kosovo status process: European concepts and policy tools of conflict resolution (1990–2005)

The EU was not prepared to address the political process of the dissolution of the former Yugoslavia. The development of a long-term institutional design took place at the expense of building practical measures to assist the self-determination process. A political approach was the only available option to address the issues of self-determination and secession. From being reactive, this approach was to develop in parallel with the events and processes that placed upon the EU a demand to act. By 2003, it transformed into a forward-looking, proactive design for the European integration of the Western Balkans. The European perspective included conceptual and institutional components applied progressively as rules for the political determination of sovereignty, changes in the definition of what constitutes conflict resolution in Kosovo from autonomy within Serbia to independence, and governance instruments extended individually to the conflict parties to ensure policy reform in line with the Community *acquis*.

Diplomatic-political principles

The EU's strategy towards the Western Balkans during the period 1991–99 remained demand-driven and focused on crisis management. Its policy tools ranged from delegations and intermediation to multilateral and unilateral political initiatives, an arms embargo, trade sanctions, etc. The effectiveness of these measures as correctives to the dynamics of the conflict was minimal. Policy coordination under the CFSP was *ad hoc* and fragmented. The EU's political initiatives were duplicated or contradicted by unilateral action. The emergent European space relevant to conflict resolution in the Western Balkans lacked coherence and did not stimulate autonomous action.

In parallel with participation in multilateral diplomacy, the EU introduced its own political and conceptual innovation into the conflict resolution process. By applying new principles of state recognition in the Western Balkans, the EU effectively altered the foundations of Europe's political order. The EU-led political approach to state sovereignty in the process of the dissolution of the former Yugoslavia combined self-determination with democracy and human rights. It largely exceeded conventional references to the concept of minority rights as a component of Westphalian sovereignty even in the absence of territorial-constitutional principles to that effect (Woodward 2001: 268). Formally, not all borders in the Western Balkans were international borders according to the post-Second World War settlement under the Helsinki Act of 1975.[14] The EU defined the dissolution of the former Yugoslavia as a *sui generis* case (Rich 1993) beyond the classical application of the sovereignty norm (Woodward 2001: 260). The new approach linked the broader considerations of human security and human rights to the *uti possedetis* principle of the right to self-determination, according to which internal borders become international (Norchi 2002; Weller 2008). From the normative perspective of qualified sovereignty the Kosovo self-determination process emerged a case of protection of human rights through territorial principles.

The work of the Badinter Commission on former Yugoslavia represents the first failure to propose a practical solution to the issue of Kosovo's self-determination. Due to the lack of agreement on a peace plan, the EU offered recognition to the Yugoslav republics which sought self-determination under the condition that they complied with international standards on minority rights. The Guidelines for Recognition were adopted under the mechanism of the European Political Cooperation and applied through the deliberations of the Badinter Commission. The Commission did not review the Kosovo application. Under the former Yugoslav Constitution, Kosovo was not formally defined as a republic with the right to secede. When internal violence escalated in 1996, the EU responded through political-diplomatic action: common positions on a trade embargo, travel restrictions for the FRY elite, and a ban on investment in Serbia. Additional sanctions followed in 1998 in the area of armaments, government financed exports, police equipment, freezing of government funds, and a flight ban.

Europeanisation of the problem: Kosovo in the EU policy process (1999–2005)

The European perspective on the 1999 Kosovo crisis

The EU response to violence in Kosovo was not isolated from the broader international involvement in the 1998–99 crisis. The EU prioritised regional stability and was opposed to independence at the time.[15] The diplomatic objective was to restore Kosovo's autonomy within Serbia and prevent military action (Ginsberg 2001: 8). In parallel with mediation and assistance efforts, the EU developed a process to create autonomous policy instruments for addressing the conflict and for developing a separate domain of interaction with the conflict parties. These processes, later to become inseparable from the EU integration objectives in Eastern Europe, were a precursor to Europeanisation. The EU Regional Approach was introduced first under a General Affairs and External Relations Council (GAERC) decision in February 1996 as the 'Royaumont process for stability and good neighbourliness in South East Europe' and incorporated into the Common Foreign and Security Policy (CFSP) in November 1998.[16]

The Regional Approach was updated by including the concept of conditionality. The General Affairs Council of 29 April 1997 defined conditionality as the core governing principle for its relations with the countries of South-East Europe which did not yet have an association. Conditionality was not linked to a direct incentive of membership in this case but to policy benefits.

It established a policy framework for promoting democracy, the rule of law, higher standards of human and minority rights, transformation towards market economies, and greater cooperation in the Western Balkans. Kosovo-related conditionality for Serbia included granting a large degree of autonomy within the borders of the FRY and establishing a real dialogue with the Kosovo Albanians on the status issue. Autonomy was defined as 'a fair legal framework going beyond the respect of minority rights'.[17]

Individual member states and the Council Presidency represented the EU position in its interaction with the Serbian government and in international talks.[18] The informal meeting of the Heads of State and Government held in the course of the NATO campaign (14 April 1999) confirmed the view on Kosovo's autonomy within Serbia in line with the Rambouillet Accords. The meeting expressed the EU's willingness to assume leadership in a future international mission in Kosovo, which the German Presidency presented in a letter to the UN Security Council.[19]

The EU participated in the political efforts for a negotiated settlement during the NATO campaign. On 6 May 1999 the G-8 meeting agreed on the principles for a solution to the Kosovo crisis (Krieger 2001: 353). In addition to its participation in international negotiations, the EU introduced a new regional instrument for the post-conflict reconstruction of the Western Balkans. The Stability Pact for Southeastern Europe was signed in Cologne on 10 June 1999.[20] The Pact established the 'European perspective', which confirmed the EU's intention to draw Southeastern Europe 'closer to the perspective of full integration' and adopted the principle of conditionality (Cortright 2007: 411). The Pact was designed to address the pan-European effects of regional conflicts (European Commission 1999: 2). It later failed to meet expectations as its mechanism of democratic reforms in exchange for economic assistance did not fully materialise (Pond 2006: 242). The Pact was conceptually important to the Kosovo conflict. It showed that the EU regarded the political solution to the crisis as contingent upon its regional stabilisation efforts.[21] A Common Strategy for the Western Balkans was pending in line with the Vienna European Council (December 1998).[22]

Acting upon a mandate from the Council, the European Commission designed the Stabilisation and Association Process (SAP) (European Commission 1999). SAP emerged as the core EU policy towards the Western Balkans after 1999. It introduced a governance perspective to the EU's involvement in conflict resolution by incorporating European standards and EU law. SAP was built on the principle of conditionality establishing a link between the EU's contractual relations with the Western Balkans and domestic reform. Access to assistance and the long-term European integration of the countries in the Western Balkans were conditional upon building democratic political institutions and a market economy.[23] The main component of the process was the legally binding instrument of bilateral Stabilisation and Association Agreements (SAAs). The original formulation of the European perspective of the Stability Pact and the SAP framework preceded the interim settlement under UNMIK (European Commission 1999). UNSC Resolution 1244 explicitly welcomed the reconstruction efforts of the EU citing the Stability Pact (Paragraph 17).

The post-1999 period marks the beginnings of the Europeanisation of the Kosovo conflict characterised by the EU's growing visibility relative to other actors and the link between conflict resolution and the European perspective of the Western Balkans. The main aspect of Europeanisation at this stage emerged through the EU effect on the institutional process of conflict resolution. The EU assumed a dual role. It was a pillar within UNMIK responsible for post-conflict reconstruction, and therefore part of the international governance structures in Kosovo. Outside UNMIK, the EU deployed autonomous action which largely outperformed UN-sponsored conflict resolution.

Economic reconstruction and institutional growth under UNMIK overlapped with the externalisation of EU governance. A European space developed through increased coordination between the EU institutional actors in an interdependent policy-making process. Kirchner and Sperling (2007: 112) note a more proactive EU involvement in the conflict after 2000 explained by the intensification of EU governance. The coherence and autonomy of the policy process was the result of cross-pillarisation of the EU's policy towards the Western Balkans which adopted the enlargement-style mechanisms of SAP.

Europeanising UNMIK governance: the EU adopts integration and Standards implementation

The formulation of a European perspective for Serbia and Kosovo within the EU policy towards Eastern Europe developed as a separate dimension of the EU's interaction with the conflict parties, complementary to the system of UNMIK governance in Kosovo. The Thessaloniki European Council of June 2003 announced a new integration strategy for the Western Balkans.[24] The Thessaloniki Agenda emphasised values, norms on regional cooperation, and democratic governance. The European integration of the region, originally introduced at the Feira Council (2000), was declared a principal objective (European Commission 2003: 3). Similarly to other tools of policy transfer, the European Partnerships model anchored the relationship with the Western Balkans within the system of EU governance.

The 2003 decision on the European integration of the region gradually led to the inclusion of more institutional actors and a policy-making process with the participation of the European Commission, the Council, and the Secretary-General/High Representative (SG/HR) for CFSP. The commonality of views was maintained through the Working Group on the Western Balkans in the Council of the European Union and materialised in Council Regulations which reflected convergence of policy positions between the

Commission (proposal, communication) and Council (legislation) with the participation of the European Parliament (Interview 1).[25]

Serbia (including Kosovo) initially remained outside the Thessaloniki Agenda as SAP was delayed due to the Kosovo crisis. The signing of the Constitutional Charter of the State Union of Serbia and Montenegro, a constitutional design strongly influenced by the EU, drew the countries closer to the process after 2003. A European Partnership with Serbia was formulated in 2004. It gradually enriched the relationship through political dialogue, conditionality, and multilateralism (Wichmann 2007: 74). The SAP established priorities for Serbia in the area of compliance with the Dayton Agreement, cooperation with the International Criminal Tribunal for the Former Yugoslavia (ICTY), constitutional and judicial reform for achieving conformity with EU standards, economic reform, and regional cooperation. For Kosovo the emphasis was on democratic governance, institutions, protection of rights, and administrative capacity. The instruments for monitoring conditionality and performance through the SAP Tracking Mechanism and the European Partnerships anchored policy implementation into the short- and medium-term objectives of the European perspective.

The EU's autonomous capacity for action under the Thessaloniki Agenda was instrumental to the objectives of UNMIK governance in Kosovo. The EU policy process and instruments developed in line with the European perspective provided for a more coherent implementation which UNMIK lacked. By 2004 the EU's involvement in the Kosovo conflict took place through its responsibility for economic reconstruction under Pillar IV of UNMIK, the Contact Group on Kosovo comprised of influential international actors, the EU member states' Liaison Office in Pristina, the European Union Monitoring Mission, and the European Agency for Reconstruction, which had established an operational centre in Kosovo in 2000 for managing the Community Assistance for Reconstruction, Development and Stabilisation (CARDS) Programme. After 2004, the EU moved beyond institutional diversity towards mutual reinforcing of the actions of all EU actors. It stepped up measures for coordination through information sharing, public communication, dialogue with local leaders, and international consultation groups.

The EU became involved in the process of consideration of Kosovo's future status by the end of 2003. Having established that delays in addressing the status question produced destabilising effects, GAERC endorsed the UNMIK-led operationalisation of the 'Standards before Status' policy in November 2003.[26] The EU adopted the Standards as principal programming priorities under the SAA. The EU's aim was to 'maintain Kosovo firmly anchored in the Stabilisation and Association process and to ensure that progress in fulfilling the UN standards remain compatible with, and reflect the relevant EU policies and the EU's values' (European Commission 2004b: 13). The 2004 Solana/Rehn report to the Council analysed the EU's contribution to the Standards Implementation Plan.[27] The report proposed the creation of links between status determination, reflected in the Standards for Kosovo initiative, and Standards monitoring under the SAP (Council of the European Union 2004: 3).

The EU's view was that the European perspective would not be held by the status issue. It would focus instead on democracy and building a multi-ethnic Kosovo in compliance with the Standards. The EU's Standards Tracking Mechanism (STM) aligned the European perspective to the Standards implementation process. Although formally under UNMIK, the Standards process was linked to the EU Thessaloniki Agenda (Council of the European Union 2004: 7). By adopting independent monitoring through the STM, the EU emerged as the only international source of consistent monitoring of standards implementation. The EU's attention to substantive issues under the Standards implementation process, such as decentralisation, was at odds with the lack of meaningful international input in the process. This discrepancy adversely affected the application of decentralisation at the post-status stage. The European perspective could not produce tangible independent results in the area of decentralisation as the latter was contingent upon implementation of standards through UNMIK. The status determination process did not make compliance with the European perspective mandatory, although it referred to the EU's political role. Political cross-referencing, short of concrete monitoring and feedback, was insufficient to guarantee compliance with the standards. Decentralisation was implemented outside the Standards process.[28] The post-status stage demonstrated that the consequences of suboptimality in this area were particularly pronounced.

The institutional coherence of the European space grew in parallel with the process of policy determination. The latter took place through the intensification of communication among the EU institutional actors and conceptualisation of Kosovo's future status within an EU perspective. The 2005 Solana/Rehn joint report of the European Commission and the Council issued proposals for the EU's conditions with regard to the status process. The EU policy was based on the principles of no return to the pre-1999 situation, Euro-Atlantic integration for Kosovo and Serbia, multi-ethnicity and protection of minorities, no change in territory, a solution compatible with European values and standards, and continued international civilian and military presence.[29] In 2005, the EU declared that, without prejudice to the United Nation's role in determining the future status of Kosovo, the Western Balkans, including Kosovo, were destined to join the EU.[30] The European Commission published an own-initiative communication addressing Kosovo's European perspective. The Commission proposed the principle of contractual relations with Kosovo which implied state-like competences (European Commission 2005). The EU acknowledged that the Standards process could lead to status determination.

Politically, the EU was ahead of the UN in the area of Standards implementation as a process of building the constitutive features of democracy in Kosovo. The 2005 declaration on Kosovo of the Brussels European Council set conditions with regard to the compatibility of the standards and status process with European values and the European prospects of the region. The EU confirmed the need for international presence at the post-status stage and expressed willingness to 'play a full part' (European Council 2005: 34). The objective was to prevent partition by contributing to a democratic Kosovo. Deliberations in GAERC focused on ensuring decentralisation as a guarantee for a multi-ethnic Kosovo.[31] The EU maintained Standards monitoring even after it became clear that UNMIK-based assessment was weak and had failed to induce adaptation.

Moving toward independence: 2005–8 and beyond – Europeanisation by extending EU governance

The launch of the process to determine Kosovo's status provides evidence of a changed institutional model of conflict resolution. This period was characterised by an emphasis on implementation. The EU adopted a differentiated approach to the conflict parties in the process of status determination. Both strategies were based on the link between the Thessaloniki Agenda, Kosovo's status, and progress toward the Euro-Atlantic integration of Serbia and Kosovo. The approach towards Serbia was based on the incentives and conditionality structure of the European perspective. The EU developed a predominantly functional-managerial approach towards Kosovo through the design of a crisis management operation.

Involvement in direct problem-solving in the status determination process emerged as the indispensable binding component of conflict resolution. Applied individually for the conflict parties, the European perspective developed independently from the status process, once again recasting conditionality in a policy, rather than membership, context. Although conflict resolution was guided through UN initiatives, the 2005 UN proposal to open a political process relied on the structuring of a viable relationship with the EU for both parties individually. The two dimensions, European perspective for the conflict parties and status determination for Kosovo, were conducive to the actual Europeanisation of conflict resolution.

Ensuring Kosovo's independence as a conflict resolution strategy
Even prior to the launch of the status determination process, the 2004 report of the UNSG Special Envoy Kai Eide on the situation in Kosovo urged the EU to take over the leadership in designing the long-term perspective of Kosovo's status in Europe.

> The EU should now start shaping its own strategy towards Kosovo. Politically, the EU will be the most important magnet both for Pristina and Belgrade. The

EU should be able to use its influence to ensure that the Kosovo Albanians commit themselves to respecting and facilitating the presence, participation and identity of the minorities ... and the EU would be able to provide incentives and disincentives for the future status negotiations and the period following them. The importance of formulating such incentives and disincentives would also apply to Belgrade.[32]

Prior to the 2004 report, the UN formula in the status process was an institutional division of labour. UNMIK maintained the approach of 'Standards before Status' and the European perspective assumed responsibility for policy transfer in the area of Standards implementation through the European Partnership.

The status process demonstrated the deepening cooperation among the EU institutional actors on tasks pertaining to the status determination process and the gradual transfer of governance actions enabling status determination under the European perspective. The consensus bodies of intergovernmentalism, the Council Presidency, European Council and the Council, as well as the supranational actors, the European Commission and the EP, increasingly shared competences for the purpose of problem-solving. The series of reports on the conceptual basis and directions for EU policy involvement, prepared by the SG/HR and the Commissioner for Enlargement at the request of the European Council during the period 2004–7 facilitated the creation of cross-pillar networks of institutional actors in the EU decision-making process. This pattern of policy-making benefited from the combined strength of Community instruments and intergovernmental consensus (Kirchner and Sperling 2007: 104–5). The European Partnership was elevated as the benchmark institutional design and a common reference for the European perspective, the PISG, and UNMIK. The establishment of contractual relations with Kosovo was seen as conditional upon status settlement and the European perspective.[33] The Commission and the Council monitored conditionality in the process of negotiation of an SAA with Serbia by postponing the signing of the Agreement at several instances. The European Commission formulated proposals with regard to the status process and monitored the cooperation of the conflict parties under the SAP. The 2006 SG/HR Solana/Rehn joint report determined that a future EU civilian mission should be based on a UNSC resolution and that it would deal with the implementation of the non-military aspects of the settlement. The 2006–7 reports recommended that the international community representative (ICR) in Kosovo at the post-status stage should be the EU Special Representative (EUSR). The reports established principles for the creation of the ICO and the EUSR position within it and defined the EU civilian mission as a crisis management operation under the European Security and Defence Policy (ESDP).[34]

GAERC maintained responsibility for policy definition in the CFSP under the general guidelines of the European Council. It was the focal point for formulating the EU's position in the conflict resolution process. GAERC implemented the guidelines of the European Council and worked with the Commission, also associated with these tasks (Yeşilada and Wood 2009: 196). In order to begin preparation for the future EU civilian mission, the Council first adopted a joint action establishing an EU Planning Team (EUPT) for the mission.[35] It was instrumental in developing a consensus decision on EULEX despite diverging national positions on the legal interpretation of Kosovo's status (Interview 2).[36]

The European Council also emerged as a source of initiative although it has maintained its primary focus on issues of the extraordinary agenda (Yeşilada and Wood 2009). The Council viewed the Kosovo conflict through the perspective of its regional approach to the Western Balkans and its system of external governance (European Council 2007, article 76).

The decision of the 2007 European Council (12–13 December) prepared the ground for the EU's leadership role in the Kosovo conflict at the post-status stage. The Council recognised the inevitability of a future unilateral action in view of the exhausted opportunities of the negotiation and the unsustainable nature of the status quo in Kosovo. It set the conditions for a UDI to establish a democratic and multi-ethnic Kosovo committed to the rule of law and to the protection of minorities. Similarly to the rules for recognition of new states of the Badinter Commission during the early 1990s, the application of political conditionality was at odds with the principle of self-determination in its post-colonial application. The latter does not set conditions on maturing or institutional capacity. According to UN Resolution 1514 (XV) (14 December 1960), 'inadequacy of political, economic, social or educational preparedness should never serve as a pretext for delaying independence' (Article 3). Without a formal reference to such background documents in international law, the Council determined that Kosovo should be treated as a *sui generis* case, similarly to the treatment of the dissolution of former Yugoslavia by the Badinter Commission in 1990–91. The Council stated its readiness to assist Kosovo through an ESDP mission. The modalities of the mission, the planning of which had started in 2006, were autonomously determined by the EU without formal coordination with the UN.

The 2007 European Council provided Serbia with important incentives. The Council suggested that Serbia's institutional capacity allowed for an upgrade in its relationship to the EU and indicated that it could advance to a candidacy stage provided that it was in compliance with the ICTY. The Council encouraged Serbia to focus primarily on the European perspective, thus separating the conflict issues from European integration. The collective preference of the EU institutional actors to maintain the European perspective separate from the conflict was at odds with the traditional interpretation of conditionality as a method of conflict resolution on behalf of influential member states. By reconfiguring conditionality, the EU modified the conventional incentives/rewards structure of offering proximity in exchange for conflict resolution.

Although the 2007 Council did not establish a link between Kosovo's independence and the European perspective of Serbia, linkage politics based on conditionality were a frequent reference in the EU relationship with Serbia, due to the intergovernmental nature of its foreign policy. On the eve of the 2007 European Council, British Prime Minister Brown and French President Sarkozy proposed that Serbia be given a positive signal in exchange for recognition of the UDI.[37] Several member states (France, Germany, Italy, and the UK) suggested 'a clear message on Kosovo' by agreeing to a rule of law mission without a new UN mandate. British Foreign Secretary Miliband proposed that the EU endorse independence for Kosovo regardless of the presence or absence of UNSC approval. Understanding that the chances for a negotiated settlement were minimal and that Russia would veto a UNSC resolution on Kosovo's independence, the EU changed its view on the need for a prior decision on the case and an authorisation of the rule of law mission by the Security Council. SG/HR Solana stated in 2007 that 'the European Union's preference has always been to have a Security Council resolution. But we cannot have a Security Council decision if there is no agreement between its members. Even without an agreement, life will go on. It's not the end of the world.'[38] The Council determined that support for Kosovo's stabilisation was a priority relative to a formal-legalistic approach to recognition.

There was, therefore, diversity of opinion among the EU member states, linkage politics, compliance pressures for Serbia, and asymmetric benefits for the conflict parties. Such political pluralism was coterminous with the EU's changed priorities in the conflict resolution process. Linkages between Serbia's recognition of Kosovo as an independent state and its own European perspective would re-emerge later, in the wake of the 2010 ICJ opinion which granted international legitimacy to the declaration of independence.

Upon Kosovo's declaration of independence on 17 February 2008 the EU institutional actors, both those operating in a supranational and those within an intergovernmental format agreed to the inevitability of independence and emphasised its *sui generis* nature. GAERC responded by a Common Position which took note of the outcome but did not formally recognise it. The emphasis was on the European perspective of the conflict parties, keeping the conflict resolution outcome separate from integration:

> It isn't a victory of the Kosovars over the Serbs, it's a victory for peace, it's a victory for common sense, and it's certainly a victory for both peoples because they're undoubtedly going to move – separately perhaps initially, but together in the very near future – closer to the European Union and towards a more peaceful Balkans.[39]

Individual member states framed the issue of independence as an element of reconciliation, not the creation of a new state. The Council converged on assisting the resolution of the conflict by separating the issues for the conflict parties. Two policy tools were agreed: the launch of a civilian mission to sustain Kosovo's independence and the integration perspective to stabilise the region, including Serbia. The decision-making process evolved into different directions for the conflict parties. The functional unity which took precedence over institutional and actor preferences was in line with the trends in EU policy-making (Stetter 2004: 726). None of the countries who had reservations about Kosovo's recognition – Cyprus, Greece, Romania, Slovakia, and Spain – objected to the deployment of the EU civilian rule of law mission. 'We took a political decision to send an ESDP mission to Kosovo. This is the clearest signal the EU could possibly give that Europe intends to lead on Kosovo and the future of the region'.[40]

The EP contributed to the cohesiveness of the EU's position achieved through cross-pillar cooperation. Parliamentary action moved further than other institutional actors in establishing a connection between the European perspective and conflict resolution. The EP's preference was for a parallel movement towards standards implementation and status deliberations.[41] In a parallel process, the EP developed a position on the EU's relationship with Serbia.[42] Parliamentary deliberations on the status issue were more explicit than the Ahtisaari Plan by directly recommending supervised sovereignty for Kosovo. The EP also urged for a more coherent approach as Kosovo's indeterminate prospects for EU membership would limit the capacity of conditionality to generate compliance (European Parliament 2007: 13–14). The EP supported the main elements in the Council's Common position but many parliamentarians expressed a preference for a negotiated settlement.[43] After Kosovo declared independence, the EP was consistent in its support for a coordinated common EU response to Kosovo's independence (Interview 3).[44] In a series of resolutions, Parliament urged the EU member states to recognise Kosovo in order to facilitate the effectiveness of its actions in Kosovo.[45]

The 2007 deliberations of the European Council and those in GAERC in February 2008 had significant consequences for the European perspective of the conflict parties. Both intergovernmental frameworks shifted the process of Kosovo's recognition to the member states. In a parallel development, decision-making under the European perspective became increasingly dependent on veto powers in the Council. Despite Commission proposals for signing the SAA with Serbia and advancing the European perspective, the workings of GAERC permitted decisive input by individual member states (i.e. the presence of veto points) in the determination of Serbia's preparedness to implement the SAA. After the signing of the Agreement on 28 April 2008 in direct encouragement of the pro-European parties in the 2008 parliamentary elections in Serbia, the Council withheld the ratification process due to insistence by the Netherlands on Serbia's full compliance with the ICTY.[46] Such developments were indicative not simply of a withdrawal on the part of the EU institutions to maintain a coherent conditionality-based approach. More importantly, they reflected the pluralist nature of European governance. There was a transfer of responsibility to the member states in the governance process along both dimensions: conflict resolution through independence for Kosovo and a European perspective for the conflict parties individually. GAERC determined that the final outcome of the conflict resolution process, Kosovo's recognition as a sovereign state, should be the prerogative of the member states as the EU did not have legal competences in the area. The consensus mechanism of the European perspective also depended on the principled views of the member states. Serbia began implementation of the SAA through the Interim Trade Agreement without formal ratification by the EU due to a sustained Dutch veto (in view of Serbia's incomplete compliance with the ICTY).

EULEX: the Europeanisation of Kosovo governance
The EU stated readiness to deploy a rule of law mission on 18 February 2008. EULEX provides evidence of the Europeanising influences of the EU's actions in Kosovo. EULEX was created following a failed plan for settlement. It borrowed the principal conditions of the CPS, the concept of 'supervised independence' through an international civilian mission and served as the link between the European perspective and international governance in Kosovo. The European Partnership and Progress Reports of the European Commission established a monitoring mechanism for Kosovo's compliance with EULEX (European Commission 2009a).

EULEX was established through a Joint Action which appointed a European Union Special Representative (EUSR) in Kosovo.[47] EULEX is status-neutral; therefore it is not a direct governance mission although it has strong executive functions. The key aspects of the mission are to ensure local ownership and a programmatic approach in fulfilment of strategic objectives of monitoring, mentoring, and advising the competent Kosovo institutions on areas related to the rule of law. EULEX demonstrates deepening institutional links among the EU actors in fulfilling governance functions on behalf of the international community. Although the functions of the EUSR and of the ISR are performed by one officer, the EUSR, they focus on different dimensions of governance. The ICR provides supervision of the implementation of the CPS while the EUSR is responsible for the EU's support and advice in connection with the political process in Kosovo.

The political approach which has guided EULEX assistance to Kosovo's functioning as an independent state while deploying the mission under UNSC Resolution 1244 which posits Kosovo as an integral part of Serbia is at odds with independence as a concept underlying the conflict resolution outcome. This contradiction was recognised in a feasibility study of the European Commission in 2009. Against the background of EULEX deployment, the Commission proposed a framework for a future relationship with Kosovo based on dialogue under SAP, a trade agreement, societal dialogue to lead to visa liberalisation, and alternatives to the SAA due to the lack of initial international recognition within the UN system (European Commission 2009b). In January 2010 the EU launched the SAP Dialogue with Kosovo in line with the European perspective. For the first time, Kosovo participated in IPA cross-border cooperation programmes with Macedonia and Albania.

The lack of a conclusive legal determination of the case, also in view of the rather technical opinion of ICJ on the legality of the Kosovo declaration of independence, has given more visibility to the individual preferences of the EU member states to the detriment of consensus decision-making in the Council. Such developments reinforce the intergovernmental nature of governance in the EU foreign policy domain (Interview 2). Kosovo's post-UDI status between sovereignty and supervised independence has altered but not diminished the scope of the EU's impact. The path of Europeanisation has shifted from an emphasis on the conflict resolution outcome, an independent democratic and multi-ethnic Kosovo, to the managerial-functional aspects of conflict resolution as a governance process. It is implemented through institutional settings and policy tools within the domain of competences assigned to the EU institutional actors (Hartlapp 2007: 656). This kind of piecemeal Europeanisation without a clear operationalisation of long-term objectives has reoriented the EU's enlargement policy in the Western Balkans toward a 'managed enlargement process' defined in terms of coherence, competences, and continuity:

> ... notwithstanding EU Member States' differing positions on Kosovo's status, the approach of diversity on recognition, but unity in engagement provides a constructive basis for progress. In line with Council conclusions, the EU can agree on measures to support Kosovo's political and economic development without prejudice to EU Member States' positions on status. (European Commission 2009b: 4)

How do actors respond? Between compliance, resource-based action, and resistance

If the autonomy and coherence of a European space of action conflict resolution is measured through the presence of a policy process of rule creation and the pressures it generates, then the evidence of the EU's impact on conflict resolution in Kosovo should be sought by tracing change at the level of institutions and actors involved in the process. Changes in the institutional logic of conflict resolution – its blueprint and pattern of communication – as well as actors' reaction to EU impact would permit one to determine whether these influences produce effects, whether Europeanisation takes place, whether it is resource-based or compliance-dominated, and to what extent it has been effective.

This task is challenging taking into account that the early EU involvement in the Kosovo conflict did not generate compliance pressures or political change conducive to conflict resolution. There was no motivation for either side to adjust to external influences (van Meurs 2004: 71). However, in parallel with the status determination process, the EU's influence on its institutional and behavioural dynamics has grown. The innovative nature of EU policy tools for addressing the conflict has generated political response and adaptation within the UN-led process, the strategies of influential actors at the status determination stage, and the conflict parties.

UN initiatives and international actors
Actors in the UN framework first acknowledged the need for an EU role in the determination of status as a political settlement and a stage in the ultimate resolution of the Kosovo conflict. The regular reports of the Secretary-General to the UN Security Council on UNMIK activities in Kosovo, the reports of Ambassador Kai Eide, the Ahtisaari process and the CSP, the Contact Group, and the Troika of influential international actors who facilitated status negotiations, all recognised the indispensable nature of the EU's presence in the process. Against the background of blocked decision-making in the Security Council in the wake of Kosovo's declaration of independence, the EU remained the only international actor to ensure the implementation of the Ahtisaari Plan even when it failed to gain acceptance by both conflict parties through negotiations.

The Contact Group on Kosovo determined a key role for the EU in the process of status determination. Following Ambassador Eide's Report submitted on 7 October 2005, the Contact Group agreed on the non-negotiable Guiding Principles about the Kosovo settlement (November 2005).[48] The principles reflected the international preference for a negotiated settlement. Its core had moved away from a legal approach to status determination by placing emphasis on the practical realisation of a democratic and multi-ethnic Kosovo as a system of governance: the implementation of standards, regional cooperation and reconciliation, decentralisation, protection of minority rights, and participation of local communities. One of the guiding principles of the settlement was compatibility with European standards and assistance with the European integration of Kosovo. The Ahtisaari Plan, which adopted the principles of the Contact Group, justified the process of status definition with the need to guarantee the European perspective of the Western Balkans:

> Kosovo is also unable to participate effectively in any meaningful process towards the European Union – an otherwise powerful motor for reform and economic development in the region and the most effective way to continue the vital standards implementation process ... Economic development in Kosovo requires the clarity and stability that only independence can provide. (United Nations 2007: 3–4)

The UN itself used the European perspective as a resource for the proposal on status settlement. Successive reports of the Secretary-General on UNMIK action in the Standards for Kosovo process established cross-references to the European Partnership and monitoring under the STM to inform the Security Council that Standards implementation continued under the European perspective.[49] Because of Russia's veto powers in the SC, UN-based instruments had a limited capacity to assist the negotiation of independence for Kosovo through a political settlement. Instead, the conflict resolution process took place as a result of EU leadership. According to Wolfgang Ischinger, EU representative on the Troika facilitating the 2007 negotiations, the US and Russia had 'expressedly accepted' that Europe was the *primus inter pares* in the mediating team.[50] UNSG Ban Ki-moon supported the EU's involvement in sustaining independence by defining Kosovo as a European issue.[51] The office of the UNSG did not obstruct EULEX and avoided a Russian veto on the mission. The UNSG was instrumental in securing approval of mission deployment by the Security Council. The UNSC Presidential Statement of 26 November 2008 unanimously authorised EULEX to deploy across the entire territory of Kosovo.[52] By transferring functions to the EU civilian mission, UNMIK's reconfiguration endorsed it with legitimacy and raised the profile of EULEX as a mechanism of international governance.[53] That this process met with the resistance of the conflict parties, for opposite reasons, provides evidence of the autonomy and centrality of the EU's role in shaping the long-term outcomes of Kosovo's independence. The process also points to a trend of gradual acceptance of its modalities by political actors through selective adaptation.

Parties to the conflict
The principal actor-centred evidence of the EU's effects on the Kosovo conflict refers to the political strategies of the conflict parties. As a result of their interaction with the EU, both Serbia and Kosovo have aligned their political objectives in a European perspective. They have accepted the EU's leadership at the post-stage and despite selective resistance have reoriented their government priorities to comply with the EU. The European perspective of Kosovo and Serbia was the only element of common understanding between the two parties during the 2007 negotiation process (Kim and Woehrel 2008: 18–19).

Noutcheva (2009) contends that political actors view the European perspective as one built on a dubious legitimacy foundation by imposing compliance and a price to pay for achieving the goals of Kosovo's independence (Noutcheva 2009: 1074, 1079). Regardless of the punitive peace argument prevalent within Serbian society (Noutcheva 2009: 1080), the European perspective has received vast acceptance reflected in high levels of support for European integration on behalf of sections of the elite and civil society.

The core of the EU involvement in the Kosovo conflict, the autonomous decision to deploy a civilian mission, illustrates this logic of Europeanisation through selective compliance and routinised behaviour. EULEX was contrary to the interests of the conflict parties. Both Serbia and Kosovo have sought to limit or even eliminate its functions. EULEX was unacceptable for Kosovo because it restated the validity of UNSC Resolution 1244. Status neutrality meant that it was not guided by the Kosovo Constitution. The problematic meaning of EULEX also arose from the fact that the CSP incorporated the mission but did not outline a mechanism or a timetable for advancement to full sovereignty. For Serbia, EULEX represented a *de facto* recognition of Kosovo's independence and withdrawal of UNSC Resolution 1244. Both parties gradually adapted to mission deployment.

Outside EULEX, EU principles and actions emerged as authoritative foundations of governance in the domestic systems of the conflict parties: a European perspective for policy reform and political pluralism in Serbia and for the functioning of constitutional order in Kosovo. Regardless of the fact that the European perspective had a different meaning for the conflict parties, they demonstrated a commitment to adopt EU preferences and policy designs. The European perspective is integral to Kosovo's independence. The latter is maintained exclusively through the EU's civilian mission. By contrast, EU pressures on Serbia through the conditionality principle of the SAA triggered a process of domestic adaptation by separating the conflict issue from European integration without a clear ranking of priorities. While both actors have embraced a European perspective, their 'Europeanness' remains unrelated to conflict resolution based on a negotiated settlement. Such 'separateness' of objectives has strengthened the EU's capacity to engage in an open-ended relationship of 'managed enlargement'.

Serbia opened talks for the signing of a Stabilisation and Association Agreement in 2005 under the condition that suspected criminals from the Bosnian war, including General Ratko Mladic, would be extradited for trial at the ICTY by the end of March 2006. The EU separated the monitoring of Kosovo under the European Partnership and reassured Serbia that its own integration aspirations 'would not be delayed by the resolution of Kosovo's status. Indeed, constructive engagement on Kosovo would ease its own path towards the European Union' (European Commission 2005: 10). Serbia did not comply with the condition on extraditions and after an extension, the EU suspended negotiations. Cooperation with the ICTY emerged as the single-issue politics of the SAA negotiation despite the multidimensional nature of monitoring under the SAP. ICTY conditionality emerged as a direct stimulus for policy reforms.

The European perspective has been a major factor for the mobilisation of domestic response to Kosovo's independence in Serbia. When the signature of the SAA failed in 2006, the governing party, the moderate nationalist Democratic Party of Serbia (DSS), and the Koštunica government reacted negatively, publicly denouncing the ICTY for being anti-Serbian, demanding that war criminals be tried by Serbian courts, and protesting against the extradition of Milošević to the ICTY. As a governing party the DSS distanced itself from the Serbian Radical Party (SRS) whose position was that Serbia should 'fight for Kosovo' in the event that Kosovo gained independence.[54] The DSS maintained moderate nationalist leanings in 2006. It formed a minority government, rather than a coalition with the pro-European Democratic Party (DS), relying on parliamentary support from the Socialist Party of Serbia (SPS), the party of former President Milošević. Instead of adjusting to the inclusive agenda of the European perspective through coalition-building or adopting a pro-European outlook, the DSS preserved its nationalist identification. It was after change in the governing coalition in 2007 that the DSS chose to form a government with the DS, compliance with the ICTY increased, and negotiations resumed (Schimmelfennig 2008: 930).

The EU affected the political opportunity structure of the 2007–8 elections in Serbia. Parliamentary elections in January 2007 strengthened the European perspective. The elections produced a coalition government of liberal pro-European parties (DS) and moderate nationalists (DSS). The EU maintained conditionality in the SAA process through the linkage between the Agreement and Serbia's cooperation with the ICTY. Despite improving cooperation and the arrest of Radovan Karadjic for crimes in the Bosnian war, the EU signed but did not ratify the SAA as Ratko Mladic remained at large.[55]

The election of a pro-European candidate in the 2008 presidential elections in Serbia days before Kosovo declared independence and subsequent pro-European coalitions in parliamentary elections provide evidence of the empowerment of political actors related to the European perspective. Upon Kosovo's declaration of independence, Prime Minister Koštunica required a revision of the entire relationship with the EU, a declaration by the Serbian Parliament, and a freeze on the SAA. The governing coalition fell apart as a result of disagreement over the course of foreign policy action in response to the unilateral declaration. The EU maintained SAA conditionality without requiring Serbia's acceptance of the declaration. The separation of the conflict issue from the European perspective was conducive to accelerated reforms, a pro-European foreign policy in anticipation of early elections, and reconciliation within the domestic system. The Socialist Party of Serbia (SPS) joined the DS to form a governing coalition as a result of the May 2008 elections. President Tadic evoked the need for a new policy of national reconciliation, not through experiences, but through policy-based measures improving the lives of citizens: 'To reconcile we all have to give up our own cherished positions in order to achieve a higher purpose.'[56] Serbia pursued democratic reforms and adoption of EU norms without abandoning its rejection of the conflict outcome. Due to the lack of advancement in meeting ICTY conditionality under the Interim Trade Agreement, the EU suspended ratification after a veto by the Netherlands in September 2008. Despite a suspended institutional process, Serbia proceeded with unilateral implementation of the Trade Agreement and submitted a formal application for EU membership in December 2009. The politics around the timing of the signing and implementation of the Agreement unfolded in parallel with the declining influence of the nationalist parties, the SRS and the nationalist line of the DSS. The pro-reform coalition of actors used the European perspective to advance Serbia's interests and presented Serbia's EU membership as a stability factor for the entire region.[57]

The evolution of domestic political discourse accordingly reoriented itself to reflect the separateness of European perspective from the conflict issue. Although political actors rank both issues high on the agenda, it is possible to determine that the European perspective is the object of a near-consensus while the status of Kosovo is characterised by diversity of opinion. Table 6.1. presents the views of political actors in Serbia on the Kosovo independence–European perspective dichotomy. The examples demonstrate also elite perceptions of the possible linkage between the two issues.

The evidence points to a resource model of Europeanisation and expanded opportunities for political competition and pluralism. Serbia's pro-European elites, including President Tadic and the DS, have kept the issues of independence and European integration separate. Reconciliation entered public discourse through the inclusion of the SPS in the governing coalition. A faction of the Serbian Radical Party led by Tomislav Nikolic differentiated itself from the nationalist ideology of the party to adopt a pro-European outlook and created the Serbian Progressive Party (SNS). The presence of resistance, behavioural change and ideological competition in direct relationship to the European perspective indicates that political actors in Serbia have 'encountered' Europe and that a process of change is under way. A pro-European consensus has emerged among the main parties due to the importance of the European perspective in Serbian electoral politics and government formation.

While the value of proximity to Europe has increased in Serbia, it remains less clear-cut in Kosovo. The coordinated nature of the declaration of independence as a result of the failed negotiations of a settlement provides evidence of the Europeanisation of the conflict resolution outcome for Kosovo. All foundational texts and government statements confirm Kosovo's European vocation. The Declaration of Independence welcomed international support referring to UNSCR 1244, a civilian presence to supervise the implementation of the Ahtisaari Plan, and an EU-led rule of law mission.[58] The Kosovo Constitution refers to Kosovo as a European state. EU membership is a declared objective of the Kosovo government.

Outside embeddedness of the constitutive features of the Kosovo polity in a European perspective, Europeanisation refers the relevance of EU governance norms to the working features of Kosovo as an independent state. The concept which unites the constitutional and governance characteristics of Kosovo's political system is that of decentralisation. Since the Standards formulation process, EU institutional actors have expressed strong

Table 6.1 The European perspective and the Kosovo conflict in Serbia's political discourse

Party	European integration	The Kosovo conflict	EU/Kosovo: key discourse interaction
DS	'Europe has no alternative' policy. A combined goal, including both Europe and Kosovo. (President Tadic, B92, 26 April 2010)	Serbia will never, under any circumstances, implicitly or explicitly, recognise the unilateral declaration of independence. (President Tadic, B92, 22 January 2010) We learned from Cyprus how to fight for Kosovo. Cyprus is a living example. (FM Jeremic, B92, 9 March 2010)	Separate issues. Evolving from unconditional to compromise: We are ready to, after the ICJ decision (on the legality of the UDI), reach compromise through dialogue. (B92: 18 March 2010) Territorial integrity is a common value of the international community. (PM Cvetkovic, 23 March 2010)
DSS	A new policy is needed for the EU. The position that there is no alternative to the EU is detrimental. (23 March 2010) A lifelong goal of having a complete Serbia with Kosovo join the EU. (Koštunica, B92, 20 March 2010)	A state-building policy that holds Kosovo as an inalienable part of Serbia. The basis for coalition politics with SNS.	'State-preserving policies'. Not separate issues. Main question: Will a united Serbia with its southern province enter the EU? (B92, 1 March 2010)
SRS	Serbia's territorial integrity as a condition for further European integration. (France 24, 9 March 2008)	Kosovo is Serbia.	The government should immediately revoke its decision to allow EULEX to deploy in Kosovo, because the only mission which should be in Kosovo is the UN mission. (4 March 2010)

Kosovo

SPS	Pro-European, DS coalition partner. (2008 elections)	Government policy: no recognition.
SNS	EU integration only with Kosovo. I do not think that we should stop the story about European cooperation and integration; we need to fulfil conditions. (Nikolic)	Abandoned nationalism? Kosovo is neither a condition for Europe, nor will Serbia ever accept for Kosovo to become a condition for Europe. European integration and solving the status of Kosovo are two separate processes. That is the policy of Serbia, but also of the EU, which does not have a united position on Kosovo. (B92, 4 March 2010) There are no more political parties in Serbia saying that they do not want to enter the EU, as long as Kosovo is a part of Serbia. (B92, 24 March 2010)
LDP	Europeanisation of Serbia. (*Serbia Today*, 28 July 2009)	Serbia has lost Kosovo. (Jovanovic, B 92, 9 March 2010) Serbs should participate in elections (in Kosovo). Whether Serbia is for Kosovo or the European Union is a fake dilemma. (B92, 13 March 2010) Serbia should meet with Kosovo officials to talk about improving the standard of living for people who live in Kosovo. (B92, 20 March 2010)

Source: B92/Key terms: Kosovo; European integration: www.b92.net/.
Note: LDP = Liberal Democratic Party.

preferences for decentralisation. The EU initially had little leverage over the process, either in its constitutional formulation or its implementation, due to the fact that reform of local government remained outside the Standards process and was pursued under the Ahtisaari Plan and the CPS. The Ahtisaari Plan provided for the ability of predominantly ethnic Serb municipalities to maintain networked connections with Serbian authorities, obtain additional funding by cooperation with Serbia, and secure Serbia's acceptance of the Plan. Decentralisation was an object of monitoring under the STM of the European Partnership, as it was crucial for the functioning of a democratic and multi-ethnic Kosovo under the European perspective.

At the time of the declaration of independence, the concept was not sufficiently implemented. Decentralisation was established as a foundational principle of the Kosovo Constitution. It captures the territorial aspect of the socially constructed nature of Kosovo's regional configurations, the municipalities, which constitute the basic unit of governance. Self-governance through local municipalities has emerged as the most controversial issue of the domestic implementation of Kosovo's independence. Decentralisation is a process without formal meaning. It lacks primary legislative powers, in contrast to devolution, which presupposes a dual polity (Cole 2004: 356). There is no clear attribution of competences. The latter are competitively determined, based on constituencies, and not federally guaranteed powers. Under decentralisation local government acts as an outpost of the state (Cole 2004: 356). Decentralisation therefore presupposes interaction. The fact that decentralisation in Kosovo is ethnically based reduces interdependence and interaction. Due to the absence of communication between the government and ethnic Serb majority municipalities in northern Kosovo, the Kosovo authorities have remained isolated from these areas. The evolving 'parallel' structures of self-governance without formal powers create a symbolic authority and a tangible legitimacy vacuum.

The implementation of decentralisation in Kosovo is in conflict with the European perspective. By creating ethnically homogeneous municipalities and endorsing them with self-governance in secondary areas, decentralisation restricts mobility and does not provide real self-governance to minorities. The initial EU view was to enable local communities to interact and implement self-governance, constructing from below a multi-ethnic Kosovo, whose final status would be secondary to democracy and democratic empowerment. In reality, decentralisation reinforces segregation. In the cases in which it is successfully implemented through local representation, it separates Kosovo's minorities from a relationship with the central institutions.

Decentralisation is unacceptable for Kosovo's political actors who demand full sovereignty and see it as an opportunity for the creation of parallel Serb structures. At the same time, decentralisation has permitted Kosovo to avoid formal recognition of its ethnically divided nature through ethnically based federalisation. EULEX represents the binding component and alleviating mechanism for such contradictory premises of polity construction. It is in the context of these political realities that the EUSR in his capacity as International Civilian Representative, acting outside EU policy deliberations, initiated a process of creation of new municipalities in majority Serb areas in northern Kosovo. The process has sought simultaneously to fill the legitimacy vacuum and extend the European perspective to the ethnic Serb minority in the absence of communication with the central government. Decentralisation has been replaced with the concept of minority integration. The EU increased its presence in northern Kosovo by opening a representation office (an 'EU house'), appointing an EU Facilitator, and increasing the visibility of projects implemented by the European Commission.[59]

EULEX governance has Europeanised the organisation of political life in Kosovo in principle but not in substance. For this reason, EU views on decentralisation and the multi-ethnic character of Kosovo have evolved during the post-status determination stage. The statements in Table 6.2 demonstrate this evolution against the background of persistent misfit between the normative value of self-determination, self-governance, and pluralism in a highly divided society.

The policy dimension of the EU's influence on Kosovo displays less conceptual controversy. It is coherently structured along the lines of a policy dialogue. Rule adoption is selective, combined with selective resistance. Kosovo benefits from the EU's advising and monitoring activities under EULEX which is instrumental to police training and keeping the Serb enclaves in northern Kosovo integrated. EULEX is otherwise regarded as a form of external control contrary to political aspirations for full sovereignty. Consistent opposition to the functional aspects of the mission, including the signing of a EULEX agreement on police cooperation with the Serbian authorities in August 2009, suggests strong adherence to the institutions of sovereignty. Although it is an element of international supervision, integral to the post-status stage, the executive competences of EULEX are at odds with the primacy of the Kosovo Constitution.

For political actors in Kosovo the conflict was resolved with the Declaration of Independence and there is no further incentive to cooperate, short of establishing contractual relations. Cooperation with the Euro-Atlantic structures for the Kosovo elites is voluntary. 'We are together, the Republic of Kosovo, the US and the EU. We have good joint achievements until now in Kosovo as a democratic and an independent state.'[60] Kosovo elites prioritise full independence and consider assisted sovereignty as a suboptimal solution. Despite the European perspective, there is little evidence of the existence of a public space with the potential for socialisation into EU norms and values. Because of the low administrative capacity of the political system and marginal viability of the Kosovo state to provide social goods, the benefits of European cooperation for the public remain limited (European Commission 2009a). The European Union is not a high salience issue in

Table 6.2 The European perspective in EU political discourse

Concept	European perspective
Standards implementation	**SG/HR Solana (2006)** Solana (S): The majority of Kosovars are Kosovars, and they do not have the differences you find in Bosnia and Herzegovina. Question (Q): No, most Kosovars are either Albanian or Serb. It is very important for them to be either Albanian or Serb. They are divided societies. S: But they will not be. Nobody is thinking about a line that would separate Albanians and Serbs. Q: At the moment there is a line - the Ibar river. S: All that will be solved ... That will be a part of the negotiations, but will require a real multi-ethnic state, where people go wherever they want, some refugees will be able to return and everyone will have the same rights as everyone else. Q: But most people do not want to live together in Kosovo. S: Then they don't comply with these standards, which are necessary to being part of Europe. Q: Which arguments does the EU have to convince Kosovo Serbs to stay in Kosovo? S: The only argument we have is our way of life. We are not going to change this because of Kosovo. If Kosovars want to become part of our family, they will have to adapt their lifestyle to the principles and values of this family, not the other way around. Q: But Kosovo Serbs are in a position where, even when internationals are present, they do not feel protected. If it were left to the Albanian majority to be responsible for this, they would feel even less protected. S: If that were the case, you could be sure Kosovo would not be part of the European family and not get the help that otherwise we are willing to give.

Monitoring, management, and assistance	*EULEX Head of Mission, Yves de Kermabon (2008–10)* Question: You have said Kosovo has European perspectives. You repeated this after the publication of the Progress Report for Kosovo 2009. Does this perspective have a timeline? When will Kosovo join the European Union? De Kermabon: There is no specific timeline because for us quality is more important than speed and substance is more important than a schedule. Whenever any country joins the European Union it has to meet all the conditions. Therefore, this work starts at home. We want to see Kosovo reinforcing its public administration, continue to reform the judiciary so that a rule of law can genuinely function in Kosovo, and intensify the fight against organised crime and corruption. These are critical issues; because the rule of law underpins every open society, every European Union society, and is therefore the starting point.
'EU house': integration of northern Kosovo	*EULEX Head of Mission, Yves de Kermabon (2010)* The objectives of the EU and EULEX for the north are the same as for the whole of Kosovo — to promote good governance, socio-economic development, the strengthening of the rule of law and local initiatives, while contributing to a stable and multi-ethnic society. The status quo is not sustainable, and therefore the EU wants to find pragmatic ways to move things forward in all these areas. *Diplomatic source, Brussels (2010)* The EU understands that we should win the hearts and souls of the northern Serbs if we want to reintegrate them. It cannot be imposed by Pristina or by some other place. As in the south of Kosovo, Serbs in the north should see the clear benefits of the EU Commission's engagement

Sources: BIRN interviews: Solana, RTK Pristina, 1 March 2006; de Kermabon, 2 February 2010, WAZ *EU Observer*, 23 March 2010.

Kosovo's domestic politics although issues related to the functioning of EULEX were present in the first post-independence local elections of November 2009.

The differences in responsiveness to EU influences in Kosovo and Serbia are due to the different social fabric of the Kosovar and Serbian societies: political pluralism and institutionalised civil society in Serbia and absence of civilian alternatives to the ethnicity-based social networks in Kosovo (Pond 2008: 107–8). The limitations of Europeanisation at the level of domestic politics remain more pronounced in Kosovo due to restricted opportunities for cross-cutting effects across its policy, political, and polity dimensions. As the European perspective is based on a contractual relationship, the extended timeframe of determination of the legality of Kosovo's independence has prevented the EU from developing a credible symmetrical relationship with the conflict parties. Such limitations reinforce the actor-centred resource-based model of Europeanisation of the Kosovo conflict without a fully autonomous mechanism of securing the desired outcome: Serbia's acceptance of an independent Kosovo.

Conclusion

The Kosovo/Serbia case is important for the big questions in this book: about the plausibility of a European model of conflict resolution, the effectiveness of conditionality derived from the mechanism of the Eastern European enlargement, and the sustainability of the alternative approach, that of separating conflict resolution from the European perspective and achieving settlement as a parallel process, not intertwined with the European perspective.

The EU's role in the resolution of the Kosovo conflict has been subsumed under EU governance dynamics. The latter's capacity to affect outcomes since the status determination stage has increased as a result of diverse policy instruments: the functionalist-managerial logic of EULEX, the European perspective of rapprochement to the perspective of European integration through policy conditionality and compliance, asymmetrical distribution of rewards and benefits, and the EU legitimising discourses. Actors' responses provide evidence of their 'encounters' with two separate models of Europeanisation: compliance-based for Serbia and resource-based for Kosovo. Although Serbia's acceptance of the Kosovo status remains an unresolved issue, its sustained preference for European integration points to the significance of Europeanising influences. Kosovo adopted a self-declared form of supervised independence, at odds with the definitive nature of the outcome.

Similarly to Cyprus, the Kosovo/Serbia case points to the need to revisit the workings of conditionality in the context of the EU enlargement policy, although from a different perspective. Membership conditionality is a key socialisation process deployed by the international institutions throughout the post-communist transition of Eastern Europe. Both Cyprus and Kosovo/Serbia demonstrate that conditionality has been modified and is now embedded in new approaches. Neither the US, nor the EU, initially applied conditionality to Kosovo and Serbia in a conventional way. The process of restructuring of relations at the post-conflict phase has relied on alternative strategies introducing a novel perspective on what constitutes settlement and conflict resolution.

The lack of a clear-cut incentives and rewards structure has determined a bottom-up process of change: the exercise of political choice through the externalisation of EU preferences. The Kosovo and Serbian elites adopted a European perspective not because the EU empowers reform-minded domestic actors and coalitions supporting conflict resolution but primarily along a sociological model – by shaping actors' perceptions of what they think they want. Political actors in Kosovo prefer independence but this idea is only possible within a European perspective. Actors make a choice that is a function of identities and interests prevalent in the EU. Although not all EU member states recognise Kosovo, they all believe in its European future as a political regime and democratic values of rule of law, respect for human rights, and regional cooperation. The strategy is possible through framing the issue as a European 'perspective' rather than an act of settlement. The emphasis in this model of impact is on future benefits rather than immediate distribution of outcomes. The EU took over from the UN in Kosovo and Europeanised the institutional dynamics of the conflict resolution process through institutional resources and policy innovation. It applied pressures and provided resources which the conflict parties could use to advance their positions (Kosovo) and reorder existing or develop new interests (Serbia).

The Kosovo case enriches our knowledge of Europeanisation. The EU does not create systematic top-down pressures through policy instruments as is the case in the conventional enlargement model. The managed enlargement model is not based on strict conditionality. It replaces the logic of Europeanisation through policy instruments with a persuasion model which is primarily actor-centred, based on changes in actors' perceptions and preferences, and externalises EU influence. The case also shows the limitations of Europeanisation through political conditionality. The actual process of state-building in Kosovo is at odds with the principle of self-determination: first, due to the requirement for protection of minority rights implemented through provisions for local self-governance which are difficult to reconcile with the majoritarian principles of the Kosovo Constitution and, second, due to the failure of the Standards before Status concept of the 2003–5 period which should have developed the foundations of a multi-ethnic Kosovo but was normatively unacceptable to the Kosovo Albanian majority. The EU thus had no viable mechanisms to affect the conflict by transforming ethnic and majority–minority relations between the conflict parties, except for the tools of external governance under the European perspective. Internationally, the European perspective subsumed other frameworks of mediation and settlement but has yet to acquire legitimacy as the ultimate system of conflict resolution.

The positive conclusion is that by Europeanising the UN-based institutional process of conflict resolution and extending the incentives and opportunities of the European perspective, the EU was capable of sustaining the conflict resolution process. In the absence of a conclusive legal determination, the EU has acted politically as a system based on the rule of law. There was no legal precedent or imperative for an EU unanimity on the recognition of independent Kosovo but the EU member states reached a consensus on assisting independence through the EULEX mission. In the absence of legal guidelines, the member states were not bound to a particular norm at the EU level. Their response to the status determination process is indicative of the Europeanising influences of integration also on the EU member states. Such influences demonstrate that European integration is not simply a gravitational model for Eastern Europe which it engages through rules and resources, but also a pluralist process of political exchange and voluntary participation.

'After all, the Balkans is ... a part of Europe?' (Banac 2009: 478).

Notes

1 US President George Bush statement, Tirana, June 2007: www.cnn.com/2007/POLITICS/06/10/bush.europe/.
2 US Secretary of State Condoleezza Rice statement, *VOA News*, 19 July 2007, http://www.voanews.com/english/archive/2007–07/2007–07–19–voa52.cfm?moddate=2007-07-19.
3 Serbia has stated that it will not recognise Kosovo even in the event that the International Court of Justice finds Kosovo's claim to independence justifiable. UN Security Council, 6144th Meeting (PM), 17 June 2009, Document SC/9683.
4 John Laughland, 'A Postmodern Declaration', *The Guardian* (online), 19 February 2008.
5 Olli Rehn, 'Lessons from EU enlargement for its future foreign policy', *Speech*, 22 October 2009, Document SPEECH/09/492. See also European Commission (2009c: 1) and Lavenex and Schimmelfennig (2009: 791).
6 FRY was comprised of Serbia (including Kosovo) and Montenegro.
7 The Contact Group was an international body of influential actors created to facilitate the settlement and implementation of sovereignty for Bosnia-Herzegovina and the resolution of the Kosovo crisis. Members of the Contact Group for Kosovo were France, Germany, Russia, the UK, the US, and Italy (since 1996).
8 On the campaigns, see Pond (1999, 2005) and Krieger (2001).
9 For details on the partition of Kosovo and the conditions of Serbia's withdrawal from the province, see Security Council Resolution 1244 authorising an international security presence in accordance with Article VII of the UN Charter and referral to preceding UNSCRs 1160, 1199, 1203, and 1239 (United Nations 1999).

10 Kai Eide, 'The situation in Kosovo', *Report to the Secretary-General of the United Nations*, ERP KiM Archive, Newsletter, 17 August 2004: www.kosovo.net/news/archive/2004/August_17/1.html.
11 Ibid, Article 49.
12 'Comprehensive Proposal for the Kosovo status settlement', 7 February 2007: www.unosek.org/unosek/en/statusproposal.html. See Weller (2008) on the negotiation process.
13 Report of the Secretary-General on the United Nations Interim Administration Mission in Kosovo, 10 June 2009, Document S/2009/300, p. 12.
14 According to the Helsinki Act (1975), the OSCE founding principles of interstate relations in Europe are: sovereign equality, refraining from the use of force, inviolability of borders, territorial integrity of states, peaceful settlement of conflicts, nonintervention in internal affairs, respect for human rights and fundamental freedoms, and equal rights and determination of peoples. See CSCE (1975), *Final Act*. CSCE: Helsinki: www.osce.org/docs/english/1990-1999/summits/helfa75e.htm.
15 EU, 2111th Council Meeting, General Affairs Council, Document PRES/98/227.
16 European Commission, 2000, *Press Release*, IP/00/65 of 21 January 2000.
17 Council Conclusions on the principle of conditionality governing the development of the European Union's relations with certain countries of south-east Europe, *Bulletin* 4-1997: http://europa.eu/bulletin/en/9704/p202001.htm.
18 Letter of the German Minister for Foreign Affairs on behalf of the European Union to Milosevic, 20 January 1999, Document 110 (Krieger 2001:195), Statement of the EU Presidency on behalf of the European Union on the conclusion of the Rambouillet conference, 23 February 1999, Document 145 (Krieger 2001: 279).
19 Letter from the Permanent Representative of Germany addressed to the President of the Security Council containing Chairman's summary of the deliberations on Kosovo at the informal meeting of the Heads of State and Government of the European Union. Document S/1999/429, 4 April 1999.
20 'A Stability Pact for South-Eastern Europe, 12 April 1999', Document 196, Krieger (2001: 354-6).
21 Common Position 1999/345/CFSP on the establishment of the Stability Pact for South-Eastern Europe, 17 May 1999, Document 202, Krieger (2001: 360).
22 Vienna European Council, 1998. *Presidency Conclusions*, 11-12 December.
23 SAP was launched at the Zagreb Summit of June 2000 and borrowed from the enlargement mechanism. Conditionality was derived from adherence to the Copenhagen criteria for acceding countries and Council Conclusions of April 1997 and June 1999. See Zagreb Summit, Final Declaration, 24 November 2000.
24 See General Affairs and External Relations Council, 2003 (2518th meeting), *Council Conclusions*, Luxembourg, 16 June 2003. Document 10369/03 (Presse 166), 19 June 2003.
25 Interview 1: Member state representative (1), GAERC (External Relations), Working Party on the Western Balkans Region, 28 June 2010, Brussels.
26 The Standards were: functioning institutions, enforcement of the rule of law, freedom of movement, right to return, market economy and economic development, clarity of property rights, normalisation of dialogue with Belgrade, transformation of the Kosovo Protection Corps (KPC), that is, a functioning state (van Meurs 2004: 68).
27 Report by Javier Solana, SG/HR for CFSP, on enhancing the EU's contribution in Kosovo, 18 February 2004, Council of the European Union, Document 6369/04, pp. 2-3.
28 Decentralisation was incorporated into the 'Comprehensive Proposal for the Kosovo Status Settlement' (UNMIK 2007: 7).
29 Summary note on the joint report by Javier Solana, EU HR for the CFSP, and Olli Rehn, EU Commissioner for Enlargement, on the future EU role and contribution in

Kosovo, Document CL05–162EN, 14 June 2005. Three subsequent notes were submitted to the Council in 2006 and 2007.
30 General Affairs and External Relations Council, 21 February 2005, Document 6420/05 (Presse 34), p. 11.
31 Press release by Jean Asselborn, 25 April 2005, GAERC meeting on the Subject of the Western Balkans and Kosovo: www.eu2005.lu/en/actualites/communiques/2005/04/25cag-balkans/index.html.
32 Kai Eide Report, n. 10, Art. 65.
33 Summary note on the joint report by SG/HR Javier Solana and Olli Rehn, EU Commissioner for Enlargement, on the state of preparations of the future EU and international presence in Kosovo, Document S111/07, 29 March 2007.
34 Summary note on the Solana/Rehn report, Document S200/06, July 2006.
35 Joint Action 2006/304/CFSP of 10 April 2006, adopted at the GAERC meeting in Luxembourg, Document EC06–095EN.
36 Interview 2: Member state representative (2), GAERC (External Relations), Working Party on the Western Balkans Region, 29 June 2010, Brussels.
37 Reference is made to UK Prime Minister Brown's address to the House of Commons, 13 December 2007: 'I think that Serbia's long-term interest truly depends on accepting the fact that relations with the EU are jeopardised if we cannot get a solution to the Kosovo problem' (www.pm.gov.uk/output/Page14070.asp).
38 HR Solana cited in *Agence Europe*, 21 November 2007.
39 French Foreign Minister Bernard Kouchner, Preliminary Statement, GAERC Press Conference, 18 February 2008: www.diplomatie.gouv.fr/en/article_imprim.php3?id_article=10846.
40 Portuguese Prime Minister Jose Socrates, Chairman of the European Council, quoted by Reuters: http://www.france24.com/france24Public/en/archives/news/world/20071215–kosovo-serbia-european-union-sarkozy-independence.php.
41 EP hearing 'EP – Kosovo – "standards and status" should go hand in hand', 26 January 2006: http://europa-eu-un.org/articles/en/article_4265_en.htm.
42 European Parliament, Committee on Foreign Affairs, 2006. Draft Report on the Future of Kosovo and the Role of the EU (Joost Lagendijk), Document 2006/2267(INI) and EP Resolution A6–0067/2007/P6–TA-PROV(2007)0097 of 29 March 2007 (*Official Journal* C 27 E, 31.1.2008, p. 207) and Report with a Proposal for a Recommendation to the Council on relations between the European Union and Serbia of the EU Committee on Foreign Affairs (Jelko Kacin, ALDE Report, Document B6–02020/2007 of 16 May 2007) and Proposal (Document 2007/2126(INI), 18 September 2007.
43 See 'Kosovo: A special case say MEPs', *Press Release*, European Parliament, REF.: 20080219IPR21734, 20 February 2008.
44 Interview 3: MEP, Group of the Progressive Alliance of Socialists and Democrats (S&D), Member of the Delegation for relations with Albania, Bosnia and Herzegovina, Serbia, Montenegro and Kosovo (DSEE), 22 June 2010, Brussels.
45 European Parliament, 'EU membership prospects for Albania and Kosovo', *Press release* REF. 20100707IPR78046, 8 July 2010.
46 The position of the Netherlands was that full cooperation with the ICTY, a core element of conditionality under the SAA, meant capture and extradition of General Mladic to the ICTY.
47 Joint Action 2008/124/CFSP of 4 February 2008, *Official Journal* L 42, 16 February 2008, p. 88.
48 Ten Guidelines principles: www.unosek.org/docref/Contact%20Group%20–%20Ten%20Guiding%20principles%20for%20Ahtisaari.pdf.
49 See Report of 29 June 2007, Document S/2007/395. See also Security Council, 5672nd meeting of 2 May 2007, Document S/PV.5672 (Provisional), p. 5.

50 RFE/RL *Newsline*, 11 (191), 12 September 2007.
51 See Patrick Moore, 'Analysis: Kosovo's rocky road to statehood', RFE/RL, 20 June 2008: www.rferl.org/content/Article/1144651.html.
52 UN Security Council, Presidential Statement, Document S/PRST/2008/44, UN Secretary-General Report on UNMIK, Document S/2008/692.
53 UN Security Council, 6144th Meeting (PM), 17 June 2009, SC/9683: www.un.org/News/Press/docs/2009/sc9683.doc.htm.
54 Statement by Tomislav Nicolic, then deputy leader of the ultranationalist Serbian Radical Party, quoted in: http://www.setimes.com/cocoon/setimes/xhtml/en_GB/features/setimes/features/2006/08/01/feature-01.
55 See report by Deutsche Welle, 'EU puts off Serbia trade decision despite Karadzic arrest': www.dw-world.de/dw/article/0,,3520791,00.html.
56 Interview with Vecernje Novosti daily, 7 July 2008: www.mfa.gov.yu/Bilteni/Engleski/b070708_e.html#N3.
57 Igor Jovanovic, 'Serbia, EU sign SAA', *Southeast European Times*, 30 April 2008: www.setimes.com/cocoon/setimes/xhtml/en_GB/features/setimes/features/2008/04/30/feature-01.
58 *Kosovo Declaration of Independence*, 17 February 2008: www.assembly-kosova.org/?cid=2,128,1635.
59 *EU Security and Defence News* (Newsletter), 4 (31 March 2010), p. 1: www.consilium.europa.eu/uedocs/cms_data/docs/pressdata/.../113640.pdf.
60 *New Kosova Report*, 'Kosovo offers own EULEX plan, final "no" on 6–points', 24 September 2009: www.newkosovareport.com.

7

Conclusion

> William the Silent, of the House of Orange, an indomitable champion of progress and tolerance in the world, once said: 'One does not need hope to act, or success to persevere.' How much greater, then, is our obligation to act and persevere; for we have hope, and we have success.
>
> Walter Hallstein (1972: 333)

This chapter reviews findings in the case studies and examines their implications for the literature on Europeanisation, European Union studies, and international conflict resolution. It presents an argument about the potential of the concept of Europeanisation and the governance perspective to explain the effects of European integration on conflicts. The chapter comments on the capacity of integration to affect conflict resolution through top-down adaptational pressures and functional expediencies relative to its role as a resource and opportunity in actor-centred processes.

Summary of the findings

The cases discussed in the empirical chapters permit the development of two lines of argument: on the substantive dimensions of the Europeanisation of conflict resolution and on the link between the European perspective on conflict resolution and conventional processes of international mediation. The core of the substantive hypothesis posits the necessary presence of a European space, the nature of EU governance effects – that they are not automatic but purposeful (the product of political action), and the responses they generate on behalf of political actors. The second argument refers to the link between European integration and issues relevant to conflict resolution in international relations theory, such as sovereignty, interdependence, peace processes, state building, and the constitutionalisation of conflict resolution. What do the findings in the individual chapters suggest about the effects of European integration on conflict resolution? Does integration bring conflict resolution closer to success? Is the EU the shorthand for conflict resolution in Europe?

According to Ladrech (1994: 84), the EU is not associated with 'revolutionary restructuring' of domestic political systems, but its effects are subtle. Olsen (2002: 934) contends that European integration is not a factor of radical change but its impact is meaningful. Jacoby (2006: 646) notes that such quiet successes are harder to spot as they look like plausible extensions to domestic trajectories rather than high-profile interventions. The evidence from the case studies points to a similar conclusion. An argument can be made that European integration is indispensable to conflict resolution because it provides a durable multilateral mechanism which sustains regional interactions and is conducive to long-term interest and value change. Similarly to other areas of inquiry, integration is a source of influence on institutions, actors, and processes pertaining to the domestic level of politics, as well as international interaction. European integration creates a variety of outcomes: transformative, institutional, and political (Hartlapp 2007). In the cases under examination those impacts have been primarily institutional and political. Without directly transforming the configuration of contested incompatibilities which conflicts represent, European integration is conducive to change in the distribution of preferences, values, and communication patterns between the parties with the potential to transform the conflict issue and lower conflict intensity. The outcomes of EU-based impact on conflict resolution are measured in terms of institutional creation, strengthening of governance structures, and politicising effects, such as growth of domestic political pluralism and actors' responsiveness to Europe. Such cumulative influences alter the institutional logic of processes of conflict resolution, determined by the relative positioning of negotiating and mediating parties, embeddedness of the constitutional features of a political settlement, and provision of a sustaining mechanism. The case studies support the argument about the Europeanisation of conflict resolution in Europe as they provide evidence of positive change along the two dimensions of the process: organisational logic, measured in terms of European influences on the blueprint for conflict resolution, institutions of settlement, and implementation, as well as change in actors' behaviour in the direction of attention and responsiveness to Europe.

Historically, the EU's involvement in such processes has ranged from advancing a new paradigm for the political organisation of the Franco-German relationship since the 1950s, to providing the institutional embeddedness of Northern Ireland's Good Friday Agreement in European norms, to extending the modalities of EU membership to the constitutive features of the political settlement in Cyprus, to direct responsibilities in state-building and reconciliation in Kosovo and Serbia.

Conflicts may not be unconditionally or immediately resolved as a result of such impacts, but in all cases the EU has provided input whose scope exceeds the objectives of reaching a settlement. In all cases international mediation has adopted EU principles and assigned a role for the EU, as a result of which the conflict resolution process has become intertwined with the dynamics of European integration. This argument challenges prior findings in the literature that European integration is more likely to generate conflict resolution effects primarily as a process of structural interdependence (Diez et al. 2008a).

Although from the perspective of domestic politics conflicts represent high-salience contested incompatibilities which reduce political space to the content of single-issue politics, all cases demonstrate that domestic interests in conflict are not homogeneous or exclusive, and that European integration has a capacity to reconfigure – unpack or rebundle – such distinctions. It acts as a factor of conflict resolution when it recasts conflict from a situation of single-issue politics into a multiple-issues arena. Change in the structure of political opportunities, leadership, and ideas matter. European integration is associated with processes of disaggregation of the conflict issue into individual high-salience issues, such as economic development, social disparities, and minority/majority relations represented by diverse societal interests. The sources of EU influence are derived from its universalist values, democratic norms of political behaviour, policy tools, incentives and resources, a *modus operandi* of institutionalisation of relationships, and legitimising discourses. Their principal value added is the opportunities and resources it provides for the conflict parties to act and re-rank their preferences towards multidimensional political objectives, rather than compromise and trade-offs. The mechanism of action of integration is that of pluralisation of interests. The extent of pluralisation accounts for the strength of the EU's impact on conflict resolution and its potential to generate transformative effects.

The evidence from the case studies points to considerable variation in the outcomes of EU involvement in conflict resolution. European integration and conflict resolution based on negotiation, mediation, and peacekeeping do not form necessarily interconnected arenas. There is also a tenuous relationship between the constitutional and political solutions to conflicts and the underlying processes of societal interaction and political mobilisation necessary to sustain them. The tendency is for European integration to acquire priority and establish itself as a higher goal for political actors, an objective valued more than gains obtained through a political settlement. In all cases regional integration serves either as a component of the settlement or its sustaining mechanism. The conflicts in Northern Ireland and Cyprus are two such examples.

The case of Northern Ireland demonstrates the cumulative impacts of regional integration. The EU's initial influence on the institutional logic of conflict resolution was weak because the parties valued a constitutional arrangement with power sharing. However, the constitutive features of the settlement adopted a European integration perspective. The cooperative environment of EU governance was indispensable to the implementation of the GFA. Its European dimension introduced new interests, channels of communication, partnerships sustaining devolution, and EU norms of nondiscrimination which shifted the standards of political behaviour towards Europe. In the case of Cyprus, the EU perspective was fully incorporated in the constitutional solution under the Annan Plan. European standards and the objective of EU membership served as the constitutive foundation of Kosovo's independence which emerged as a stable outcome of conflict resolution replacing a negotiated settlement. In the cases of Serbia and northern Cyprus, European integration emerged as a higher strategic goal than domestic preferences for a distributive settlement, and altered actors' perceptions of the value of settlement. The prospect of the EU accession of a united Cyprus was the principal coalition-building resource for advancing new interests in northern Cyprus after 2002. In the absence of a negotiated outcome, the context of EU membership further affected the dynamics of the Cyprus conflict by causing polarisation and shifts in public opinion. The salience of European issues continued to increase at the post-accession stage. However, the EU did not simultaneously provide resources for cross-border and intercommunal cooperation as an instrument of conflict resolution in Cyprus. Such resources remained contingent upon the political settlement and limited the transformative capacity of the European perspective. Despite such limitations, European integration accelerated the resumption of talks after 2008.

On Europeanisation

By transforming integration from an outcome into an explanatory variable, Europeanisation has offered important conceptual and analytical advantages in the examination of the case studies. Europeanisation approximates the EU's effects on conflict resolution to the impact of European integration on the domestic systems and actors. It demonstrates that such effects unfold according to multiple logics. Conventional accounts of the EU's influence on international outcomes grant ontological priority to its structural qualities to the detriment of political agency (Diez *et al.* 2008a) or approximate it to an institutional actor and a normative power (Manners 2002).

International institutions are associated with the binding rules of conduct and agreements which affect actors' behaviour. Evidence on the workings of international organisations suggests that actors have a variety of occasions to violate the rules of the regime. By contrast, there has been surprisingly little contention with regard to the EU's international roles pointing to the high legitimacy of the impact. The evolution of attitudes towards European integration is towards more, rather than less, acceptance. Such findings point to the need to better contextualise prior research which has found that integration may induce unintended and negative dynamics, not necessarily conducive to conflict resolution (Bourne 2003b; Noutcheva *et al.* 2004; Stetter *et al.* 2008: 221).

In order to differentiate European integration from institutional influences, its impact on conflict resolution should be examined based on the assumption that political agency is a constitutive element of the process. The effects of European integration cannot be reduced to those of interdependence and path dependency. In contrast to institutionalist theorising, Europeanisation demonstrates that European integration is not only a process of rule-making and rule adoption but also a resource and an opportunity for domestic actors to make reference to Europe and solve problems even in the absence of direct pressures. Europeanisation advances the new institutionalist perspective in integration theory by adding a political dimension. It looks beyond institutional outcomes, conventionally defined as compliance and identity change, and focuses on the political processes of choice, implementation, and empowerment (Olsen 2007). Its emphasis on interaction provides a better approach to examining domestic change in the context of European integration than propositions of global convergence, structural power, isomorphism, or institutional resilience. In short, Europeanisation contributes to uncovering the mechanism of action of integration as a political, rather than as an economic or an institutional, process. Europeanisation permits one to test the principal hypotheses in this study on the historical relevance and nature of integration influences on conflict resolution in Europe.

The two hypotheses on Europeanisation
Although the Europeanisation of conflicts has 'many faces' and displays across-case variation, the evidence suggests that there is a historical trend of subsuming conflict resolution dynamics under the logic of European integration. Such findings enrich Olsen's reconciliation thesis which holds that the principal role of European integration is that of maintaining a 'politically organised cooperative community in Europe' (Olsen 2007: 65). The historical argument does not suggest that all conflicts in Europe are resolved exclusively through European integration because it was originally formulated as a project of reconciliation and peace. European integration is not simply a recurring learning experience or reconciliation discourse, but a pattern of interactions. The reconciliation discourse is not based on actors' learning alone. It is embedded in the EU's policy-making dimension and sustained through the system of European governance. All cases provide evidence of the connection between the historical evolution of European integration and EU governance.

The Europeanisation through governance perspective approximates the EU's influence on conflict resolution to Europeanisation in other domains, emphasising the interplay between policy actions, political mobilisation, and EU discourses. The difference in the governance approach is that it permits an untangling of the ways in which European integration interacts with local actors.

CONCLUSION

The problem with interaction is that domestic interests in conflict situations tend to be highly aggregated. The opportunities to contribute to conflict resolution by building coalitions with pacifist and reform-minded elites are limited. All cases indicate that EU governance has served as the only viable corrective to the single-issue politics of conflicts. Historically, the sources of integration influences have been diverse, but they are all governance-based: institutional structures for joint policy-making in the Franco-German case, policy tools based on partnerships, programming, and cross-border cooperation in Northern Ireland, enlargement policy through conditionality, membership asymmetry, and direct assistance effects in the Cyprus conflict, and the instruments of foreign policy and enlargement in the Kosovo/Serbia case. The historical proposition on Europeanisation is related also to a less discussed issue in the literature on EU governance: that of its changing nature. There is a different mix of policy tools, political action, and discourse applied as material, cognitive, and normative resources to individual aspects of the conflict that the EU affects: communication between the parties and grievances (Northern Ireland), political organisation for settlement (Kosovo, Cyprus), or acceptability and sustainability of the outcome (Serbia). The measures of behavioural change range from expanded opportunities for subnational actors (Northern Ireland) to pressures for reform and resources for political mobilisation (Serbia) to lack of opposition to institutional arrangements in a European context (Serbia, northern Cyprus) and consensus over the goals of integration (all cases).

Exploring the relationship between the historical and substantive dimensions of Europeanisation is instrumental to addressing a key question on the Europeanisation agenda: is there a historically consistent and necessary link between European integration and conflict resolution? The chapters collectively demonstrate that although EU governance has a systemic quality as a *modus operandi* of European integration, there is no single 'EU' model of conflict resolution. The common features of the governance perspective are those of policy ideas and design, resource allocation, and implementation. Specific tools vary from managing diversity, implementing the rule of law, correcting for peripherality and marginalisation, and reconciliation initiatives. Early Europeanisation models are based on the assumption that the EU's involvement in conflict resolution reflects a permanent common preference valid for all conflicts and that preference is to prevent secession. Efforts to keep Bosnia-Herzegovina, Cyprus, and Serbia-Montenegro (prior to 2006) together are an expression of such priorities. The case of Kosovo demonstrates that there is no 'one size fits all' model but instead a contextualised governance process combining case-specific policy ideas, instruments, and political action. Theory posits European governance as a multi-mode, non-hierarchical network system (Wallace *et al.* 2005). A uniform governance process may not apply across cases. However, the case studies suggest that a common feature of the Europeanisation framework of conflict resolution is the triggering mechanism of misfit. The political recognition of misfit (institutional, policy, and normative) is a necessary condition for the tools and actors of European integration to get involved. This triggering mechanism was present in the own-initiative reports and resolutions of the European Parliament on the conflict in Northern Ireland, and the 1993 Opinion of the European Commission on Cyprus's eligibility for EU membership, as well as Commission initiatives and joint reports with the Secretary-General/High Representative on CFSP to the Council on Kosovo. The pluralist nature of European governance explains why there is no single source of EU impact on conflict resolution. There are multiple points of political initiative to trigger the process.

The structures and mechanisms of interaction under the system of EU governance therefore matter. European integration is not only a combination of pressures, incentives, and resources, but also a process of engagement. In order to alter the expectations and beliefs of political actors, integration needs to be 'present' in the domestic politics of the conflict parties as a governance system comprised of networks or institutionalised relationships (Della Porta and Caiani 2006: 80). European integration is more likely to be successful if it applies tools and resources which define its role beyond that of a context or opportunity for political action. In parallel with the increasing institutional proximity of the conflict parties to the EU, the conflict resolution process becomes more actor-centred. As the Cyprus case demonstrates, the capacity of European integration to have pressure and incentives effects diminishes accordingly.

On the EU framework of conflict resolution. How does Europeanisation take place?

The presence of a European space

The chapters demonstrate the necessity for a European space to exist as an arena relevant to conflict resolution which generates compliance pressures, provides resources, and creates opportunities for political reform. Governance tools, resources, and cognitive roadmaps have to be present for Europeanisation to take place. Symbolic references to integration are insufficient to induce a process of political change, otherwise indispensable for conflict resolution. Exadaktylos and Radaelli (2009) have argued that there is no responsiveness to EU influences without engagement and sources of impact.

In addition to the misfit proposition valid in other areas of Europeanisation research (Caporaso 2007; Cowles et al. 2001), the proposition on the necessity of a European space relevant to conflict resolution is an important common empirical finding in the case studies. Depending on its coherence and salience, the public sphere of European integration may be conducive to change in conflict dynamics and actors' preferences for conflict resolution and reconciliation. This regional public sphere was originally conceptualised by Jean Monnet as 'new politics'. It has evolved historically as institutionalisation of interdependencies, discourse and norm of reconciliation, expansion of the public domain through the pluralisation of interests and coalitions, and resources for political actors to advance new interests.

The idea of Europe is not only a normative structure or a normative power (Manners 2002) but a material and cognitive resource. The Franco-German case demonstrates the logic of creating peace by small steps and 'practical achievements': through problem-solving tools, capacity-building, and solidarity, as reflected in the ideas of the Schuman Declaration. Such measures may be contrasted with the 'symbolic' accession of Cyprus in the context of the conflict resolution process, which contained no problem-solving or solidarity-building mechanism. The case of the Greek Cypriot community indicates that the normative argument, that it is desirable to resolve conflicts in the expectation of EU membership, is not sufficient to generate agreement to the terms of a political settlement. The model depends on actors' proactive usage of Europe (Radaelli and Franchino 2004: 951).

Europe as a legitimising discourse
Similarly to other areas of Europeanisation in which domestic political actors use references to Europe in order to legitimise change (Schmidt 2004), all cases demonstrate that actors regard European integration as a source of conflict resolution. Strategies for political reform in Serbia, northern Cyprus, and Northern Ireland used a legitimising discourse anchored in Europe, similarly to domestic policy reform associated with the adoption of the single currency, gender equality, citizenship, employment, and other policies (Cowles *et al.* 2001).

A pro-European discourse does not mean that actors necessarily identify with Europe, but that they use the ideological legitimation of the reconciliation discourse for political action in order to advance their interests in the conflict resolution process. European integration has not fundamentally changed actors' identities in conflict. The cases of the DUP and Sinn Féin in Northern Ireland, nationalist elites in Cyprus, and mainstream political parties in Kosovo and Serbia demonstrate that social and political interests remain embedded in the concept of sovereignty and ethnic–national identity. However, political actors realise the importance of EU-derived economic benefits and political opportunities and seek participation in integration for their respective communities, thus opening new opportunities for domestic competition.

The model of outcome creation: pressures, resources, and political opportunities

Rather than looking for policy, polity, and political effects, the argument about the transformative nature of governance is based on the interaction occurring between policy tools, styles, and dialogues, and political mobilisation. The case studies indicate that the EU has the capacity to alter the constellation of domestic interests and the structure of political opportunities. The level of aggregation of political interests is an important intervening variable in all cases. Interest pluralisation may be slow due to elite intransigence sustained through constituency support. While Europeanisation depends on the constellation of domestic factors, such as influential actors, veto players, and other intervening variables, it affects the very constellation of domestic political interests and structures. Domestic resonance and veto points are not fixed and do not have a constant input; they change as a result of Europeanising influences. In the Franco-German case, the functional approach to separating cooperation in the coal and steel industry from the definitive political settlement through a peace treaty acted as a breakthrough mechanism for the pluralisation of domestic interests. In the case of Northern Ireland, the EU contributed to a parallel reconceptualisation of the conflict issue through policy innovation addressing issues of peripherality, economic deprivation, cross-border and cross-community cooperation, equality, nondiscrimination, and diversity.

At the same time, the cases demonstrate that a model of EU involvement in conflict resolution based on pressures and conditionality alone does not guarantee compliance and conflict resolution. Conflict reflects incompatible values and preferences. Unless opportunities develop to alter them, the high aggregation of societal interests around the conflict issue cannot trigger adaptation as it does in other areas in which top-down pressures affect actors' cost–benefit calculation. Credibility and plausibility of reward are applicable only to situations where the conflict parties are outside the EU membership base. If the EU is an internal actor to the conflict situation, the plausibility of reward is minimal. The Cyprus case demonstrates this point. Additional elements, such as control over agenda-setting, institutional procedures, and ideological resources, provide a more contextualised understanding of the workings of compliance (Moravcsik 1994). By shaping the agenda of conflict resolution and the modalities for discussion of alternative proposals, in parallel with demands and incentives for compliance, the EU expands the win-set for a given format of conflict resolution. It makes cooperation between the conflict parties possible by emphasising the significance of the European perspective. The expanded compliance model was applied vis-à-vis Serbia during the period 2006–9. While the EU observed strict conditionality in the process leading to the signature of the Stabilisation and Association Agreement (SAA), it also steered domestic politics towards prioritising a European perspective. Through linkages between the timing of the institutional procedure which led to the signing and ratification of the SAA, the electoral process in Serbia, and Kosovo's declaration of independence, the EU raised the domestic political costs of non-adoption of the European perspective to a prohibitively high level. Similarly, the discursive legitimation of EU values and ideas reshaped actors' preferences for conflict resolution which lowered the costs for adapting to EU pressures. In all cases, the shift of domestic preferences towards Europe has taken place in parallel with growing pluralism and political openness created through the legitimation of a strengthened institutional relationship with the EU.

Such findings point to the need for revisiting EU membership conditionality as a mechanism of conflict resolution in the wider Europe established in the literature so far (Coppieters *et al.* 2004). The Europeanisation of conflict resolution through the conditionality instruments of EU governance is a type of policy transfer and a way of structuring the relationship between the EU and the conflict parties. The underlying link is developed through the agenda-setting process, leaving political actors with few alternative options for pursuing conflict resolution outside European integration, a restricted set of institutional procedures for voicing opposition, and ideological legitimation of a certain path of conflict resolution endorsed by the EU and steered into a European perspective. Such approaches leave domestic political actors parties to a conflict with limited options to resist settlement and lower the political costs of accepting its distributive nature.

The evidence suggests that the costs of opposing EU initiatives and decisions relevant to conflict resolution have increased in all cases. Despite the failure of the Annan Plan to bring about a constitutional settlement in Cyprus, direct intercommunal talks have been reinstated. The discourse on conflict resolution as a political priority of Turkey's EU accession, while met with resistance, has not led to a reversal of its foreign policy course. Rising electoral support for nationalist politicians within the Greek and Turkish Cypriot communities has not led to an escalation of the conflict. On the contrary, intercommunal talks are shaped by the need to respond positively to the EU's expectations for resolving regional issues. The declining costs of opposition to EU initiatives and decision-making have strengthened the conflict resolution agenda and the autonomy of the EU proposals. Questions about the opportunities for participation in European integration are central to the conflict resolution discourse in northern Cyprus and Serbia. In Kosovo, where the domestic public sphere prioritises self-determination and sovereignty, the costs of unilateralism have increased. Political elites continue to lower their resistance to EU-based initiatives.

According to Jacoby (2006), domestic reform occurs through a coalition between external actors (including the EU) and domestic reformers. However, the issue area of conflict resolution makes it difficult for external actors to engage in a coalition-building process with reformers and empower local constituencies in support of conflict resolution, unless a change in values and preferences takes place. European integration is more effective when it offers an independent perspective with the potential to emerge as a broadly shared political preference. The EU approach to inducing political change is therefore one of capacity- rather than coalition-building.

The capacity-building model is better positioned to advance conflict resolution than a top-down model relying on pressures and incentives, as the latter generates reactive responses. The top-down model is more likely to induce resistance and entrenchment, if no new interests are created. Incentives, such as membership or funding opportunities, are limited if they do not provide actors with resources for problem-solving. The Franco-German case illustrates the importance of building problem-solving capacity through European integration. As a result of the reconceptualisation of the bilateral relationship into a multilateral functionalist arrangement, actors acquired direct problem-solving capacities, a new arena for political action, and new policy ideas. In all cases, the domestic legitimation of the European integration was high and grew in parallel with the strengthening of EU governance initiatives.

Explaining variation in outcomes
The success of conflict resolution is measured in terms of reduction of conflict intensity, increasing tolerance, weakening salience of veto points, empowerment of reformers, increased capacity for problem-solving, and the consolidation of European integration. The Europeanisation literature explains variation in outcomes with the presence of mediating factors, such as institutional structures, aggregation of societal cleavages, veto players, and social institutions (Börzel and Risse 2000; Cowles *et al.* 2001; Schmidt 2002).

The findings in the empirical chapters point to a second source of variation based on the proposition about interaction effects between the policy, political, and polity dimensions of EU governance. Following this argument, low levels of EU impact on conflict resolution are explained by the limited transferability of pressures across the policy, political, and institutional dimensions of integration. The EU's policy influences in Kosovo and Cyprus have remained isolated from domestic politics. The idea of Europe often remains isolated from political discourse and polity traditions despite the policy effects of European governance. The ambiguity of the European perspective based on universalist values does not resonate with nationalist ideas reflected in concepts of self-determination and territorial exclusivity otherwise typical of the single-issue context of conflict. The benefits of EU membership may not be the primary objective of conflict parties which prioritise statehood (Coppieters *et al.* 2004). The opportunity for cross-cutting influences between the policy, political, and institutional domains of European integration compensate for that inherent limitation. The Cyprus case demonstrates that, in the presence of intervening variables, membership conditionality either has not performed or has been dropped, while the policy and polity effects of Europeanisation have been significant. Cyprus, Northern Ireland, and Kosovo apply varieties of policy conditionality thus redefining the prevalent conceptualisation of the Europeanisation of conflict resolution as EU membership conditionality. The latter type of conditionality has remained a valid tool of conflict resolution in the case of Serbia.

Revisiting conditionality as a tool of Europeanisation

The application of conditionality to conflict resolution is a widely cited tool of EU influence (Coppieters *et al.* 2004; Diez *et al.* 2008b; Tocci 2007). The presence of unresolved conflicts is at odds with EU norms of the rule of law, democratic governance, and membership criteria. The resolution of conflicts as a condition for EU membership is therefore normatively defined, although its practical application is primarily incentives-based (Buiter 2005: 30).

As the cases above indicate, membership conditionality implemented through the incentive and punishment structures of the EU enlargement process does not engage the broader aspects of programming conditionality and compliance applied to individual policy domains, such as the EU regional and cohesion policy, the single internal market, and the foreign policy domain outside enlargement. A broadened conceptualisation of conditionality offers a better assessment of the scope and modalities of EU impact on conflict resolution.

Buiter (2005: 31) distinguishes between process and institutional conditionality as two distinct types of conditionality valid with regard to members and non-members alike. Process conditionality pertains to political or governance issues. Membership conditionality is institutional and reflects EU influences associated with its enlargement policy. This type of conditionality places the burden of terminating conflicts on political systems and communities that have the incentive of acquiring EU membership. The requirement for such prior actions necessarily excludes the EU as an agent of conflict resolution. The incentive structure of a future membership lacks credibility as it fails to formulate a process of tying performance to political action for resolving conflicts. The principal deficiency of models which link the conflict resolution effects of European integration to membership conditionality is the limited space they reserve for interaction between the EU and the conflict parties as political actors. Because conflict resolution is a condition for membership, there is no necessity for the EU to apply resources with a capacity to induce learning, provide assistance and resources, and facilitate consensus-building. Membership conditionality in the area of conflict resolution usually applies to cases of acute contradiction with EU norms where no domestic consensus exists, political objectives are contested, and no institutional capacity to attain them develops. This case is the exact opposite to conditionality defined as the fulfilment of policy conditions according to the blueprint for programme-based conditionality developed by the international financial institutions (IFIs) with an emphasis on macro-economic stability, sound institutions, economic growth, and poverty reduction. It is this latter type of conditionality that the EU increasingly applies to conflict situations by opening up communication channels and offering assistance and resources, such as pre-accession aid. Conditionality in this sense is not about actions and responses but about incentives, accommodation, modified opportunity structures, and a shift towards new values and interests replacing entrenched ones.

It is obvious that the EU's enlargement policy increasingly has distanced itself from membership conditionality. The dynamics of conflict resolution in Cyprus and Kosovo demonstrate the rationale of de-linking EU membership from conflict resolution but guiding the process through the conditionality of its policy preferences and norm adherence. As the case of Turkey demonstrates, membership conditionality has a limited and rather short-term effectiveness.

When conflict resolution is applied as a condition for establishing an institutional proximity between the EU and the conflict parties, the relationship is based on governance and political principles which link political and economic reform to conflict resolution. Conditionality is not simply an *ex ante* instrument to resolve conflicts but a question of preferences and the desired end-state of a process of domestic reform and adaptation. EU membership conditionality is therefore not only institutional but a type of policy conditionality which sets mutually acceptable goals and outlines effective ways of achieving them through policy dialogue and local ownership. Similarly to IFIs' process conditionality, EU conditionality has shifted from an *ex ante* to an *ex post* type which functions as a problem-solving device. It does not require the resolution of conflicts in order to gain access to the benefits of EU membership (although the membership perspective is not excluded) but relies on the anticipated benefits of the EU's engagement in domestic reform. *Ex post* conditionality provides policy designs, supports institutions, builds a capacity to act, and develops into a monitoring device for progress in the implementation of European norms and principles of governance. It is process- and performance-oriented rather than exclusively linked to conflict resolution as a condition for EU membership.

From this perspective, the evidence of limited effectiveness of conditionality in the case studies is explained by its asymmetrical application which undermines its legitimacy in developing local ownership. The failure to implement conditionality in the case of the Greek Cypriot community and the contrasting application of conditionality vis-à-vis Turkey has created a highly asymmetrical situation which undermines the effectiveness of key EU policy tools.

The outcomes of conditionality across cases demonstrate that Europeanisation is a primarily rational process, although it differs from propositions about the rational socialisation influences of international institutions according to Schimmelfennig *et al.* (2006). Europeanisation is not limited to cost–benefit calculations and automatic adjustment but implies local ownership and actor consensus on the desired goals and benefits. The latter include freedoms, participation in European integration through partnerships, economic growth, market access, and mobility. Monitoring is achieved through action plans, progress reports, and benchmarking which permits the conflict parties to develop relationships with the EU independently, albeit in the same direction. This latter broadened conditionality model was implemented in the Kosovo/Serbia case.

Europeanisation and international conflict resolution

The second group of conclusions derived from the case studies refers to the macro-political perspective on conflict resolution. The empirical findings permit the addressing of key issues in the international relations literature on conflict resolution with regard to sovereignty, interdependence, peace, international organisation, secession, and constitutional versus political approaches to settlement.

On sovereignty and interdependence
The patterns of Europeanisation revealed in the case studies show that European integration does not replace the notion of sovereignty as an organising political principle. France and Germany eventually developed bilateral cooperation outside the EEC. Northern Ireland maintains a strictly constitutional solution of power sharing and devolution within the nation-state. Cyprus still debates sovereign rights. Kosovo's sovereignty status is being determined through classical Westphalian notions of statehood, independence, and external recognition. In all these cases, European integration has facilitated the process of conflict resolution achieved through viable political communities and, more importantly, enriched the constitutive solution with post-sovereignty features.

By contrast, the case studies fail to validate the interdependence thesis which posits a deterministic relationship between the creation of interdependencies between the parties to a conflict and conflict resolution. All cases demonstrate some degree of interdependence, strengthened through a European perspective, but the findings point to high variation in the gains achieved through interdependence only. Outcomes vary from a balanced relationship in Northern Ireland and the classical Franco-German reconciliation, to limited interdependence between the two Cypriot communities despite EU membership, to a triangular relationship in the Kosovo/Serbia case whereby the conflict parties have remained functionally independent and pursue a European perspective separately.

Territorial organisation of politics: constitutional solutions

It is a widely shared claim that conflict resolution through separation, assimilation, and negotiated solutions may produce a settlement but not the resolution of conflicts. The implementation of settlement requires structural techniques which change the institutional format of the conflict by altering the incentive structures of political actors (Horowitz 1990: 121). The principal constraint of international conflict resolution is that mediation stops when such structural incentives are created. Such structural approaches are territorial autonomy and electoral systems. According to Horowitz (1990), both represent policy instruments which ultimately do not resolve conflict as they function at the level of elites and hierarchical political organisations within groups. Most of these outcomes do not address the ontological needs of individuals and communities in conflict for security, identity, and human development (Montville 1990: 535). The constitutionalisation of conflict resolution provides a framework and no content for the termination of conflicts. Both violence and electoral process have served as an expression of the Northern Ireland conflict by allowing the parties to maintain opposing political goals in a system of governance without consensus (Rose 1990: 133).

The structural–constitutional methods of settlement and conflict resolution need a sustaining mechanism. Such arrangements do not ultimately depend on structure but on process. Conflicts also evolve and settlement often is unable to match an evolving configuration of political and societal interests. As Reiterer (2003: 27) contends, the Cyprus conflict was different in 1960, 1964, and 1974. Similarly, important aspects of the Northern Ireland conflict have moved from constitutional issues to issues of governance. Devolution under the GFA is not a complete structure and has required a sustaining process.

The changing preferences of international mediation from power sharing (Northern Ireland) to majoritarian models (Kosovo) suggest that consociational arrangements have a limited capacity to perform. They are not governance and performance-oriented systems as they tend to fragment policy-making (Rothchild and Roeder 2005). While guaranteeing minority rights and the policy interests of the conflict parties through elite accommodation, power sharing depends on the strict segmentation of social groups. It reinforces distinct group-based vertical political structures which undermine the very functioning of the system based on minority veto. An overarching consensus through the shared legitimacy of the consociational arrangement is difficult to achieve. Societal cohesion in a post-conflict environment is lacking as sustainable political structures depend on inter-elite bargaining on behalf of groups separated by formal boundaries. Northern Ireland and Cyprus demonstrate that communities remain divided and such arrangements tend to reinforce divisions. Elite accommodation remains separate from societal forces. Social pressures for conflict resolution remain minimal as a new culture of social partnerships does not develop spontaneously unless new common identities emerge. The cases of Northern Ireland and Cyprus demonstrate that identity change has yet to take place.

At the other end of the spectrum, majoritarian constitutional forms lack the constitutional rigidity of formal separate jurisdictions that sustain autonomy, although they guarantee performance. Minority rights are protected through self-governance. Although implemented in territorial terms through decentralisation, self-governance does not ensure the policy representation of minority interests. As a constitutional method of conflict resolution, the concept of decentralisation, short of federalism, is an unstable arrangement and is conceptually controversial (Lake and Rothchild 2005: 112). Authority in decentralised systems is neither shared nor dispersed. It pertains only to secondary and tertiary policy areas, such as health care, education, and local services. Similarly to power sharing, decentralisation reinforces segmentation without guaranteeing minority protection and participation in policy formulation in primary areas. It effectively reinforces the losing position of minorities by preventing them from forming cross-cutting alliances with other groups along functional principles. The Kosovo case demonstrates that decentralisation cannot exist as a method of governance only. It is inseparable from the constitutional demarcation of competences between the central and the subnational level of policy-making. The power dividing principles of the Kosovo settlement have become unsustainable due to the lack of legitimacy for the ethnic Serb minority.

The only possible corrective and sustaining process in all cases of constitutionalisation of political settlement is one based on governance, not government. The case studies examined in this book demonstrate that the EU has had diverse influences on conflict situations under all varieties of constitutional arrangements: from pooled sovereignty (France/Germany) and power sharing (Northern Ireland) to bizonal federalism and territorial division (Cyprus) to constitutional accommodation of minority self-governance short of federalism (Kosovo/Serbia). All cases demonstrate that European integration has offered additional structural incentives by enhancing political processes of exchange, cooperation, and compromise.

The constitutionalisation of conflict resolution therefore may be questioned on principled and performance grounds. The issues of conflict resolution through settlement and sustained management of the outcome are not fully separable. A coherent political community based on commonality of objectives, common interests, empathy, and values which are at the origin of conflict transformation and reconciliation may not be attained through constitutional forms alone.

A reflection on European integration, democracy, and conflict resolution
Findings in the literature point to the role of domestic actors in conflict resolution, suggesting that international solutions cannot be imposed. The success of international administration in conflict situations depends on the

domestic constellation of forces and a commitment to democracy (Tansey 2009: 226). For this reason, conflict resolution has moved away from purely constitutional solutions, unless a sustaining process is in place to manage diversity and recreate common interests.

The relationship between self-determination, democracy, and governance is not always underlined in the literature but is central to explaining the EU's role in international conflict resolution. Ladrech (1994: 79) has noted that a certain detachment occurs through European-level influences on domestic politics, as the nation-state is not exclusive in framing the relationships between networks and structures. Participation in European integration leads to differentiation at the domestic level understood as the creation of new interests and enhanced competition on functional terms. While such interests do not necessarily produce interdependencies, they are conducive to increased political pluralism.

In all cases discussed in this book, such democracy gains may be linked to a growing appreciation for the European Union. The latter's positive influence on democracy in Europe is traced back to the post-Second World War origins of European integration, the democratic rules for self-determination in former Yugoslavia advanced by the Badinter Commission, the 1993 Copenhagen criteria for EU membership, the pluralist principles of EU policy-making, and treaty-based adherence to democratic values in the EU's enlargement and foreign policy.

The policy recommendation that follows refers to the need to establish complementarity between constitutional and political approaches to settlement and conflict resolution by encouraging domestic political pluralism.

Bibliography

Ackerman, A. (1994), 'Reconciliation as a peace-building process in postwar Europe: The Franco-German case', *Peace and Change* 19 (3): 229–50.
Adams, G. (1994), *Free Ireland: Towards a Lasting Peace*. Niwot, CO: Roberts Rinehart Publishers.
Adenauer, K. (1965), *Erinnerungen 1945–1953*. Stuttgart: Deutsche Verlags-Anstalt.
Ágh, A. (1999), 'Processes of democratization in the East Central European and Balkan states: Sovereignty-related conflicts in the context of Europeanization', *Communist and Post-Communist Studies* 32: 263–79.
Albert, M., Diez, T. and Stetter, S. (2008), 'The transformative power of integration: Conceptualizing border conflicts'. In Diez, T., Albert, M. and Stetter, S. (eds), *The European Union and Border Conflicts: The Power of Integration and Association*, 13–32. Cambridge: Cambridge University Press.
Allen, D. (2005), 'Cohesion and structural funds'. In Wallace, H., Wallace, W. and Pollack, M. (eds), *Policy Making in the European Union*, 213–41. Oxford: Oxford University Press.
Anderson, J. (2002), 'Europeanization and the transformation of the democratic polity, 1845–2000', *Journal of Common Market Studies* 40 (5): 793–822.
Anderson, J. and Goodman, J. (1994a), 'Northern Ireland: Dependency, class and cross-border integration in the European Union', *Capital and Class* 54 (Autumn): 13–23.
Anderson, J. and Goodman, J. (1994b), 'European and Irish integration: Contradictions of regionalism and nationalism', *European Urban and Regional Studies* 1 (1): 49–62.
Arthur, P. (1994), 'Negotiating the Northern Ireland problem: Track one or track two diplomacy?', *Government and Opposition* 25 (4): 403–18.
Aspinwall, M. and Schneider, G. (eds) (2001), *The Rules of Integration: The Institutionalist Approach to European Studies*. Manchester: Manchester University Press.
Auel, K. and Benz, A. (2005), 'The politics of adaptation: The Europeanisation of national parliamentary systems', *The Journal of Legislative Studies* 11 (3/4): 372–93.
Aughey, A. (1990), 'The troubles in Northern Ireland: 20 years on', *Talking Politics* 3 (1): 17–22.
Aughey, A. (2005), *The Politics of Northern Ireland: Beyond the Belfast Agreement*. Abingdon and New York: Routledge.
Avery, G. and Balfour, R. (eds) (2008), 'The Balkans in Europe: Containment or transformation? Twelve ideas for action', *EPC Working Paper* 31. Brussels: European Policy Centre.
Axt, H.-J., Milososki, A. and Schwarz, O. (2006a), 'Europäisierung – ein weites Feld. Literaturbericht und Forschungsfragen', *Politische Vierteljahresschrift* 28 (1): 136–49.
Axt, H.-J., Schwarz, O. and Wiegand, S. (2006b), 'The Greek-Macedonian name dispute in the light of the "hexagon of conflict resolution"', *Politicka Misla* 4 (16): 67–77.
Bache, I. (2000), 'Europeanization and partnership: Exploring and explaining variations in policy transfer', *Queen's Papers on Europeanisation* 8/2000.
Bache, I. (2008), *Europeanization and Multilevel Governance: Cohesion Policy in the European Union and Britain*. Boulder and New York: Rowman and Littlefield Publishers.
Bahcheli, T. (2001), 'The lure of economic prosperity versus ethno-nationalism: Turkish Cypriots, the European Union option, and the resolution of the conflict in Cyprus'. In

Keating, M. and McGarry, J. (eds), *Minority Nationalism and the Changing International Order*, 203–22. Oxford: Oxford University Press.

Bahcheli, T. (2006), 'Turkey's quest for EU membership and the Cyprus problem'. In Joseph, J. (ed.), *Turkey and the European Union: Internal Dynamics and External Challenges*, 161-78. Basingstoke: Palgrave Macmillan.

Banac, I. (2009), 'What happened in the Balkans (or rather ex Yugoslavia)?', *East European Politics and Societies* 23 (4): 461–78.

Banchoff, T. and Smith, M. P. (eds) (1999), *Legitimacy and the European Union: The Contested Polity*. London: Routledge.

Barnett, M. and Duval, R. (2005), 'Power in International Politics', *International Organization* 59 (1): 39–75.

Barry, J. (2005), 'Northern Ireland, identities and Europe'. In Robyn, R. (ed.), *The Changing Face of European Identity*, 186–206. Abingdon and New York: Routledge.

Ben-Porat, G. (2005), 'Between power and hegemony: Business communities in peace processes', *Review of International Studies* 31 (2): 325–48.

Benz, A. and Eberlein, B. (1999), 'The Europeanization of regional policies: Patterns of multi-level governance', *Journal of European Public Policy* 6 (2): 329–48.

Berger, F. (1997), 'Les sidérurgistes français et allemands face à l'Europe: Convergence et divergences de conception et d'intérêts 1932–1952', *Journal of European Integration History* 3 (2): 35–52.

Bew, P. and Meehan, E. (1994), 'Regions and borders: Controversies in Northern Ireland about the European Union', *Journal of European Public Policy* 1 (1): 95–111.

Beyer, H. (1986), *Robert Schuman: L'Europe par la Reconciliation Franco-Allemande*. Lausanne: Fondation Jean Monnet pour l'Europe, Centre de Recherches Européennes.

Bitsch, M.-T. (1995), 'La première institution internationale: Du nouveau sur l'histoire de la haute autorité de la Communauté Européenne du Charbon et d'Acier', *Journal of European Integration History* 1 (1): 128–41.

Bitsch, M.-T. (2004), 'La triple option de Paris: Pour une France supranationale et sectorielle autour d'un noyau franco-allemand'. In Wilkens, A. (ed.), *Le Plan Schuman dans l'Histoire: Intérêts Nationaux et Projet Européen*, 149–68. Brussels: Bruylant.

Blankenhorn, H. (1980), *Verständnis und Verständigung, Blätter eines politischen Tagebuchs 1949 bis 1979*. Frankfurt: Propyläen Verlag.

Blockmans, S., Wouters, J. and Ruys, T. (eds) (2010), *The European Union and Peacebuilding: Policy and Legal Aspects*. The Hague: Asser Press.

Börzel, T. (1999), 'Towards convergence in Europe? Institutional adaptation to Europeanisation in Germany and Spain', *Journal of Common Market Studies* 39 (4): 573–96.

Börzel, T. (2002a), *States and Regions in the European Union: Institutional Adaptation in Germany and Spain*, Cambridge: Cambridge University Press.

Börzel, T. (2002b), 'Pace-setting, foot-dragging, and fence-sitting: Member state responses to Europeanization', *Journal of Common Market Studies* 40 (2): 193–214.

Börzel, T. and Risse, T. (2000), 'When Europe hits home: Europeanization and domestic change', *European Integration online Papers* (EIoP) 4 (15): http://eiop.or.at/eiop/texte/2000–015a.htm.

Börzel, T. and Risse, T. (2003), 'Conceptualizing the domestic impact of Europe'. In Featherstone, K. and Radaelli, C. (eds), *The Politics of Europeanization*, 57–80. Oxford: Oxford University Press.

Börzel, T. and Risse, T. (2007), 'Europeanization: The domestic impact of European Union politics'. In Jørgensen, K., Pollack, M. and Rosamond, B. (eds), *Handbook of European Union Politics*, 483–504. London: SAGE Publications.

Bossuat, G. (1995), 'Les hauts fonctionnaires français et le processus d'unité en Europe occidentale d'Alger à Rome (1943–1958)', *Journal of European Integration History* 1 (1): 87–110.

Bossuat, G. (2001), *Les Fondateurs de l'Europe Unie*. Paris: Belin.
Boulding, K. (1972), *The Economics of Peace*. Freeport, NJ: Books for Libraries Press.
Bourne, A. (2003a), 'European integration and conflict resolution in the Basque country, Northern Ireland and Cyprus', *Perspectives on European Politics & Society* 4 (3): 391–415.
Bourne, A. (2003b), 'The EU, conflict and cooperation within member states', *Perspectives on European Politics & Society* 4 (3): 529–35.
Bourne, A. (ed.) (2004), *The EU and Territorial Politics in Member States: Conflict or Cooperation?* Leiden: Brill Academic Publishers.
Breakwell, G. (2004), 'Identity change in the context of the growing influence of European Union institutions'. In Herrmann, R., Risse, T. and Brewer, M. (eds), *Transnational Identities: Becoming European in the EU*, 25–39. Lanham, MD: Rowman & Littlefield Publishers, Inc.
Bromberger, M. and Bromberger, S. (1969), *Jean Monnet and the United States of Europe*. New York: Coward-McCann.
Bruce, S. (2007), *Paisley: Religion and Politics in Northern Ireland*. Oxford: Oxford University Press.
Brugmans, H. (1965), *L'Idée Européenne*. Bruges: De Tempel.
Buckland, P. (1979), *The Factory of Grievances: Devoted Government in Northern Ireland 1921–1939*. Dublin: Gill and Macmillan.
Buiter, W. (2005), 'Country ownership: A term whose time has gone'. In Koeberle, S., Bedova, H., Silarszky, P. and Verheven, G., *Conditionality Revisited: Concepts, Experiences, and Lessons*, 27–32. Washington, DC: The World Bank.
Bull, H. (1982), 'Civilian power Europe: A contradiction in terms', *Journal of Common Market Studies* 21 (1–2): 149–64.
Buller, J. (2006), 'Contesting Europeanization: Agents, institutions and narratives in British monetary policy', *West European Politics* 29 (3): 389–409.
Bulmer, S. (1983), 'Domestic politics and European Community policy-making', *Journal of Common Market Studies* 21 (4): 349–63.
Bulmer, S. (1985), 'The European Council's first decade: Between interdependence and domestic politics', *Journal of Common Market Studies* 24 (2): 89–104.
Bulmer, S. (2005), 'The EU and its member states: An overview'. In Bulmer, S. and Lequesne, C. (eds), *The EU and its Member States: An Overview*, 1–21. Oxford: Oxford University Press.
Bulmer, S. (2007), 'Theorizing Europeanization'. In Graziano, P. and Vink, M. (eds), *Europeanization: New Research Agendas*, 46–58. Basingstoke: Palgrave Macmillan.
Bulmer, S. and Lequesne, C. (eds) (2005), *The Member State and the European Union*. Oxford: Oxford University Press.
Bulmer, S. and Radaelli, C. (2005), 'The Europeanization of national policy'. In Bulmer, S. and Lequesne, C. (eds), *The EU and its Member States: An Overview*, 338–59. Oxford: Oxford University Press.
Bursens, P. (2007), 'Europeanization of state structures'. In Graziano, P. and Vink, M. (eds), *Europeanization: New Research Agendas*, 121–37. Houndmills and New York: Palgrave Macmillan.
Bussière, E. (1997), 'Les milieux économiques face à l'Europe au XXième siècle', *Journal of European Integration History* 3 (2): 5–21.
Byrne, S. (2001a), 'Tranformational conflict resolution and the Northern Ireland conflict', *International Journal on World Peace* 18 (2): 3–22.
Byrne, S. (2001b), 'Consociational and civic society approaches to peacebuilding in Northern Ireland', *Journal of Peace Research* 38 (3): 327–52.
Caporaso, J. (2007), 'The three worlds of regional integration theory'. In Graziano, P. and Vink, M. (eds), *Europeanization: New Research Agendas*, 23–34. Houndmills and New York: Palgrave Macmillan.

Caporaso, J. and Stone Sweet, A. (2001), 'Conclusion: Institutional logics of European integration'. In Stone Sweet, A., Sandholtz, W. and Fligstein, N. (eds), *The Institutionalization of Europe*, 221–36. Oxford: Oxford University Press.

Caporaso, J. and Wittenbrinck, J. (2006), 'The new modes of governance and political authority in Europe', *Journal of European Public Policy* 13 (3): 471–80.

Charillon, F. (2005), 'The EU as a security regime', *European Foreign Affairs Review* 10: 517–33.

Checkel, J. (2001), 'Why comply? Social learning and European identity change', *International Organization* 55 (3): 553–88.

Checkel, J. (2005), 'International institutions and socialization in Europe: Introduction and framework', *International Organization* 59 (4): 801–26.

Christiansen, T. (1997), 'Tensions of European governance: Politicized bureaucracy and multiple accountability in the European Commission', *Journal of European Public Policy*, 4 (1): 73–90.

Christiansen, T., Jørgensen, K. and Wiener, A. (eds) (2001), *The Social Construction of Europe*. London: Sage.

Christou, G. (2006), 'The European Union: What role in the Cyprus conflict?', *International Spectator* 41 (2): 19–31.

Cole, A. (2004), 'Devolution and decentralization in Wales and Brittany: A framework for evaluation', *International Journal of Urban and Regional Research* 28 (2): 354–68.

Cole, A. and Drake, H. (2000), 'The Europeanization of the French polity: Continuity, change and adaptation', *Journal of European Public Policy* 7 (1): 26–43.

Conseil de l'Europe-Assemblée consultative-Commission des Affaires générales (ed.) (1953), *Le statut futur de la Sarre*: www.ena.lu/report_marinus_van_der_goes_van _naters_future_status_saar_26_august_1953-2-35853.

Constaninou, C. and Papadakis, Y. (2002), 'The Cypriot state(s) *in situ*: Cross-ethnic contact and the discourse of recognition'. In Diez, T. (ed.), *The European Union and the Cyprus Conflict: Modern Conflict, Postmodern Union*, 73–97. Manchester: Manchester University Press.

Coppieters, B. (2007), 'Kosovo merits "special status as part of the EU"'. *Policy Brief* 143 (October 2007). Brussels: Centre for European Policy Research.

Coppieters, B., Huysseune, M., Emerson, M., Tocci, N. and Vahl, M. (2003), 'European institutional models as instruments of conflict resolution in the divided states in the European periphery'. *CEPS Working Document* 195 (July 2003). Brussels: Centre for European Policy Studies.

Coppieters, B., Emerson, M., Huysseune, M., Kovziridze, T., Noutcheva, G., Tocci, N. and Vahl, M. (2004), *Europeanization and Conflict Resolution: Case Studies from the European Periphery*. Ghent: Academia Press.

Cortell, A. and Peterson, S. (2001), 'Limiting the unintended consequences of institutional change', *Comparative Political Studies* 34 (7): 768–99.

Cortright, D. (2007), 'Sanctions and stability pacts: The economic tools of peacemaking'. In Zartman, W. (ed.) *Peacemaking in International Conflict: Methods and Techniques*, 385–418. Washington, DC: United States Institute of Peace.

Coufoudakis, V. (2006), *Cyprus: Contemporary Problem in Historical Perspective*. Minneapolis: Modern Greek Studies, University of Minnesota.

Council of the European Union (1995), *General Affairs Council, Conclusions*, 6 March. Brussels: General Secretariat of the Council.

Council of the European Union (2003), 'Protocol No 10 on Cyprus', *Official Journal of the European Union* L 236/955 (23 September 2003).

Council of the European Union (2004), 'Report of SG/HR Solana on enhancing the EU contribution in Kosovo', *Document* 6369/04. Brussels, February 17, 2004.

Council of the European Union (2005), *Presidency Conclusions*, Brussels European

Council, 16 and 17 June 2005. Brussels: Council of the European Union.
Council of the European Union (2005), *Enlargement: Turkey. Declaration by the European Community and Its Member States* (21 September 2005: Brussels). Document 12541/05 (Presse 243).
Council of the European Union (2006), *Council Conclusions*, Brussels, 14–15 December.
Court of Auditors (2000), 'Special report No 7/2000 concerning the International Fund for Ireland and the Special support programme for peace and reconciliation in Northern Ireland and the border counties of Ireland, together with the Commission's replies'. *Official Journal of the European Communities* C146 (25 May 2000). Brussels: European Communities.
Cowles, M. G., Caporaso, J. and Risse, T. (eds) (2001), *Transforming Europe. Europeanization and Domestic Political Change*. Ithaca, NY: Cornell University Press.
Daviter, F. (2007), 'Policy framing in the EU', *Journal of European Public Policy* 14 (4): 654–66.
De Bièvre, D. and Neuhold, C. (eds) (2007), *Dynamics and Obstacles of European Governance*. Chetenham: Edward Elgar.
Defrance, C. (2004), 'La France et l'autorité internationale de la Ruhr'. In Wilkens, A., Gerbet, P., Schwabe, K., Bitsch, M.-T., and Bossuat, P. (eds), *Le Plan Schuman dans l'Histoire: Intérêts Nationaux et Projet Européen*, 123–45. Paris: Bruylant.
De Gaulle, C. (1970), *Discours et Messages. Tome II: Dans l'Attente*. Paris: Plon.
Delanty, G. (1996), 'Northern Ireland in a Europe of regions', *The Political Quarterly* 67 (2): 127–34.
Della Porta, D. and Caiani, M. (2006), 'The Europeanization of public discourse in Italy: A top-down process?', *European Union Politics* 7 (1): 77–112.
Demetriou, O. (2008), 'Catalysis, catachresis: The EU's impact on the Cyprus conflict'. In Diez, T., Albert, M. and Stetter, S. (eds), *The European Union and Border Conflicts: The Power of Integration and Association*, 64–93. Cambridge: Cambridge University Press.
de Reuck, A. (1984), 'The logic of conflict: Its origins, development, and resolution'. In Banks, M. (ed.), *Conflict in World Society: A New Perspective on International Relations*, 96–111. New York: St. Martin's Press.
Deutsch, K. (1966), 'Integration and arms control in the European political environment: A summary report', *American Political Science Review* 60 (2): 354–65.
Deutsch, K. *et al.* (1957), *Political Community and the North Atlantic Area: International Organization in the Light of Historical Experience*. Princeton: Princeton University Press.
Diez, T. (1999), 'Speaking "Europe": The politics of integration discourse', *Journal of European Public Policy* 6 (4): 598–613.
Diez, T. (2000), 'The imposition of governance: Transforming foreign policy through EU enlargement', *Copenhagen Peace Research Institute Working Paper* (August 2000), CIAO: www.ciaonet.org/wps/dit04/index.html.
Diez, T. (2001), 'Europe as a discursive battleground: Discourse analysis and European integration studies', *Cooperation and Conflict* 36 (1): 5–38.
Diez, T. (ed.) (2002a), *The EU and the Cyprus Conflict: Modern Conflict, Postmodern Union*. Manchester: Manchester University Press.
Diez, T. (2002b), 'Introduction: Cyprus and the European Union as a political and theoretical problem'. In Diez, T. (ed.), *The EU and the Cyprus Conflict: Modern Conflict, Postmodern Union*, 1–13. Manchester: Manchester University Press.
Diez, T. (2002c), 'Last exit to paradise? The European Union, the Cyprus conflict, and the problematic "catalytic effect"'. In Diez, T. (ed), *The European Union and the Cyprus Conflict: Modern Conflict, Postmodern Union*, 139–62. Manchester: Manchester University Press.
Diez, T. (2002d), 'Conclusion: Cyprus and the European Union – an opening'. In Diez, T. (ed), *The European Union and the Cyprus Conflict: Modern Conflict, Postmodern Union*, 203–12. Manchester: Manchester University Press.

Diez, T. (2006), 'The EU and the transformation of conflictual constitutional systems'. In Giegerich, T., *The EU Accession of Cyprus: Key to the Political and Legal Solution of an 'Insoluble' Ethnic Conflict?*, 219–31. Baden-Baden: Nomos.

Diez, T., Albert, M. and Stetter, S. (2006), 'The European Union and border conflicts: The transformative power of integration', *International Organization* 60 (3): 563–93.

Diez, T., Albert, M. and Stetter, S. (eds) (2008a), *The European Union and Border Conflicts: The Power of Integration and Association*. Cambridge: Cambridge University Press.

Diez, T., Albert, M. and Stetter, S. (2008b), 'Introduction'. In Diez, T., Albert, M. and Stetter, S. (eds), *The European Union and Border Conflicts: The Power of Integration and Association*, 1–12. Cambridge: Cambridge University Press.

Diez, T. and Pace, M. (2007), 'Normative power Europe and conflict transformation'. Paper presented at the 2007 EUSA Conference, Montreal.

Diez, T. and Tocci, N. (2009), 'Conclusion'. In Diez, T. and Tocci, N. (eds), *Cyprus: A Conflict at the Crossroads*, 293–300. Manchester: Manchester University Press.

Dixon, P. (2000), 'European integration and Irish disunity'. In Byrne, S. and Irvin, C. (eds), *Reconcilable Differences: Turning Points in Ethnopolitical Conflict*, 174–89. West Hartford: Kumarian Press.

Duchêne, F. (1972), 'Europe's role in world peace'. In Mayne, R. (ed.), *Europe Tomorrow: Sixteen Europeans Look Ahead*, 32–47. London: Fontana.

du Toit, P. (2003), 'Why post-settlement settlements?', *Journal of Democracy* 14 (3): 104–18.

Eberlein, B. and Kerwer, D. (2002), 'Theorising the new modes of European Union governance', *European Integration online Papers* (EIoP) 6 (5): http://eiop.or.at/eiop/texte/2002-005a.htm.

Eberlein, B. and Kerwer, D. (2004), 'New governance in the European Union: A theoretical perspective', *Journal of Common Market Studies* 42 (1): 121–42.

Economides, S. (2005), 'The Europeanization of Greek foreign policy', *West European Politics* 28 (2): 471–91.

Eilstrup-Sangiovanni, M. and Verdier, D. (2005), 'European integration as a solution to war', *European Journal of International Relations* 11 (1): 99–135.

Emerson, M. (2002), 'The wider-Europe as the European Union's friendly Monroe Doctrine'. *CEPS Policy Brief* 27. Brussels: Centre for European Policy Studies, 2002.

Emerson, M. (2008), 'The struggle for a civilised wider European order: Elements for a European security strategy', *CEPS Working Document* No. 307 (October).

Emerson, M. and Noutcheva, G. (2004), 'Europeanisation as a gravity model of democratisation'. *CEPS Working Document* 214: 1–27.

Emerson, M., Vahl, M., Coppieters, B., Huysseune, M., Koviridze, T., Noutcheva, G. and Tocci, N. (2004), 'Elements of comparison and synthesis'. In Coppieters, B., Emerson, M., Huysseune, M., Kovziridze, T., Noutcheva, G., Tocci, N. and Vahl, M., *Europeanization and Conflict Resolution: Case Studies from the European Periphery*, 233–56. Ghent: Academia Press.

Epstein, R. and Sedelmeier, U. (2008), 'Beyond conditionality: International institutions in postcommunist Europe after enlargement', *Journal of European Public Policy* 15 (6): 795–805.

Eriksen, E. (2006), 'The EU – a cosmopolitan polity?', *Journal of European Public Policy* 13 (2): 252–69.

European Commission (1960), *Third General Report on the Activities of the Community*. Brussels: European Economic Community.

European Commission (1984), *Communication from the Commission to the European Parliament Concerning the Impact of Community Policies and Actions in Northern Ireland*. COM(84) 613 final. Brussels: European Commission.

European Commission (1989), *Community Support Framework 1989–93 for the Development and Structural Adjustment of the Regions Whose Development Is Lagging*

behind (Objective 1): United Kingdom (Northern Ireland). Brussels: EC, Commission.
European Commission (1993), 'Commission opinion on the application by the Republic of Cyprus for membership'. COM (93) 313 final, 30 June 1993. *Bulletin of the European Communities*, Supplement 5/93.
European Commission (1994), 'A Special Support Programme for Peace and Reconciliation in Northern Ireland'. *Communication from the Commission to the Council and the European Parliament.* COM(94) 607 final, 7 December 1994. Brussels: Commission of the European Communities.
European Commission (1998a), *Peace and Reconciliation: An Imaginative Approach to the European Programme for Northern Ireland and the Border Counties of Ireland.* Luxembourg: Office for Official Publications of the European Communities.
European Commission (1998b) 'Regular report from the Commission on Cyprus' progress towards accession': http://ec.europa.eu/enlargement/archives/pdf/key_documents/1998/cyprus_en.pdf.
European Commission (1999), *Communication from the Commission to the Council and the European Parliament on the Stabilisation and Association process for the countries of South-Eastern Europe.* COM(1999) 235 final, 26 May 1999. Brussels: Commission of the European Communities.
European Commission (2001), *Communication from the Commission on Conflict Prevention.* COM(2001) 211 final, 11 April 2001. Brussels.
European Commission (2003), 'Wider Europe—Neighborhood: A New Framework for Relations with our Eastern and Southern Neighbors'. *Communication from the European Commission to the Council and the European Parliament.* COM(2003) 104 final. Brussels: European Commission.
European Commission (2004a), *Proposal for a Council Regulation on the special conditions for trade with those areas of the Republic of Cyprus in which the Government of Cyprus does not exercise effective control.* COM(2004) 466 final (2004/0148 (ACC)).
European Commission (2004b), 'The Stabilisation and Association process for South East Europe', *Report from the Commission* COM(2004) 202 final.
European Commission (2004c), 'Commission Proposes Comprehensive Measures to End Isolation of Turkish Cypriot Community'. *Press Release* IP/04/857. Brussels: European Commission.
European Commission (2005), 'A European future for Kosovo'. *Communication from the Commission.* COM(2005) 156 final, 20 April 2005. Brussels: Commission of the European Communities.
European Commission (2006), 'Report on the International Fund for Ireland pursuant to Article 5 of Council Regulation (EC) No 177/2005'. *Communication from the Commission* COM(2006) 563 final. Brussels: Commission of the European Communities.
European Commission (2007a), Flash Eurobarometer No. 203: EU attitudes in the UK. Brussels: European Commission.
European Commission (2007b), 'Annual Report 2006–2007 on the implementation of Community Assistance under Council Regulation (EC) No 389/2006 of 27 February 2006 Establishing an Instrument of Financial Support for Encouraging the Economic Development of the Turkish Community'. *Communication from the Commission to the European Parliament and the Council,* COM(2007) 536 final. Brussels: Commission of the European Communities.
European Commission (2007c), *The European Commission, 1958–72: History and Memories.* Luxembourg: Office for Official Publications of the European Commission.
European Commission (2008a), *Commission Staff Working Document on the Report of the Northern Ireland Task Force.* SEC(2008) 447, 7 April 2008. Brussels: Commission of the European Communities.

European Commission (2008b), 'Annual report on the implementation of Council Regulation (EC) 866/2004 of 29 April 2004 and the situation resulting from its application', *Communication from the Commission* COM(2008) 529 final, 27 August 2008, Brussels, Commission of the European Communities.

European Commission (2008c), *Commission staff working document, Turkey 2008 Progress Report accompanying the Communication by the Commission to the European Parliamentand the Council 'Enlargement Strategy and Main Challenges 2008–2009'*, SEC(2008) 2699, 5 November 2008. Brussels.

European Commission (2009a), 'Kosovo under UNSCR 1244/99 2009 Progress Report'. Commission Staff Working Document. SEC(2009) 1340, 14 October 2009. Brussels: Commission of the European Communities.

European Commission (2009b), 'Kosovo – Fulfilling Its European Perspective'. *Communication from the Commission to the European Parliament and the Council.* COM(2009) 5343, 14 October 2009. Brussels: Commission of the European Communities.

European Commission (2009c), *Enlargement Strategy 2009*: http://ec.europa.eu /enlargement/pdf/key_documents/2009/strategy_paper_2009_en.pdf.

European Council (1997), *Luxembourg European Council, Presidency Conclusions* (12–13 December).

European Council (1999), *Helsinki European Council, Presidency Conclusions* (10–11 December).

European Council (2004), 'Council Regulation (EC) No 866/2004 of 29 April 2004 on a Regime under Article 2 of Protocol No 10 to the Act of Accession', *Official Journal of the European Union L 161* (30 April 2004).

European Council (2005), *Presidency Conclusions*. Brussels, 16–17 June 2005.

European Council (2006a), 'Council Regulation (EC) No 389/2006', *Official Journal of the European Union L 65/5*: 5–8.

European Council (2006b), *Presidency Conclusions*. Brussels, 14–15 December 2006.

European Council (2007), *Presidency Conclusions*. Brussels, 14 December 2007.

European Economic and Social Committee (2008), 'Opinion of the European Economic and Social Committee on the Role of the EU in the Northern Ireland Peace Process'. *Document* SC/029–CESE 1686/2008. Brussels: EESC: www.eesc.europa.eu/documents /opinions/ces1686–2008_ac_en.doc.

European Parliament (1964), *Towards Political Union: A Selection of Documents*. Luxembourg: European Parliament (Political Committee).

European Parliament (1981), *Report on Community Regional Policy and Northern Ireland* (May 4, 1981, Rapporteur S. Martin). Document 1–177/81. Brussels: European Parliament.

European Parliament (1982), *Selection of Texts Concerning Institutional Matters of the Community from 1950 to 1982*. Luxembourg: European Parliament (Committee on Institutional Affairs).

European Parliament (1983), 'Report on EEC-Cyprus economic and trade relations', *Working Documents 1983–1984*. Document 1–501/83. Brussels: European Communities.

European Parliament (1984a), 'Report drawn up on behalf of the Political Affairs Committee on the situation in Northern Ireland' (Rapporteur Mr. Haagerup). *European Parliament Working Document* 1–1526/83, 9 March.

European Parliament, (1984b), *Debates*, No. 2–316 (12 September).

European Parliament (1987), 'Report on the regional problems of Ireland' (Rapporteur: John Hume). *Document* A2–109/87. Brussels: European Parliament.

European Parliament (1990), 'Rapport sur l'Action de Développement Régional de la Communauté en Faveur de l'Irlande du Nord au Royaume-Uni' (Rapporteur Sylviane Ainardi). *Documents* PE: 1990/0277 A3. p. 18. Luxembourg: European Parliament.

European Parliament (2004), 'Resolution on Cyprus', *Official Journal of the European*

Union C 104E (30 April 2004), 720–22.
European Parliament (2005), 'Recommendation on the Proposal for a Council regulation Amending Regulation (EC) No 1260/1999'. *Session Document* A6–0001/2005. Brussels: European Parliament.
European Parliament (2006), 'European Parliament Resolution on Turkey's progress towards Accession'. P6_TA(2006)0381. Brussels: European Parliament.
European Parliament (2007), 'European Parliament Resolution on the future of Kosovo and the role of the EU'. P6_TA(2007)0097. Brussels: European Parliament.
European Union (2002), 'Consolidated Version of the Treaty on the European Union', *Official Journal of the European Communities* C 325/5, 24 December 2002.
European Union (2003), 'Protocol No 10: On Cyprus to the Act of Accession', *Official Journal of the European Union* (23 September 2003), 955.
European Union (2008a). 'Consolidated version of the Treaty on European Union', *Official Journal of the European Union* C/115 (9 May 2008): 13–45.
European Union (2008b). 'Consolidated version of the Treaty on the functioning of the European Union', *Official Journal of the European Union* C/115 (9 May 2008): 47–199.
Exadaktylos, T. and Radaelli, C. (2009), 'Research design in European studies: The case of Europeanisation', *Journal of Common Market Studies* 47 (3): 507–30.
Farrell, M. (ed.) (2005), 'EU external relations: Exporting the EU model of governance?', *European Foreign Affairs Review* 10 (4): 451–62.
Featherstone, K. and Radaelli, C. (eds) (2003), *The Politics of Europeanization*. Oxford: Oxford University Press.
Feld, W. (1981), *West Germany and the European Community: Changing Interests and Competing Policy Objectives*. New York: Praeger.
Feldman, L.G. (1999a), 'The principle and practice of reconciliation and German foreign policy: Relations with France, Israel, Poland and the Czech Republic', *International Affairs* 75 (2): 333–56.
Feldman, L.G. (1999b), 'Reconciliation and legitimacy: Foreign relations and enlargement of the European Union'. In Banchoff, T. and Smith, M. (eds), *Legitimacy and the European Union: The Contested Polity*, 66–90. London and New York: Routledge.
Féron, E. and Lisaniler, F. G. (2009), 'The Cyprus conflict in a comparative perspective: Assessing the impact of European integration'. In Diez, T. and Tocci, N. (eds), *Cyprus: A Conflict at the Crossroads*, 198–216, Manchester: Manchester University Press.
FitzGerald, G. (1972), *Towards a New Ireland*. London: Charles Knight and Co.
Fondation Jean Monnet pour l'Europe (FJME) (1985), *L'Europe: Une Longue Marche*. Lausanne: Centre de Recherches sur l'Europe.
Forsyth, M. (1967), 'The political objectives of European integration', *International Affairs (Royal Institute of International Affairs 1944)* 43 (3): 483–97.
Forsyth, M. (1981), *Unions of States: The Theory and Practice of Confederation*. New York: Holmes & Meier Publishers.
Franck, T. (1992), 'The emerging right to democratic governance', *American Journal of International Law* 86 (1): 46–91.
Frevert, U. (2005), 'Europeanizing Germany's twentieth century', *History & Memory* 17 (1–2): 87–116.
Frost, B. (1991), *The Politics of Peace*. London: Darton, Longman and Todd.
Funck, B., Pizzani, L. and Buncko, M. (2003), 'Overview'. In Funck, B. and Pizzani, L. (eds), *European Integration, Regional Policy, and Growth*, 1–17. Washington, DC: The World Bank.
Gallagher, T. (2001), *Outcast Europe: The Balkans, 1789–1989: From the Ottomans to Milošević*. London and New York: Routledge.
Galtung, J. (1973), *The European Community: A Superpower in the Making*, Oslo: Universitetsforlaget.

Garrett, G. and Weingast, B. (1993), 'Ideas, interests and institutions: Constructing the European Community's internal market'. In Goldstein, J. and Keohane, R. (eds), *Ideas and Foreign Policy: Beliefs, Institutions and Political Change*, 173–206. London: Cornell University Press.

Geiger, T. (2000), 'Europeanization on the periphery: Irish elite responses to European integration'. In Harmsen, R. and Wilson, T. (eds), *Europeanization: Institutions, Identities and Citizenship. Yearbook of European Studies* 14: 105–33.

George, A. and Bennett, A. (2005), *Case Studies and Theory Development*. Cambridge and London: MIT Press.

Gerbet, P. (2004), 'La naissance du Plan Schuman'. In Wilkens, A. (ed.), *Le Plan Schuman dans l'Histoire: Intérêts Nationaux et Projet Européen*, 13–51. Brussels: Bruylant.

Gerbet, P., de La Serre, F. and Nalifyan, G. (eds) (1998), *L'Union Politique de l'Europe: Jalons et Textes*. Paris: Documentation Française.

Giegerich, T. (2006), 'The EU accession of Cyprus and the fate of the Annan Plan – concluding remarks'. In Giegerich, T. (ed.), *The EU Accession of Cyprus – Key to the Political and Legal Solution of an 'Insoluble' Ethnic Conflict?* (Proceedings of the International and Interdisciplinary Conference held in Bremen on 14–15 May 2004), 253–80. Baden-Baden: Nomos.

Gillingham, J. (1991), *Coal, Steel, and the Rebirth of Europe, 1945–1955: The Germans and French from Ruhr Conflict to Economic Community*. Cambridge: Cambridge University Press.

Gillingham, J. (2003), *European Integration, 1950–2003: Super State or New Market Economy?* Cambridge: Cambridge University Press.

Gillingham, J. (2006), 'The German problem'. In Dinan, D. (ed.), *Origins and Evolution of the EU*, 55–83. Oxford: Oxford University Press.

Ginsberg, R. (1999), 'Conceptualizing the European Union as an international actor: Narrowing the theoretical capabilities-expectations gap', *Journal of Common Market Studies* 37 (3): 429–54.

Ginsberg, R. (2001), *The European Union in International Politics: Baptism by Fire*. Lanham: Rowman & Littlefield Publishers, Inc.

Ginsberg, R. (2007), *Demystifying the European Union: The Enduring Logic of Regional Integration*. Lanham: Rowman & Littlefield Publishers, Inc.

Glenn, J. (2004), 'From nation-states to member states: Accession negotiations as an instrument of Europeanization', *Comparative European Politics* 2 (1): 3–28.

Goetz, K. (2000), 'European integration and national executives: A cause in search of effect?', *West European Politics* 23 (4): 211–31.

Goetz, K. (2006), 'Territory, temporality and clustered Europeanization', *Political Science Series*. Vienna: Institute for Advanced Studies.

Goldsmith, M. (2003), 'Variable geometry, multilevel governance: European Integration and subnational government in the new millennium'. In Featherstone, K. and Radaelli, C. (eds), *The Politics of Europeanization*, 112–33. Oxford: Oxford University Press.

Goodman, J. (1996), *Nationalism and Transnationalism: The National Conflict in Ireland and European Union Integration*. Aldershot: Avebury Press.

Goodman, J. (1998), *Dis/Agreeing Ireland: Contexts, Obstacles, Hopes*. Pluto Press: London.

Goodman, J. (2000), *Single Europe, Single Ireland? Uneven Development in Process*. Dublin and Portland, OR: Irish Academic Press.

Gorz, A. (1967), *Strategy for Labor: A Radical Proposal*. Boston: Beacon Press.

Gourevitch, P. (1978), 'The second image reversed: The international sources of domestic politics', *International Organization* 32 (4): 881–912.

Grabbe, H. (2001), 'How does Europeanization affect CEE governance? Conditionality, diffusion and diversity', *Journal of European Public Policy* (Special Issue) 8 (6):1020.

Grabbe, H. (2003), 'Europeanization goes east: Power and uncertainty in the EU accession process'. In Featherstone, K. and Radaelli, C. (eds), *The Politics of Europeanization*, 303–27. Oxford: Oxford University Press.

Grabbe, H. (2006), *The EU's Transformative Power: Europeanization Through Conditionality in Central and Eastern Europe*. Basingstoke: Palgrave Macmillan.

Graziano, P. and Vink, M. (eds) (2007), *Europeanization: New Research Agendas*. Basingstoke: Palgrave Macmillan.

Greer, J. (2001), *Partnership Governance in Northern Ireland: Improving Performance*. Aldershot: Ashgate.

Grossman, E. (2006), 'Europeanization as an interactive process: German public banks meet EU state aid policy', *Journal of Common Market Studies* 29 (3): 255–67.

Grote, J. and Lang, A. (2003), 'Europeanization and organizational change in national trade associations: An organizational ecology perspective'. In Featherstone, K. and Radaelli, C. (eds), *The Politics of Europeanization*, 225–54. Oxford: Oxford University Press.

Gruner, W. (2007), 'The German debate on Europe: Expectations – positions – perceptions – ideas (1945–2005)'. In Bitsch, M.-T., Loth, W. and Barthel, C. (eds), *Cultures Politiques, Opinions Publiques et Intégration Européenne*, 61–86. Brussels: Buylant.

Guelke, A. (1988), *Northern Ireland: The International Perspective*. Dublin: Gill & Macmillan.

Guelke, A. (ed.) (2004), *Democracy and Ethnic Conflict: Advancing Peace in Deeply Divided Societies*. New York: Palgrave Macmillan.

Gurr, Ted R. (1968), 'A causal model of civil strife: A comparative analysis using new indices', *American Political Science Review* 62 (4): 1104–24.

Güven-Lisaniler, F. and Rodriguez, L. (2002), 'The social and economic impact of EU membership on Northern Cyprus'. In Diez, T. (ed.), *The European Union and the Cyprus Conflict: Modern Conflict, Postmodern Union*, 181–202. Manchester: Manchester University Press.

Haas, E. (1968), *The Uniting of Europe: Political, Social, and Economic Forces, 1950–1957*. Stanford, CA: Stanford University Press.

Haas, E. (1970), 'The Study of regional integration: Reflections on the joy and anguish of pretheorizing', *International Organization* 24 (4): 607–44.

Haas, E. (2001), 'Does constructivism subsume neo-functionalism?'. In Christiansen, T., Jørgensen, K. E. and Wiener, A. (eds), *The Social Construction of Europe*, 22–31. London: Sage.

Hadjipavlou-Trigeorgis, M. and Trigeorgis, L. (1993), 'Cyprus: An evolutionary approach to conflict resolution', *Journal of Conflict Resolution* 37 (2): 340–60.

Hainsworth, P. (1981), 'Northern Ireland: A European role?', *Journal of Common Market Studies* 20 (1): 1–15.

Hainsworth, P. and Morrow, D. (1993), 'Northern Ireland: European region – European problem', *Études Irlandaises* 18: 131–46.

Hakki, M. (ed.) (2007), *The Cyprus Issue: A Documentary History 1878–2007*. London and New York: I.B. Tauris.

Hallstein, W. (1961), *Economic Integration and Political Unity in Europe*. London: Information Service of the European Communities.

Hallstein, W. (1972), *Europe in the Making*. London: Allen & Unwin.

Hamber, B. and Kelly, G. (2004), 'A working definition of reconciliation', *Occasional Paper*. Belfast: Democratic Dialogue.

Hamber, B. and Kelly, G. (eds) (2005a), 'Reconciliation: Rhetoric or relevant?' *Report* 17 (February 2005). Belfast: Democratic Dialogue: www.brandonhamber.com/publications/report-dd17.pdf.

Hamber, B. and Kelly, G. (2005b), 'Views from Northern Ireland'. In Hamber, B. and Kelly, G. (eds), *Report* 17 (February 2005), 21–33. Belfast Democratic Diologue.

Hannay, D. (2006), 'Cyprus: Lessons from the debacle of 2004 and the way ahead', *The Round Table* 95 (383): 95–100.

Harmsen, R. and Wilson, T. (eds) (2000), 'Europeanization: Institution, identities and citizenship', *Yearbook of European Studies*, 14.

Harpaz, G. (2007), 'Normative power Europe and the problem of a legitimacy deficit: An Israeli perspective', *European Foreign Affairs Review* 12: 89–109.

Harris, E. (2003), 'New forms of identity in contemporary Europe', *Perspectives on European Politics and Societies* 4 (1): 13–33.

Hartlapp, M. (2007), 'On enforcement, management and persuasion: Different logics of implementation policy in the EU and the ILO', *Journal of Common Market Studies* 45 (3): 653–74.

Hasenclever, A., Mayer, P., and Rittberger, V. (2008), *Theories of International Regimes*. Cambridge: Cambridge University Press.

Haverland, M. (2005), 'Does the EU cause domestic developments? The problem of case selection in Europeanization research', *European Integration Online Papers* (EIoP) 9:2: http://eiop.or.at/eiop/texte/2005–002a.htm.

Haverland, M. (2007), 'Methodology'. In Graziano, P. and Vink, M. (eds), *Europeanization: New Research Agendas*, 59–70. Basingstoke: Palgrave Macmillan.

Hayward, K. (2003), 'The region between state and nation: British and Irish conceptions of Northern Ireland as a region', *Perspectives on European Politics and Societies* 4 (3): 417–45.

Hayward, K. (2006), 'National territory in European space: Reconfiguring the island of Ireland', *European Journal of Political Research* 45 (6): 871–1021.

Hayward, K. (2007), 'Mediating the European ideal: Cross-border programmes and conflict resolution on the island of Ireland', *Journal of Common Market Studies* 45 (3): 675–93.

Hayward, K. and Wiener, A. (2008), 'The influence of the EU towards conflict transformation on the island of Ireland'. In Diez, T., Albert, M., and Stetter, S. (eds), *The European Union and Border Conflicts: The Power of Integration and Association*, 33–63. Cambridge: Cambridge University Press.

Héritier, A. and Knill, C. (2001), 'Differentiated responses to European policies: A comparison'. In Adrienne Héritier, D. Kerwer, C. Knill, D. Lehmkuhl, M. Teutsch and A. C. Douillet (eds), Differential Europe: The European Union Impact on National Policymaking, 257–94. Boulder, New York, and Oxford: Rowman and Littlefield.

Hettne, B. (1991), 'Security and peace in post-Cold War Europe', *Journal of Peace Research* 28 (3): 279–94.

Hettne, B. and Söderbaum, F. (2000), 'Theorising the rise of regionness', *New Political Economy* 5 (3): 457–74.

Hettne, B. and Söderbaum, F. (2005), 'Civilian power or soft imperialism? The EU as a global actor and the role of interregionalism', *European Foreign Affairs Review* 10 (4): 535–52.

Hill, C. (1993), 'The capabilities-expectations gap, or conceptualizing Europe's international role', *Journal of Common Market Studies* 31 (3): 305–28.

Hill, C. (ed.) (1996), *The Actors in Europe's Foreign Policy*. London: Routledge.

Hill, C. and Wallace, W. (1996), 'Introduction: Actors and actions'. In Hill, C. (ed.), *The Actors in Europe's Foreign Policy*. London: Routledge.

Hix, S. (1998), 'The study of the European Union II: The "new governance" agenda and its rival', *Journal of European Public Policy* 5 (1): 38–65.

Hoffmann, S. (1966), 'Obstinate or obsolete: The fate of the nation state and the case of Western Europe', *Daedalus* 95 (3): 862–915.

Hooghe, L. (1995), 'Subnational mobilisation in the European Union', *West European Politics* 18 (3): 175–98.

Horowitz, D. (1990), 'Making moderation pay: The comparative politics of ethnic conflict management'. In Montville, J. (ed.), *Conflict and Peace-Making in Multiethnic Societies*, 115–30. Lexington, MA: Lexington Books.

Howell, K. (2004), *Europeanization, European Integration and Financial Services: Developing Theoretical Frameworks and Methodological Perspectives*. London: Palgrave Macmillan.

Hume, J. (1996), *A New Ireland: Politics, Peace and Reconciliation*. Boulder, CO: Roberts Rinehart Publishers.

Hurrell, A. and Fawcett, L. (1995), 'Conclusion'. In Fawcett, L. and Hurrell, A. (eds), *Regionalism in World Politics: Regional Organization and International Order*. Oxford: Oxford University Press.

ICG (2006), 'The Cyprus stalemate: What next?', *Europe Report* 171 (8 March 2006).

ICG (2008), 'Reunifying Cyprus: The best chance yet', *Europe Report* 194 (23 June 2008).

Imig, D. and Tarrow, S. (2000), 'Political contention in a Europeanising polity', *West European Politics* 23 (4): 73–93.

Inglehart, R. (1967a), *The Socialization of 'Europeans': Nation Building in Western Europe* (Doctoral Dissertation). Chicago: University of Chicago, Department of Political Science.

Inglehart, R. (1967b), 'An end to European integration', *American Political Science Review* 61 (1): 91–105.

Irvin, C. and Byrne, S. (2004), 'The perception of economic aid in Northern Ireland and its role in the peace process'. In Neuheiser, J. and Wolff, S., *Peace at Last? The Impact of the Good Friday Agreement on Northern Ireland*, 132–52. New York and Oxford: Berghahn Books.

Jacoby, W. (2006),'Inspiration, coalition, and substitution: External influences on post-communist transitions', *World Politics* 58 (4): 623–51.

Jacquot, S. and Woll, C. (2003), 'Usage of European integration – Europeanisation from a sociological perspective', *European Integration online Papers* (EIoP) 7 (12): http://eiop.or.at/eiop/texte/2003–012a.htm.

Jandt, F. E. (1973), *Conflict Resolution Through Communication*. New York, Evanston, San Francisco, London: Harper & Row.

Jeffery, C. (2000), 'Sub-national mobilization and European integration: Does it make any difference?', *Journal of Common Market Studies* 38 (1): 1–23.

Jeong, H.-W. (2005), *Peacebuilding in Postconflict Societies, Strategy and Process*. Boulder, CO: Lynne Rienner Publishers.

Jørgensen, K. E. (1997), 'PoCo: The diplomatic republic of Europe'. In Jørgensen, K. (ed.), *Reflective Approaches to European Governance*, 167–80. Basingstoke: Macmillan Press and New York: St. Martin's Press.

Joseph, J. (ed.) (2006), *Turkey and the European Union: Internal Dynamics and External Challenges*. London: Palgrave Macmillan.

Jupille, J., Caporaso, J. and Checkel, J. (2003), 'Integrating institutions: Rationalism, constructivism, and the study of the European Union', *Comparative Political Studies* 36 (1/2): 7–40.

Kassim, H. (2003), 'Meeting the demands of EU membership: The Europeanization of national administrative systems'. In Featherstone, K. and Radaelli, C. (eds), *The Politics of Europeanization*, 83–111. Oxford: Oxford University Press.

Kassim, H. (2005), 'The Europeanization of member state institutions'. In Bulmer, S. and Lequesne, C. (eds), *The EU and its Member States: An Overview*, 285–316. Oxford: Oxford University Press.

Kearney, R. (1997), *Postnationalist Ireland*. London: Routledge.

Kelstrup, M. (1990), 'The process of Europeanization: On the theoretical interpretation of present changes in the European regional system', *Cooperation and Conflict* XXV: 21–40.

Kennedy, D. (1994), 'The European Union and the Northern Ireland question'. In Barton, B. and Roche, P. (eds), *The Northern Ireland Question: Perspectives and Policies*, 166–88. Aldershot: Ashgate.

Kennedy, D. (2000), 'Europe and the Northern Ireland problem'. In Kennedy, D. (ed.), *Living with the European Union: The Northern Ireland Experience*, 148–68. Basingstoke: Macmillan Press Ltd.

Ker-Lindsay, J. (2007), 'The policies of Greece and Cyprus towards Turkey's EU accession', *Turkish Studies* 8 (1): 71–83.

Kim, J. and Woehrel, S. (2008), 'Kosovo and U.S. foreign policy: Background to independence', *CRS Report for Congress* RL31053. Washington, DC: Congressional Research Service.

Kirchner, E. (2006), 'The challenge of European Union security governance', *Journal of Common Market Studies* 44 (5): 947–68.

Kirchner, E. and Sperling, J. (2007), *EU Security Governance*. Manchester: Manchester University Press.

Knill, C. (2001), *The Europeanisation of National Administrations: Patterns of Institutional Change and Persistence*. Cambridge: Cambridge University Press.

Knill, C. and Lehmkuhl, D. (1999), 'How Europe matters: Different mechanisms of Europeanization', *European Integration online Papers* (EIoP) 3 (7): http://eiop.or.at/eiop/texte/1999–007a.htm.

Knill, C. and Lehmkuhl, D. (2002), 'The national impact of European Union regulatory policy: Three Europeanization mechanisms', *European Journal of Political Research* 41 (2): 255–80.

Koenig-Archibugi, M. (2004), 'Explaining government preferences for institutional change in EU foreign and security policy', *International Organization* 58 (1): 137–74.

Kohler-Koch, B. (1996), 'Catching up with change: The transformation of governance in the European Union', *Journal of European Public Policy* 3 (3): 359–80.

Kohler-Koch, B. (1999), 'The Evolution and transformation of European governance'. In Kohler-Koch, B. and Eising, R. (eds), *The Transformation of Governance in the European Union*, 14–35. London: Routledge.

Kohler-Koch, B. (2002), 'European networks and ideas: Changing national policies?', *European Integration online Papers* (EIoP) 6 (6): http://eiop.or.at/eiop/texte/2002–006a.htm.

Kohler-Koch, B. (2003), 'Independent European governance'. In Kohler-Koch, B. (ed.), *Linking EU and National Governance*, 10–23. Oxford: Oxford University Press.

Kohler-Koch, B. and Eising, R. (1999), *The Transformation of Governance in the European Union*. London: Routledge.

Krasner, S. (1999), *Sovereignty: Organized Hypocrisy*. Princeton, NJ: Princeton University Press.

Krieger, H. (2001), *The Kosovo Conflict and International Law: An Analytical Documentation 1974–1999*. Cambridge: Cambridge University Press.

Kronenberger, V. and Wouters, J. (eds) (2005), *The EU and Conflict Prevention: Policy and Legal Aspects*, The Hague: Asser Press.

Krotz, U. (2007), 'Parapublic underpinnings of international relations: The Franco-German construction of Europeanization of a particular kind', *European Journal of International Relations* 13 (3): 385–414.

Lacher, H. and Kaymak, E. (2005), 'Transforming identities: Beyond the politics of non-settlement in North Cyprus', *Mediterranean Politics* 10 (2): 147–66.

Ladrech, R. (1994), 'Europeanization of domestic politics and institutions: The case of France', *Journal of Common Market Studies* 32 (1): 69–88.

Laffan, B. (1996), 'The politics of identity and political order in Europe', *Journal of Common Market Studies* 34 (1): 81–102.

Laffan, B. (1997), 'The European Union: A distinctive model of internationalisation?', *European Integration online Papers* (EIoP) 1 (18): http://eiop.or.at/eiop/texte/1997–018a.htm.

Laffan, B. (2006), 'Managing Europe from home in Dublin, Athens and Helsinki: A comparative analysis', *West European Politics* 29 (4): 687–708.

Laffan, B. and Payne, D. (2003), 'INTERREG III and cross-border cooperation in the Island of Ireland', *Perspectives on European Politics and Societies* 4 (3): 447–73.

Lake, D. and Rothchild, D. (2005), 'Territorial decentralization and Civil War settlements'. In Roeder, P. and Rothchild, D. (eds), *Sustainable Peace: Power and Democracy after Civil Wars*, 109–32. Ithaca and London: Cornell University Press.

Larat, F. (2005), 'Present-ing the past: Political narratives and the justification of Europe', *German Law Journal* 6 (2): 273–90.

Larrabee, S. (1977), *Balkan Security*. Santa Monica, CA: RAND Corporation.

Lavenex, S. (2004), 'EU external governance in the "wider Europe"', *Journal of European Public Policy* 11 (4): 680–700.

Lavenex, S. and Schimmelfennig. F. (2009), 'EU rules beyond EU borders: Theorizing external governance in European politics', *Journal of European Public Policy* 16 (6): 791–812.

Lefort, B. (2001), *Une Europe Inédite: Documents des Archives Jean Monnet*. Villeneuve d'Ascq: Presses Universitaires du Septentrion.

Liebfried, S. and Wolf, W. (2005), 'Europeanization and the unraveling European nation state: Dynamics and feedback effects', *European Foreign Affairs Review* 10 (4): 479–99.

Lijphart, A. (2004), 'Constitutional design for divided societies', *Journal of Democracy* 15 (1): 96–109.

Lindberg, L. and Scheingold, S. (1970), *Europe's Would-be Polity: Patterns of Change in the European Community*. Englewood Cliffs: Prentice Hall.

Lipgens, W. and Loth, W. (eds) (1988), *Documents on the History of European Integration: The Struggle for European Union by Political Parties and Pressure Groups in the West European Countries 1945–1950* (Volume 3). Berlin and New York: Walter de Gruyter Inc.

Lippert, B., Umbach, B. and Wessels, W. (2001), 'Europeanization of CEE executives: EU membership negotiations as a shaping power', *Journal of European Public Policy* 8 (6): 980–1012.

Loriaux, M. (2008), *European Union and the Deconstruction of the Rhineland Frontier*. Cambridge: Cambridge University Press.

Loth, W. (1988a), 'General introduction'. In Lipgens, W. (ed.), *Documents on the History of European Integration. Vol. 3: The Struggle by Political Parties and Pressure Groups in Western European Countries 1945–1950*, 1–16. Berlin: De Gruyter.

Loth, W. (1988b), 'French political parties and pressure groups in the discussion on European Union'. In Lipgens, W. (ed.), *Documents on the History of European Integration. Vol. 3: The Struggle by Political Parties and Pressure Groups in Western European Countries 1945–1950*, 17–125. Berlin: De Gruyter.

Magen, A. (2006), 'The shadow of enlargement: Can the European neighbourhood policy achieve compliance?', *The Columbia Journal of European Law* 12 (2): 384–427.

Mair, P. (2004), 'The Europeanisation dimension', *Journal of European Public Policy* 11 (2): 337–48.

Mallinson, W. (2005), *Cyprus: A Modern History*. London: I. B. Tauris.

Manners, I. (2002), 'Normative power Europe: A contradiction in terms?', *Journal of Common Market Studies* 40 (2): 235–58.

Manners, I. (2008), 'The normative ethics of the European Union'. *International Affairs* 84 (1): 45–60.

March, J. and Olsen, J. (1984), 'The new institutionalism: Organizational factors in political life', *American Political Science Review* 78 (3): 734–49.
March, J. and Olsen, J. (1995), *Democratic Governance*. New York: The Free Press.
March, J. and Olsen, J. (1998), 'The institutional dynamics of international political orders', *International Organization* 52 (4): 943–69.
Marcussen, M., Risse, T., Engelmann-Martin, D., Knoepf, H. J. and Roscher, K. (1999), 'Constructing Europe? The evolution of French, British, and German nation state identities', *Journal of European Public Policy* 6 (4): 614–33.
Markovitz, A. and Reich, S. (1997), *The German Predicament: Memory and Power in the New Europe*. Ithaca: Cornell University Press.
Marks, G., Hooghe, L. and Blank, K. (1996), 'European integration from the 1980s: State centric v. multi-level governance', *Journal of Common Market Studies* 34 (3): 341–78.
Massey, A. (2004), 'Modernisation as Europeanisation', *Policy Studies* 25 (1): 19–33.
Mastenbroek, E. and Kaeding, M. (2006), 'Europeanization beyond the goodness of fit: domestic politics in the forefront', *Comparative European Politics* 4 (4): 331–54.
Mathison, S. (1988), 'Why triangulate?', *Educational Researcher* (March 1988): 13–17.
Matlary, J. H. (1997), 'Epilogue: New bottles for new wine'. In Jørgensen, K. (ed.), *Reflective Approaches to European Governance*, 201–13. Basingstoke: Macmillan Press.
Maurer, A., Mittag, J. and Wessels, W. (2003), 'National systems adaptation to the EU system: Trends, offers, and constraints'. In Kohler-Koch, B. (ed.), *Linking EU and National Governance*, 53–81. Oxford: Oxford University Press.
Mayer, H. (1996), 'Germany's role in the Fouchet negotiations', *Journal of European Integration History* 2 (2): 39–59.
McCall, C. (1998), 'Postmodern Europe and the resources of communal identities in Northern Ireland', *European Journal of Political Research* 33 (3): 389–411.
McCall, C. and Williamson, A. (2000), 'Fledgling social partnership in the Irish border region: European Union "community initiatives" and the voluntary sector', *Policy & Politics* 29 (3): 397–410.
McGarry, J. (ed.) (2004), *Northern Ireland and the Divided World: The Northern Ireland Conflict and the Good Friday Agreement in Comparative Perspective*. Oxford: Oxford University Press.
McGarry, J. (2006), 'Europe's limits: European integration and conflict management in Northern Ireland'. In McGarry, J. and Keating, M. (eds), *European Integration and the Nationalities Question*, 272–89. Abingdon and New York: Routledge.
McGarry, J., Keating, M. and Moore, M. (2006), 'Introduction: European integration and the nationalities question'. In McGarry, J. and Keating, M. (eds), *European Integration and the Nationalities Question*, 1–20. Abingdon and New York: Routledge.
McGarry, J. and O'Leary, B. (1995), *Explaining Northern Ireland: Broken Images*. Oxford and Malden, MA: Blackwell Publishers.
McGarry, J. and O'Leary, B. (eds) (2004), *The Northern Ireland Conflict*. Oxford: Oxford University Press.
McSweeney, B. (1996), 'Security, identity and the peace process in Northern Ireland', *Security Dialogue* 27 (2): 167–78.
Milward, A. (1992), *European Rescue of the Nation State*. London: Routledge.
Mitchell, C. R. (1991), 'Classifying conflicts: Asymmetry and resolution', *Annals of the American Academy of Political and Social Science* 518 (1): 23–38.
Mitchell, S. (2002), 'A Kantian system? Democracy and third-party conflict resolution', *American Journal of Political Science* 46 (4): 749–59.
Mitchell, G. (1999), *Making Peace*. Berkeley, Los Angeles and London: California University Press.
Mitrany, D. (1975), *The Functional Theory of Politics*. London: London School of Economics and Political Science: Martin Robinson.

Monnet, J. (1978), *Memoirs*. Garden City, NY: Doubleday & Company, Inc.
Montville, J. (1990), 'Epilogue: The human factor revisited'. In Montville, J. (ed.), *Conflict and Peacemaking in Multiethnic Societies*, 535–41. New York: Lexington Books.
Moravcsik, A. (1994), 'Why the European Union strengthens the state: Domestic politics and international cooperation', *Working Paper Series* 52, Harvard University, Center for European Studies.
Moravcsik, A. (1998), *The Choice for Europe: Social Purpose and State Power from Messina to Maastricht*. Ithaca, NY: Cornell University Press.
Muir, M. (1966), *Quelques Aspects de l'Opinion Publique Française d'une Fédération Européenne*. Thesis. Strasbourg: University of Strasbourg.
Murphy, M. (2007), 'Europeanization and the sub-national level: Changing patterns of governance in Northern Ireland', *Regional and Federal Studies* 17 (3): 293–315.
Murray, G. and Tonge, J. (2005), *Sinn Féin and the SDLP: From Alienation to Participation*. New York: Palgrave Macmillan.
Natali, D. (2004), 'Europeanization, policy arenas, and creative opportunism: The politics of welfare state reforms in Italy', *Journal of European Public Policy* 11 (6): 1077–95.
Norchi, C. (2002), 'Kosovo's evolving contest: Security, policy and sovereignty', *Conference paper*, CIAO database 02/02: http://ciaonet.org/conf/noc03.
North, R., Koch, H. and Zinnes, D. (1960), 'The integrative functions of conflict', *The Journal of Conflict Resolution* 4 (3): 355–74.
Noutcheva, G. (2009), 'Fake, partial and imposed compliance: The limits of the EU's normative power in the Western Balkans', *Journal of European Public Policy*, 16 (7): 1065–84.
Noutcheva, G., Tocci, N., Coppieters, B., Koviridze, T., Emerson, M. and Huyseeune, M. (2004), 'Europeanization and secessionist conflicts: Concepts and theories'. In Coppieters, B., Emerson, M., Huysseune, M., Kovziridze, T., Noutcheva, G., Tocci, N. and Vahl, M., *Europeanization and Conflict Resolution: Case Studies from the European Periphery*, 13–62. Ghent: Academia Press.
Nugent, N. (1997a), 'Cyprus and the European Union: A particularly difficult membership application', *Mediterranean Politics* 2 (3): 53–75.
Nugent, N. (1997b), 'EU enlargement and "the Cyprus problem"', *Journal of Common Market Studies* 38 (1): 131–50.
Nugent, N. (2006), 'Cyprus and the European Union: The significance of its smallness, both as an applicant and a member', *Journal of European Integration* 28 (1): 51–71.
Nugent, N. and Paterson, W. (2003), 'The political system of the European Union'. In Hayward, J. and Menon, A. (eds), *Governing Europe*, 92–109. Oxford: Oxford University Press.
Obradovic, D. (1996), 'Policy legitimacy and the European Union', *Journal of Common Market Studies* 34 (2): 191–221.
O'Cleireacain, S. (1983), 'Northern Ireland and Irish integration: The role of the European Communities', *Journal of Common Market Studies* 22 (2): 107–21.
OFMDFM – Office of the First Minister and Deputy First Minister (2005), *A Shared Future Policy and Strategic Frameworks for Good Relations in Northern Ireland*. Belfast: OFMDFM.
Oğuzlu, T. (2002), 'The EU as an actor in the solution of the Cyprus dispute: The questions of "how"?', *Journal of Ethnopolitics and Minority Issues in Europe* 2/2002: www.ecmi.de/jemie/download/Focus2-2002_Oguzlu.pdf.
O'Hearn, D. (2008), 'How has peace changed the Northern Irish political economy?', *Ethnopolitics* 7 (1): 101–18.
Olsen, J. (2002), 'The many faces of Europeanization', *Journal of Common Market Studies* 40 (5): 921–52.
Olsen, J. (2007), *Europe in Search of Political Order: An Institutional Perspective on*

Unity/Diversity, Citizens/Their Helpers, Democratic Design/Historical Drift and the Co-existence of Orders. Oxford: Oxford University Press.

Page, E. (2003), 'Europeanization and the persistence of administrative systems'. In Hayward, J. and Menon, A. (eds), *Governing Europe*, 61–73. Oxford: Oxford University Press.

Panke, D. (2007), 'The European Court of Justice as an agent of Europeanization? Restoring compliance with EU law', *Journal of European Public Policy* 14 (6): 847–66.

Papadimitriou, D., Petrov, P. and Greiçevci, L. (2007), 'To build a state: Europeanisation, EU actorness and state-building in Kosovo', *European Foreign Affairs Review* 12 (2): 219–38.

Paraskevopoulos, C. (2001), *Interpreting Convergence in the European Union: Patterns of Collective Action, Social Learning and Europeanization*. Basingstoke: Palgrave.

Paraskevopoulos, C. and Leonardi, R. (2004), 'Introduction: Adaptational pressures and social learning in European regional policy – cohesion (Greece, Ireland and Portugal) vs. CEE (Hungary, Poland) countries', *Regional and Federal Studies* 14 (3): 315–54.

Parsons, C. (2004), *A Certain Idea of Europe*. Ithaca: Cornell University Press.

Parsons, C. (2007), 'Puzzling out the EU role in national politics', *Journal of European Public Policy* 14 (7): 1135–49.

Pentland, C. (1973), *International Theory and European Integration*. New York: The Free Press.

Pevehouse, J. and Russett, B. (2006), 'Democratic international governmental organizations promote peace', *International Organization* 60 (4): 969–1000.

Pierre, J. and Peters, G. (2000), *Governance, Politics and the State*. New York: St. Martin's Press.

Pierson, P. (1993), 'When effect becomes cause: Policy feedback and political change', *World Politics* 45 (4): 595–628.

Polat, N. (2002), 'Self-determination, violence, modernity: The case of the Turkish Cypriots'. In Diez, T. (ed.), *The European Union and the Cyprus Conflict: Modern Conflict, Postmodern Union*, 98–116. Manchester: Manchester University Press.

Pollak, A. (ed.) (1993), *A Citizen's Inquiry: The Opsahl Report on Northern Ireland*. Dublin: Lilliput Press.

Pollack, M. (2005), 'Theorizing the European Union: International organization, domestic polity, or experiment in new governance?', *Annual Review of Political Science* 8: 357–98.

Pond, E. (1999), 'Kosovo: Catalyst for Europe', *The Washington Quarterly* 22 (4): 77–92.

Pond, E. (2005), 'Kosovo and Serbia after the French non', *The Washington Quarterly* 28 (4): 19–36.

Pond, E. (2006), *Endgame in the Balkans: Regime Change, European Style*. Washington, DC: Brookings Institution Press.

Pond, E. (2008), 'The EU's test in Kosovo', *The Washington Quarterly* 31 (4): 97–112.

Pope, H. (2009), 'Turkish Cypriots serve notice on peace talks', *International Crisis Group*: www.crisisgroup.org/home/index.cfm?id=6073&l=1.

Prange, H. (2003), 'Rethinking the impact of globalisation on the nation-state: The case of science and technology policies in Germany', *German Politics* 12 (1): 23–42.

Probert, B. (1978), *Beyond Orange and Green: The Political Economy of the Northern Ireland Conflict*. London: Zed Press Ltd.

Puchala, D. (1970), 'Integration and disintegration in Franco-German relations, 1954–1965', *International Organization* 24 (2): 183–208.

Quaglia, L. and Radaelli, C. (2007), 'Italian politics and the European Union: A tale of two research designs', *West European Politics* 30 (4): 924–43.

Rabier, J.-R. (1965), *L'Information des Européens et l'Intégration de l'Europe*. Brussels: Université Libre de Bruxelles.

Radaelli, C. (2000a), 'Policy transfer in the European Union: Institutional isomorphism as

a source of legitimacy', *International Journal of Policy and Administration* 13 (1): 25–43.
Radaelli, C. (2000b), 'Whither Europeanization? Concept stretching and substantive change', *European Integration online Papers* (EIoP) 4:8 (2000): http://eiop.or.at/eiop/texte/2000-008a.htm.
Radaelli, C. (2003), 'The Europeanization of public policy'. In Featherstone, K. and Radaelli, C. (eds), *The Politics of Europeanization*, 27–56. Oxford: Oxford University Press.
Radaelli, C. (2004), 'Europeanisation: Solution or problem?', *European Integration online Papers* (EIoP) 8 (16): http://eiop.or.at/eiop/texte/2004-016a.htm.
Radaelli, C. and Franchino, F. (2004), 'Analyzing political change in Italy', *Journal of European Public Policy* 11 (6): 941–53.
Radaelli, C. and Pasquier, R. (2007), 'Conceptual lenses'. In Graziano, P. and Vink, M. (eds), *Europeanization: New Research Agendas*, 35–45. Houndmills and New York: Palgrave Macmillan.
Radaelli, C. and Schmidt, V. (2004), 'Conclusions', *West European Politics*, 27 (2): 364–79.
Ragin, C. (1987), *The Comparative Method. Moving Beyond Qualitative and Quantitative Strategies*. Berkley, CA: University of California Press.
Reiterer, A. (2003), *Cyprus: Case Study about a Failure of Ethno-National Understanding*. Frankfurt: Peter Lang.
Rhodes, R. A. W. (2003), 'What is new about governance and why does it matter?'. In Hayward, J. and Menon, A. (eds), *Governing Europe*, 162–76. Oxford: Oxford University Press.
Rich, R. (1993), 'Recognition of states: The collapse of Yugoslavia and the Soviet Union', *European Journal of International Law* 4 (1): 36–65.
Richmond, O. (2002), 'The multiple dimensions of international peacemaking'. In Diez, T. (ed.), *The European Union and the Cyprus Conflict: Modern Conflict, Postmodern Union*, 117–36. Manchester: Manchester University Press.
Rieker, P. (2006), *Europeanization of National Security Identity: The EU and the Changing Security Identities of the Nordic States*. London and New York: Routledge.
Risse-Kappen, T. (1996), 'Exploring the nature of the beast: International relations theory and comparative policy analysis meet the European Union', *Journal of Common Market Studies* 34 (1): 53–80.
Risse, T, Caporaso, J. and Cowles, M. (2001), 'Introduction'. In Cowles, M., Caporaso, J. and Risse, T. (eds), *Transforming Europe: Europeanization and Domestic Change*, 1–20. Ithaca: Cornell University Press.
Rittberger, B. (2001), 'Which institutions for post-war Europe? Explaining the institutional design of Europe's first community', *Journal of European Public Policy* 8 (5): 673–708.
Robertson, A. (1973), *European Institutions: Cooperation, Integration, Unification*. London: Stevens & Sons; New York: Matthew Bender.
Robyn, R. (2005), 'Conclusion'. In Robyn, R. (ed.), *The Changing Face of European Identity*, 227–35. Abingdon and New York: Routledge.
Roeder, P. (2005), 'Power dividing as an alternative to ethnic power sharing'. In Roeder, P. and Rothchild, D. (eds), *Sustainable Peace: Power and Democracy after Civil Wars*, 51–82. Ithaca and London: Cornell University Press.
Roeder, P. and Rothchild, D. (eds) (2005), *Sustainable Peace: Power and Democracy after Civil Wars*. Ithaca: Cornell University Press.
Rosamond, B. (2000), *Theories of European Integration*. New York: St. Martin's Press.
Rose, R. (1971), *Governing Without Consensus: An Irish Perspective*. Boston: Beacon Press.
Rose, R. (1976), *Northern Ireland: Time of Choice*. Washington, DC: American Enterprise Institute for Public Policy Research.

Rose, R. (1990), 'Northern Ireland: The irreducible conflict'. In Montville, J. (ed.) *Conflict and Peacemaking in Multiethnic Societies*, 133–50. New York: Lexington Books.

Rothchild, D. and Roeder, P. (2005), 'Power sharing as an impediment to peace and democracy'. In Roeder, P. and Rothchild, D. (eds), *Sustainable Peace: Power and Democracy after Civil Wars*, 29–50. Ithaca: Cornell University Press.

Ruane, J. and Todd. J. (1996), *The Dynamics of Conflict in Northern Ireland: Power, Conflict and Emancipation*. Cambridge: Cambridge University Press.

Ruane, J. and Todd, J. (2007), 'Path dependence in settlement process: Explaining settlement in Northern Ireland', *Political Studies* 55 (2): 442–58.

Ruggie, J. (1993), 'Territoriality and beyond: Problematizing modernity in international relations', *International Organization* 47 (1): 139–74.

Rupnik, J. (2005), 'Europe's challenge in the Balkans', *ESF Working Paper* 18 (January 2005), 4–6. Brussels: Centre for European Policy Studies.

Salmon, T. (2002), 'The EU's role in conflict resolution: Lessons from Northern Ireland', *European Foreign Affairs Review* 7 (3): 337–58.

Sandholtz, W. (1993), 'Choosing union: Monetary politics and Maastricht', *International Organization* 47 (1): 1–39.

Sandholtz, W. (1996), 'Membership matters: Limits of the functional approach to European institutions', *Journal of Common Market Studies* 34 (3): 401–29.

Sandholtz, W. and Stone Sweet, A. (eds) (1998), *European Integration and Supranational Governance*. Oxford: Oxford University Press.

Sbragia, A. (2000), 'The European Union as coxswain: Governance by steering'. In Pierre, J. (ed.), *Debating Governance*, 54–90. Oxford: Oxford University Press.

Scharpf, F. (2000), 'Notes towards a theory of multilevel governing in Europe', *MPIfG Discussion Paper*, 5. Max-Planck-Institute für Gesellschaftsforschung.

Scharpf, F. (2001), 'European governance: Common concerns vs. the challenge of diversity', *Max Planck Institute for the Study of Societies Working Paper* 01.

Schattschneider, E. E. (1935), *Pressures and the Tariff*. New York: Prentice-Hall.

Scheingold, S. (1970), 'Domestic and international consequences of regional integration', *International Organization* 24 (4): 978–1002.

Schellenberg, J. (1996), *Conflict Resolution: Theory, Research, and Practice*. Albany, NY: State University of New York Press.

Schimmelfenning, F. (2007), 'Europeanization beyond Europe', *Living Reviews in European Governance*: www.livingreviews.org/lreg-2007-1.

Schimmelfennig, F. (2008), 'EU political accession conditionality after the 2004 enlargement: Consistency and effectiveness', *Journal of European Public Policy* 15 (6): 918–37.

Schimmelfennig, F., Engert, S. and Knobel, H. (2006), *International Socialization in Europe: European Organizations, Political Conditionality, and Democratic Change*. Basingstoke: Palgrave Macmillan.

Schimmelfennig, F. and Sedelmeier, U. (eds) (2005), *The Europeanization of Central and Eastern Europe*. Ithaca: Cornell University Press.

Schimmelfennig, F. and Wagner, W. (eds) (2004a), 'Symposium: External governance in the European Union', *Journal of European Public Policy* (Special Issue) 11 (4).

Schimmelfennig, F. and Wagner, W. (eds) (2004b), 'Preface: External Governance in the European Union', *Journal of European Public Policy* 11 (4): 657–60.

Schmidt, V. (1997), 'Discourse and (dis)integration in Europe: The cases of France, Germany, and Great Britain', *Daedalus* 126 (3): 167–99.

Schmidt, V. (2002), 'Europeanization and the mechanics of economic policy adjustment', *Journal of European Public Policy* 9 (6): 894–912.

Schmidt, V. (2004), 'The European Union: Democratic legitimacy in a regional state?' *Journal of Common Market Studies* 42 (4): 975–99.

Schmidt, V. (2005), 'The role of discourse in European democratic reform projects',

European Integration online Papers (EIoP) 9 (8): http://eiop.or.at/eiop/texte/2005–008a.htm.

Schmitter, P. (1996), 'Examining the present Euro-polity with the help of past theories'. In Marks, G., Scharpf, F., Schmitter, P. and Streek, W., *Governance in the European Union*, 1–14. London: SAGE Publications.

Schwabe, K. (2004), 'L'Allemagne, Adenauer et l'option de l'intégration à l'Ouest'. In Wilkens, A. (ed.), *Le Plan Schuman dans l'Histoire: Intérêts Nationaux et Project Européen*, 81–105. Brussels: Bruylant.

Sciarini, P., Fischer, A. and Nicolet, S. (2004), 'How Europe hits home: Evidence from the Swiss case', *Journal of European Public Policy* 11 (3): 353–78.

Sepos, A. (2008), *The Europeanization of Cyprus: Polity, Policies, and Politics*. Houndmills and New York: Palgrave Macmillan.

SEUPB (2007), *PEACE III: EU Programme for Peace and Reconciliation 2007–2013. Draft Operational Programme*. Belfast: SEUPB.

Sifft, S., Brüggemann, M., Kleinen-V. Königslöw, K., Peters, B. and Wimmel, A. (2007), 'Segmented *Europeanization*: Exploring the legitimacy of the European Union from a public discourse perspective', *Journal of Common Market Studies* 45 (1): 127–55.

Simpson, J. (1984), 'European community policies and Northern Ireland'. In Simpson, J. (ed.), *European Community Policy in Northern Ireland*, 1–19. Belfast: Queen's University.

Sinn Féin (1984), *Report of the New Ireland Forum*. Dublin: Sinn Féin.

Sjøstedt, G. (1977), *The External Role of the European Community*. Westmead: Saxon House.

Sjursen, H. (2006), 'The EU as a '"normative" power: How can this be?', *Journal of European Public Policy* 13 (2): 235–51.

Smith, M. L. (2000), 'The European connection and public opinion'. In Kennedy, D. (ed.), *Living with the European Union: The Northern Ireland Experience*, 169–96. Houndmills: Macmillan Press Ltd.; New York: St. Martin's Press.

Smith, M. L. (2004), 'Toward a theory of EU foreign policy-making: Multi-level governance, domestic politics, and national adaptation to Europe's common foreign and security policy', *Journal of European Public Policy* 11 (4): 740–58.

Smolnikov, S. (2008), 'Conflating economic power and diplomacy: How the EU could contribute to making Kosovo's independence legitimate and safeguard peace in the Western Balkans', *American Diplomacy* (22 April 2008).

Spaak, P.-H. (1969), *Combats Inachevés. Tome II: De L'Espoir aux Déceptions*. Paris: Fayard.

Stefanova, B. (2006), 'Regional integration as a system of conflict resolution: The European experience', *World Affairs* 169 (2): 81–93.

Stelandre, Y. (1996), 'Les pays du Benelux, l'Europe politique et les négociations Fouchet (26 juin 1959–17 avril 1962)', *Journal of European Integration History* 2 (2): 21–38.

Stetter, S. (2004), 'Cross-pillar politics: Functional unity and institutional fragmentation of EU foreign policies', *Journal of European Public Policy* 11 (4): 720–39.

Stetter, S., Mathias, A. and Diez, T. (2008), 'Conclusion'. In Diez, T., Albert, M., and Stetter, S. (eds), *The European Union and Border Conflicts: The Power of Integration and Association*, 220–36. Cambridge: Cambridge University Press.

Stevenson, J. (1998), 'Peace in Northern Ireland: Why now?', *Foreign Policy* 112 (Fall): 41–54.

Stone Sweet, A., Sandholtz, W. and Fligstein, N. (eds) (2001), *The Institutionalization of Europe*. Oxford: Oxford University Press.

Sturm, R. and Dieringer, J. (2005), 'The Europeanization of regions in Eastern and Western Europe: Theoretical perspectives', *Regional and Federal Studies* 15 (3): 279–94.

Talmon, S. (2001), 'The Cyprus question before the European Court of Justice', *European Journal of International Law* 12 (4): 727–50.

Talmon, S. (2006), 'The European Union – Turkey controversy over Cyprus or a tale of two treaty declarations', *Chinese Journal of International Law* 5 (3): 579–616.

Tansey, O. (2009), *Regime-Building: Democratization and International Administration*. Oxford: Oxford University Press.

Tavares, R. (2004), Contribution of macro-regions to the construction of peace: A framework of analysis', *Journal of International Relations and Development* 7 (1): 24–47.

Teague, P. (1996), 'The European Union and the Irish peace process', *Journal of Common Market Studies* 34 (4): 549–71.

Thatcher, M. (2004), 'Winners and losers in Europeanisation: Reforming the national regulation of telecommunications', *West European Politics* 27 (2): 284–309.

Thielemann, E. (2000), 'Europeanisation and institutional compatibility: Implementing European regional policy in Germany', *Queen's Papers on Europeanization* 1 (4).

Tocci, N. (2000), 'The "Cyprus question": Reshaping community identities and elite interests within a wider European framework', *CEPS Working Document* No. 154 (September 2000). Brussels: Centre for European Policy Research.

Tocci, N. (2004), 'Conflict resolution in the European neighbourhood: The role of the EU as a framework and as an actor', *EUI Working Paper RSCAS* No. 2004/29. Florence: European University Institute.

Tocci, N. (2005), 'Conflict resolution in the neighborhood: Comparing EU involvement in Turkey's Kurdish question and in the Israeli-Palestinian conflict', *Mediterranean Politics* 10 (2): 125–46.

Tocci, N. (2007), *The EU and Conflict Resolution: Promoting Peace in the Backyard*. London and New York: Routledge.

Tocci, N. and Kovziridze, T. (2004). 'Cyprus', *Journal on Ethnopolitics and Minority Issues in Europe* (Special Focus), 1/2004, Chapter 2: http://ecmi.de/jemie/download/1–2004Chapter2.pdf.

Töller, A. (2004), 'The Europeanization of public policies – understanding idiosyncratic mechanisms and contingent results', *European Integration online Papers* (EIoP) 8 (9): http://eiop.or.at/eiop/texte/2004–000a.htm.

Tonge, J. (2005). *The New Northern Irish Politics?* London: Palgrave Macmillan.

Tonra, B. (1997), 'The impact of political cooperation'. In Jørgensen, K. (ed), *Reflective Approaches to European Governance*, 181–98. Basingstoke: Macmillan Press; New York: St. Martin's Press.

Tonra, B. (2001), *The Europeanisation of National Foreign Policy: Dutch, Danish and Irish Foreign Policy in the European Union*. Aldershot: Ashgate.

Trauner, F. (2009), 'From membership conditionality to policy conditionality: EU external governance in South Eastern Europe', *Journal of European Public Policy*, 16 (5): 774–90.

Treib, O. (2008), 'Implementing and complying with EU governance outputs', *Living Reviews in European Governance* lreg-2008-5: http://europeangovernance.livingreviews.org/Articles/lreg-2008-5/.

Tsebelis, G. and Yataganas, X. (2000), 'Veto players and decision-making in the EU after Nice: Policy stability and bureaucratic/judicial discretion', *Journal of Common Market Studies* 40 (2): 283–307.

Türkes, M. and Gökgöz, G. (2006), 'The European Union's strategy towards the Western Balkans: Exclusion or integration?', *East European Politics and Societies* 20 (4): 659–90.

Tziampiris, A. (2000), *Greece, European Political Cooperation and the Macedonian Question*. Aldershot, Burlington USA, Singapore, Sydney: Ashgate.

Udalov, V. (1991), 'The concept of balance of power and U.S.–Soviet intereaction', *The ANNALS of the American Academy of Political and Social Science* 518 (1): 165–76.

United Nations (1999), *Resolution 1244 (1999) Adopted by the Security Council at its 4011th Meeting on 10 June 1999*. New York: United Nations.

United Nations (2005), 'Letter dated 7 October 2005 from the Secretary-General addressed to the President of the Security Council', *Document* S/2005/635 (Annex 'A Comprehensive review of the situation in Kosovo'): www.unosek.org/docref/KaiEidereport.pdf.

United Nations (2007), 'Letter dated 26 March 2007 from the Secretary-General addressed to the President of the Security Council', *Document* S/2007/138 (Annex 'Main provisions of the Comprehensive Proposal for the Kosovo Status Settlement'): www.unosek.org/docref/report-english.pdf.

United Nations Mission in Kosovo (UNMIK) (2007), 'Assessment of Standards goals to April 2007', *Report* (20 April 2007): http://www.unmikonline.org/standards/docs/Consolidated_Annex_april2007.pdf.

Usher, J. A. (1985), 'The scope of community competence – its recognition and enforcement', *Journal of Common Market Studies* 24 (2): 121–36.

Vachudova, M. (2005), *Europe Undivided: Democracy, Leverage, and Integration after Communism*. New York: Oxford University Press.

Vanhoonacker, S. (1989), 'La Belgique: Responsable ou bouc émissaire de l'échec des négociations fouchet?', *Res Publica* 31 (4): 513–26.

Van Houten, P. and Wolff, S. (2008), 'The dynamic of ethnopolitical conflict management by international and regional organizations in Europe', *Journal of Ethnopolitics and Minority Issues in Europe* 1 (2008): www.ecmi.de/jemie/download/1–2008: www.ecmi.de/jemie/download/1-2008-Houten_Wolff.pdf.

van Meurs, W. (2004), 'Kosovo's fifth anniversary—on the road to nowhere?', *The Global Review of Ethnopolitics* 3 (3–4): 60–74.

Varnava, A. and Faustmann, H. (eds) (2009), *Reunifying Cyprus: The Annan Plan and Beyond*. London: I. B. Tauris.

Vassallo, F. (2003), 'Another Europeanisation case: British political activism?', *Working Paper* 61. Brighton: Sussex European Institute.

Verney, S. (2009), 'From consensus to conflict: Changing perceptions of the Cyprus issue in the European Parliament, 1995–2006'. In Diez, T. and Tocci, N. (eds), *Cyprus: A Conflict at the Crossroads*, 124–46. Manchester: Manchester University Press.

Voorhoeve, J. (2007), *From War to the Rule of Law: Peace Building after Violent Conflicts*. Amsterdam: Amsterdam University Press.

Wæver, O. (1998), 'Insecurity, security, and asecurity in the West European non-war community'. In Adler, E. and Barnett, M. (eds), *Security Communities*, 69–118. Cambridge: Cambridge University Press.

Wallace, H. (2005), 'An institutional anatomy and five policy modes'. In Wallace, H., Wallace, W. and Pollack, M. (eds), *Policy Making in the European Union*, 49–90. Oxford: Oxford University Press.

Wallace, H., Wallace, W. and Pollack, M. (eds) (2005), *Policy Making in the European Union*. Oxford: Oxford University Press.

Wallensteen, P. (2002), *Understanding Conflict Resolution*. London, Thousand Oaks, New Delhi: SAGE Publications.

Wallensteen, P. and Axell, K. (1994), 'Conflict resolution and the end of the Cold War, 1989–93', *Journal of Peace Research* 31 (3): 331–46.

Weiler, J. H. H. (1991), 'The transformation of Europe', *The Yale Law Journal* 100 (8): 2403–83.

Weller, M. (1999), 'The Rambouillet conference on Kosovo', *International Affairs* 75 (2): 211–51.

Weller, M. (2008), 'Negotiating the final status of Kosovo', *Chaillot Paper* 114. Paris: EU Institute for Security Studies.

Wessels, W. and Linsenmann, I. (2002), 'EMU's impact on national institutions: Fusion towards a "*Gouvernance Économique*" or fragmentation?'. In Dyson, K. (ed.), *European*

States and the Euro: Europeanization, Variation, and Convergence, 53–77. Oxford and New York: Oxford University Press.
Whittaker, D. (1999), *Conflict and Reconciliation in the Contemporary World*. London: Routledge.
Wichmann, N. (2007), *Democratisation Without Societal Participation? The EU as an External Actor in the Democratisation Processes of Serbia and Croatia*. Berlin: LIT and London.
Wiener, A. and Diez, T. (eds) (2004), *European Integration Theory*. Oxford: Oxford University Press.
Wilkens, A. (ed.) (2004), *Le Plan Schuman dans l'Histoire: Intérêts Nationaux et Projet Européen*. Brussels: Bruylant.
Wilkens, A., Möller, H. and Hildebrand, K. (eds) (1997), *Die Bundesrepublik Deutschland und Frankreich: Dokumente 1949–1963*. Munich: Saur.
Williamson, J. (ed.) (1983), *IMF Conditionality*. Washington, DC: Institute for International Economics.
Wincott, D. (2004), 'Policy change and discourse in Europe: Can the EU make a "square meal out of a stew of paradox"?', *West European Politics* 27 (2): 354–63.
Woodward, S. (2001), 'Compromised sovereignty to create sovereignty: Is Dayton Bosnia a futile exercise or an emerging model?'. In Krasner, S. (ed.), *Problematic Sovereignty: Contested Rules and Political Possibilities*, 252–300. New York: Columbia University Press.
Wozniak Boyle, J. (2006), *Conditional Leadership: The European Commission and European Regional Policy*. Lanham: Lexington Books.
Wurm, C. (ed.) (1995), *Western Europe and Germany: The Beginnings of European Integration*. Oxford: Berg Publishers.
Yeşilada, B. and Wood, D. (2009), *The Emerging European Union*. Boston: Longman.
Zaborowski, M. (2004), *Germany, Poland and Europe: Conflict, Cooperation and Europeanization*. Manchester and New York: Manchester University Press.
Zielonka, I. (1998), *Explaining Euro-Paralysis: Why Europe Is Unable to Act in International Politics*. Basingstoke: Palgrave Macmillan.
Zielonka, I. (2007), 'Plurilateral governance in the enlarged European Union', *Journal of Common Market Studies* 45 (1): 187–209.
Zürn, M. and Checkel, J. (2005), 'Getting socialized to build bridges: Constructivism and rationalism, Europe and the nation-state', *International Organization* 59 (4): 1045–79.

Index

Accession Treaty *see* Cyprus
acquis see community *acquis*
Adams, Gerry 103
Adenauer, Konrad 47, 48, 56, 57, 65, 70
additionality 39
Agenda 2000 128, 132
Ahtisaari, Martti 154
Ahtisaari Plan 154, 166, 169, 173, 176
Aid Regulation 137, 141
Alsace 44, 52
Anastasiou case 126
Anglo-American bizone 49
Anglo-Irish Agreement (1985) 89, 98, 100, 103, 112
Anglo-Irish Treaty (1921) 82
Ankara Protocol *see* EC-Turkey customs union
Annan, Kofi 122, 154
Annan Plan 117, 123, 126, 133, 134–5, 137, 145n.5, 188, 195

Badinter Commission 157, 164
  Guidelines for Recognition 157
Ban Ki-moon 155, 170
Benelux countries 49
Beyen Plan 66
Bildt, Carl 145n.2
Blankenhorn, Herbert 73, 78n.29
Bonn Agreement 78n.22
Bosnia-Herzegovina 14, 191

Boutros-Gali, Boutros 122
Briand, Aristide 47
British Irish Council 83, 100
  see also Good Friday Agreement
British-Irish Intergovernmental Conference *see* Good Friday Agreement
British rebate 87
De Brún, Bairbre 105

CAP *see* Common Agricultural Policy
Carolingian Empire 44
Carter, James 98
Caucasus 2
CDU *see* Christian Democratic Union
CFSP *see* Common Foreign and Security Policy
Charlemagne 44
Christian Democratic Union 48
Churchill, Winston 1, 47
Cleridis, Glafkos 122
Clinton, William 98
Coakley, John 113
Common Agricultural Policy 87
Common Foreign and Security Policy 5, 20n.2, 33, 117, 118, 134, 157
  European Security and Defence Policy 164, 166
  Secretary-General/High Representative 159, 163, 165, 192

common market 51, 52, 55
community *acquis* 123, 125, 129, 130, 131, 134, 136, 138, 139
Community Initiative 90
Community Support Programme 92
Comprehensive Proposal for the Kosovo Status Settlement 154, 167, 169, 171, 176
conditionality 14, 19, 20, 34, 36, 38, 39, 43n.1, 119, 127, 128, 129, 130, 139, 144, 151, 157, 162, 164, 166, 172, 180, 195, 197–9
  membership 14, 116, 117, 136, 141, 143,151, 196, 197–9
conflict 38, 42, 194
  context of 38
    single-issue 23
  definition 7
  European governance and 14
  Europeanisation of 35
  frozen conflicts 7
  institutional logic 37
  intercommunal conflict 7, 16
    see also Cyprus conflict
  protracted 8, 10
  secessionist 34
  stages 16
  status 41
  transformation 38, 42, 85, 150
conflict resolution 5, 7, 13, 18, 22, 150, 152, 187, 196, 199–201
  constitutionalisation of 200
  domestic conditions of 9
  Europeanisation of (definition) 13, 23, 36
  institutional logic 25, 98, 134, 187, 188
  external sources 8
  method of 16
  measurement 7
  outcome 38
  politics of 38
  theories 32
consociationalism 98

consociational arrangements 200
Consultative Assembly (France) 49
Contact Group on Kosovo 19, 153, 160, 169, 182
  Guiding Principles about the Kosovo settlement 169
  Troika 169, 170
Coudenhove-Kalergi, Richard 1
Council of Europe 4, 49, 58, 62
  Consultative Assembly 49
  Council of Ministers 49
Council of Ministers, EEC/EU 87, 100, 125
Council of the European Union 138, 159, 160, 168
  see also Council of Ministers
  Regulations 159
CPS see Comprehensive Proposal for the Kosovo Status Settlement
cross-border cooperation 150
  see also Northern Ireland
CTP see Republican Turkish Party
customs union 7, 18, 59, 66, 123, 131
Cvetkovic, Mirko 174
Cyprus 17, 116–44, 187, 191, 192, 193, 194, 198
  Association Agreement, EC 14, 120, 124
  Comprehensive Settlement 135
  conflict 3, 118–19, 120–3, 128, 139, 188, 189, 200
    intercommunal talks 19, 120, 195
    transformation 34
  Constitution 121, 132
  EU Accession Treaty 123, 135
    Act of Accession 135, 137
      Protocol 10 135, 137
    Act of Adaptation 123, 135
  Guarantor states 121, 132
  Referendum (2004) 123, 135
  Republic of 122, 123, 125, 127, 128, 133, 137, 145n.1

Dayton Agreement 160

decentralisation 201
  see also Kosovo
Delors, Jacques 90
Democratic Party 172, 173
Democratic Party of Serbia 171
Democratic Unionist Party 102, 104, 105–7, 111, 193
Denktash, Rauf 122, 129, 133
desecuritisation 4, 120, 150
Deutsche Kohlenbergbauleitung 54
Deutsche Kohlen-Verkaufsgesellschaft 55–7
devolution 39, 85, 86, 89, 96, 100, 104, 112, 188, 199, 200
Direct Trade Regulation 138, 140
discourse
  (Euro-) European, EU as 39, 40, 108–11, 193
  peace and reconciliation 46
DKBL *see Deutsche Kohlenbergbauleitung*
DKV *see Deutsche Kohlen-Verkaufsgesellschaft*
Dowes Plan 47
Downing Street Declaration (1993) 83, 99
DS *see* Democratic Party
DSS *see* Democratic Party of Serbia
Duc de Sully (Maximilian de Béthune) 1
Dulles, John Foster 53
DUP *see* Democratic Unionist Party

Eastern Europe 33, 157
Eastern European enlargement 33, 118–19, 129, 139, 143–4, 180
ECSC *see* European Coal and Steel Community
  ECSC Treaty 55, 56, 57, 58–65 *passim*
  ECSC Working Document 55
EC-Cyprus Association Agreement (1973) 19, 124
EC-Cyprus Parliamentary Committee 125
ECJ *see* European Court of Justice
EC Mediterranean policy 124
EC-Turkey customs union 123, 127, 129, 139, 140
  Ankara Protocol 139, 140
EDC *see* European Defence Community
EEC *see* European Economic Community
EESC *see* European Economic and Social Committee
Eide, Kai 154, 162, 169
Elysée Treaty 18, 46
  see also Franco-German Treaty for Cooperation
EP *see* European Parliament
EPC *see* European Political Cooperation
ERDF *see* European Regional Development Fund
Erdogan, Recep Tayyip 133
Eroğlu, Derviş 142
ESDP *see* Common Foreign and Security Policy
EU *see* European Union
EU-Cyprus relationship 19
EU-Cyprus Joint Parliamentary Committee 129
EU governance 7, 8, 24, 27, 32, 41, 141, 151, 152, 159
  definition 22
EU House 177
EULEX *see* European civilian rule of law mission (Kosovo)
EU Planning Team (Kosovo) 164
EU regional policy 97
Eurofederalism 150
European Agency for Reconstruction 160
European Coal and Steel Community (ECSC) (1951) 7, 18, 20, 45, 46, 55, 57, 69, 74
  High Authority 64, 65

political union 69
European Commission 88, 89, 90, 92, 95, 122, 125, 127, 130, 135, 137, 138, 141, 159, 160, 161, 163, 166, 167, 177
  opinion on Cyprus 122, 125, 126, 127, 192
European Council 88, 125, 127, 128, 129, 135, 141, 144, 159, 163, 166,
  Brussels (2005) 162
  Corfu (1994) 126
  Council Presidency 128, 163
  Edinburgh (1998) 129
  Feira (2000) 159
  Helsinki (1997) 122, 127, 130, 131, 132
  Luxembourg 122, 129, 132, 133
  Stuttgart (1983) 98
  Thessaloniki (2003) 159
    Agenda 160, 161
  Vienna (1998) 158
European Court of Justice 126, 135, 141
European Defence Community 57, 61
European Economic and Social Committee (EESC) 16, 95
European Economic Community (EEC) (1957) 18, 20, 45, 52, 58, 66, 67, 74
  Messina Declaration 66
  EEC/Rome Treaty 66, 75, 87
  Paris Summit (1961) 70
    Paris Communique 70
  political community 69, 70
European Federalist Movement 4
European governance 7, 11, 26, 94, 191, 192
  see also governance; EU governance
European integration 12, 23, 84, 111, 112, 113, 119, 190, 196, 199
  community method 27, 70, 71
  conditioning variable 37
  and conflict resolution 46
  definition 5

independent variable 5, 37, 39
Europeanisation
  causal process 38, 40
  definition 24–5
  discursive practice as a 28
  Eastern Europe 151
  effects 35, 152, 180
  foreign policy 33
  heuristic device as a 23
  integration theory and 23–4
  interaction effects 36, 97
  intervening variables 34
  misfit proposition 36, 39, 117, 120, 136, 192
  model
    bottom-up 37, 40, 97, 101, 129, 132
    see also resource, coalition-building
    compliance 32, 38, 40, 180
    coalition-building 40, 120, 196
    resource 98, 104, 120, 143, 173, 180
    top-down 30, 36, 40, 97, 113, 119, 120, 129, 138, 140, 143, 144, 196
  necessary condition for 30, 39
  'old' and 'new' 24
  policy domain 31, 36, 39
  policy effects 28, 112
  polity domain 37
  polity effects 28, 99–101, 112
  politics domain of 37, 180
  political effects 28, 37, 101–8, 112
  sociological hypothesis 38
  sociological institutionalist model 31
European Parliament 16, 18, 88, 95, 105, 127, 130, 138, 141, 160, 166, 192
  Foreign Affairs Committee 140
  High Level Contact Group for relations with TCC 138
  Parliamentary Assembly 71
European partnership 39, 90, 159, 160,

163, 167
European Political Cooperation 88, 113, 124, 157
European Regional Development Fund 87
European Social Fund 87
European space 7, 23, 39, 96, 124, 192–3
European Union (EU) 2
  actorness 5, 6
  enlargement policy 181
  institution 6
  multiperspectival polity 6
  regional policy 86
  system of governance 12
  Monitoring Mission 160
European Union civilian rule of law mission (Kosovo) 19, 164, 166, 167, 171, 177, 180, 182
European Union Special Representative 155, 163, 167, 177
  see also International Civilian Representative

federalism 4, 49
  federalist idea 51
Federal Republic of Yugoslavia 158, 182
Fouchet Committee 70
  Fouchet Plan (Nov 1961) 71, 72, 75
framing 43n.2, 129
France 16, 45–51, 53–75
Franco-German case 16, 17, 87, 191, 193, 194, 196
Franco-German Peace Treaty (1955)
Franco-German relationship 17, 44, 47, 53, 57, 62, 187
  enmity 17, 53, 65, 74, 75, 76
  peace 48, 53, 61, 65
  rivalry 51
  tariff agreement (1950) 56
  trade 56
  Agreement (1954) 63
Franco-German reconciliation 3, 15, 18, 44, 46, 47, 48, 51, 52, 57, 65, 69, 72, 76, 102, 199
Franco-German Treaty for Cooperation (Elysée Treaty) (1963) 18, 45, 69–74
Franco-Saar conventions 60
Franco-Saar economic and monetary union 59, 60, 61, 63
FRY see Federal Republic of Yugoslavia
functionalism 3

G-8 158
GAERC see General Affairs and External Affairs Council
de Gaulle, Charles 48, 67, 69, 70, 72, 73, 74
General Affairs and External Affairs Council 126, 128, 129, 157, 160, 162, 165, 166, 167
  Solana/Rehn report 160, 161
German Bundestag 73
German coal industry 56
German Empire 45
German problem 49, 53
  see also German question
German question 53, 58
  see also German problem
Germany 45–51, 53–75
van der Goes van Naters 62, 63
Good Friday Agreement (1998) 80, 96, 100, 112, 187, 188, 200
governance 8, 11–12, 43, 82, 85, 90, 97, 119, 120, 190, 202
  definition 6, 8
  effects 33
  externalisation 7
  multi-level 85, 86, 150
  multi-level networks and 11
  new institutionalism and 12
  perspective 24, 113
  system of 12
Government of Ireland Act (1920) 82, 91

Greco-Turkish relations 121
 rapprochement 127
Greece 121, 124, 128, 129, 130, 132, 142
Greek Cypriot
 community 121, 123, 131, 198
 elite/side 118, 121, 122, 123, 127, 130, 134, 137, 138, 143
 government 122, 125, 126, 135, 137
Greek Cyprus *see* Cyprus, Republic of
Green Line 121, 137
 see also Cyprus conflict
Green Line Regulation 137

Haagerup Report 88, 89
Hallstein, Walter 186
Herriot, Edouard 1
Hugo, Victor 1
Hume, John 81, 98, 102
hurting stalemate 10

IAR *see* International Authority for the Ruhr
ICG *see* International Crisis Group
ICJ *see* International Court of Justice
ICTY *see* International Criminal Tribunal for the former Yugoslavia
IFI *see* International Fund for Ireland
imperial subvention 82
 see also Northern Ireland conflict
institutionalism 21n.7, 190
 see also new institutionalism
integration 29, 52
 see also European integration; regional integration
 economic 48
 interdependence as 34
 negative 31
 positive 31, 86
 peace and reconciliation rationale 36
integration theory 4, 26, 190
interdependence 4, 20, 26, 32, 38, 186, 199
 structural 22, 118, 188
intergovernmental 165, 168
intergovernmentalism 4, 163
 intergovernmental cooperation 98
 intergovernmental institutions 49
International Authority for the Ruhr 53–7
international conflict 7
 see also conflict
International Civilian Office (Kosovo) 155, 163
International Civilian Representative (Kosovo) 155, 167, 177
International Court of Justice 148
 advisory opinion on Kosovo 148, 149, 155, 168
International Criminal Tribunal for the former Yugoslavia 160, 164, 166, 172
 conditionality 171, 172
International Crisis Group 117
International Fund for Ireland 89, 92, 99
international mediation 16
international organisation 3
 functionalist approach 3
 see also functionalism; integration theory
international socialisation 26, 150
INTERREG 92, 96, 100, 101
Ireland 113
 'island economy' 113
Ischinger, Wolfgang 170

JHA *see* Justice and Home Affairs
Jeremic, Vuk 174
Justice and Home Affairs 20n.2

Karadjic, Radovan 172
Kellogg-Briand Pact (1928) 47
de Kermabon, Yves 178
KLA *see* Kosovo Liberation Army
Konzerns 54, 56

Korean War 57
Kosovo 14, 19, 20, 148–85, 187, 191, 193, 195, 198, 199, 200
  autonomy 158
  conflict 3, 16, 153–5, 191, 199
  conflict resolution 154, 156
    Europeanisation of 154
  constitution 155, 171, 173, 176, 177, 181
  decentralisation 161, 169, 173, 176–7
  Declaration of Independence (2008) 14, 155, 173, 195
  Declaration of independence (1991) 153
  European perspective 153, 159, 161, 164, 167, 168, 170, 171, 182
  Provisional Institutions of Self-Governance 154, 163
  Republic of 148
  Standards before Status 154, 163, 170, 176, 181, 183n.26
    Standards Implementation Plan 160, 161, 163, 173
  status determination (process) 150, 161
    see also Ahtisaari Plan; Comprehensive Proposal for the Kosovo Status Settlement
  sui generis case 149, 164, 165
  supervised independence 154, 167, 168
  unilateral declaration of independence 148, 164, 165
Kosovo Liberation Army 153
Kosovo/Serbia conflict see Kosovo conflict
Koštunica, Vojislav 171, 172, 174

Ladrech, Robert 36
Law 27 (1950) 55
Law 75 see Property Law 75
League of Nations 58
Leibnitz, Gottfried-Wilhelm 1

Lemass, Seán 91
liberal internationalism 22
London Agreements (1948) 54
Lorraine 44, 51, 55–9 *passim*, 62
Lotharingia 51, 64
Luxembourg Treaty (1955) 64, 65
Luxembourg Treaty (1956) 64

Maastricht Treaty 84, 100, 125
Mann, Heinrich 1
Makarios III, Archbishop
Mann, Thomas 1
Marshall Plan (1947) 53, 54
Martin Report 88
Martin, Simone 88
  see also Martin Report
Mason, Roy 98
Memorandum for a European Union (1928) 47
Messina Declaration see European Economic Community
Milošević, Slobodan 172
Mitchell, George 98
Mitrany, David 3
Mladic, Ratko 171, 172
Monnet, Jean 7, 51, 53, 61, 193
Morgenthau, Hans 53
multi-level governance see governance

Napoleonic Wars 45
National Assembly (France) 49, 56, 61
National Unity Party 12
NATO 49, 52, 72
  Kosovo campaign 158
neofunctionalism 4
  see also integration theory
new institutionalism 12
New Ireland Forum 89
Nikolic, Tomislav 173, 175
Nietzsche, Friedrich 1
northern Cyprus 123–6 *passim*, 128, 130, 131, 132, 134, 140, 141, 142, 189, 191
Northern Ireland 3, 16, 17, 76,

79–113, 188, 191, 192, 193, 199, 200
all-Ireland economy 84, 104
conflict 81, 200
  European dimension 18, 81–4, 102
  Troubles, the 83
cross-border cooperation 84, 85, 86, 91, 100, 112
settlement
  see also Good Friday Agreement
peace process 80, 104
peripherality 85
reconciliation 80
shared society 105
Northern Ireland Assembly 83, 92,
  see also Good Friday Agreement
Northern Ireland Executive 83, 92, 104, 105
  see also Good Friday Agreement
North-South Ministerial Council *see* Good Friday Agreement

Olsen, Johan 33, 190
O'Neill, Terence 91
O'Neill, Tip 98
open method of coordination 27
Organisation for European Economic Cooperation (1948) 49
Organisation for Security and Cooperation in Europe 183n.14
  Helsinki Act 183n.14

Paisley, Ian 104
Paris Agreements (1953) 62
partnership 99, 112
  see also European partnership
peace dividend 84, 89, 90, 95, 99, 112
PEACE Programme 89, 92, 94–7, 99, 100, 104, 106, 112
  see also Special Support Programme for Peace and Reconciliation
Peyrefitte, Alain 78n.29
Petersberg Agreements 54

Philip, André 48
Pleven, René 71
Pleven Plan 57
Poland 60
policy transfer 86, 99, 112
Pond, Elizabeth 148
power 34
power sharing 81, 83, 84, 86, 102, 109, 121, 123, 133, 188, 199, 200, 201
process tracing 15, 40
Property Law 75 54

Quigley, George 113

rational choice 30
Rambouillet talks 153
  Accords 158
Realpolitik 48, 58,
reconciliation 4, 7, 9, 33, 48, 49, 76, 92, 102, 105, 112, 173, 187
  see also Franco-German reconciliation
  definition 9–10
  hypothesis 33, 116
  intercommunal 18
  norm of 7
Reconstruction and Modernisation Plan 53, 59
regional integration 10, 20n.3
  peace process as a 18
  regionalism as 27
regionalisation 20n.3
regionalism 5, 20n.3, 86, 151
Rehn, Olli 160, 161, 184n.29
Republican Turkish Party 142
Republic of Kosovo *see* Kosovo
Rhineland 47, 51, 53
Robinson, Peter 111
Roland, Romain 1
Rome Treaty *see* European Economic Community
Rosenau, James 26
Rousseau, Jean-Jacques 1
Royaumont process 157

Ruhr 18, 46, 51, 59
Ruhr Authority 49, 53–7
  see also International Authority for the Ruhr (IAR)
Ruhr Statute 54, 56, 57
Russia 60, 170

SAA see Stabilisation and Association Agreement
Saar, the 53, 56, 58–65
  see also Saar issue
  settlement 46
  préalable sarrois 61
  Europeanisation 62–5
  Saar Statute 62, 64
  Referendum 64
Saar issue 18, 46, 65
  van Naters Plan 62
de Saint Pierre, Bernadin 1
SAP see Stabilization and Association Process
Schmidt, Karl (Carlo) 49
Schuman Declaration (1950) 52, 55, 57, 193
Schuman, Robert
SDLP see Social Democratic and Labour Party
security community 4
Security Council see United Nations
security externalities 5
secession 16
self-determination 16, 81, 148, 149, 177, 195, 196, 202
  uti possedetis principle 156
Serbia 148–85 *passim*, 187, 189, 193, 194, 195
  European perspective 159, 162, 167, 170, 182, 193
  Application for EU membership 172–3
Serbian Progressive Party 173
Serbian Radical Party 172, 173
Set of Ideas (Cyprus) 122, 125, 132
  see also Boutros-Gali

settlement 9, 22, 38, 122, 195, 200
  consociational arrangements/majoritarian models 200
SEUPB see Special EU Programme Body
SF see Sinn Féin
SFIO (Section Française d'Internationale Ouvrière) 48
SFRY see Socialist Federal Republic of Yugoslavia
SG/HR see Secretary-General/High Representative
Single European Act (1986) 89, 103
single European market 86
Sinn Féin 84, 101–7, 193
SNS see Serbian Progressive Party
Social Democratic and Labour Party 83, 102
Social Democratic Party 49, 57
socialisation 31, 33, 113
Socialist Federal Republic of Yugoslavia 153
  see also Yugoslavia
  Constitution (1974) 153, 157
Socialist Party of Serbia 172, 173
sociological institutionalism 30
Solana, Javier 160, 161, 178, 184n.29
Solana/Rehn report see General Affairs and External Affairs Council
Sorel, Georges 1
sovereignty 34, 72, 81, 82, 85, 104, 121, 126, 150, 153, 154, 168, 171, 176, 177, 186, 193, 195, 199, 201
  joint 119
  pooled 151
  shared 49
  supervised 166
  Westphalian 156
Spaak, Paul-Henri 66, 71
SPD see Social Democratic Party
Special EU Programme Body 101
Special Support Programme for Peace and Reconciliation (PEACE) 90
SPS see Socialist Party of Serbia

SRS *see* Serbian Radical Party
Stabilisation and Association
 Agreement 158, 160, 163, 166,
 167, 171, 172, 194
 Interim Trade Agreement (Serbia)
 167, 172
Stabilisation and Association Process
 (SAP) 19, 158, 159, 160, 163, 168,
 171, 172
 Standards Monitoring (Kosovo) 161
 Standards Tracking Mechanism 160,
 176
Stability Pact for Southeastern Europe
 159, 159
Standards Tracking Mechanism *see*
 Stabilisation and Association
 Process
St Andrews Agreement 84
State Union of Serbia and Montenegro
 160, 191
STM *see* Stabilisation and Association
 Process
Stresemann, Gustav 47
Structural and Cohesion Funds, EU
 86, 87, 90
subsidiarity 86, 100
sui generis see Kosovo
Sunningdale Agreement (1973) 83,
 102
supranational governance 4
supranationalism 21n.7
 supranational actors 163, 165

Tadic, Boris 172, 173, 174
Talat, Mehmet Ali 142
TCC *see* Turkish Cypriot community
Tocci, Nathalie 34, 128
transnationalism 11
Treaty of Guarantee 122, 145n.16
Treaty of Rome (1957) 20n.2
Treaty of Westphalia 44
Treaty on European Union 20n.4
Treaty on the functioning of the
 European Union 141

triangulation 15
Trimble, David 104
Turkey 121, 124, 126, 128, 129, 130,
 131, 132, 133, 136, 138–40, 144,
 198
Turkish Cypriot
 community 121, 123, 126, 128, 129,
 131, 133, 134, 135, 139, 140,
 142, 145n.1
 elite/side 118, 121, 122, 123, 127,
 130, 132, 133, 142, 143
Turkish Federated State 122, 127
Turkish Republic of Northern Cyprus
 122, 127, 145n.1

UBP *see* National Unity Party
UDI *see* Kosovo
Ulster plantations 82
Ulster Unionist Party 83, 102, 104,
 105
UN *see* United Nations
UN Security Council *see* United
 Nations
UNFICYP *see* United Nations
 Peacekeeping Mission in Cyprus
United Kingdom 121
United Nations 121, 122, 123, 125,
 127, 129, 130, 131, 143, 161, 162,
 163, 165, 169, 181, 182
 General Assembly 155
 Secretary-General 15, 122, 169
 Security Council 15, 124, 127, 149,
 153, 154–5, 163, 165, 169, 170
 Resolution 1244 (1999) 153, 154,
 159, 171, 173, 182
UNMIK *see* United Nations Mission
 in Kosovo
United Nations Peacekeeping Mission
 in Cyprus 121
United States of Europe 1, 47, 48, 54
United Nations Mission in Kosovo
 153, 155, 159, 160, 162, 169
 Six-Point Plan 155
UUP *see* Ulster Unionist Party

Valéry, Paul 1
Versailles Treaty (1919) 46, 47, 58, 59
veto points 31

war
  see also Napoleonic Wars
  First World War 45, 51, 57, 58
  Franco-Prussian War (1870–71) 45
  Second World War 45, 47, 49, 76
  German war industry 45
  War of the Palatinian Succession 45
Warndt coal mine 59, 64
Western Balkans 2, 7, 20, 148, 151, 152, 159, 161, 168
  Common Strategy 158
  European perspective 152, 156, 158
  Regional approach (1997) 19, 157
Western European Union 58, 62
Western powers 53
  Council of Foreign Ministers 53
WEU *see* Western European Union

Young Plan 47
Yugoslav Constitution
  see Socialist Federal Republic of Yugoslavia
Yugoslavia, former 153

EU authorised representative for GPSR:
Easy Access System Europe, Mustamäe tee 50,
10621 Tallinn, Estonia
gpsr.requests@easproject.com

www.ingramcontent.com/pod-product-compliance
Ingram Content Group UK Ltd.
Pitfield, Milton Keynes, MK11 3LW, UK
UKHW021848140426
5217IPUK00022B/1653